30/1

AN

Churchill and his Airmen

Churchill
and his Airmen

Vincent Orange

GRUB STREET • LONDON

Published by
Grub Street
4 Rainham Close
London
SW11 6SS

Copyright © Grub Street 2013
Copyright text © Vincent Orange 2013

British Library Cataloguing in Publication Data
Orange, Vincent, 1935-
 Churchill and his airmen.
 1. Churchill, Winston, 1874-1965–Military leadership.
 2. Great Britain. Royal Air Force–Officers–History–
 20th century. 3. World War, 1914-1918–Aerial operations,
 British. 4. World War, 1939-1945–Aerial operations,
 British.
 I. Title
 940.4'4'941-dc23

ISBN-13: 9781908117366

Cover design by Sarah Driver
Edited by Sophie Campbell
Book design and artwork by:
Roy Platten, Eclipse – roy.eclipse@btopenworld.com

Printed and bound by MPG Ltd, Bodmin, Cornwall

Grub Street Publishing only uses
FSC (Forest Stewardship Council) paper for its books.

Contents

Acknowledgements

Above all, to Sandra. I can handle a keyboard, but as for getting my text, pictures and maps to the other side of the world, I depend entirely upon her skills. I am also grateful to my friend Robin Stevens, former Librarian at the University of Canterbury. With the help of his colleagues, Bronwyn Matthews, Tim O'Sullivan, Rosie Sykes and Dave Clements, they obtained for me essential books and articles from the Library, despite its partial closure as a result of Christchurch's earthquakes.

David McIntyre, at one time head of the History Department, has long been a valued adviser and in particular I have benefitted from his excellent work on the rise and fall of the Singapore naval base. Errol W. Martyn, an expert on RNZAF history, was helpful in the early stages of this work.

Overseas, I am now – and always will be – grateful to the late Air Commodore Henry Probert, head of the Air Historical Branch in London, his successor, Sebastian Cox, and his right hand man, Sebastian Ritchie, whose book on airborne forces was an essential aide. Across the Atlantic, I have valued for many years the advice and information offered to me by my dear friends, Mrs Yvonne Kinkaid, senior historian at Bolling Air Force Base in Washington DC and Tami Davis Biddle at Duke University of North Carolina, whose book *Rhetoric and Reality in Air Warfare* has been a constant guide. Last, and by no means least, I am grateful for the support of my publisher, John Davies, who did not fuss when pneumonia prevented me from meeting our original deadline.

Vincent Orange
Christchurch, New Zealand
September 2012

PUBLISHER'S NOTE

At the proof reading stage of this book, sadly Professor Vincent Orange passed away. He will be sorely missed. It was his wish that the text be published without footnotes, to make it more easily accessible to the general reader.

For Sandra Rosina Orange, my dear wife

1

New Worlds to Conquer, 1908-1914

Zeppelins and Aeroplanes

Winston Churchill's aviation interests began at the age of thirty-three in 1908 when he read reports of the flight tests carried out by Count Ferdinand von Zeppelin's airships in Germany. These tests caused ever-increasing alarm in Britain: neither ships nor armies had threatened her in living memory, but the airship might.

David Lloyd George (Chancellor of the Exchequer) was so disturbed by these reports that he proposed the formation of a coalition government to deal with such an unprecedented danger. Although nothing more useful than cries of alarm followed, Zeppelins – all imaginary – were regularly reported to be flying over British coasts in years when Europe was more or less at peace.

Shortly after the German alarm sounded in 1908 came another alarm from France, a traditional enemy though currently a suspicious friend. In July 1909 Louis Blériot flew across the Channel from Calais to Dover in barely half an hour. Churchill was among those who realised that practical flying machines (Zeppelins and aeroplanes) would soon affect the age-old conduct of war on land and at sea. He was then president of the Board of Trade and announced that the development of an aviation industry would be filled with immense consequences for everyone at home and abroad. The War Office did not share his excitement glumly referring, in July 1910, to the 'unwelcome progress' of aerial navigation, an opinion with which the Admiralty 'concurred generally'. Nevertheless, as soon as Churchill became First Lord of the Admiralty in October 1911, his fertile mind and vivid imagination turned to recruiting pilots and ground crews and he sought instruction in the art of flying himself.

'To describe Churchill as taking a close interest in his work,' wrote Peter Rowland, 'would probably be the understatement of all time. He flung himself into it.' He would hold that appointment for three years and seven months: 'The most memorable of my life', he wrote, long after he had earned enduring fame as Prime Minister during the Second World War.

In the winter of 1912-1913 a wave of Zeppelin mania swept across Britain. Citizens saw them everywhere and in February 1913 Churchill assured the Committee of Imperial Defence that Germany's huge airships had actually flown over parts of eastern England. Could the War Office and/or the Admiralty build their own airships or would it be better to develop aeroplanes capable of challenging these monsters? The War Office merely fretted, but the Admiralty – goaded by Churchill – began to set up a chain of coastal aerodromes, primarily for working with ships at sea.

John Seely, Under-Secretary of State at the War Office, discussed the formation of an air corps with David Henderson, its designated head, in 1912. 'What is the best method to pursue,' he asked Henderson, 'in order to do in a week what is generally done in a year?' The army and the navy had at that time about nineteen qualified pilots between them, whereas France had about 263, 'so we are what you might call behind.' As for Germany, she would have 180 aeroplanes in the west on the outbreak of war in August 1914.

Early hopes for a unified air service gradually evaporated with the Admiralty determined to keep command of one and the War Office just as anxious to control the other. Air-minded navy officers were keen to develop fighting and bombing aeroplanes, whereas air-minded army officers thought more of developing stable platforms in the sky to observe enemy movements and direct artillery fire. Churchill had at first been greatly impressed by the potential threat of airships if war broke out, but was gradually won over by the much greater potential of the aeroplane.

Two Wings and a School

Demands in newspapers and in Parliament for the government to foster aviation with more enthusiasm had obliged Prime Minister Herbert Asquith, in November 1911, to invite Henderson (Director of Military Training) and an army staff captain, Frederick Sykes, to look into the matter. Both of them had qualified as pilots during that year and in April 1912 Asquith accepted their recommendation that a Royal Flying Corps, comprising an Army Wing and a Naval Wing – with a Central Flying School to serve both – should be created. Sykes commanded the Army Wing from 1912 to 1914 and Henderson was appointed Director of Military Aeronautics in September 1913. They are the first two in a long line of distinguished airmen who might fairly be called Churchill's.

The aeroplane, they supposed, would be most useful in spotting for artillery and carrying out (or preventing) reconnaissance; eventually it might engage in aerial combat with enemy aircraft. They ordered a biplane designed by Geoffrey de Havilland that was stable enough to permit useful observation by airmen, who were later able to take thousands of valuable photographs. This machine – the BE 2 and improved versions – was built in a new Royal Aircraft Factory at Farnborough in Hampshire.

War Office reliance on the Farnborough factory, which attempted to monopolise airframe design and production, but failed to encourage engine development, caused outrage in the newspapers. The Admiralty, especially when Churchill took charge, refused to succumb to its pressure. Murray Sueter was Director of the Air Department from 1911 to 1915 and helped to create a Royal Naval Air Service (RNAS) out of the Naval Wing. Sueter encouraged the development of aircraft capable of carrying torpedoes and set up an Anti-Aircraft Corps for London. He had in mind aircraft for coastal and fleet reconnaissance, submarine and mine detection, defence against air raids and offence against enemy bases. He chose to rely on private industry for the Naval Wing's aircraft and found in Churchill a strong supporter. Sueter was clearly one airman who was important when Churchill's mind turned to aviation matters.

An Honourable, Dangerous Profession

Terms of service for naval airmen, wrote Churchill, in December 1911, 'must be devised to make aviation for war purposes the most honourable, as it is the most dangerous, profession a young Englishman can adopt'. Young men, he ruled, must be in effective – and aggressive – command, learning all they can about bomb dropping and the use of machine guns. The army, by contrast, thought its airmen should think mainly of observation and the avoidance of combat.

Churchill had required the Royal Navy to concentrate on acquiring aeroplanes, not airships, in 1911 and in the following year oversaw the launching of its first seaplanes. He then changed his mind about airships, on observing the progress made by Germans with their Zeppelins. In December 1912 he admitted in Parliament that Germany, 'has won a great pre-eminence' in airships and expressed 'anxiety' about the threat they posed to dockyards, machine shops and ships in British harbours: all of them 'absolutely defenceless'. He also foresaw that generals and admirals would compete to control naval aircraft.

When presenting his estimates of naval expenditure to the House of Commons in March 1912, Churchill had said that he wished to see 'a thoroughly good and effective development' of naval air power 'and money will not stand in the way of the necessary steps'. He thought the products of the Royal Aircraft Factory inadequate and looked to private companies for a source of more efficient machines. The Naval Wing became a successful weapon and played an important part in stimulating Britain's aircraft industry into building efficient aircraft for the army as well as the navy.

In the event of war, Churchill doubted whether the War Office could provide sufficient aircraft for both home defence and to assist ground forces in France. By 'various shifts and devices', he later wrote, he began to arrange for more aircraft to protect harbours, oil tanks and other 'vulnerable points'.

He called for an air service separate from both the Admiralty and the War Office, but the time was not ripe for such a radical idea.

Aeroplanes could not yet be flown at night, Churchill learned in 1913. Consequently, Zeppelins had a great advantage. Also, they flew so steadily that they could easily defend themselves with accurate gunfire and might well be protected, as some alleged experts supposed, from return fire by a non-inflammable outer layer. The time had come, he argued, 'when we must develop long-range airships of the largest type'. In July 1913 he ordered the construction of two rigid and four non-rigid airships and had 'good hopes' of 'building a vessel which in every respect will be equal to the latest on the Continent'. But his earlier opposition to the airship had left the navy too far behind to catch up and he was obliged to make a deal with the War Office to obtain use of the army's airships.

With regard to defence against German airships, Churchill thought ground gunners, aided by searchlights, would force them to fly higher, even if they were unable to hit them. That should at least make accurate bombing more difficult. Extinguishing ground lights would be a great help and so too would aeroplanes, if and when pilots learned to fly in darkness. But defence was only part of the answer: Zeppelins 'must be kept away altogether and that will only be done by attacking them', he said, in their bases as well as en route to and from their targets. This emphasis on offence (always a prime consideration for Churchill in peace or war) persuaded him that the aeroplane was superior to the airship, which was merely 'an enormous bladder of combustible and explosive gas'. It was not, he rightly believed, invulnerable to bullets and could surely be destroyed by aeroplanes attacking from above and dropping a string of bombs 'like a whiplash across the gas bag'.

Churchill firmly supported the development of seaplanes, working from coastal bases, to protect ships at sea. As early as October 1913, he had recommended that the Royal Navy needed armed aircraft able to carry out long-range reconnaissance (operating from ships at sea as well as bases ashore) and also to protect ports and coastal shipping. When seaplanes are devised that can carry torpedoes, he thought, they 'may prove capable of playing a decisive part in operations against capital ships'. In *Flight*'s opinion, the government was reluctant to spend sufficiently on aviation. 'We frankly do not envy the task of the First Lord', wrote the editor, Stanley Spooner, in October 1913. Churchill was obliged to fit in with both his professional advisers and with the Treasury which, 'to put it mildly', is never anxious to support new ventures. But Spooner was convinced that Britain must match 'the iron-hard determination' of Germany to develop air power.

Even so, Churchill confidently asserted in November 1913: 'The British seaplane, although still in an empirical stage, like everything else in this sphere of warlike operation, has reached a point of progress in advance of anything done elsewhere.' This was thanks to Commander Charles Samson 'and his band of brilliant pioneers'. Samson became one of those fighting men who always delighted Churchill for their skill, courage and above all their aggressive temperament.

Losing his Ethereal Virginity

Churchill lost what he called his 'ethereal virginity' in 1912 when he made his first flight and during the following year began a determined attempt to qualify as a pilot. All pilots, actual and hopeful, were delighted to learn that the First Lord of the Admiralty himself, a person so eminent and almost as old as Methuselah (he was then thirty-eight) should attempt to master so dangerous a skill. 'We are in the Stephenson age of flying', he told one of his instructors. 'Now our machines are frail. One day they will be robust, and of value to our country.' He had lessons at Upavon in Wiltshire, but Colonel Hugh Trenchard (commanding the flying school there) was unimpressed by his 'wallowing about the sky' and decided that he was 'altogether too impatient for a good pupil'. However his opinion would weigh more if Trenchard had ever shown any skill as a pilot himself.

In October 1913 Churchill told his wife Clementine about 'a very jolly day in the air' over Eastchurch on the Isle of Sheppey in Kent and places nearby: 'A delightful trip on which I was conducted by the redoubtable Samson.' Quite apart from the thrill of flying, which no-one of any earlier generation had enjoyed, Churchill relished excitement, novelty, and the thrill of being above the clouds. Unlike almost all his fellow-politicians, he rarely missed an opportunity to fly during the next forty years. 'It has been as good as one of those old days in the South African war,' he happily reminisced to Clementine, 'and I have lived entirely in the moment, with no care for all those tiresome party politics and searching newspapers, and awkward by-elections, and sulky Orangemen, and obnoxious Cecils and smug little Runcimans.'

Churchill became the first cabinet minister to 'control' (with a qualified pilot beside him) an aeroplane in flight. This was in a Short biplane, with Gilbert Wildman-Lushington. *The Pall Mall Gazette* was impressed, but other newspapers were critical of the risks he took and envious of the publicity he attracted so easily and enjoyed so obviously. That approval was not undermined, in the newspaper's opinion, when Lushington was killed shortly after his flights with Churchill. It was 'simply one of those fortuitous circumstances,' the *Gazette* wrote, somewhat callously, 'which have a habit of happening.'

Lushington had written to his fiancé on 30 November, just two days before his fatal accident. 'I started Winston off on his instruction about 12.15 and he got so bitten with it I could hardly get him out of the machine, in fact except for about forty-five minutes for lunch we were in the machine till about 3.30. He showed great promise and is coming down again for further instruction and practice.' Lushington had made a good impression and was invited to dine aboard the Admiralty yacht *Enchantress* that night, seated at the right hand of the First Lord. 'He was absolutely full out and talked hard about what he was going to do.' Had the young pilot lived he would undoubtedly have been given every opportunity to make his name.

Churchill kept on flying during 1914, both as passenger and pilot, until he was persuaded, especially by his wife, to give up – which he did, most reluctantly. 'This is a wrench,' he told her on 6 June, 'because I was on the verge of taking my pilot's certificate. It only needed a couple of calm mornings; and I am confident of my ability to achieve it very respectably.' This was a misplaced confidence, because he had already had ample flights to qualify if he had been skilful enough. He admitted that 'the numerous fatalities of this year' justified her anxiety.

'Anyhow, I can feel I know a good deal about this fascinating new art. I can manage a machine with ease in the air, even with high winds, and only a little more practice in landings would have enabled me to go up with reasonable safety alone. I have been up nearly 140 times, with many pilots, and all kinds of machines, so I know the difficulties and the joys of the air well enough to appreciate them and to understand all the questions of policy which will arise in the near future.'

Nothing ever daunted Churchill's self-confidence for long.

Fairy Godfather

As John Morrow wrote, Churchill 'became the darling of the aviation press' and in January 1914, *The Aeroplane* magazine described him as 'the fairy godfather' of naval aviation. As was typical of Churchill in all his offices, he paid great attention to detail. In December 1913, for example, he had told Sueter to ensure that the seaplanes currently being designed should have comfortable seats for the pilots: at present, manufacturers were not paying sufficient attention to this need. Also, designs must ensure that both engines and wireless sets should be easy to fit and replace. In another December message to Sueter, Churchill gave specific instructions about the equipment of a new Sopwith machine to be used for special reconnaissance. It must have a well-sheltered cockpit for two pilots seated side by side with complete dual control, a full instrument panel and be ready for service by February next.

Churchill took the closest interest in everything to do with the infant service by firing off a constant stream of minutes dealing with landing places, navigation, promotions, terms of service, working conditions aboard aircraft and airships, design and construction, methods of spotting submarines, rates of pay, details of uniforms, leisure activities and, not least, anything said or done by the Admiralty or the War Office suggesting that airmen were inferior to sailors or soldiers. At the same time, he was adamant that 'young gentlemen' wishing to join the Naval Wing were not to become a 'mere mixture of pilot and mechanic'. They must also receive a proper military training.

Sadly, during 1914 divergent approaches to aviation between the Admiralty and the War Office led to a split, with the navy setting up its own training school at Eastchurch. By July 1915 the Admiralty in 'a unilateral declaration of independence' had officially turned its wing into a separate service. This despite the fact that Churchill, while First Lord, and Lord Haldane (chairman of the Sub-Committee of the Committee of Imperial Defence) had spoken strongly in favour of a united air service. 'Tremendous strides have been made', wrote Spooner in March 1914 during the past year, especially in naval aviation. As Churchill pointed out, 'the creation of an entirely new branch of armaments is not a thing that can be done in a day ... sheds, plants, appliances and land, as well as the actual instruments of aviation' take time to emerge. But Spooner remained convinced that the work should already have begun: 'As soon, indeed, as the recognition was first born that aviation was destined to play an important, possibly a vital, part in the warfare of the immediate future.'

At that time, March 1914, the RNAS had about 100 aeroplanes of which sixty were seaplanes; there were 125 officers and 500 men in the service and by the end of the year those numbers were expected to reach 180 officers and nearly 1,500 men. Five seaplane bases had been established and two more were under construction. Spooner again:

> 'This new service is thoroughly naval in spirit and character, but at the same time it contains, and must contain, a large element of civilians, both officers and mechanics... The seaplane has a great future before it. We cannot doubt that it will play an effective part in military and naval arrangements. We are without doubt in numbers, quality and experience far in front of any other country in our seaplane work.'

On 20 March 1914 Churchill circulated to his Cabinet colleagues a paper on a 'Proposed Aircraft Expedition to Somaliland' in response to a massacre carried out by a local ruler, the so-called 'Mad Mullah'. The Mullah's wealth, wrote Churchill, is in camels and livestock, so 'very considerable damage could be inflicted on him, apart from actual offensive operations, by stampeding his stock and keeping them from the wells. Stephen Roskill thought this the first appearance of a proposal to use aircraft 'in a counter-insurgency role in colonial territories – later termed "air control"'. As it happened, retribution did not follow for the Mullah until 1920, but from then on rebels against imperial authority in many places east of Suez would feel the impact of air control.

Meanwhile, in May and June 1914, Churchill proposed that Sueter be appointed Inspecting Captain of the Naval Wing as well as Director of the Air Department in the Admiralty. His two principal assistants should be Francis Scarlett, commanding the seaplane ship and managing the central office, and Samson, commanding the Eastchurch Naval Flying School and the war squadron there. Samson should not, ruled Churchill, give up his flying duties, 'for which his qualifications are pre-eminent'. Oliver Schwann (who would, in April 1917, change his name to a more English-sounding Swann) should stay at the Admiralty, 'where his technical knowledge and administrative abilities are at present indispensable'.

2

Airmen at War,
1914-1915

Across the Channel

By 4 August 1914, when Britain declared war on Germany, Churchill had already shown himself to be a strong supporter of the development of air power, especially at sea. As early as the 7th he sent Field Marshal Horatio Kitchener (Secretary of State for War) a copy of 'the scheme worked out between the Naval and Military Wings for the patrol of the east coast'. He did not have enough machines to patrol the whole coast and proposed to leave everything north of the Humber as well as around Dover to the army, while the navy put three or four seaplanes around the Firth of Forth and the Tyne. 'Experience shows,' he said, 'that unless numbers are available, no regular patrol can be maintained by aeroplanes day after day.' The 'experience' he spoke of, in the very first days of the war, came from pre-war patrols, supplemented by his exceptional imagination. Two days later, Churchill proposed to set up a base for seaplanes and aeroplanes somewhere along the Dutch coast from which to 'report all movements in the Heligoland Bight and later attack with explosives the locks of the Kiel Canal or vessels in the canal'.

Churchill was determined to use whatever air strength he could muster. On 1 September he told Sueter: 'The largest possible force of naval aeroplanes should be stationed in Calais or Dunkirk.' It was very likely, he thought, that Zeppelins would attempt to attack London. 'The proper defence is a thorough and continual search of the country for seventy to 100 miles inland with a view to marking down any temporary airship bases or airships replenishing before starting to attack.' Any airships found were to be attacked at once. Samson and Eugene Gerrard were to have charge of this duty.

On the same day, 1 September, Churchill asked the French Ministry of Marine for permission to place some thirty or forty naval aeroplanes at Dunkirk or a similar place, supported by perhaps as many as sixty armoured cars and 300 men able to set up temporary bases as far as fifty miles inland. Francis Villiers, Britain's minister to Belgium, reported to Edward Grey (Foreign Secretary) on 4 September that Gerrard had arrived in Antwerp with six aeroplanes and support equipment. He proposed to make it a base for attacks on Cologne, Düsseldorf and other cities to deter Zeppelin raids on either British or French troops or across the Channel on targets in England.

As Malcolm Cooper wrote, Churchill can rightly be considered 'the father of naval air power' and as early as September 1915 Arthur Balfour, who succeeded Churchill as First Lord of the Admiralty – and was by no means an unqualified admirer – wrote that 'contribution' is too small a word to use for the part he played in naval aviation: 'you were the onlie [sic] begetter', of that service.

Two months later, on 13 November, Vice-Admiral Sir Charles Coke wrote to Churchill. He had recently met a young flying officer on a train (who took him for a civilian) and asked: 'Where would the Naval Flying Service have been but for Mr Churchill's energy and foresight?' Coke agreed: 'Mr Churchill not only deserved the gratitude of the RNAS, but that of the entire service and the country, for his untiring efforts both before and after war was declared.'

Britain's First 'Finest Hour'

In August 1914 the old Army Wing, now the Royal Flying Corps, was sent to France to support the British Expeditionary Force: sixty-three machines in total, all with French-built engines and nearly half of them designed abroad. The War Office, charged with home defence, had no useful aircraft on hand, but was not overly concerned because the war was not expected to last long. Churchill, with more imagination and with naval aviation mainly in mind, accepted responsibility for Britain's air defence on 3 September. He was starting at the bottom, with no anti-aircraft guns, no searchlights, no system to give early warning of intruders and his fifty usable aeroplanes and seaplanes had been built by eight different manufacturers, one of them German. All were inadequate: slow, poorly armed and unable to climb to the height of Zeppelins and they could not yet fly in darkness.

In answer to those who criticised the navy's slow start to defend Britain from aerial attack, Lieutenant Richard Davies, one of the First Lord's flying instructors, snapped: 'They have pissed on Churchill's plant for three years – now they expect blooms in a month.' At any moment, Churchill later recalled, 'half a dozen Zeppelins might arrive to bomb London or, what was more serious, military targets like Chatham, Woolwich or Portsmouth'. He would eventually anticipate by twenty-six years what is often said to be 'Britain's Finest Hour' (the effective air defence against the Luftwaffe in the summer of 1940) by issuing instructions for the deployment of aeroplanes, the installation of guns and searchlights, the illumination of aerodromes and instructions to the police, firemen and civilians who might be attacked from the air. Such bombardment, he said bluntly, 'must be endured with composure'.

On the Attack

Churchill had more than defence in mind, despite the weakness of his forces. Asquith's daughter Violet, a lifelong friend, later wrote, 'a purely defensive role was alien to his spirit'. He saw 'no use' in waiting for the enemy to come: 'Only offensive action could help us.'

He proposed to control the air in a radius of 100 miles from Dunkirk. 'I decided immediately to strike by bombing from aeroplanes' at Zeppelin sheds in Germany and conquered parts of Belgium and France, to prevent enemy airships from reaching the British coast. In the first week of the war, Sueter proposed the bombing of Zeppelin sheds in Germany, targets 'bigger than a battleship and more vulnerable than the Crystal Palace'. Churchill readily approved and on 8 October 1914 an aeroplane flew from Antwerp to Düsseldorf, destroying, with two 20-lb bombs, a hangar in which lay a Zeppelin.

Late in November, four Avro machines were secretly shipped in their crates from a factory in Manchester to Belfort in eastern France and bombed Zeppelin works at Friedrichshafen on Lake Constance. Two of the Avros returned safely from a round-trip of 250 miles. These were 'the first strategic aeroplane raids of the war'. But Churchill was obliged to leave the Admiralty in May 1915. Years later, Trenchard thought the Admiralty's failure to back his use of air power cost the Allies dearly.

Charles Samson – an airman whom Churchill already admired – took his Eastchurch squadron to the Continent and 'in buccaneering fashion had sent armoured cars marauding through Belgium'. He undertook to bomb the Zeppelin sheds at Cologne and Düsseldorf from Antwerp with his 'motley force' of aeroplanes. 'Deficiencies in material,' he said, 'had to be made good by daring.' This was a demand Churchill would often repeat in both world wars.

The first air raid on enemy territory was carried out on 22 September 1914. Three days later, on the 25th, Churchill wrote to the Foreign Secretary, Edward Grey. A Zeppelin had dropped two bombs into Ostend: 'A town of no military significance.' Churchill proposed to have his naval airmen in Antwerp drop two on a German town in retaliation. He was displeased by Grey's response. It was too soon for such action, Grey said, and would serve no useful purpose because the Germans have more aircraft than we have; they could hit us harder than we could hit them.

Churchill never liked to accept that the odds were against him and heartily approved when on 17 October Spenser Grey reported a second raid on enemy territory. Reginald Marix had bombed and destroyed a shed containing a new airship at Düsseldorf on 9 October. Grey, taking off about the same time, failed to find an airship shed in Cologne, but bombed a railway station there. These attacks, being unprecedented, caused what in later years would seem to be excessive alarm.

When the army's retreat placed him out of range of the Rhine sheds, Samson had his men attack the Zeppelin factory at Friedrichshafen and sheds at Ludwigshafen. They attacked from Belfort in eastern France, close to the frontiers with Germany and Switzerland on 21 November. The violation of their neutrality provoked cries of outrage from members of the Swiss parliament. Churchill told the Foreign Secretary that his airmen avoided Swiss territory whenever possible, but in his view many Swiss were pro-German and he should: 'Tell them to go and milk their cows.' The Foreign Secretary was not amused. Ever fearful of ruffling feathers overseas, he expected 'a real row with Switzerland', but somehow the crisis passed with no blood spilt.

On Christmas Day 1914, Churchill sent three seaplane carriers to attack German shipping at Cuxhaven. 'The result,' wrote Paul Halpern, 'was the first significant encounter between aircraft and warships, and a preview of the great air-sea battles of future wars.' Although the fact was the seaplanes achieved nothing on this occasion.

Defending London

Churchill had submitted a memorandum to the Cabinet on 22 October 1914, enclosing a report by Sueter: 'The Defence of London against Aerial Attack'. At Kitchener's request, the Admiralty had undertaken the aerial defence of Britain, but it must be clearly understood, wrote Churchill, 'that no attempt can be made to protect residential areas, and only points of special military significance can be guarded, and those only in a very partial and limited degree'. He did not think aerial attack 'can yet produce decisive military results, but I cannot feel that our arrangements to cope with it are yet in a satisfactory state. Loss and injury, followed by much public outcry, will probably be incurred in the near future.'

In January 1915, however, Churchill admitted that 'there is no known means of preventing the airships coming and not much chance of punishing them on their return. The unavenged destruction of non-combatant life may therefore be very considerable.' England's best ally at present was bad weather. Despite the widespread fear of airships, Churchill remained convinced – and rightly so – that the answer to them was improved aircraft, working with guns and searchlights, helped by wireless communication to get early warning of intruders. The Germans, however, 'thought it worthwhile to attack London merely for the purpose of injuring and terrorising the civil population and damaging property', so he told the War Council on 7 January 1915, and 'there was no means of preventing it'.

Jealousy Between Wings

As early as November 1914, disputes were arising between Britain's two air wings. Lord French (commanding British forces on the Continent) wrote to

Churchill on the 14th, claiming that he should decide who attacks what and where. Churchill replied politely, telling French that he had ordered his naval airmen to keep 'entirely clear' of the British front, 'and to work only on the flank with the French and Belgians'. In another letter he told French that the only way to prevent Zeppelins from bombing England was by destroying them in their bases. That was an Admiralty, not a War Office, responsibility and included guarding Britain and shipping seeking her ports against attack by submarines or surface ships. 'There is a good deal of jealousy,' Churchill told Kitchener on 3 December, 'between the head people in the two wings.' However he had no doubt that 'a friendly arrangement can be arrived at'.

On 23 December he did his best to achieve this when he offered Kitchener a squadron of naval aircraft. At the same time, he recognised the value both officers and men already placed on squadron spirit by stipulating: 'They shall be kept together as a unit and shall not be broken up and dispersed, so as to destroy their identity as a single naval squadron among the various army squadrons; and that they shall not be treated in any manner inferior to that in which army squadrons are treated.'

The First 'Bloody Paralyser'
In December 1914 Churchill authorised work on the construction, by Frederick Handley Page, of a heavy bomber. Although Page is often described as the father of this weapon, Sueter deserves much of the credit. He rejected the early drawings: 'Look, Mr Page – what I want is a bloody paralyser, not a toy.'

The prototype of what would become (but not until the next war) Britain's enormous fleet of 'bloody paralysers' was Page's twin-engined 0/100, which first flew in December 1915. The history of strategic bombing throughout both wars reveals, as Tami Davis Biddle wrote, 'the tension between imagined possibilities and technical realities'. Neither defence nor offence in the air were yet serious factors in the war, but Churchill pressed for better anti-aircraft guns, searchlights and for the police and fire brigades to be organised to deal with the casualties and destruction caused by bombing. Attempts were made to reduce urban lighting and to illuminate open land, as a decoy. Telephone links between airfields were created and night flying began. Incendiary bullets and 'anti-Zeppelin grenades' were soon produced.

Fisher in Love
As soon as the war began, Churchill's thoughts had turned increasingly to Admiral Sir John Fisher, who had retired as First Sea Lord in 1910. Fisher had been one of the great seamen of his age and Churchill, who knew nothing about war at sea, naturally looked to an expert for support and guidance on his appointment as First Lord. He was untroubled by the fact that Fisher turned seventy in 1911 or that he had made many bitter enemies. For his part, Fisher – never a man to measure his words – said that he 'fell desperately in

love with Winston Churchill. I think he's quite the nicest fellow I ever met and such a quick brain that it's a delight to talk to him.' Fisher became one of very few men for whom Churchill had a high regard. Although exasperated by his unsteady temperament, wild language and contempt for systematic work, Churchill forgave all for his aggressive temperament.

Churchill's 'penchant for me,' said Fisher, 'was that I painted with a big brush and was violent!' It was hardly, as Richard Ollard wrote, 'a marriage of true minds' and they would eventually do their best to ruin each other. Fisher loved to quote an epitaph written about one of Nelson's captains: 'Death found him fighting.' Churchill conducted a secret correspondence with Fisher for more than two years until he felt able to force through his re-appointment as First Sea Lord on 30 October 1914.

A Northern Adventure Denied

Churchill had plans made for the capture of Borkum, largest of the East Frisian Islands, plans that he never abandoned. In his postwar memoirs, *The World Crisis*, he claimed that he had always favoured a northern adventure and regarded a southern undertaking 'only as an interim measure'. It is certainly true that in January 1915 he had said that Borkum was 'the key to all northern possibilities, whether defensive against raid or invasion, or offensive to block the enemy in, or to invade either Oldenburg or Schleswig-Holstein'. From there, Churchill believed, the Royal Navy could threaten Germany's major naval bases. Early in January, Fisher, Kitchener and Asquith all agreed that a base at Borkum offered great possibilities.

In a memorandum of 24 March 1915 Churchill mentioned: 'a complete aviation park, specially organised for landing on an island, comprising sixty aeroplanes and seaplanes.' On or about the fifth day of the attack: 'The main flying base will be landed, and a permanent aeroplane patrol at 8,000 feet will be established to attack all Zeppelins or hostile aircraft, and take what steps are necessary to establish an effective mastery of the air.' Instead of a northern adventure, which seemed feasible, it was suddenly decided to attempt a southern push that never promised well and ended in disaster.

A Southern Adventure Approved

Fisher joined Churchill in approving the decision early in 1915 to seize the Dardanelles, as a means of helping Russia and threatening the Central Powers on a new front, opposing mainly Turks and subsequently Austrians, both regarded as easier to defeat than Germans. The adventure had many founders before it became clear that it had failed; many of them then did their best to blame Churchill, its most vocal advocate. Neither he nor they forgot or forgave during the rest of their lives.

Back in 1904, Fisher had sensibly concluded that storming the Straits would be 'mightily hazardous' and Churchill himself – no less sensibly – had written in 1911 that 'it is no longer possible to force the Dardanelles, and nobody should expose a modern fleet to such a peril'. Carlo D'Este, among a host of historians, has asked the root question: 'Just how was a naval force expected to capture Gallipoli?'

Even so, both Churchill and Fisher changed their minds and willingly abandoned a promising prospect in the near north in favour of a less encouraging venture in the far south. They did so because Sackville Carden (commanding a squadron off the Dardanelles) casually informed them on 3 January 1915 that he thought it might be possible. This became a decisive turning point in Churchill's career and indeed the war. He had uncharacteristically accepted Foreign Office pressure in September 1914 to appoint Carden in place of an excellent officer, Arthur Limpus, who had a thorough knowledge of the Turkish navy and the waters in and around the Dardanelles. This was done for the absurd reason that it was thought improper – 'ungentlemanly' – to take advantage of Limpus's expertise. Carden had been a blameless peacetime superintendant of the Malta dockyard and had no experience of handling ships at sea. He was incapable of holding a wartime command and eager to retire, which he duly did on l5 March 1915, six weeks before the Dardanelles venture began.

Churchill had written to Fisher on 13 January about making an aeroplane base on the Turkish island of Tenedos, about twenty miles south of the Dardanelles.

'We cannot rely on French seaplanes for our spotting. The army has developed a system of wireless telephone from aeroplanes spotting for artillery, which is most effective. Full details of this should be at once obtained and some of the machines fitted accordingly.'

'But Fisher was a broken reed, as Churchill failed to realise. Old and worn out and nervous', wrote Herbert Richmond, Assistant Director of Operations at the Admiralty, in his diary on 19 January. 'It is ill to have the destinies of an empire in the hands of a failing old man, anxious for popularity, afraid of any local mishap which may be put down to his dispositions.' As late as 21 April Fisher wrote to Admiral Sir John Jellicoe (commander of the Grand Fleet) urging him to demand aeroplanes to protect his ships in the North Sea and the Atlantic from Zeppelins. 'You must write direct to the First Lord and ask for them at once, before they are all sent to the Dardanelles,' adding, in typically extravagant language: 'where they are now going by dozens!'

Air Power at the Dardanelles

The campaign, launched on 25 April 1915, was fought mainly by soldiers and sailors, but airmen did bear part of the burden. Churchill ordered the captain of HMS *Phaeton* to take Ian Hamilton, appointed commander of the proposed assault on the Gallipoli Peninsula, and his staff to Lemnos (an island forty miles west of the entrance to the Straits) on 13 March. *Phaeton* was also to 'embark as many seaplanes and aeroplanes, with their personnel, as can reach you before the time of sailing and for which you have room'. Carden signalled to Churchill on the eve of his retirement: 'Seaplanes at 2-3,000 feet have experimented in locating mines, these are clearly visible at eighteen feet depth and further trials are in progress.' John de Robeck (Carden's successor, another officer unfit for wartime command) reported on 19 March that 'major damage' had been caused to ships by drifting mines which seaplanes had not spotted.

A naval squadron (of twelve aeroplanes, plus some armoured cars) under the command of 'the redoubtable' Samson, 'a born fighter', arrived at Lemnos in April. They photographed and mapped Turkish defences, dropping small bombs whenever they could. During May, a landing strip was constructed at Helles so that observers could report important information as quickly as possible. At a meeting of the War Council on 14 May (three days before he was obliged to leave the Admiralty) Churchill said 'aeroplanes, including those capable of carrying heavy weights, should be despatched' to the Dardanelles, in addition to numerous other resources, 'to make preparations for a regular siege', in an attempt to rescue an operation already failing at a heavy cost in lives and material. Next day, the 15th, he sent a telegram to de Robeck telling him that he was planning to send him strong aerial reinforcements:

'... including machines to carry 500-lb bombs. This is more than equivalent to a 15-inch high explosive shell. The propriety and expediency of an air attack on Constantinople should be considered. The Arsenal, the German Embassy, shipping in the harbour etc., would afford fair objects of attack, and would have serious moral effect on the population.'

However such attacks were never made. As its strength gradually increased, the navy's aircraft – including two kite balloons – moved to Imbros in August, under the overall command of Sykes. On 23 November, Samson reported that 179 bombs each of 100-lbs weight had been dropped and 507 25-lbs on numerous targets, causing – it was believed – considerable panic as well as damage. In addition, Charles Edmonds, flying a Short seaplane over the Sea of Marmara struck and sank a Turkish steamer with a torpedo: one of the earliest such aerial victories. But co-operation with the other services had not yet been organised and reconnaissance aircraft were often in danger from naval shells, while soldiers fired at all aircraft, British and Turkish. Aircraft reported the location and movements of enemy forces at Suvla *before* the landings, but as Steel and Hart wrote, 'intelligence is of no value if it is not used'.

'The outstanding originality, the skill in improvisation, and the great gallantry' of Samson and his co-pilots, wrote Stephen Roskill, 'sheds a ray of light on a scene which is otherwise one of unmitigated gloom.' On 2 May 1915, Samson reported to Sueter from the *Ark Royal* (Britain's first seaplane-carrier, converted from a tramp steamer) at Mudros Bay, on the island of Lemnos. 'We live in the air all day and it is taking it out of our machines', of which only six were usually available. The BE 2c was little use, but Farmans were fast (75 mph) and could carry wireless, two 100-lb bombs and do whatever task required.

'It was rotten seeing the soldiers get hell at the landing places', Samson added. 'Knowing the defences, I did not believe they would be able to get ashore.' But they did, 'although the Turks and Germans have got awfully strong positions our men have got their blood up, as the Turks are such devils to the wounded... I honestly believe that our aeroplanes have given the Turks a healthy feeling of dread.'

Samson looked and behaved just like a pirate, recalled Richard Davies, who was himself a hero, awarded a Victoria Cross for saving the life of a downed airman during this campaign. Charles Samson left the Mediterranean near the end of 1915 to work on anti-Zeppelin defences along England's north-eastern coasts. He reached the rank of air commodore in the RAF, but died in 1931, aged only forty-eight. A man for wartime, greatly admired by Churchill, he had not thrived in peacetime.

Churchill wrote to Arthur Balfour, his successor at the Admiralty, on 22 July 1915. Frederick Sykes, he said, had visited him on his return from the Dardanelles and told him that only five aeroplanes, on average, were flying each day. 'If this is true, it is very discreditable to the Naval Wing.' The local organisation must be poor, but clearly the Air Department is failing 'to grasp the importance of the aviation services at the Dardanelles'. Churchill recalled a minute he had sent to Fisher on 13 May advising the despatch of 'large reinforcements of aeroplanes and seaplanes', but nothing was done before they both left office. At least thirty aeroplanes and seaplanes, thought Churchill, should be operating daily in that area and he again advocated bombing 'strategic targets' in Constantinople.

A Disaster Too Many

Fisher backed off from the southern venture when he realised – late in the day – that a purely naval assault was intended, unsupported by soldiers. Troops were eventually assigned to this operation, but few of them were well trained in their own skills and not at all in combination with seamen or airmen. 'Grand strategic concepts are fine things,' wrote Robert Rhodes James, 'but it is of value to have the wherewithal to accomplish them. It is also desirable to have a clear conception of the advantages that will accrue from success and some thoughts on the price that would have to be paid for failure.'

Yet Fisher did not resign until 15 May, feebly claiming that 'by the traditions of the service' he should support the First Lord. He was mentally deranged by then and had fled from the Admiralty to lurk in a nearby hotel. Asquith personally ordered him back to his duty. Insofar as he thought at all, Fisher supposed that his actions would get rid of Churchill (which they did) and force a reversal of the Dardanelles policy (which they did not). Much to his surprise, Fisher was dismissed.

The true test of a general, wrote the Duke of Wellington, was to know when to retreat and dare to do it. Churchill, so fond of using past examples to suit current ambitions, overlooked this opinion and, like Fisher, was surprised – as well as mightily offended – at his dismissal from the Admiralty. Few historians accept his eloquent attempt, prolonged for the rest of his life, to wriggle out of his share of responsibility for a disaster that cost 47,000 British, French and Anzacs killed or missing; many more suffered sickness. Turkish losses were heavier – about 68,000 killed or missing – but they were not defeated.

In March 1916, at a time when he was a mere backbencher, desperate for further office, Churchill chose to advocate in Parliament Fisher's re-appointment as First Sea Lord. This amazing proposal was received with astonishment and dismissed out of hand. As Martin Gilbert wrote, he 'was shattered by the hostile, mocking reactions to his proposal'. He did not, however, accept that his opponents might be right and wrote to Fisher on 14 May 1916: 'Don't lose heart. I am convinced destiny has not done with you.' But it had, although Fisher never abandoned hope of a third return to the top of the naval tree until he died in 1920.

Park at Gallipoli
Keith Park, who later became a famous fighter pilot and commander of air forces, served as an artilleryman at Gallipoli. He was much impressed by the outstanding Australian soldier, William Birdwood ('Birdie' to the troops, 'the Soul of Anzac' in the history books) and tried to follow many of his precepts during the rest of his career: attention to detail; regular tours of inspection; indifference to personal danger and, not least, Birdwood's recognition that the uniformed civilians of a wartime army would not respond easily to barrack-square discipline. Gallipoli marked Park both physically and mentally, as it did everyone who served there. He saw and shared in the squalor so often unavoidable on 'active service', suffered from the exceptional bungling of those responsible for a disastrous campaign and would be among the commanders of other combined operations in Britain, the Mediterranean and the Far East who did their best to avoid the mistakes made at Gallipoli.

Expanding Naval Air Power
When Churchill gave up his sinecure (Chancellor of the Duchy of Lancaster) on the fringes of power in November 1915, *Flight*'s editor thought it a sad day for Britain's air services. He had, in fact, been little more than a eunuch in a harem, disregarded by all the movers and shakers. Churchill and Fisher

were replaced by Balfour (as First Lord of the Admiralty) and Admiral Henry Jackson (as First Sea Lord). They brought: 'tranquility in place of conflict and turmoil to Whitehall; but it was the tranquility of prudence and discretion, not of calm, decisive action.'

Roskill believed that 'the seeds of the bitter harvest of 1917, when the Admiralty lost control of its air service, were sown in the conflagration of May 1915'. Balfour did not think that the navy should be involved in the defence of London and on 18 June 1915 the Admiralty asked the War Office to resume this task, which – in accordance with its stately procedures – it actually did eight months later. French, recently superseded as head of the armies in France, was appointed in February 1916, even though he knew nothing whatsoever about the problems of defending London from aerial attack.

Had Churchill survived in office, Roskill thought 'the offensive possibility of an air torpedo attack on the enemy fleet in harbour would have been given higher priority and pressed ahead with greater vigour'. As early as October 1914 Churchill had imagined both purpose-built aircraft carriers and the launching of aircraft from capital ships and even barges: aircraft that would land close to their 'mother' vessel on returning from a mission.

Before the Dardanelles campaign began, Churchill had presided over a conference in the Admiralty on 3 April 1915. Sueter and all the more senior naval airmen attended: among them, Francis Scarlett, Spenser Grey and Arthur Longmore. They discussed enlarging and strengthening the service's number of aeroplanes and seaplanes to use for bombing, dropping torpedoes, photo-reconnaissance and attacking enemy shipping, not forgetting the need for many training machines. Curtiss seaplanes, supplied from the United States, were not yet adequate, but Churchill pointed out that these machines, 'and in fact all aeroplanes and seaplanes delivered from America, must be considered as an addition to our forces': they *must* be made efficient. We have 'passed the stage of daring exploits,' he said, 'and must acquire the power to strike heavy blows which will produce decisive effects on the enemy's fighting strength.'

He had in mind a series of 'smashing blows', like a naval bombardment, which would disrupt Germany's ability to continue the war. At least two or three tons of explosives, he stipulated, should be dropped on one target during the night in a single operation.

Neville Jones thought that if Churchill had not lost office in May 1915: 'Britain might have possessed a strategic bomber force as early as 1916.' Shortly after this conference, on 15 April, Churchill told Sueter the 'standards of daring and achievement,' by naval airmen 'are rising and so many officers perform excellent work that it is no longer possible except now and then to deal with every case of a fine exploit. Every month, therefore, you will submit to me the names of officers and men who in the opinion of the Air Department are deserving of notice or reward.'

On 30 May 1915, almost two weeks after his dismissal from the Admiralty, Churchill composed a memorandum on the RNAS. It had expanded from ninety-eight officers and 575 men in August 1914 to 875 officers and more than 8,000 men in just nine months. It also included armoured car squadrons and anti-aircraft guns. About 250 machines were ready to fly at any time and by the end of 1915 they would have about 500 trained pilots, as well as those under-training and allowing for those killed or found unsuitable.

Air Lord?
Sueter wrote 'Notes on the Formation of an Air Department', dated 10 June 1915. He sent a copy to Churchill, who revised and forwarded them to Asquith late in June. At that time, he believed the prime minister might set up an air department and invite him to head it. His friends encouraged this hope: James Garvin (editor of the *Observer*) for example, wrote to him on 22 June saying 'I wish you were Air Lord'. Churchill continued to believe that he might be given charge of all air matters until May 1916, when Asquith set up an Air Board, under Lord Curzon: a former Viceroy of India, who knew as much about aviation as French did about aerial defence.

Like Sueter, Churchill had hoped to bring both air services under a single head before the end of 1915 in an attempt 'to make the British air service indisputably the largest, most efficient, and most enterprising of any belligerent power'.

Maurice Bonham Carter (who had married Violet and was now Asquith's secretary), sent the proposal to Maurice Hankey, secretary of both the CID and the Dardanelles Committee. 'It looks to me,' he added, 'like a scheme for providing Winston with something to do.' The Military Wing, thought Bonham Carter, 'is a success largely because it has been developed and trained as a branch of the army and with military objects strictly in view': unlike the Naval Wing, which had degenerated 'into a crowd of highly-skilled but ill-disciplined privateersmen. What is wanted is to make the Naval Wing more "Naval", rather than more "Aerial".' Hankey, not a man made for office in the hurly-burly of wartime improvisation, and no friend of Churchill, agreed.

3

A War for Germany to Win, Under the Sea, 1914-1918

The Most Formidable Thing

Had there been more submersible torpedo-boats (U-boats, as German submarines are known), Germany might well have survived or even won the war by isolating the British Isles. As we shall see, Hitler's Germany might also have triumphed at sea a generation later. Fortunately, those leaders – civilian and military – who rule us pay little attention to history. The U-boat's defeat in the Great War would be brought about mainly by Britain's long-overdue decision, in 1917, to use heavily-armed destroyers to convoy merchant ships sailing for British ports with aircraft and airships lending an increasingly valuable hand.

Convoys forced U-boats to risk contact with these escorts, on the surface and in the air, in their hunt for merchant ships. By November 1918, more than 100 airships and thirty-seven out of forty-three maritime squadrons in home waters were engaged in anti-submarine duties. Although aircraft found it difficult to destroy U-boats, 'they exercised, when employed as close and distant escorts to convoys, a most decisive effect: they rendered convoys virtually immune from successful attack.'

One bonus for the British was the surprising success of the De Havilland 6. More than 2,000 examples of this training machine had been hastily produced for the RFC, which found in 1918 that it had no use for them. It was saved by an Admiralty request for aircraft patrols off the coasts of north-eastern England and Scotland. Although slow and lightly-armed, U-boat captains did not know this and prudently took evasive action whenever a DH 6 was sighted. This frail machine thus became one of the most 'cost effective' weapons in Britain's air armoury. By the middle of 1918, Churchill announced, with his usual exaggeration, that the U-boat has been 'definitely defeated'.

Although the Royal Navy had begun to build its own submersibles years before the war began, the Germans overtook the British in quantity and quality production. 'We can wound England most seriously by injuring her trade', wrote Admiral Friedrich von Ingenohl, commander of Germany's High Seas Fleet. 'The gravity of the situation demands that we should free ourselves from all scruples which certainly no longer have justification.' As Arthur Hezlet (a submariner) wrote in 1960, submersibles were 'an independent weapon' that achieved great success, given its defensive weakness and small numbers.

A War Zone at Sea

On 4 February 1915 Germany declared that the waters around Great Britain and Ireland would be regarded, from the 18th, as 'a war zone'. Any vessel found therein was liable to be sunk; her crew and any passengers would have to take to the lifeboats, if they could, and hope to be rescued. In response to President Woodrow Wilson's protests unrestricted attacks were abandoned, but by the end of 1915 U-boats had sunk more than 1,000,000 tons of shipping, and would achieve even greater success in 1916. As more U-boats became available, it seemed to German naval and military chiefs that a war-winning weapon was to hand and they advocated a resumption of 'unrestricted warfare' in 1917.

They calculated that even if the United States declared war – which she did on 6 April – victory could be achieved before American soldiers were mobilised, trained, equipped and shipped across the Atlantic on voyages which might see many of them drowned as a result of U-boat attacks. The U-boat, wrote Walter Page (US Ambassador in Britain) in 1917 'is the most formidable thing that the war has produced, by far, and it gives the German the only chance he has to win'.

Aircraft and Airships

Aircraft would become of increasing value in the fight against U-boats. An improved version of the Short Type 184 seaplane, the Curtiss H12 Large America flying boat (developed from an earlier type by Commander John Porte, 'a designer and innovator of genius') and the excellent Felixstowe F2a all proved their worth. In April 1917, a 'Spider Web' patrol system, based on the North Hinder Light Vessel and linked to Felixstowe and Great Yarmouth was set up in the North Sea. It formed an octagon sixty miles in diameter and permitted the systematic search of some 4,000 square miles of sea, right across the preferred path of U-boats looking for targets. Although flying boats rarely sank or even damaged U-boats, they did force them to submerge, where they had to travel slowly and risked exhausting their electric batteries.

Flying boats were greatly helped by non-rigid airships, especially those of the NS (North Sea) class. Airships were able to hover, allowing extended observation, and carried a far heavier load of fuel and weapons plus the large wireless sets needed to send and receive messages clearly and promptly. By the end of 1917, it had been learned that aircraft attacking submarines needed to be able to drop a bomb containing at least 300-lbs of explosive, fitted with both an impact and a delayed-action fuse, to have any hope of causing serious damage. Their chief value, however, was as a deterrent: obliging U-boats to submerge and lose contact with their prey.

A Veritable Cemetery

No aircraft had sunk a U-boat when 1917 began and during the first four months of that year U-boats sank more than 900 ships. Many were ocean-going vessels on which Britain's supplies depended and the number of neutral nations sending ships to her ports fell to a quarter of the total in 1916. At the end of March 1917 Maurice Hankey feared that 'we may yet be beaten at sea' and news from the Western Front was just as bad. The battle of Arras in April turned into the costliest of British offensives and a French offensive in the same month ended in a disaster from which the French army scarcely recovered during the remainder of the war. In the air, the RFC lost more than 300 pilots: many of them young men with fewer than twenty hours' solo flying trying to cope with better-equipped and far more experienced enemies. The American declaration of war in April could bring no comfort for months to come.

'The great approach route to the south-west of Ireland,' wrote Churchill in April 1917, 'was becoming a veritable cemetery of British shipping, in which large vessels were sunk regularly day by day about 200 miles from land...' The U-boat was rapidly undermining not only the life of the British islands, but the foundations of the Allies' strength; and the danger of their collapse in 1918 began to loom black and imminent.

Most British or French citizens were unaware of this extreme danger because their governments did not release information about shipping losses and journalists were strictly censored. The impact of German air raids on England, beginning in May, could not be hidden from the general public, although officials did their best.

Convoys and Air Cover

Since the war began, the navy had escorted every vessel carrying troops to and from the Western Front 'without ever losing a man, horse or gun at sea'. Escort had traditionally been a prime task, but the Compulsory Convoy Act was repealed in 1872. Thereafter, naval officers persuaded themselves that it was enough to patrol *routes*, rather than to escort *ships*; to act offensively and not defensively. As Donald Macintyre wrote, this was like having 'a single rifleman trying to protect a caravan in the Sahara by strolling at random to and fro along the route'.

David Beatty (commanding the Grand Fleet) sent the first of a stream of letters from January 1917 onwards to the Admiralty pressing for a greatly-improved and expanded RNAS to focus on support for the fleet and anti-submarine work. The secretary of the new Air Board (headed by Lord Cowdray) arranged the transfer from the Ministry of Munitions of responsibility for the supply and design of aeroplanes and seaplanes; a responsibility which the Admiralty had 'clung to with the utmost tenacity' in 1916.

Churchill – still out of office – addressed his fellow MPs in April 1917 on what he called 'the whole story of the muddle in the air services since the beginning of the war'. He was especially severe in his criticism of the House of Commons for having allowed control to pass out of its hands. The pilots, he believed, had excellent qualities, but they suffered heavy casualties both in training and combat as a result of inadequate machines and poor organisation. He recalled that as long ago as March 1916 MPs had criticised that muddle. A committee was formed, as usual in Britain, drawn from members on both sides of the House and an Air Board was created under Lord Curzon, but it had no real powers and therefore achieved nothing. Churchill blamed Curzon 'for taking the responsibility without proper power and authority' and the House 'for relaxing its vigilance, for being so easily put off'.

Curzon's successor, Cowdray, resigned in June and *Flight* thought Churchill should be appointed Air Minister: a 'man of imagination', ready to act. He had always taken a deep interest in aviation, especially at sea, overcoming powerful opposition from 'Old Navy' officers. In addition, 'even his worst enemies never denied him the possession of outstanding ability as statesman and administrator'. Arnold Bennett, an immensely popular novelist and playwright, also backed Churchill: 'If Germany had imagination,' he wrote, 'she would concentrate in the air for the remainder of the war. She may yet do so.'

Leslie and Henderson

Beatty was supported by two men who made a vital contribution to victory in the war at sea: Norman Leslie (a civil servant in the new Ministry of Shipping) and Reginald Henderson (a junior officer, later an admiral). They discovered that the number of ocean-going vessels arriving and departing – the only ones that mattered – was, at most, about twenty a day. The Admiralty had been working on a figure of 5,000 because unthinking officials were counting every movement of every ship above 300 tons along every coast and concluded, reasonably enough, that such an enormous number could not be escorted. In fact, hundreds of vessels were already carrying essential coal to France, in what the Admiralty was pleased to call 'controlled sailings' without suffering any significant loss.

Reflecting on these dismal events after the war, Churchill got to the root of the matter: 'There was in fact very nearly as good a chance of a convoy of forty ships in close order slipping unperceived between the patrolling U-boats as there was for a single ship', given the vast extent of the sea. Moreover, wireless messages could deflect convoys from areas known to be dangerous. Better still, the escorting destroyers – being closely gathered – would have better prospects of sinking or at least driving away U-boats.

A Convoy Committee was set up on 17 May 1917, which began to organise a worldwide system of protection, but on 20 June the First Sea Lord, John Jellicoe, told the newly-created War Policy Committee (not including Churchill) that 'owing to the great shortage of shipping due to German submarines, it would be impossible for Great Britain to continue the war in 1918'. The 'bombshell', as Douglas Haig noted in his diary, alarmed everyone present. Jellicoe was by then exhausted and despondent, yet he retained his high office for a further five months. Meanwhile, more anti-submarine vessels, including eighteen American destroyers, were being employed and the RNAS was expanding and taking on more efficient aircraft.

Even so, it was not until April 1918 that losses of merchant ships fell below 300,000 tons per month and in that month the construction of ships exceeded losses for the first time since unrestricted attacks began. Worse still, from a German point of view, U-boats proved unable to prevent an ever-increasing flow of American soldiers across the Atlantic and into France. Improving surface defences were greatly helped throughout 1918 with aircraft directed by naval commanders. Yet the Admiralty's deep-seated faith in submarine-hunting operations (a dogmatism seen at its most obdurate in the Mediterranean) was still as alive and vigorous in 1918 as in previous years. Admiral Sir William Jameson, writing in 1965, concluded that the U-boat was 'foiled rather than defeated', but only by a narrow margin: between February 1917 and November 1918, it sank well over 3,000 British and Allied ships and killed nearly 15,000 merchant seamen.

A Massive Campaign

The war at, under and over the sea had grown massively by the time of the Armistice. On the Allied side, over 300 destroyers, more than 4,000 auxiliary vessels and thirty-five submarines, assisted by no fewer than 500 flying boats, seaplanes and land planes, together with 100 airships, were at work. Opposing them were about 120 operational U-boats. This was in addition to the immense effort needed to produce and lay a vast number of mines and nets. The number of men required to man this gigantic force was approximately 14,000, with probably another 500,000 to build, refit and support them generally.

During 1918, aviation had become a weapon to be taken seriously, rather than the annoyance it had been at the beginning. David Beatty and other air-minded naval officers had hoped to create a force of torpedo-carrying seaplanes and ships capable of taking them to within hitting range of the German fleet in its harbours, but the necessary ships, aircraft and weapons were still under development at the time of the Armistice. Even so, naval aviation had become a valuable weapon for spotting U-boats, attacking enemy coasts and shipping as well as protecting those of Britain and her allies.

The U-boat had severely shaken the British government and the first article of the Armistice terms required the Germans to surrender them all. In 1921, when representatives of the five largest naval powers met in Washington, Britain strongly advocated the abolition of all submarines. She argued that this weapon was only effective as a commerce raider and asserted that it was of no value as a military weapon, which was obviously untrue, as would be revealed – even more plainly – after the outbreak of another war in 1939.

4

A New Way to Wage War:
The First Battle of Britain, 1914-1918

Acorns and Oaks

Statistically, the first 'Battle of Britain' was a minor episode in a long and fearfully destructive war: no more than fifty-one attacks were made by airships and fifty-two by aeroplanes and yet these raids burned deep into many British memories, causing great oaks to grow from these little acorns. As well as the notorious (but largely ineffectual) airship raids, twin-engined Gothas and the much larger Giants struck at English targets on average once a fortnight for a whole year and caused widespread unrest among civilians, many of whom were engaged in war production. Politicians therefore gave serious attention to their fears and this eventually led to the uniting of the RFC and the RNAS in a 'Royal Air Force'.

Although the actual casualties and damage caused by German attacks were so slight, in comparison to the horrors of the Western Front, Gallipoli and Mesopotamia, the government was obliged to divert significant forces to home defence. Memories of those attacks would influence post-war planning around the world, most notably in Britain, Germany and the United States. Giulio Douhet (an Italian theorist), Hugh Trenchard in the RAF, Billy Mitchell and Alexander de Seversky in the United States were to air power what Carl von Clausewitz was to ground power and Alfred Thayer Mahan to sea power: philosophical theorists, articulators for a new doctrine of military power, prophetic historians of a new age, polemical pamphleteers whose faith in 'airy navies' was unbounded. As we shall see, Churchill had plenty to say and write about air power as soon as Hitler came to power in Germany.

A Tactical or Strategic Weapon?

It was the Germans, using airships at first and then much more useful aeroplanes, who first attempted strategic bombing. To meet the aerial threat during the Great War, the British evolved all the complex paraphernalia of defence that would be revived, expanded and improved – notably with the addition of chains of radar stations – to counter Hitler's aggression: guns;

fighters; barrage balloons; wireless detection networks; observer posts; searchlights; shelters and telephone communications. The question would be asked again, much more insistently: can bombers destroy industries, fuel resources and undermine civilian will to resist and thereby win, or at least shorten, a war?

After 1918, the Germans decided that the military results of so-called *strategic* bombing had not justified the expenditure and consequently built a *tactical* air force in the 1930s geared primarily to army support: there were no long-range heavy bombers intended to destroy industrial or military resources or to undermine civilian morale far from the front lines. In Britain, by contrast, German air raids left deep scars because the Channel and the North Sea could now so easily be crossed. Air enthusiasts harped constantly on the dangers of aerial attack and on the need to develop a force capable of effective retaliation: it was the British, not the Germans, who had 'a bomber obsession' prior to and during World War Two; it was Lloyd George who first said, in 1917, that the bomber would always get through.

One or two German aeroplanes had dropped a few small bombs along the English coast, the first on a garden near Dover Castle on Christmas Eve, 1914. No-one was hurt and the damage was trivial. By then, more than 1,000,000 Europeans had already been killed or wounded in five months of war (quite apart from horses, cows and other animals as well as immense destruction of property), but this petty incident at Dover confirmed what Churchill had been saying ever since the Germans and French built effective flying machines: a new method of waging war now existed that would, sooner or later, plague mankind.

On New Year's Day 1915 Churchill warned the War Council that he had heard rumours of a night attack on London by up to twenty airships, an attack which the navy would be powerless to prevent. Fisher (First Sea Lord) was greatly disturbed. A terrible massacre was imminent, he believed, and could only be prevented if one German prisoner was shot for every Briton killed by an air raid. No such massacre took place and Fisher's bizarre proposal was rejected out of hand. He promptly offered his resignation to Churchill, who unwisely rejected it. No-one doubts Fisher's past achievements for the Royal Navy, but this proposal should have alerted Churchill – long before the Gallipoli disasters – to the fact that Fisher was no longer fit for high office, least of all in wartime.

Defending London

Churchill outlined plans for the defence of London in January 1915, claiming that within the London-Sheerness-Dover triangle about sixty British aeroplanes, armed with rifles firing incendiary bullets, were on constant call and even that some pilots were prepared to charge Zeppelins: this kamikaze spirit was not so alien to Britons of that generation as we may now like to believe. In fact, the Germans had only nine airships available, but on the 19th two Zeppelins actually attacked coastal targets. They caused few casualties and little damage, but were untroubled by the defences, ground or air, either coming or going.

After he left the Admiralty in May 1915, Churchill promoted the case for an independent Air Department 'to supply, maintain and organise' all aircraft, especially those charged with the defence of London and other possible targets, while leaving 'command and military control' to navy and army commanders. The two wings would draw together and by the end of 1915, he thought, 'the British air service' would be 'indisputably the largest, most efficient, and most enterprising of any belligerent power' and he was willing to command it.

Those in power, however, no longer attended to Churchill's opinions. In July 1915 the Admiralty declared the RNAS to be an integral part of the Royal Navy and in September Balfour appointed a non-airman, Rear-Admiral Vaughan-Lee, as Director of Admiralty Air Services. Sueter, obviously the man best qualified, was overlooked. Although 'brilliantly inventive', he was 'impatient of authority' and therefore relegated to supervision of aircraft construction. In October, when he again proposed the formation of a Royal Air Service, he was exiled to the Mediterranean. Churchill, even more out of favour than Sueter, spent some months late in 1915 and early in 1916 as an army officer on the Western Front.

Although politics at home remained his obsession, he was also concerned both about Britain's air defence and her capacity to attack German targets. 'There is no excuse,' he wrote to his wife on 17 January 1916, 'for our not having command of the air. Since I left the Admiralty, the whole Naval Wing has been let down, and all our precious ascendancy has been dissipated.' In another letter to Clementine on the 20th he commented on an assertion in the House of Commons by Harold Tennant (Under-Secretary of State for War and Margot Asquith's brother) that German aeroplanes never, or rarely, flew across British lines: an assertion that 'reads amusingly here. The flying officers tell me a sad tale of their difficulties and the utter want of knowledge and drive that characterises the present War Office administration.'

He was convinced that if he were in charge, Britain would have 'supremacy today'. Jennie, his mother and London agent, told him on 3 February that the 'poor aviation department seems to be doing badly, kicked from pillar to post'. There was even a rumour that Fisher might be recalled to head it.

'I do not think they will want me for Air', Churchill told Clementine on 10 February 1916. His mind now returned to the idea of seizing Borkum and provoking a northern adventure. It would be 'one sure and certain remedy for a prevention of air raids on England', he thought, because 'a really strong air station' would permit us to destroy Zeppelins in their sheds and attack German military targets. 'But be sure no-one will have the nerve for that', he sighed: it will be thought 'less risky' to try and put a roof over England 'in a purely futile defensive'. By 14 February Churchill had heard that Curzon was likely to be Air Minister. 'Well, I do not care', he told Clementine. 'I could have done it well. But I am under the vague displeasure of the press: and Asquith's interests, as I told you, will best be served by my disappearance, temporary or final.'

There was, in fact, nothing 'vague' about opposition to Churchill in most newspapers and he cared very much about his lack of office: 'it riles me to see how ungrateful they are. But for my personal struggles we should not have had *half* the air service we have today.' He complained to his wife again on the 20th: the Germans 'sail about unmolested overhead, watching the shooting and scorning our anti-aircraft guns. There is no doubt who is master of this air!' Other hands were at work, however. In April 1916 Felton Vesey Holt was brought to England from France and set up the first purely air defence formation: a wing of two squadrons, about twenty aeroplanes in each. These were truly 'the first of the few'. By the end of July Holt's wing had expanded to five squadrons and was re-named 'The Home Defence Wing'. It was the embryo of Dowding's Fighter Command, formed twenty years later.

Attacking the Enemy

On 25 March 1916 Churchill wrote to Clementine, quoting with approval a speech made in the House by Noel Pemberton Billing in which he called for an Air Board to frame a unified air policy and encourage an 'active offensive air force'. Churchill then added: 'Fancy Tennant admitting that the preparations made by Seely and me had given them command of the air for ten months at the beginning of the war,' a command subsequently lost. 'Was there ever such a confession!' In another letter to his wife on 30 March Churchill again spoke warmly of Pemberton Billing: 'His speeches are genuine products; and the facts are incontrovertible. It all shows the uselessness of Balfour except as a counsellor. He does not comprehend action in any form.'

In May 1916 came one of Churchill's most important speeches on air power, commending 'the triumph of the aeroplane'. Only his 'hornets' – as he called the fighter aircraft he had once controlled – could have prevented Zeppelins from raiding 'every fine day' and forced them to strike only at night, 'almost blindfolded'. Without his hornets, he continued, after twenty-two months of war, no important enemy military or naval targets had been destroyed.

An Air Department was needed, Churchill argued, with the power to override obstruction from the other services. It should be 'one unified, permanent branch of imperial defence, composed exclusively of men who will not think of themselves as soldiers, sailors, or civilians, but as airmen'. That service might 'possibly, at no distant date... become the dominating arm of the war'. Whereas submarines and mines have 'robbed the navy of its rights' and the deadlock on land has prohibited the movement of the army, 'the air is free and open. There are no entrenchments there. It is equal for the attack and for the defence.' Britain must obtain 'that aerial supremacy which is, perhaps, the most obvious and most practical step towards a victorious issue from the increasing dangers of the war'.

Churchill attacked the Air Board as a mere attempt to parry the demand for an Air Ministry, predicting a 'first class row', which duly came in August 1916 when the Admiralty – bypassing Curzon – was granted nearly £3,000,000 by the Treasury for aeroplanes and engines. Curzon was incensed. Although he did not think a unified service could be set up in wartime, he asked that the Air Board be given responsibility for the 'supply, design, inspection and finance' of aeroplanes and engines; he also asked that the Admiralty be required to appoint an additional Sea Lord with responsibility for naval aviation. Asquith would not decide, Balfour refused to co-operate and for these and many other reasons Asquith's government collapsed in December 1916. Curzon, among those who brought Asquith down, promptly left the Air Board to become Lord President of the Council under new Prime Minister Lloyd George.

London's First Air Raid

It was not until 28 November 1916 that London was hit by a daylight raid regarded by historians as 'among the most audacious of the war'. A single-engined LVG CIV biplane, with a two-man crew, took off from an airfield near the Belgian coast, intending to drop six 20-lb bombs on the Admiralty buildings in Whitehall. The bombs, dropped from a great height – 13,000 feet – landed 'commendably close' and ten Londoners were injured. The incident made little stir because on that same day RFC pilots destroyed two Zeppelins, provoking widespread jubilation. The gallant crew of the LVG would cause London no more harm because they made a forced landing near Boulogne and were captured by the French. *The Times*, however, was perturbed by their deed: the aeroplane, being 'relatively cheap and elusive' had 'far more dangerous possibilities than the large and costly Zeppelin'.

Eight months later, in July 1917 after a formation of German bombers struck at London, Lovat Fraser, a leader-writer on *The Times*, wrote:

'If I were asked what event of the last year has been of most significance to the future of humanity, I should reply that it is not the Russian Revolution, nor even the stern intervention of the United States in a sacred cause, but the appearance of a single German aeroplane flying at high noon over London last November.'

Aerial defences were barely tested before 25 May 1917 when twenty-one Gotha GIV twin-engined bombers, planning to attack London, were foiled by thick cloud and chose Folkestone on the Kent coast instead, where there was a large military camp as well as an important harbour. The Gothas were not challenged over England, helped by French's bizarre order (in effect since March 1916) forbidding anti-aircraft gunners, except those along the coast, from firing at aircraft 'even if recognised as hostile'.

Eventually, seventy-four fighters chased the Gothas home, but managed only to damage one between them. Folkestone suffered nearly 300 casualties, a third of them fatal. The defences had been designed to cope with night raiders and it was not easy, as John Bushby wrote, 'to switch overnight from whale harpooning to mosquito swatting'.

A widespread uproar followed, exacerbated by French's foolish edict and what *The Times* called a 'childish and dangerous' reluctance to allow the raid to be reported. William Robertson, head of the army, summoned important officials to London to consider national defence. Henderson, now Director-General of Military Aviation, represented the RFC. He tried to revive his earlier proposal for the development of airborne radio-telephony, but the Admiralty objected, fearing that such experiments might interfere in its own communications with warships. Henderson was one of Britain's earliest military pilots, having learned to fly in 1910 at the age of forty-eight and had 'nursed and reared' the RFC since its creation. He refused to press the Admiralty over the wireless issue, and French would not revoke his no-fire order.

Gothas over London

A few days later, on 13 June 1917, fourteen Gothas reached London. They bombed and returned to their Belgian base, virtually unchallenged either from the ground or in the air. They had killed or injured nearly 600 Londoners, many of them children. The outcry over the Folkestone raid was redoubled and the War Minister, Lord Derby, when asked if any of the raiders had been shot down could only offer this lame answer: 'I am afraid not. There are some doubts about one, but I would not like to say for certain,' adding that Lord French 'is doing all in his power to secure this city.'

Zeppelins, attacking by night, were not a serious threat, but aeroplane raids in daylight certainly were. Lloyd George and his War Cabinet, responding to vehement public demands, required Haig and Trenchard to release two Sopwith squadrons, one equipped with the SE 5a and the other with Pups, from the Western Front, for service at home. They complied, most reluctantly. But these excellent fighters, far more capable in aerial combat than the useless BE 2cs hitherto deemed sufficient for home defence, were needed, especially if further Gotha raids were to be punished.

The Gothas returned to London on 7 July: twenty-one of them, entirely unopposed, 'as if they were in a peacetime parade', recalled one witness. They flew so low, wrote another, 'their approach was so leisurely, and so well-kept was their fan-like formation, that to suppose they were enemies was preposterous'. As before, British defences, both on the ground and in the air, achieved little and more than 300 Londoners were killed or injured. Nearly 100 aircraft of twenty different types eventually took to the air: undirected and uncoordinated, they suffered several casualties. One Gotha was shot down, provoking an unseemly squabble between the Admiralty and the home defence forces as to who deserved the credit. British newspapers howled while those in Germany exulted. We had not been so 'humiliated and disgraced', wrote the *Daily Mail*, since a Dutch fleet sailed up the Medway in 1667. A corresponding wave of outrage led to the destruction of properties owned or managed by persons with German names.

Anger was widespread, but it did not last and there was no pressure to sue for terms. MPs and some public officials feared that lower-class persons would panic and were most surprised to find that they had not. Basil Liddell Hart, who became a well-known commentator on military matters, shared that surprise. In 1925 he wrote of 'women, children, babies in arms, spending night after night huddled in sodden fields, shivering under a bitter wintry sky'. Now thoroughly excited, he invited his readers to imagine all England's cities wrecked: 'Whitehall a heap of ruins, the slum districts maddened into the impulse to break loose and maraud... Would not the general will to resist vanish?'

Haig, Tiverton, Smuts, Ashmore

Setting aside such post-war extravagance, many politicians and public officials were outraged in 1917 to learn that two squadrons of effective fighters had returned to France just before the raid. Haig was ordered to send them back to England, but in fact – with Trenchard's support – sent only one. Robertson told Haig: 'I am inclined to think that we need a separate air service, but that would be a big business.' Although Haig agreed on that point, he had placed a high value on aircraft ever since he took command on the Western Front, for making maps based on photographic reconnaissance, for artillery spotting and for flying offensive patrols, 'to engage the enemy well over their lines, thus preventing German aircraft from interfering with the RFC's army co-operation types'.

In March 1915, on learning that some gunners were reluctant to follow corrections proposed by airmen, he bluntly told them that he would not tolerate reliance on 'early Victorian methods'. Throughout the rest of the war, Haig worked closely with Trenchard, giving him vital support in ensuring that the RFC was properly supplied and resisting efforts by some artillery commanders to have aircraft placed under their command.

During 1915, Major Lord Tiverton (later Second Earl of Halsbury) had begun to study the problems of dropping bombs accurately. As Biddle wrote, he may 'legitimately be considered one of the first true analysts of air warfare' and most of his opinions would be confirmed in both world wars. In September 1917, he identified key target areas in Germany which had machine shops or steel works or produced the chemicals needed in explosives. Heavy, concentrated raids on these areas would weaken enemy fighting capacity at the front lines. Tiverton also advised on the location of bases, the need for accurate navigation, the number of sorties one could expect from each bomber and the transport and storage of bombs. He underlined the fact that rain, wind and cloud – as well as enemy defences – would often upset plans and advocated daytime bombing, when factories would be fully manned, in order to cause casualties or at least oblige men to stop work and seek shelter.

As it happened, Tiverton was a generation ahead of his time and most of Britain's light bombing raids were devoted to ground support. Tiverton, as John Ferris wrote, argued that 'victory through air power would stem from rapier strikes against precise elements of an enemy's economy', whereas Trenchard thought of 'smashing its morale with a battleaxe'. Both believed that their chosen weapon 'would produce quick, cheap, cost-effective, and decisive triumphs'.

Lloyd George wanted 'a fresh and able mind, free from departmental prejudices' to deal with a growing crisis. His choice fell on Jan Christian Smuts, once a Boer rebel, now a devoted ally, whose decisions would lead to the creation of a Royal Air Force in April 1918. Smuts soon decided that all defence forces should be under a single commander: an airman, because 'the aeroplane is by far the most important means of defence'.

A London Air Defence Area was set up at the end of July 1917, covering all of south-east England as well as the capital, and for once a man with appropriate skills was found to command it: Edward Ashmore. A pilot and artillery expert, he would play a vital role in the development of Britain's air defences during and after the war. He is 'the father of all modern air defence systems', devising a standardised method of reporting for every defence unit. Each unit passed information on a basic grid to a map table in his headquarters. Ashmore emphasised the importance of co-ordination between aircraft and those who supported on the ground: guns; searchlights; observers and those manning sound indicators (although these last proved useless).

Haig and Trenchard, whose eyes never left the Western Front, objected to this diversion of resources, but the War Cabinet readily agreed to the popular clamour for an effective system of home defence. Ashmore had made, what would prove to be in both world wars, a critical decision to assign guns priority over London, ordering aircraft to patrol *beyond* the city, where they would be, in theory, safe from 'friendly fire'. Equally important was a system employing coastal watchers and telephone operators charged to give defending fighters enough warning to take off in time to harass approaching raiders, as well as to attack them on their return to Belgium. These measures, together with prevailing westerly winds and the frailty of the bombers, brought daylight raiding to an end in August.

Smuts's second report, of 17 August 1917, changed the course of history, since it came down strongly in favour of the creation of an Air Ministry, uniting the two services. Then followed his famous forecast, which became a sacred text for generations of airmen:

'The day may not be far off when aerial operations, with their devastation of enemy lands and destruction of industrial and populous centres on a vast scale, may become the principal operations of war, to which the older forms of military naval operations may become secondary and subordinate.'

And yet, as Malcolm Cooper wrote, Smuts 'had no specialised knowledge of the subject and was dependent only on whatever advice he could find readily to hand'. Henderson was virtually the only senior aviation officer who agreed with Smuts that there should be a separate service. Eric Geddes, First Lord, reflecting Admiralty opinion, was reluctant to agree, but Beatty's support for Smuts – backed by Lloyd George – carried the day.

Still No Air Ministry
Smuts's thoughts were not original, but they were well timed. Soon after Zeppelin raids began in 1915 newspapers had demanded a 'Ministry of Aeronautics' and Churchill, already recognised as 'an ardent believer in air power', was proposed as a suitable Air Minister. Asquith's supporters could not stomach his return to office and chose instead to create what they called 'a Joint Air War Committee' with Lord Derby (Director-General of Recruiting) as chairman to mediate squabbling between the services for aeroplanes and supplies. The committee was purely advisory and Derby resigned after a few weeks. It was 'quite impossible', he told Asquith, 'to bring the two wings closer together' unless they were amalgamated into a single service. Asquith promptly appointed Curzon as 'president of the Air Board', but Kitchener (speaking for the army) and Balfour (for the navy) ensured that the Board had no independent powers.

Now, after Smuts had reported in August 1917, the War Cabinet charged the Air Board in consultation with the War Office and the Ministry of Munitions, to increase aircraft production and create more squadrons for both the RFC and the RNAS. Haig argued that the most effective step of all against Gotha raids would be the capture of the Belgian coast. He had his way and after 250,000 British soldiers had been killed, injured or captured, the offensive was called off. The Gotha bases remained in German hands, although they were frequently raided by naval aircraft.

5

'Winston is Back':
Minister of Munitions, 1917-1918

Bolo House

'We who are concerned with the air all live in one house', recalled John Baird, the Air Board's parliamentary secretary. That was the Hotel Cecil: 'An architecturally deplorable, dreadful building' on the Strand, popularly known as Bolo House, in memory of a notorious French swindler, Bolo Pasha, who was executed for his sins. According to the Air Ministry's first historian, it was full of 'Bolo Brigadiers, Strand Subalterns and Kingsway Captains', doing nothing to help the war effort. There were exceptions: Henderson had an office there; so did Godfrey Paine, newly-appointed Fifth Sea Lord; and William Weir, Minister of Munitions.

Aviation had grown enormously since the outbreak of war and its management needed a separate building: an important practical step towards independence from the Admiralty and the War Office, both absorbed by worries over conducting war at sea and on land. By March 1918, the RFC had over 100 operational squadrons in Britain and France, with another seventeen in the Mediterranean and the Middle East; the RNAS had forty in Britain and France, plus five in the Mediterranean. Many other squadrons were either employed in training or in the process of forming.

By the end of the war, the RAF would have a strength of nearly 300,000 officers and men, about 14,000 of them pilots, and there were nearly 23,000 aeroplanes on charge. Aviation had become a significant factor in Britain's armament, as it had in France and Germany.

Back in Office

Zeppelins were no longer a serious threat to England, but Gothas were. Within ten days of the raid on London on 7 July Lloyd George had called on Smuts and also offered the Ministry of Munitions position to Churchill. Christopher Addison, the current minister, had written to Lloyd George on 4 June about the need to 'get Winston in quick as the more it is talked about the more opportunity there is for opposition to gather'. Addison asked for three weeks, 'so as to pave the way for Winston if you wished him to follow me'. The Prime Minister gave him six, and then it could have been said, as it actually was in September 1939: 'Winston is back.'

He might well have been brought back as Air Minister, if Lloyd George had accepted the advice of Smuts, given on 6 June. Munitions, he said, offered less scope for his 'constructive ability and initiative, and with effective help from America our aerial effort might yet become of decisive importance not only in the anti-submarine campaign but also on the Western Front in the next twelve months'. Churchill would prefer Munitions, Smuts told Lloyd George, but would accept the Air 'if real scope is given to him', together with control of 'the higher patronage'.

Lord Derby was distressed at the prospect of Churchill's return to office. It was provoking 'rather bitter political controversy', he wrote on 8 June to Haig. Were he to be made chairman of the Air Board, Derby foresaw the 'eventual downfall' of the government. Next day, Lord Cowdray, currently president of the Air Board, had his say. Production of aircraft would increase if Churchill took over from him, he admitted to Lloyd George, but: 'Winston will see that he, and he alone, gets all the credit from the very brilliant achievements of the air services which may have a very material effect on the duration and success of the war.' A bewildering comment: meaning, presumably, that the efforts of this 'dangerously ambitious man' might shorten the war.

The wisest comment came from Churchill's Aunt Cornelia: 'My advice is to stick to Munitions, and don't try to run the government.' *The Morning Post* – to say nothing of all his former colleagues – knew what she meant. 'That dangerous and uncertain quantity,' the *Post* wrote on 3 August, 'is back again in Whitehall. We do not know in the least what he may be up to, but from past experience we venture to suggest that it will be everything but his own business.'

The Times asserted that 'the crying need for 1917 is for aeroplanes, as it had been for shells in 1915. The government must be compelled to realise that the aeroplane will be the ultimate and deciding factor of the war.' Churchill agreed that Britain needed to strengthen her air forces and urged the War Cabinet, yet again, on 7 July to seize Borkum. Air bases there would threaten vital targets in Germany. All her dockyards and anchorages could be 'brought under continuous bombing by night and day from quite short distances. Aerial observation would reveal each morning the exact disposition of the German fleet.'

Nothing was done about Borkum, but by 17 July Churchill was Minister of Munitions and 'head of the greatest productive department of the empire', with his headquarters in the Hotel Metropole in Northumberland Avenue, handy for Whitehall. He wrote to William Weir, Director-General of Aircraft Production, on the 30th. 'We need an immediate conference with the Air

Board, under the presidency of a member of the War Cabinet (Smuts, for choice), to frame a clear view of war policy in the air during the coming year.'

Clouds of Aeroplanes

Churchill attended a War Cabinet meeting on 24 August where he said that he strongly favoured the creation of an Air Ministry and was confident that there were natural and intimate bonds linking the two services. The personnel, he thought, would consist of 'men who would make it their life-long profession', plus others 'who would be lent temporarily to the air service', before returning in due course to the army or the navy. He reminded his colleagues that 'our American allies are inclined to the view that victory would be achieved by the side which obtained complete command of the air'.

With such thoughts in mind, he proposed a great and increasing extension of aircraft manufacture, diverting skilled workmen and essential materials from shell production. For too long, he told the Munitions Council on 4 September, the air force had been 'the drudge of the other services'. Now, however, there were 'only two ways of winning the war, and they both begin with A. One is aeroplanes and the other is America. That is all that is left. Everything else is swept away.' Prophetic words, in this war and the next.

Churchill's 'imagination and boldness', in Lloyd George's words, countered the Admiralty's claim to 'super-priority upon all supplies'. The development of aeroplanes, said Churchill, was now 'clearly before us as a great expansive feature of the campaign of 1918'. *Flight*'s editor agreed: 'The future and the safety of the British Empire lie as much in the air as on the sea.'

During October 1917 Churchill argued that 'air predominance' would make possible attacks on German communications and bases. It would 'paralyse the enemy's military action' by compelling him to devote more resources to defence than to attack. 'All attacks on communications and on bases should have their relation to the main battle' because it is not 'reasonable to speak of an air offensive as if it were going to finish the war by itself'.

Churchill was determined to replace men with machines as far as possible with 'masses of guns, mountains of shells, and clouds of aeroplanes'. This last was a more complex task than any other war material supply because of rapid changes in aircraft design, high wastage of men and machines and the problems of linking airframe to engine supply.

His appointment was welcomed by Weir, now Controller of Aeronautical Supply. Both men were efficient, hard-working managers, determined to get value for money from suppliers and workmen who thought – but not for long – that they could be bamboozled as easily as officials in the War Office and the Admiralty. The ministry prioritised labour and materials for tanks, transport and agricultural machinery as well as aviation. They reduced the number of aircraft types and engines already in service without impeding the development of better types and engines and hugely expanded the work force, including women. By the end of 1917 Churchill presided over the largest aviation industry in the world.

'We Deserve to Lose the War'

It was, however, an industry often at odds with the Air Board, heavily dependent on French engines (some of them poorly built), suffering fiascos by producing insufficiently tested British engines, plagued by a shortage of skilled workers and numerous strikes. By January 1918 Trenchard was complaining that the situation was 'hopeless', like a 'comic opera' and 'we deserve to lose the war'.

Weir had often allowed 'enthusiasm to outrun discretion' in accepting airframes and engines and in promising large-scale production, but Henderson, Robert Brooke-Popham and Sefton Brancker, under Cowdray's presidency of the Air Board, share the responsibility. Henderson, for example, said at a board meeting on 16 October 1917: 'When the French had adopted any machine or engine on a large scale they had been proved to be wrong.' This absurd comment, wrote John Morrow, was made 'while English engines self-destructed all around him'.

Lloyd George welcomed the creation of an independent Air Ministry, wrote Morrow, as a means of 'vaulting the "snail's pace"' of operations on the Western Front and bringing the prospect of victory closer. But nearly all the military and civilian officials consulted by Smuts opposed unifying the air services. Henderson was the chief exception, apart from Lloyd George, and his opinion weighed heavily with Smuts.

Henderson is today virtually unknown while Trenchard is frequently regarded as the father of the RAF. He certainly had the loudest voice, earning him a widely-used nickname 'Boom'. Lord Beaverbrook, who kept a beady eye on everyone who mattered in and around Whitehall, disagreed: 'Trenchard was a father who tried to strangle the infant at birth though he got the credit for the grown man.'

Trenchard's Constant Offensive

'The Germans never shared the Trenchardian notion that fighting aircraft could only be effective in an offensive role', wrote Malcolm Cooper. 'The concentration of German fighters in large formations over their own territory was not, as the RFC command assumed, the reaction of an enemy being gradually beaten down, but rather that of a numerically-inferior opponent organising his forces to fight at best advantage in support of an army that was itself on the defensive.' That point – understood by every able commander since organised warfare began – was ignored by Trenchard. He and his advisers persuaded themselves that heavy British casualties somehow proved that German losses were heavier.

Sefton Brancker, Director of Air Organisation at the War Office, offered this astounding comment to Trenchard in September 1916: 'I rather enjoy hearing of our heavy casualties as I am perfectly certain in my own mind that the Germans lose at least half as much again as we do.' Brancker, safely ensconced in Whitehall, would continue to 'enjoy' the loss of British airmen for the rest of the war and Trenchard shared his pleasure.

As head of the RFC in France, Trenchard was Haig's man. Haig wrote in his diary for 28 August 1917 that Trenchard was 'much disturbed' by the prospect of an Air Ministry, 'just at a time when the Flying Corps was beginning to feel that it had become an important part of the army'. He had somehow earned pilot's wings in 1912 in thirteen days with a total flying time of sixty-four minutes, but he had a strong personality, considerable bureaucratic skills and the shrewdness to cultivate influential persons – military, civilian, royal – before and during the war. He also paid the closest attention to the press. His emphasis on constant offensive appealed strongly to many Victorians, Churchill among them, who regarded it as gallant and honourable.

If Trenchard had had his way, there would have been no RAF in 1918. Years later, he wrote: 'I thought that if anything were done at the time to weaken the Western Front, the war would be lost and there would be no air service, united or divided.' Henderson, he admitted, 'had twice the insight and understanding that I had. He was prepared to run risks rather than lose a chance which he saw might never come again. He did so with no thought of self-interest, and it is doubtful whether the RAF or Britain realises its debt to him, which is at least as great as its debt to Smuts.' Trenchard's 'insight and understanding' were severely limited. He was aware that many of his aircraft were inadequate and most of his air crews poorly trained, but persuaded himself that their efforts were destroying large numbers of German aircraft and undermining German morale, which, of course, they were not.

The word 'morale' resonated constantly in the minds of Trenchard and his admirers. It reflected and highlighted the qualities valued by upper-middle-class Victorian and Edwardian society: courage; initiative; resourcefulness; tenacity and will-power, as opposed to acquiring practical skills as a result of intensive training and thinking seriously about effective tactics. Jack Slessor, a Trenchard admirer, disdained the morale of 'foreigners' if faced – as in the Great War – by British bombing: 'Your toothpick worker,' he wrote (apparently under the impression that foreigners made a great many of those items), 'will go to ground again even if he has not already left the area, which is more likely.' Thus wrote a man who rose to the highest rank in the RAF and is regarded as one of its foremost thinkers.

Under Trenchard, aerial strength was never grouped into areas most seriously threatened at a particular time, but spread thinly across the whole Western Front. The RFC, encouraged to concentrate on aerial combat, failed to focus its attention on protecting those aircraft who were making a more positive contribution to winning the war: attempting to locate enemy artillery batteries; taking photographs of troop movements and offering close support to ground forces.

On 24 August 1917, Smuts reported to the War Cabinet and was invited to draft appropriate legislation for the creation of an Air Ministry and at once asked for the full-time assistance of Henderson, who gave up his position as head of the RFC. Eric Geddes, First Lord of the Admiralty, refused to accept that the proposed Air Ministry should include the RNAS, even though he knew nothing about aviation (or indeed war at sea). Haig's concern did not extend beyond the Western Front, but fortunately the Germans came to the rescue of Smuts and Henderson by launching a night offensive.

Night Attacks
Shortly after 11 pm on 3 September 1917 a number of Gothas bombed a drill hall at Chatham naval barracks, killing or injuring more than 200 naval ratings. The raid was totally unexpected and the defences, ground and air, offered no effective resistance. On the following night, the Gothas came again, five of them following the Thames to London, where 'thousands of lights', as one German pilot recalled, guided them. They were untroubled by ground or air defences, and although only ninety Londoners were killed or injured, as loud an outcry followed as when day bombers struck at Folkestone and London earlier in the year.

The *Manchester Guardian* demanded 'overwhelming supremacy in the air to redeem our shores from outrage' and denounced the attacks as the worst event 'since the Normans conquered England': a ludicrous exaggeration from a newspaper with a reputation for usually sensible reporting.

Ashmore decided to set up a balloon barrage around London. An apron of long dangling streamers was to be held aloft by three to five balloons joined together by heavy steel cables. Anchored at three points, the apron could be raised as high as 10,000 feet. More impressive in theory than in practice, very few were actually erected and none served any useful purpose. A better idea proved to be the use of night fighters helped by searchlights and given a broad search zone free of ground fire. Sound locators, like massive ear trumpets, were also tried. 'Such were the beginnings,' wrote Raymond Fredette, 'of an early-warning system against German bombers. In the next war Britain would have something better.'

Fortunately for Britain, the Gothas – even improved models – were always too few, too under-powered and too lightly-loaded to mount persistent and heavy attacks on London. During August they were, in any case, directed to attack the Channel ports, where men and supplies for Haig's Flanders offensive were building up.

Beginning on 24 September 1917, the Germans used Gothas and also their first four-engined 'Giants' against targets in England. About twice the size of

Gothas, they were technically far ahead of their time, carrying a heavy bomb load, several machine guns for defence and were robust enough to withstand punishment. In twenty-eight sorties, none were destroyed by ground or air defences. Although their bombing caused few casualties or damage, it made thousands of Londoners take refuge in underground railway stations while others fled into the country. Nightshift work was seriously disrupted and when daylight came transport services were overloaded as men and women tried to pick up their usual routines.

Anti-aircraft guns had blindly fired numerous shells, making a tremendous noise that was believed to be encouraging, but they hit no enemy aircraft. Night fighters did no better, for all their determination. As in the daylight raids, low cloud, rain, strong headwinds, navigational errors, light bomb loads and the near-impossibility of hitting any designated target saved London from serious damage. Heavy landings on return flights caused more losses than combat.

Lynching the Cabinet?

Lloyd George called an emergency meeting of the War Cabinet and, naturally, set up another committee: this one under Smuts, included Churchill and Ashmore. French gloomily predicted that London's artillery defences would 'cease to exist' in a few months because gun barrels would be worn out. Churchill reported that he was arranging to have barrels relined at the rate of twenty a month, but the Cabinet decided that the entire production of 3-inch guns, planned to equip merchant ships in October, should instead be assigned to London.

As Minister of Munitions, Churchill was concerned about factory production. He asked for a report on current output at Woolwich Arsenal. It was well down on what it should be, but the authorities were more concerned about press coverage of the raids, claiming that it generated panic. Among those panicking was Lord Cowdray: 'When London is half levelled,' he wailed, 'someone will have to be lynched, presumably the Cabinet, since no-one else has any clear responsibility.'

Lloyd George ordered newspaper editors to restrict their coverage and not publish photographs, pointing out that since the war began traffic accidents had killed or injured many more Londoners than air raids. Owners of bombed-out buildings were required to conceal the damage and shelters were provided under some public buildings.

What Londoners did not know was that of ninety-two Gothas sent out in October, only fifty-five crossed the Channel and fewer than twenty reached London. Five sorties by Giants achieved little. The Germans lost thirteen bombers and others were destroyed at their Belgian bases when the British launched their own attacks. On the last night of October, twenty-two Gothas dropped a great many small incendiary bombs, but most failed to ignite and as usual cloudy weather compounded navigational errors. About thirty persons were killed or injured: seven of these casualties (one fatal) were caused by shrapnel from British gun fire. Night fighters achieved nothing, but several of the Gothas were destroyed while attempting to land on fog-shrouded aerodromes.

Offence, Defence, Resilience

Churchill thought it 'improbable' that terrorising aerial attacks could compel 'the government of a great nation to surrender'. Most people would welcome a good system of dugouts or shelters and firm control by the authorities. They would soon realise that the casualties and destruction caused by bombers were less grave than they feared. In Britain, he said, 'we have seen the combative spirit of the people roused, and not quelled, by the German air raids'.

Effective air defence in England needed a ground-to-air radio telephone network. Although work was in progress, this had not been achieved by the end of 1917. Ashmore, however, improved other aspects of ground defence. For example, he had searchlights grouped and placed those working with night fighters under the control of air squadron commanders. He also did his best to see that observer posts were capably manned and provided with a direct telephone link to his headquarters.

More of everything was needed – guns, fighters, searchlights – because there was a high risk of massive German raids in 1918, especially after the winter was over, and some Londoners panicked on any night when aircraft were heard or guns fired. Late in January 1918, on a rare clear evening, the Germans caused more than 200 casualties, a quarter of them fatal. Overall, though, the raids by Zeppelins, Gothas and Giants did not, from a German point of view, justify their immense expense and the heavy losses suffered by carefully-trained crews.

Churchill backed Ashmore and helped to provide 'adequate' protection against air raids, especially at factories and ports, well aware of the danger of panic and consequent loss of production. 'Nothing that we have learned of the German population to endure suffering justifies us in assuming that they could be cowed into submission or, indeed, that they would not be rendered more desperately resolved by them.' It is a great pity that Churchill's reflections on the limited impact of aerial bombing were not accepted as a 'general doctrine' when the RAF came into existence. Too many officers preferred to believe what Trenchard and his acolytes claimed: that German defences against British bombers could not match those of Britain and that German resilience under aerial attack could not match that of Britons.

'There is good reason to believe,' said Churchill in October 1917, 'that if the war lasts until 1919 aeroplane warfare by bombing and counter-bombing and the general struggle for mastery in the air by heavier-than-air machines will require the whole of our available resources and energies.' Godfrey

Paine, Fifth Sea Lord, objected. He needed aluminium to complete the building of rigid airships and most of the skilled labour required would be supplied by women. He wrote:

'The Admiralty War Staff have repeatedly pointed out that they consider one effective rigid airship to be equal to six light cruisers, and judging by the use made of these aircraft by the Germans, this is fully borne out. As submarines grow in size and radius of action, so their operations will continue to extend to greater distances from the coast and far out into the Atlantic, where these rigid airships should be of the utmost value for convoy work and submarine scouting, etc.'

At the Battle of Jutland and on several other occasions the lack of such airships had deplorable results.

The End of German Air Raids
A massive German offensive began on the Western Front on 21 March 1918 and some three weeks later, on 15 April, Haig sent out a signal which alarmed many who received it: 'With our backs to the wall, each one of us must fight to the end.' That was a period when German air raids on England, timed to coincide with the offensive on land, might have had serious consequences. But there were no air raids in March or April, partly because the bomber force had been gravely weakened by its earlier efforts and partly because its strength was devoted to support of the ground forces. In the middle of May, however, four major raids were aimed at targets in England: on the night of the 19th, about 250 Londoners were killed or injured and over 1,000 homes and business premises were destroyed or damaged. But anti-aircraft guns and night fighters shot down or drove away most of the bombers in what proved to be the last attack of the war.

The German aerial offensive against England killed more than 400 people and seriously injured ten times as many. Among these casualties were thirty-eight killed and about 200 injured either by British anti-aircraft fire or in air-raid shelter stampedes. Grievous losses, but light by Great War standards. They were, moreover, unprecedented and no-one knew – before the Armistice – how much greater they might grow. The damage caused was estimated at nearly £3,000,000. Despite claims made at the time, the diversion of guns and aircraft to home defence was never a serious drain on the Western Front, although memories of the raids were kept green by many Britons in the years between the wars.

The RFC's 'Finest Hour'
As soon as trench lines became established on the Western Front, artillery became an essential weapon and airmen became an important ally for

gunners, providing them with thousands of photographs and in 1917, as John Terraine wrote, the RFC enjoyed its 'finest hour' by carrying out 'a meticulous aerial survey of the whole British front, which the Royal Engineers translated into the first really reliable map'. Gunners were then able to identify and attack particular targets.

This ground-air co-operation lasted until the Armistice 'and it is one of history's extraordinary circumstances that it took until 1942 for the penny to drop in the next war': thanks, above all, to Tedder and Coningham (officers whom we shall meet anon). Attempts were also made to destroy railways and rolling stock behind enemy lines, to give support to land forces advancing (or retreating) and to drop small arms ammunition and food supplies.

Retaliation

Meanwhile, in response to growing public demands, Haig and Trenchard had been ordered in 1917 to prepare a bomber force to hit German cities. Both were unwilling. Every aeroplane available, they objected, was needed for the proposed Flanders offensive and in any case Trenchard had few that could reach targets in Germany. Since May 1916, the navy had had a base at Luxeuil in eastern France from which raids could have been made on German war industries.

Trenchard opposed this initiative and was backed by Henderson, but plans to revive it came early in 1917 from Weir, representing the Ministry of Munitions on the Air Board. Trenchard, still loyally backing Haig's Flanders offensive, resisted. He had no suitable machines, but C. G. Grey (editor of *Aeroplane*) pointed out that nothing was being done to build such machines: 'The Germans,' he wrote, 'have developed a special branch of warfare which we have neglected in a manner which can only be described as idiotic.'

As early as December 1914, Handley Page had begun work on his heavy bomber, 'a bloody paralyser', as Sueter demanded. But without Churchill's drive the project faltered and the RNAS did not receive its first twin-engined Handley Page 0/400 (an improved version of his 0/100) until November 1916.

Its performance surpassed that of the Gotha, but in September 1917 only eighteen were serving the naval squadrons in Dunkirk. The RFC did not build *any* until the Cabinet ordered reprisal raids and Trenchard chose to dismiss it as 'a useless type'. Despite his opposition, these bombers, and some other single-engined types of little value as bombers, were formed into 41 Wing at Ochey (in north-eastern France, near Nancy) under the command of Cyril Newall, a lifelong Trenchardist who rose to the RAF's highest rank.

On 17 October, his bombers carried out the RFC's first long-range attack on a German target in daylight and a week later the navy's Handley Pages made their first night raid, both on a factory near Saarbrücken. In May 1918 Newall admitted that 'the material effect' of bombing had been slight, but claimed that 'the moral effect had been considerable'. That claim, untested but fervently asserted, would become an article of faith with Trenchardists.

Weir organised an 'Independent Air Force' (independent, he meant, of the Anglo-French armies on the Western Front), intended to focus on bombing targets in Germany. The IAF came into existence on 5 June with Trenchard in command and Newall as his deputy, with five squadrons at Ochey.

In August Churchill wrote to Louis Loucheur, French Minister of Munitions, about plans for long-distance bombing. This was the time, he said, to attack targets in Germany, launching a combined offensive in darkness as well as daylight. We needed only more reliable Liberty engines for our bombers. He told Lloyd George in September that Haig placed a high value on the work of aircraft. In Britain, however, as in Germany, the threat of aerial attack aroused public outcries and obliged the authorities to divert guns and aircraft to home defence, even though the casualties and destruction caused by air raids were very light.

Trenchard knew this, but asserted in his final despatch (December 1918) that 'the moral effect of bombing stands undoubtedly to the material effect in a proportion of twenty to one': an assertion later regarded as an established fact by many airmen. German anti-aircraft crews showed themselves to be formidable opponents, but many British theorists overlooked that fact after 1918. During the Great War, flak brought down nearly 1,600 British and French aircraft over the Western Front: 260 of them in the last four weeks of fighting. As soon as the Armistice was signed, Trenchard returned the IAF to Haig's command. Salmond, who succeeded Trenchard, was annoyed by his eagerness 'to pass on an unwanted baby and clear out with all speed'.

At Last an Air Ministry

Meanwhile, early in October 1917, Cowdray told Admiral Mark Kerr, in 'strictest confidence', that there was to be no Air Ministry. Kerr, the first flag officer to qualify as an air pilot, prepared a memorandum later described by himself as 'The Bombshell'. The Germans, he believed, were building a large force of heavy bombers that would be capable of destroying factories everywhere in London and south-eastern England. To counter this danger, wrote Kerr, 'the Air must have a Ministry with executive power, and also priority of output for a while', even though he recognised the need for aircraft to combat submarines and fight enemy aircraft on the Western and other fronts. The government, already moving in that direction, introduced an Air Force Bill to Parliament early in November.

Reginald Barnes (with whom Churchill went to Cuba in 1895 and was now a brigadier-general on the Western Front) strongly favoured improving the air force: 'real supremacy in the air,' he told his old friend on 1 November 1917, would be 'the difference between winning and losing this war.' Bombing, although still in its infancy, 'is going to make it impossible for the weaker side in the air to fight'. Barnes and his men had just endured continuous bombing in darkness without being able to do anything about it and he wanted Churchill 'to open people's eyes at home to this'. Churchill replied on the 15th: your letter 'confirms my views I have long held'.

William Joynson-Hicks (a Conservative MP) 'thankfully welcomed' the Bill to create an air force. He had urged the creation of an independent striking force ever since 1912 and early in the war asked for 'continuous raids of some 400-500 aeroplanes dropping bombs on the Rhine bridges and the giant Krupp factory at Essen... Many of us who have been called fanatics have felt that there is a chance of the war being decided in the air.' The air force now to be created should not be merely a wartime measure, but survive into peacetime. The Bill easily passed both Houses and the royal assent needed to make it law was given on 29 November 1917.

Cowdray expected to become the first Air Minister. Lloyd George, however, invited Lord Northcliffe, a newspaper magnate, to take on the task. He rejected the offer on 16 November in a letter to *The Times* (which he owned) complaining about 'men in various positions of authority who deserved punishment, but were being retained and even elevated'.

Cowdray resigned on the same day, in a letter also published in *The Times*. He had been deeply offended to read in that newspaper the first intimation that Lloyd George wished to appoint a new Air Minister. Lloyd George replied at once: he had wished 'to secure at the head of the Board the services of one who was personally acquainted with the organisation of the air service in America, and who was therefore in a better position to co-ordinate the energies of the two countries'. He asked Cowdray to stay on until the Air Force Bill became law, but he refused.

Cowdray wrote to Churchill on 28 November. Although he was sorry to leave the Air Board, he had 'every kind regard and thankfulness for your devotion to the needs of the air services'. Lloyd George immediately appointed Lord Rothermere, another newspaper magnate, as president of the Air Board and then, on 3 January 1918, made him first Secretary of State for the Air Force. Trenchard was appointed chief of the Air Staff (CAS) on the 18th, despite being opposed to the idea of a separate air force.

Churchill told Rothermere on 26 January that he hoped to produce about 2,000 aircraft that month and 3,000 by June as well as 4,000 engines: 'we ought to go on building up the size and scale of our air forces' during the next eighteen months. He was aware, he said, of research requiring new types of aircraft and asked Rothermere to make provisions for these. In March, Churchill asked the War Cabinet to consider a new offensive strategy for 1919 based on aircraft and tanks: 'A strategy proceeding by design through crisis to decision, not mere waste and slaughter sagging slowly downwards into general collapse.' He wanted to double Britain's air strength. Victory could be achieved, he thought, if the air force could drop not five but 500 tons of bombs each night on German cities and manufacturing establishments.

A Powerful Air Force

Churchill's main work in the summer of 1918 was building weapons of all kinds for use in 1919, the first year in which he thought victory would be possible. He was living permanently in the Hotel Metropole where he demonstrated, as throughout his public life, an exceptional capacity for sheer hard work, day after day; and for ensuring that everyone over whom he had authority also worked harder than they thought possible. The hotel, he said, 'enables me to work to the last moment before dinner, to get papers when I come back after, and to begin with shorthand assistance as early as I choose in the morning'.

As late as 15 September he still had in mind campaigns in 1919, as he told Clementine: he intended to arm perhaps fifteen American divisions, nearly 500,000 men, and was buying 2,000 or 3,000 aircraft from the United States 'for the bombing of Germany' by British pilots. He hoped to drop mustard gas 'on the Huns to the extent of nearly 1,000-tons by the end of this month'.

A month later, however, Clementine urged her husband to come home. 'Even if the fighting is not over yet, your share of it must be', she wrote on 18 October. She wanted him to be praised as 'a reconstructive genius', and not only as 'a mustard gas fiend, a tank juggernaut and a flying terror'. 'Could not your munitions workers be set to build lovely garden cities, pull down slums and make furniture for their new homes?' The answer, then and later, was always, 'No'.

The RNAS, neglected since Churchill's departure from the Admiralty, welcomed independence, but 'nearly all the experienced and far-sighted naval airmen turned over to the Royal Air Force', wrote Stephen Roskill. 'The loss of that band of pioneers was perhaps the greatest single cause of the trials and tribulations which later afflicted the Fleet Air Arm, and which endured right into World War II.' Trenchard did not believe the new service could survive even in wartime and had found it impossible to work with Rothermere, resigning on 19 March.

Rothermere was happy to see him go, as he later wrote to Bonar Law (Chancellor of the Exchequer): Trenchard had a 'dull unimaginative mind', he believed he knew everything about aviation and would 'within twelve months have brought death and damnation to the air force'. In particular, Trenchard insisted on ordering large numbers of obsolete aeroplanes.

Smuts agreed that Trenchard should go and so Lloyd George appointed Major General Frederick Sykes in his place on 12 April. Henderson, passed over again, also resigned and Rothermere, unable to stand criticism in those newspapers he did not own, and already depressed by the recent death of a second son, left office on 25 April. Trenchard would happily have accepted Haig's offer to command an infantry brigade, but Lloyd George, responding to a vehement rumpus in the press, instructed Weir to find him another job in aviation.

'Never has there been an arm,' Churchill declared, 'to which more encouraging prospects were open than the British flying service at present.' Within a year, he predicted, it would be the most powerful in the world. Therefore, he urged, no major offensive should be launched on the Western Front until the Allies had aerial superiority. When this appeared to have been achieved by August 1918, he wrote: 'This is the moment to attack the enemy [with an aerial bombing offensive] to carry the war into his own country.' Then smash his morale and to 'harry his hungry and dispirited cities without pause or stay' on the eve of winter. 'While the new heavy French machines ... will strike by night at all the nearer objectives, the British [will bomb] not only by night but in broad daylight far into Germany.'

During 1918, Britain's air strength had increased rapidly as her factories produced nearly 56,000 air frames and engines. At the time of the Armistice, more than 300 aircraft were appearing every day and thousands more were on order; 100 large factories were at work and half of all orders placed by Churchill's ministry were for aviation materials.

After the war, the British had an opportunity to discover what bombing of German cities, factories and communications had actually achieved. They could not deny that only minor damage had been caused, but many years later, an American historian, George Williams, concluded that the Air Ministry was more interested in 'advocacy than accuracy'. Tami Biddle agreed: Trenchard used his authority 'to protect his own record and his own version of the war effort'. Natural enough, but he 'closed off deeper and more searching analyses of what bombing had or had not accomplished in the war'. Trenchard, as Malcolm Smith wrote, was 'a master of the wholly unfounded statistic'.

On 28 January 1919, Weir spoke warmly of the work done by Churchill's ministry for the RAF. It had been part of 'the greatest example of state organisation ever carried through in any country'. And so Churchill ended the war as he had begun it: in charge of a formidable weapon, well able to defend Britain and attack her enemies.

6

Keeping the Royal Air Force Alive, 1919-1925

Linking the Services?

'Don't put Churchill in the War Office', wrote Leo Amery to Lloyd George on 27 December 1918. Amery had been at Harrow with Churchill and believed he knew him well. A Conservative MP since 1911, he was about to leave the War Cabinet, where he had been an assistant secretary and move to the Colonial Office as a parliamentary under-secretary. The army, he told Lloyd George, was 'terrified' at the prospect of Churchill in the War Office: what he needs is scope for 'adventure and advertisement' and would do well in the Air Ministry.

Lloyd George ignored Amery's plea and asked Churchill if he wanted the War Office or the Admiralty. 'My heart is in the Admiralty', he replied on the 29th. Perhaps it would be best, he continued, to link the Air with the Admiralty: 'though aeroplanes will never be a substitute for armies, they will be a substitute for many classes of warship. The technical development of the air falls naturally into the same sphere as the mechanical development of the navy; and this becomes increasingly true the larger the aeroplane grows.' Early in January, however, the Prime Minister decided not to link air and sea power. It was a decision with permanent consequences. Instead, Churchill was offered land and air power (the War Office and the Air Ministry).

Saving an Infant

In *Aftermath*, the last volume of his Great War memoirs, Churchill wrote about his 'Armistice Dream' whereby the League of Nations would preserve world peace by controlling 'war from the air' because the aeroplane threatened 'the safety and even the life of whole cities and populations'. If a major war came again, he foresaw the 'wholesale, unlimited, and perhaps, once launched, an uncontrollable' process of destruction.

Lloyd George's decision to appoint Churchill minister for two departments was unpopular with many men in public life, who had long resented (and/or envied) his elevation at such a young age to so many offices and his exceptional success as a journalist and orator. His able management of the Ministry of Munitions was not held to outweigh the disasters suffered by the Royal Navy, especially at Gallipoli: disasters for which he was believed to be primarily responsible.

Aviation enthusiasts feared that the newly-created Air Ministry would disappear because the War Office and the Admiralty were keen to divide its assets between them. At that time, Trenchard opposed independence and Henderson refused a commission in the RAF. He found a non-military role in Geneva as Director-General of the League of Red Cross Societies. Trenchard and Henderson have subsequently been lauded as fathers of the RAF, but without Churchill the infant would have died. There was, however, force in the argument that not even Churchill could successfully manage two major offices.

The Times asked: 'Can any single man cover the huge span of both these departments of the army and the air? We gravely doubt it.' *Flight* agreed: the notion that any one man could fill both posts at the same time 'is simply an absurdity', but reminded readers that it was Churchill, at a time when few of his colleagues believed in a future for aviation, who had the foresight to create a naval air service. 'Had it not been for him and Commodore Sueter the probability is that the war would have found the navy minus aircraft altogether.'

As early as January 1919 Churchill said: 'The air force is the arm which stands alone and midway between the land and sea services, where they clash it rules.' In February he underlined that point: 'There is no question of subordinating the Royal Air Force' to the other services or allowing them to divide its assets. However, he took surprisingly little interest in the development of *civil* aviation. McCormack wrote that his 'malign influence on civil air policy would linger until the Second World War'. It is certainly the case that Britain, then a state with world-wide interests, failed to develop efficient long-distance aircraft, civilian or military, between the wars. Germany's Junkers Ju 52 first flew in 1932 and the American Douglas DC-3 in 1935: the RAF had nothing comparable.

The fate of the RAF rested with Churchill. By March 1920, it had been reduced to twenty-five squadrons and about 28,000 officers and men, but he had said in February 1919 that its integrity, unity and independence 'will be sedulously and carefully maintained' Weir did not wish to continue as Air Minister and advised Churchill to appoint Trenchard, who would devote the rest of his life to fostering the interests of that service. Churchill agreed that should there be another war, the bomber would by then have become a decisive weapon and could only be wielded by an independent air force.

Splendid Titles

In February 1919, Churchill intended to appoint Trenchard as First Air Lord, but that splendid style of naming – borrowed from the Royal Navy – was soon dropped and he became merely chief of the Air Staff. Likewise, Sykes would not be Second Air Lord, but Controller-General of Civil Aviation, while Edward Ellington became Director-General of Aircraft Production (later Supply and Research), rather than Third Air Lord. Robert Groves, alas, was never to be Fourth Sea Lord even briefly: instead, he would serve as Trenchard's deputy and Director of Air Operations. Churchill intended 'to make this post of much wider scope and importance than at present'. Groves would be appointed to command RAF units in the Middle East later that year and his death in an aircraft accident near Cairo in 1920 made it easier for Trenchard to reign over the new service.

To ensure the 'distinct and independent character' of the RAF Churchill wisely ordered that ranks, titles and uniforms be 'deliberately differentiated' from those of the older services. Perhaps it is just as well that such suggestions as 'Ensign', 'Reeve', 'Banneret' and 'Ardian' went the way of the various 'Air Lords'. Instead, a range for officers from 'pilot officer' to 'marshal of the Royal Air Force' took root. The non-commissioned ranks got their own hierarchy: corporal, sergeant and warrant officer survived from army days, but with the addition of 'AC2' and 'AC1' (aircraftman 2nd and 1st Class, leading aircraftman (LAC) and later senior aircraftman (SAC). There was also 'flight sergeant', senior to sergeant. These new ranks had a significant impact on the team spirit and self-respect of both officers and men from that time on.

Churchill refused to appoint a Secretary of State for Air because, he told his friend F. E. Smith (Lord Birkenhead and Lord Chancellor) in March 1919, the service is too small to justify that status, although one day it may take the prime place in our defensive organisation. Meanwhile, Churchill wanted 'a thoroughly efficient RAF which will last year after year in good condition and be a credit to the country'. Squadron identities were to be preserved; technical development (the service's 'life blood') was to be encouraged and also general education for recruits.

Feeding the Infant Cheaply

Churchill found work for the RAF that was not merely important but cheaper than anything the other services could offer. The RAF was 'one element' in a modern defence force: 'modern' in 1920s language meant 'cheap'. He rejected the proposal of Sykes (then CAS) for a large, expensive air service in these days of 'economy and disarmament'. Trenchard therefore replaced Sykes and submitted a much more modest proposal, and even that was trimmed by Churchill. No major war was in prospect for at least ten years, therefore, 'we have to aim at quality and progress rather than quantity and immediate war power'. But he reminded Lloyd George on 1 May 1919 that even a small RAF would be expensive. 'All the arts and sciences are involved. Only the most skilful mechanics and highest paid craftsmen are of any use: only the best materials will serve.'

Churchill presented Trenchard's memorandum on the permanent

organisation of the RAF to Parliament in December 1919. Trenchard – well aware that money was tight – concentrated on building a sound framework, one which could, at need, be expanded. Small elements would work with the army and the navy respectively, while the main portion 'will grow larger and larger and become more and more the predominating factor in all types of warfare'.

Should it Survive?

Churchill presented the estimates for the coming year to Parliament in March 1921. Two years ago, he said, he was faced with clearing away 'the gigantic debris and enormous mass of material' left over from the war and thought it would take five years 'to make an efficient, self-respecting, well-disciplined, economically-organised air force'. In fact, progress had been more rapid than he hoped, thanks to 'continuity of administration' and hard work by all ranks.

'No more complicated service has ever been brought into existence in this world... Almost every known science and art practiced among men is involved in aeronautical research.' Only the ablest men can learn to be efficient pilots and also to master 'aerial war-gunnery, bombing, torpedoing, photography, wireless telegraphy, spotting for artillery, observing, and other functions of that kind'. It follows therefore that the RAF needs many schools or training centres where every aspect of military aviation is going to be taught and studied. The system is still far from complete, but eventually the RAF will 'become a great technical university for the nation, with the glamour and traditions of a gallant service super-added'.

There were now twenty-eight fully-formed service squadrons, Churchill continued, twenty-one of them overseas: six in Egypt and Palestine; five in Mesopotamia; eight in India; one on the Rhine and one at Malta. The 'equivalent' of three more are in Ireland, three were working with the navy and one was employed in England: 'giving refresher courses to pilots'. Four more were to begin forming in April, and 'we propose this year to begin the formation on a very small scale of a Territorial Air Force' of six squadrons, stationed near large cities, 'with a small nucleus of regular air mechanics', backed by volunteers.

'I am very anxious to illustrate how foolish and wasteful it would be,' said Churchill, 'if we were to take advice which is pressed upon us from more than one quarter at present. Now that the war to end war is over, we need only civil, not military, aircraft. But we still need to defend Britain and her empire.' Properly handled, the RAF 'will become a substitute to a very important extent both for soldiers and ships'.

However, the Committee of Imperial Defence learned in November 1921 that the RAF had only three squadrons in Britain, whereas France had as many as forty-seven. Churchill had left the Air Ministry in April of that year and *The Times* wrote that: 'He leaves the body of the British flying service well nigh at that last gasp when a military funeral would be all that was left for it.' Due to his 'incredibly inadequate rule... the soul had all but departed'.

According to John Ferris, the Air Ministry under Churchill had overcome its 'gravest political problems' and 'despite his usual cavalier disregard for consistency, he provided an admirable blueprint for reform', recognising that after a long and costly war the most the RAF could hope for was secure foundation.

Several MPs objected to his control of both the Air Ministry and the Colonial Office. He tried to answer those who suggested that he had too many fish to fry, by remarking that fish were not the problem: he simply had too little batter (too little money). More seriously, they were concerned that little was being done to foster civil aviation. Money was tight in those post-war years and civil aviation did indeed suffer even more than the RAF. *Flight* was sharply critical of Churchill in these days. He remained very much 'the fighting man', wrote Spooner, and the sooner he handed over the Air Ministry to a civilian the better. Spooner believed, with good reason, that during the years 1919-1921 Churchill had hoped to add a third office, the Royal Navy, and become Britain's first Minister of Defence. But that was very much a step too far, in years when admirals and generals had no thought of unification and were determined to divide air power between themselves, ending the RAF's independence. Had it not been for Churchill, they would have had their way and nothing said or done by Trenchard would have thwarted them.

Sueter (now Rear-Admiral Sir Murray) 'was exceedingly caustic', recorded Spooner on 11 August 1921, 'regarding alleged shortcomings of air force units operating with the navy'. Churchill, said Sueter, was turning the RAF 'into an air military force, which is being developed exactly like a guards regiment, but that is of very little use to the navy'. In some recent combined manoeuvres, the airmen were so incompetent that they located a submarine in Dorchester, Dorset: about twelve miles from the nearest deep water. 'That,' said the gallant admiral, with some justification, 'is not what is wanted in the navy.' Clearly, commented Spooner: 'There is a screw loose somewhere.'

In November 1922, ~~Arthur Balfour~~ *Andrew Bonar Law* replaced Lloyd George as Prime Minister and proposed to liquidate the RAF. Churchill was at that time out of office – indeed, out of Parliament – but an inquiry by the Committee of Imperial Defence recommended that it survive. Defence spending, as always in peacetime, was unpopular with many voters and as late as 1932 Maurice Hankey (Secretary of the Cabinet and of the CID) wrote: 'It would be worth a lot to get rid of submarines and aircraft, which I have advocated for a long time.' As for Churchill his understanding of what aircraft might do did not advance. For example, he still believed in the late 1930s that 'even a single well-armed vessel will hold its own against aircraft' and that the RAF's concentration on forward-firing guns for fighters was ill-advised and that turret-armed fighters would prevail in aerial combat.

Imperial Policeman

'The first duty of the Royal Air Force', as Churchill and Trenchard agreed, 'is to garrison the British Empire', as cheaply as possible. Churchill was ahead of most military men (or politicians) in urging the development of troop-carrying aircraft, but those built were few and poorly designed. He had in mind the possibilities of what would become 'aerial policing' since as early as March 1914, when the so-called 'Mad Mullah' (Mohammed Abdullah Hassan) massacred members of the Somaliland Camel Corps. During unrest in Egypt in 1919 and again in 1921 aircraft were used to bomb and strafe 'rebels'. Egypt was a vital base for British control of the Middle East and as a staging-post on long flights to India and the Far East. Aircraft gave valuable service in Mesopotamia, the north-west frontier of India and Aden, where 'policing' (keeping the peace, protecting farmers and herders from raiders) was more emphasised than 'control'.

Palestine posed greater problems for Britain in the late 1930s than could be solved with the resources available. Ships and troops were also employed in preserving imperial rule, but aircraft were highly mobile and usually invulnerable to opponents who were 'uncivilised', 'primitive' and lightly-armed. Loudspeakers were a useful weapon for airmen to overawe the restless and warn them of the consequences of 'rebellion'. As the Governor-General of the Sudan put it: airmen were 'swift agents of government'. Churchill's support for aerial policing was confirmed in 1920 when the RAF successfully subdued the Mullah of Somaliland at a cost of only £30,000 instead of a projected cost of £7,000,000 needed to finance a military expedition. It was the first time, he reported to Parliament in February 1920, that airmen had enjoyed 'the general direction' of soldiers and seamen.

Irish rebels, however, could not be subdued in the same fashion. They could perhaps be dispersed, wrote Churchill on 1 July 1920, 'by machine-gun fire or bombs, using, of course, no more force than is necessary to scatter and stampede them': a foolish remark for a man who was supposed to understand what aircraft and weapons could do. On 24 September, he told Trenchard that his forces in Ireland were too weak and should be strengthened, to protect armoured cars and scatter rebel gatherings. The situation was worse by April 1922 when Churchill urged that aerodromes be set up in the north and around Dublin, so that 'hostile concentrations might be dealt with from the air or retaliatory measures taken in case of aggressive attack upon the British forces'.

Iraq the Centrepiece

For Mesopotamia (now known as Iraq), Churchill suggested 'a series of defended areas in which air bases could be securely established'. Strong aerial forces could operate from these and 'enforce control, now here, now there... long lines of communication that eat up troops and money' would not be needed. Trenchard, encouraged by Churchill, supported 'air control' of Britain's imperial territories, because it gave his infant RAF an important role to play and also because it did indeed prove to be much cheaper than ground forces and cost many fewer British casualties. In Iraq, for example, five RAF squadrons were successfully substituted in 1921 for thirty-three imperial battalions, reducing the annual cost of the garrison to £2,000,000, a tenth of the army cost.

Churchill had emphasised to Trenchard that the aim was not to defend Iraq from invasion, but to maintain 'internal security'. Aircraft would be able to bomb or machine gun from the air, as well as transport soldiers at need, and supply them. From a central position in Baghdad, 'any point' could be quickly reached and 'reinforced or relieved'. Air control would permit 'substantial economies' and could be extended over all imperial trade routes and even to Ireland.

Henry Wilson (head of the army) was bitterly opposed to an independent air force and refused to be impressed by Churchill's advocacy of aerial policing. By July 1921, writing to Henry Rawlinson (C-in-C India), he had thought of a satisfying insult: 'I do not believe in Winston's ardent hopes of being able to govern Mesopotamia with hot air, aeroplanes and Arabs.'

Later in March 1921 Churchill, now Colonial Secretary, told Laming Worthington-Evans (his successor as Secretary of State for War) that the War Office was refusing to allow an air squadron to be moved from India to Mesopotamia. This squadron was needed there and Churchill asked Worthington-Evans 'to give directions which will bring to an end what is an extraordinary interference with the affairs of another department'. Churchill's advocacy of aerial policing was crucial in protecting the RAF's independence. Churchill was also concerned about resistance to Trenchard's desire to establish three aerodromes in Trans-Jordan.

Aeroplanes would mark out a 'desert route' to Mesopotamia, he told his Cabinet colleagues in April 1921, which 'would have a very salutary effect upon the Arabs' and significantly shorten the journey time between the two. Wilson approved. Writing to Walter Congreve (commanding ground forces in Egypt and Palestine) he said Churchill intended to use aeroplanes to drop bombs along the chosen route: falling onto a white surface they would throw up the black sub-soil, thus forming a chain of black dots. Wilson urged Congreve to help make it easier for aircraft to fly between Egypt and Mesopotamia. The advantages were obvious, but Churchill had a struggle to overcome the 'obdurate' resistance of Austen Chamberlain, Chancellor of the Exchequer.

In March 1922, Churchill 'scored a great victory', in Spooner's opinion, for his account in Parliament of the RAF's work in Iraq. As Sccly observed, 'for the first time in history we see the young air force taking charge of a big country, with the older services ancillary to it'. Although Seely had disagreed with Churchill over his holding of two ministries, he supported him wholeheartedly now that he was Colonial Secretary and welcomed his 'most interesting experiment' in Iraq: four 'little rebellions' in the past year had all been settled with few casualties on either side.

Churchill was already certain, in March 1922, that if war 'on a great scale suddenly broke out again', air power would play a vital part. To keep 'this new arm, with its measureless possibilities, in perpetual thraldom to the army or the navy' would be a major mistake. An independent air force will, moreover, take over many duties hitherto carried out by the Royal Navy, such as long-range reconnaissance, anti-submarine operations, attacks upon troop transports, and do so more effectively and cheaply.

Rawlinson wrote to Trenchard in April: 'I know that you and Winston are pressing to replace British troops in India with aeroplane squadrons. At the moment, he refused to agree, but if your air policy succeeded in Iraq, he would reconsider.' As for Beatty (First Lord of the Admiralty) he assured Hankey in August that there was 'not the smallest chance of Mr Churchill being able to bring about an arrangement between the two services' with regard to the RAF's continued independence. This was the same Beatty who had supported Churchill's efforts in the last year of the war to combine air and sea power against the U-boat threat.

The RAF formally took control of Iraq on 1 October 1922 with John Salmond in command of a formidable force: more than 1,000 officers and men (plus eight female nurses) had left Southampton aboard the *Braemar Castle* on 14 September. It was the first time the RAF had chartered a ship exclusively for its own drafts. The total strength in Iraq would amount to about 3,000 persons when they arrived, including four armoured car companies, signals personnel, an armoured train and a water transport section. Eight squadrons (one of Sopwith Snipes, one of Bristol fighters, four of De Havilland 9as and two of Vickers troop-carriers, one of Vernons and the other Victorias) were to be stationed at three bases – Hinaidi, Mosul and Shiva – and all eight were equipped with twelve aircraft and reserves.

Some six months later, on 14 March 1923, Samuel Hoare (now Secretary of State for Air) reported to Parliament that the problem they were trying to solve in Iraq was 'control without occupation' and if they succeeded the experiment would be extended throughout the Middle East. In India, the senior RAF officer now had direct access to the viceroy and his headquarters lay close to those of the army.

At the Dardanelles, the air units sent there had shown that on 'active service soldiers, sailors and airmen could all work harmoniously together'. In David Omissi's opinion, air power preserved Britain's influence for a generation: without such a cheap alternative to military occupation, 'it is likely that the British presence would have been curbed or ended' and Turkey might well have absorbed large parts of an Arab kingdom.

'Regrettable Accidents'

Air control was well established by 1933 when Flight Lieutenant Edgar Kingston-McCloughry described it in a prize-winning essay.

'Mountain, desert, marsh and swamp offer no obstruction to aircraft which, ignoring such barriers, can penetrate to the source of trouble... Against this arm uncivilised people are almost helpless, for they have practically no means of retaliation, and our bases and important centres are easily defended by land forces.'

Action against rebels made their 'existence wretched and intolerable'. Far fewer native casualties were suffered than in the days of army control, and the cost to Britain, in lives and money, was far less. 'Air control,' he concluded, 'resembles the quick, clean incisive sweep of a surgeon's knife which cuts out a cancerous growth.' Incidental casualties – to women, children or innocent bystanders – were unavoidable prices to pay for preserving order. The Air Ministry did its best to conceal 'regrettable accidents', but no airmen in those years could seriously claim that aircraft were capable of 'precision' bombing or ground strafing. Worse still, was the practice of dropping delayed-action bombs, intended to kill those who believed the raid was over.

Although Churchill left the War Office in February 1921, he remained Secretary of State for Air and the Colonies until April, when to the great delight of Stanley Spooner, the Air Ministry got its own Secretary of State – Frederick Guest – although he was at a loss to understand the appointment of a former soldier with no aviation experience and currently a politician who has had 'a quiet parliamentary life'. On the other hand, Guest was Churchill's complaisant cousin and remained in office until October 1922. Seely would have been a better choice, 'welcomed by the friends of aviation', in Spooner's opinion, 'having regard for his fearlessly expressed views upon the vital importance of seeing that the British Empire is supreme in the air'.

Churchill was 'extremely shocked' in July 1921 to learn that the RAF had fired on women and children at Nasiriyah. It was 'a disgraceful act', he told Trenchard, who blamed political officers for demanding that 'a special example should be made of an exceptionally unruly tribe'. On 30 May Trenchard had been told by Group Captain Amyas Borton that eight aircraft had fired upon tribesmen enjoying a picnic, chasing them into a lake where they made easy targets. Trenchard was rightly concerned that if the news got out, 'there would be a charge of "frightfulness" against the force'.

A week later, on 7 June, Churchill told Percy Cox, High Commissioner in Iraq, that aircraft must be used 'with the greatest circumspection', and never to support 'purely administrative measures, such as collection of revenues'. He assured Cox on 8 July that he believed in 'the legitimate use of air power', reiterating his hopes for 'order and happiness in Mesopotamia ... a state with an Arab ruler protected by contingents of British, Indian and native troops and Imperial Air Forces'.

No action was taken against Borton, however, who reported cheerfully to Trenchard on 23 August that a bombing raid had killed eight men and fifty-seven livestock. 'I am most pleasantly surprised at these results, as I had anticipated a purely moral effect', wrote Borton. A year later, in June 1922, he told Trenchard that a rebel village had been entirely destroyed by ground troops after a raid in which a hundred bombs were dropped: the village had been 'a hot bed of malcontents'. Trenchard did not complain. He was by no means alone among RAF officers who had no qualms about severely punishing 'restless natives' in any territories ruled by Britain. They were not as 'extremely shocked' as was Churchill at such incidents.

'I am a great believer in air power,' said Churchill in 1922, 'and will help it forward in every way' thus resisting a return of aviation controlled by the older services. Any country which neglected air power would in the event of war find itself 'fatally situated' and therefore aviation must be developed as an 'independent conception', essential to bolster Britain's defence against 'the most deadly attack, one from the air, if ever such a danger arose again'.

Churchill told Austen Chamberlain in March 1922 that he had discussed the RAF with Billy Mitchell, head of the American flying service, who had travelled all round Europe, studying air organisations, and regarded the RAF as a model for every nation. He told Churchill about the chaos prevailing in the United States over waste and duplication caused by the army and the navy running their own separate services.

The Chanak Crisis

This 'dramatic and bizarre' crisis erupted early in September 1922, when Mustafa Kemal – also known as 'Atatürk' – hero of Gallipoli in 1915 and now head of a popular rising against both the moribund sultanate and foreign occupation of Turkish territory, advanced to the Dardanelles Straits, having destroyed a large force of Greek invaders in Asia Minor.

Atatürk threatened a small British garrison in Chanak (Çanakkale), a town of strategic significance on the Asian coast opposite Kilid Bahr. Lloyd George, Curzon (Foreign Secretary) and Churchill were all determined to resist him. 'If the Turks take the Gallipoli peninsula and Constantinople,' asserted Churchill with his usual exaggeration at a Cabinet meeting on 7 September, 'we shall have lost the whole fruits of our victory [in the Great War] and another Balkan war would be inevitable.'

Ordered on 29 September to deliver an ultimatum requiring Atatürk to withdraw from Chanak, Charles Harington (commanding Allied forces in Turkey) wisely refused. Atatürk, also cleverly, did not attack British garrisons there or elsewhere. On 11 October an agreement obliged Lloyd George to accept a demand for a drastic revision of the humiliating Treaty of Sèvres (August 1920) and Atatürk agreed to tolerate a British presence in a 'neutral zone', enclosing all the coasts of the Sea of Marmara from Gallipoli to Constantinople. In July 1923, after nine months of negotiation in Lausanne, Turkey was freed from foreign occupation and shortly afterwards a republic was proclaimed, with Atatürk as first president.

A powerful fleet had been sent by the British government to the region and Trenchard sent four squadrons, one of them commanded by Arthur Tedder, later to become a great Allied commander and the only one known to have been rescued from a watery grave (in May 1918) by a Japanese destroyer; a distinction of which, in his whimsical way, he was inordinately proud. The danger of a major war over Chanak ended, in fact, on the day after Tedder arrived in Constantinople. Yet all British forces remained in the region throughout the months of diplomatic negotiations.

This tedious standby did certainly help Tedder's emergence as a likely senior officer, but he later reflected that an opportunity had been missed at Constantinople to accustom all three services to the idea of working together. Serious casualties would have been suffered if fighting had begun, as a consequence of their failure to do so. Here lie the roots of Tedder's particular strength as a commander in the Second World War: his constant concern to combine the efforts of all services. As for Churchill, he lost his hitherto safe Dundee seat in October 1922 and was out of Parliament for the next two years.

Interlude: 1923-1933
'Wilderness Years'

Churchill was now moving away from the Liberal Party back into the Conservative fold after twenty years and was re-elected to Parliament, calling himself a 'Constitutionalist', as member for Epping, Essex, in October 1924. He was one of the biggest boulders in a Conservative landslide in that year's General Election and was promptly appointed Chancellor of the Exchequer, to his surprise and delight, by Prime Minister Stanley Baldwin. It was a high position for which he was unqualified. He nevertheless retained it for five years and sensibly passed swiftly over them in his memoirs. He severely cut expenditure on the armed services, thereby setting up a situation against which he would rail so eloquently in the 1930s.

Those services (with the exception of the RAF's Fighter Command) were poorly equipped and manned in September 1939 and without American supplies and support would have suffered even heavier losses in the early years of the war. During 1933, when Churchill began to give serious attention to German re-armament and British weakness, the RAF had numerically fallen to sixth place in the world: 'the Royal Navy had a smaller complement of men than at any time for forty years; the condition of the British Army was the most hapless of all.'

As always, wrote Robert Blake, Churchill pressed 'with enthusiastic extremism the case for whatever department he headed', while he headed it. Peter Gretton agreed: he became 'absorbed in his task, whatever it was, and fitted himself with mental blinkers,' which allowed him to disregard other points of view and other issues. 'Rigorous economy' became his watchwords.

Throughout the years from 1911 to 1922, he had been an aviation enthusiast, but during the years from 1922 to 1933, other interests absorbed him. As far as his relations with airmen are concerned, these are his real 'wilderness years'. In David MacGregor's opinion, Churchill was a 'cheapskate' as Chancellor, a man who 'strenuously opposed Admiralty plans for warship construction, naval aviation development, and a Singapore naval base'.

Consequently, thanks in part to Churchill's conduct for five years in a powerful office, Britain's ability to face the dictators from 1933 onwards was seriously weakened. On the other hand, as Christopher Bell argued, Churchill did back the creation of a base in Singapore, against both Treasury advice and the Labour Party. Bell fairly observed 'the propensity of historians to place Churchill at the centre of events and, consequently, to treat him as the only member of the decision-making process who mattered' and concluded that 'the most serious damage to the armed services was inflicted, as Churchill himself argued, after he left office'.

In 1925 he returned Britain to the 'gold standard', as in the days of his youth, which meant, in practice, low wages, massive unemployment and poor returns for exports. Britain was not 'a land fit for heroes' and resounding speeches could not make it so. The services were a prime target for cuts in expenditure (essential, so he was advised). Despite Trenchard's protests, he ruled that for economic reasons RAF expansion, due to be completed in 1931, must be delayed until 1940, thus ensuring 'very considerable economies'.

Relations with France were good, he thought; Germany posed no threat; Italy and the Soviet Union needed watching, China and Japan did not matter. He told Samuel Hoare (Secretary of State for Air) on 20 September 1925:

'You would be surprised to hear all the quarters in which misgivings are felt upon the subject [of an independent RAF]. My own view is strictly in favour of a separate air force on the merits, subject only to the query: "can we afford it?" As you know, I am animated by the most friendly feeling to you and to Trenchard and am most earnestly desirous of maintaining that close co-operation of which you speak.'

In October 1925, Churchill assured Trenchard that 'I have not at all altered my views as to the desirability of a separate air force, so far as efficiency and leadership in the air are concerned'. But the cost 'is another matter, and I am not convinced that large savings would not result from the less satisfactory solution of division'. Churchill admitted to Trenchard that he was being bitterly reproached by the navy and under cruel pressure and cuts must be made because: 'Everything now turns on finance.'

In the event, the RAF survived, but its budget was cut by thirty per cent. Churchill said that he regretted this cut. In December 1926 he told Francis Bridgeman (First Lord of the Admiralty) that 'the much-abused air force put up with a devil of a lot, if you look at the dwellings they live in and compare them with the fine permanent barracks of the navy and army, particularly the navy'. A year later, in December 1927, he complained to Baldwin that he was 'repulsed by every department, except the Air Ministry', when seeking to reduce expenditure.

Churchill wrote to Richard Hopkins (a senior Treasury official) in December 1927 about Trenchard's idea 'that with flying boats he could take over most of the naval duties now performed in the Persian Gulf by small cruisers'. Churchill wanted Hopkins to look into the costs and discuss with Trenchard what could be done. On 16 January 1928 he asked Bridgeman to reduce the Admiralty's estimated expenditure for the coming year. It was essential, said Churchill, that Bridgeman consult the Air Ministry regarding a great expenditure proposed on an untested new anti-aircraft weapon: was it likely to be justified by the probable results against aircraft attack? Later that month, on the 29th, he wrote to Baldwin. 'There is a widespread feeling – in my opinion well founded – that the Admiralty give less value for money than either of the other two services.'

The Ten-Year Rule
In his first month as Chancellor – November 1924 – Churchill asked the Committee of Imperial Defence to consider extending the Ten-Year Rule (a rule that he had initiated in 1919, supposing that Britain would not be engaged in a major war during the next decade). This was done informally until December 1928 when the government accepted his wish to extend it from a date that began anew each day. Throughout the years from 1919 to 1932 it remained in force. The rule helped the Chancellor to control service expenditure and thereby played a part in encouraging the policy of appeasement against which that same Chancellor would later protest, especially when he realised that neither Baldwin nor Chamberlain would give him another office.

The RAF fared better than the other services between the wars and Churchill argued that reducing its budget should not in any way hamper the development of ideas; it would merely 'check mass production until the situation demanded it' and so avoid expenditure on armaments that might be obsolete when required. In spite of his deep interest in military history, he was as naive as most other politicians in supposing that fully-equipped and trained fighting men could be conjured into existence at little more than a moment's notice. Consequently, he never admitted that the Ten-Year Rule endangered Britain or the empire.

According to Ernle Chatfield (Third Sea Lord, 1925-1928; later First Sea Lord and later still Minister for Co-ordination of Defence) the rule made realistic military planning impossible. In memoirs written early in the war he denounced the 'crushing, soul-destroying influence' of the rule. The decision to extend it in 1928 was particularly distressing. 'Gagged and bound hand and foot', the service departments 'were handed over to the Treasury Gestapo. Never has there been such a successful attempt to hamstring the security of an empire.' Hankey agreed with Chatfield.

In 1948, after *The Gathering Storm* (Churchill's version of events in the 1930s) was published, Hankey wrote to *The Times*, claiming: 'Several service people and ex-ministers have begged me to write on the subject.' The 'whole official world' knew that Churchill was responsible for the rule and the higher ranks in the services 'have never forgiven him'. British rearmament after 1933, wrote Hankey, had been severely constrained by the 'dangerous and demoralising' impact of the rule, which had badly damaged both the fighting services and the arms industry and Churchill could not 'escape some responsibility for our misfortunes'. The rule seriously undermined Britain's aircraft industry, in Barnett's opinion: it was 'one of Churchill's least happy contributions to English [sic] history'.

'The Largest Aircraft Producer in the World'

Between 1924 and 1932, wrote Tami Biddle, 'RAF procurement expenditure increased rather than declined, and in the mid-1920s the Air Ministry spent a higher proportion of its total budget on research and development than the Admiralty or the War Office', and by 1940 Britain was 'the largest aircraft producer in the world'. On the other hand, RAF officers did too little thinking – as opposed to making assertions – about the practicalities of their obsession with *offence*. They made plenty of noise, but were found wanting when the war began in 1939 and it was not until 1942 that deeds began to match that noise. Fortunately for Britain and all those who feared a total and permanent German victory in 1940, some officers *had* been quietly thinking and acting, so that an effective defence, at least in daylight, was available in that crucial year.

Amery wrote to Baldwin on 11 March 1929 about the danger of entrusting Churchill after the election (due on 30 May) 'with his long-cherished dream of co-ordinating the fighting services'. That danger never arose because the Conservatives were defeated and Churchill was furious at finding himself once again out of office. More than a decade would pass before he returned to ruling circles. One of his last acts as Chancellor was to resist the Admiralty's demand for a larger Fleet Air Arm. The days when he fostered naval aviation were over, but most influential naval officers were content with such aircraft as gradually found their way into service.

These were the years when the United States and Japan overtook the British seaborne empire in number and quality of both aircraft and aircraft carriers. During the Great War, the RNAS had learned to use land-based aircraft effectively for protection of ports and convoys, but after that war, the RAF lost this expertise. The Imperial Japanese Navy benefitted 'because its air force was trained by British officers who used the RNAS as a model. Between the wars, alone in the world, Japan developed land-based maritime strike forces' and these were used to good effect in 1941 and 1942.

If Churchill had Died in December 1931

In December 1931, Churchill was nearly killed on 5th Avenue in New York. He looked the wrong way before stepping off into the path of a car travelling at more than 30 mph. Although he was in great pain, he remained conscious and when a policeman pressed him for details of the accident, he correctly insisted that it was entirely his own fault. Had he died, there would still have been British politicians and military leaders to speak out against German and Italian aggression, but they would probably have been no more concerned than he was about danger from Japan. There would still have been a spectacular expansion of the RAF, but the army would still have been untrained and poorly-equipped for operations anywhere. As for the Royal Navy, it too would have been hard-pressed.

With Churchill long gone, who was there to stand up to the formidable Chamberlain and his numerous supporters? Not Anthony Eden. He had his chance in 1938-1939, but lacked the guts to seize it. As late as April 1939, a public opinion poll gave him thirty-eight per cent support as the next Prime Minister if Chamberlain resigned and only seven per cent each to Halifax and Churchill. On the outbreak of war, Chamberlain excluded him from the centre of events by offering him the Dominions Office, a backwater post without membership of the War Cabinet, and he accepted it. It is possible, of course, that Eden might have developed a more assertive character in the absence of Churchill, but it seems more likely that he would have proven to be as 'realistic' a Prime Minister as Chamberlain.

Lloyd George, a known admirer of Hitler, might well have made more of a stir in Churchill's absence. He would not have been averse to playing the part of Hitler's puppet. In Churchill's absence, Halifax would have urged Chamberlain to hang on in 1940, bearing in mind that there would have been no invasion of Norway without Churchill demanding it. Neither Attlee (the Labour Party leader) nor Sinclair (Liberal leader) had Churchill's assets: A small but devoted group of supporters; galvanic energy; an unrivalled power of oratory when words really mattered; a simple British patriotism; a real sense of destiny that he was the chosen man to save the nation; above all, an extraordinary optimism and confidence against all the odds.

Under Chamberlain and following Hitler's victories in Western Europe, Britain would have negotiated an armistice with Hitler: an armistice acceptable, if not popular, with many Britons whose memories of the Great War were still vivid, enhanced by years of lurid, if not lucid, writing on the impact of aerial bombardment and even more memorable newsreels of the destruction caused in China, Spain, Poland and Western Europe. Axis control of the Mediterranean and the Middle East would have permitted an undistracted campaign against the Soviet Union that might well have been victorious. The United States would eventually have prevailed against Japan, if she chose to attack Pearl Harbor, but the war in the east would surely have been longer and more bloody.

It is certain that the United States would have taken no part in the war across the Atlantic: how could she, without bases in the British Isles? Had Churchill died in December 1931, some other Briton might have emerged during the 1930s to oppose appeasers and pacifists alike, to inspire and bully his fellow-citizens into 'their finest hour'. But it is hard to think who that might have been. Although he made many mistakes during the crucial decade, 1934 to 1945, Churchill towered head, shoulders and torso over everyone else in British public life, and never quite fell out with his essential American and Soviet allies.

7

Agitation over Singapore, 1921-1942

What Kind of Fortress?
Britain had no dry dock east of Malta which could take capital ships and therefore if she wished to defend her empire in the Far East, should it be seriously threatened, a secure sea-fortress on Singapore Island was needed. That island, about the same size as the Isle of Wight, lay at the southern tip of a peninsula ruled by Malay sultans under British authority. A combination of valuable rubber plantations, tin mining and a superb harbour generated immense wealth in the whole region. The proposed sea-fortress – with an air and seaplane base nearby at Seletar – had to be on the northern coast, in order not to upset the merchants wheeling and dealing around Keppel Harbour and Singapore City on the southern coast.

The decision to build was taken in June 1921, but little was actually done throughout the 1920s, apart from endless argument between the services and the Treasury about what should be done. The Admiralty and the War Office believed that several huge guns, supported by submarines, would deter a major threat from enemy warships. The Air Ministry argued that torpedo-bombers, escorted by fighters, would prove to be an effective – and far cheaper – substitute. Most British observers, including Churchill, assumed that a fortress at the southern end of 200 miles of jungle was safe from land attack. They supposed that the jungle was far denser than in fact it was and, in any case, the danger was not great. Time and time again, Churchill would assert, in his confident way, that Japan could not possibly mount a serious challenge to Singapore.

In the 1920s, Churchill had hoped for 'an imaginative development of air power' which would allow for both a 'cheaper and more effective method of defence'. In December 1924, for example, he said the best way to defend Singapore would be by an expansion of its aerial defences, rather than the Admiralty's wish for gun batteries and submarines. A 'large economy' would be achieved and 'heavy bombing machines' offered an effective deterrent. Churchill assured Prime Minister Baldwin in December 1924 that war with Japan was not a serious possibility 'in our lifetime'. Only if she threatened to invade Australia (or, presumably, New Zealand) would Britain be concerned. Some Admiralty officials were less confident and pressed for developing a fully-equipped naval base in Singapore.

In fact, naval aviation and the base at Singapore both suffered severely under Churchill as an economy-first Chancellor of the Exchequer. The Naval Staff had proposed building four aircraft carriers during the next twelve years and sufficient aircraft for them, but Churchill delayed action, arguing that British air power at sea was already superior to that of Japan and the United States. Many senior naval officers shared this mistaken opinion.

Churchill supported the RAF's ambitions for Singapore because they would cost much less than the navy required. The result of inter-service quarrelling and the Treasury's wish to save money ensured that all imperial territories in the Far East were vulnerable if in fact Japan did threaten them. Inter-service co-operation was dismal; the air force chose airfield sites that the army could not defend, the navy failed to advise the air force of ship movements requiring air cover, and few civilians – public servants or merchants – supposed that Japanese ambitions might reach as far as Malaya and Singapore. As Prime Minister Stanley Bruce, of Australia, said in 1923, 'While I am not quite clear as to how the protection of Singapore is to be assured, I am quite clear on this point, that apparently it can be done.' Words that echo an ancient theatrical saw: 'It will be alright on the night.'

A Remarkable Theory

During 1925 Churchill accepted Trenchard's 'remarkable theory', as Ferris described it, 'that the same squadrons in Asia could simultaneously replace infantry on the north-west frontier of India, cruisers for trade protection in the Indian Ocean, and 15-inch guns at Singapore', while the mere *threat* that these squadrons could be sent there would deter Japanese aggression. Even more 'remarkable' was the fact that Churchill, with his long interest in all matters military, should have accepted such nonsense. Worse still, continual squabbles between the three services, as well as the conviction of successive governments that Far Eastern territories could be held on the cheap are the 'key roots' of disasters there.

There was always, as Raymond Callahan wrote, 'a large element of fantasy about the "Singapore strategy"', for it was based on a belief that Japan would never be so bold as to attack Britain's Far Eastern territories, but even if she did, the attack would only come when those territories were ready to resist until a relieving fleet arrived. 'Churchill was certainly a party to this fantasy, which was a convenient one for an economising Chancellor fighting a major battle to hold down the naval estimates.'

Not a Priority

A 'grand tournament of bureaucratic jousting', as David McIntyre called it, was played out for many years until Japanese, German and Italian aggression gradually provoked a certain amount of action. In May 1932, John Salmond (Trenchard's successor as CAS) asserted yet again that guns were not essential, aircraft were mobile and could now hit, with bombs or torpedoes, whatever targets they aimed at. He really seems to have believed this. Singapore, he claimed, would be adequately protected with one division of soldiers, six squadrons of aircraft and had no need of big guns. The Japanese were not to be equated with Germans or even Italians as a major threat.

Salmond's opinions did not prevail and in February 1938, 'amidst much ceremonial posturing', Sir Shenton Thomas, Governor of the Straits Settlement, formally opened a dry dock in Singapore in a ceremony attended by the Japanese consul-general. But the base was far from complete and C. G. Grey was quoted in the *Straits Times* on 26 February as saying that Singapore's defences 'are the laughing stock of any intelligent Asiatic': an opinion that evidently cut no ice in Whitehall. For months the dock served only as a swimming pool and workers there remarked in 1940: 'We'll just about finish it in time for the Japanese.' They were not far wrong.

The Air Ministry had proposed in 1934 to spread aircraft 'in penny packets' around the empire. Ten squadrons were to be devoted to imperial defence (three in Singapore, others in Hong Kong, Penang, Ceylon and Aden) to reinforce thirty-five already overseas. Another twenty would be provided for the Fleet Air Arm. Only ten would be added to the forty-two already assigned to home defence.

Chamberlain rejected these proposals and in October 1935 it was decided that thirty-three new squadrons would be provided at home and only four for imperial defence (three of them in Singapore) and three-and-a-half for the FAA. From then on, the Air Staff was reluctant to send squadrons abroad: in October 1940, the commanders in the Far East estimated that they needed nearly 600 aircraft (to protect Malaya, Burma, Borneo and Hong Kong). The chiefs of staff decided that about half that number would suffice, but in December 1941 there were only 180 serviceable and seventy-nine of them were an inadequate American fighter, the Brewster Buffalo.

In February 1937 the chiefs of staff had warned ministers that threats at 'both ends of the empire' and from Italy in the middle meant that unless diplomacy resolved these issues 'only very great military and financial strength can give the empire security'. Although Singapore got more coastal guns and several more airfields were built on the island and in the Malayan Peninsula, by the summer of 1939 British defence planners in London had decided that the Mediterranean mattered more than anywhere in the Far East or the Pacific.

Philip Babington (RAF commander in the Far East) wrote to Slessor, Director of Plans in the Air Ministry. There was no certainty, he thought, that any part of the Royal Navy would reach Singapore in the foreseeable future and therefore asked for the island's air defences to be doubled, from the existing eight squadrons to sixteen, making a total of 250 aircraft. This was not done.

In London the old fantasy was revised. The time before the 'fortress' of Singapore could be relieved by the Royal Navy was officially increased from seventy to ninety days in July 1939 and then in September to six months. Churchill, both before and after he returned to office, agreed with these extensions. 'On no account,' this backbencher told Neville Chamberlain in March 1939, 'must anything which threatens in the Far East divert us from this prime objective', of securing control of the Mediterranean.

A Naked Empire

Churchill breezily recommended that the Prime Minister should tell the Australians and New Zealanders 'the whole story and they will come along'. They were not vital interests, as Churchill made clear in his first message to President Roosevelt after becoming Prime Minister in May 1940: 'I am looking to you to keep that Japanese dog quiet in the Pacific.' This at a time when the United States had very weak land and air forces, although its fleet was large and powerful. Churchill 'culpably neglected' the defence of Britain's territories in the Far East, 'even willfully preferring to reinforce the air strength of the Soviet Union' after June 1941.

In June 1939 the Japanese blockaded the British Concession in Tientsin on the Chinese coast, south-east of Beijing. Britain came dangerously close to declaring war on Japan over this crisis, but realised, almost at the last moment, that she could not face warfare against Germany, Italy *and* Japan at the same time.

As soon as war with Germany began, Australia and New Zealand stood by Britain. The two Dominions, thought Chamberlain's 'War Cabinet', should retain most of their strength at home until Japan's response to Germany's invasion of Poland became clear. Churchill, back in office as First Lord of the Admiralty, argued that Dominion forces should at once join British in France.

At a meeting in November 1939, the Australians – represented by Richard Casey, Minister of Supply – wanted to know what Britain intended to do about Singapore. Churchill produced a paper repeating a promise made in 1937 that the Far East came before the Mediterranean in British planning. Singapore, he declared, was a 'fortress armed with five 15-inch guns', a garrison of 20,000 men and plenty of aircraft. It could only be taken after a siege lasting for several months by an army of at least 50,000 men and during that time a British fleet would arrive.

The Japanese, 'a prudent people', said Churchill, would not embark upon such a mad enterprise. Chamberlain thought the Dominions might take Churchill's paper to mean that if Japan entered the war, Britain would abandon the Mediterranean in order to reinforce Singapore. Casey was concerned that no battleships would be at Singapore until after Japan made a move, but Churchill took a hard line: the navy could not keep battleships 'tethered' at Singapore to meet a possible threat. Casey gave way and Churchill praised New Zealand for taking 'a much more realistic view of the situation'. Both Dominions agreed to send men to the Far East.

Brooke-Popham in the Hot Seat

Air Chief Marshal Sir Robert Brooke-Popham retired in March 1937 and was then appointed Governor of Kenya. Amazingly, in November 1940 – at the ripe old age of sixty-two – he was recalled to active service and sent to Singapore with a very small staff. He was to command all British soldiers and airmen in Burma, Malaya, Singapore and Hong Kong. Naval units were expressly excluded from his authority because they answered, as always, only to the Admiralty.

He had never even visited the Far East and had no authority over the civilian administration or the business community and relations with the French, Dutch and Americans were whatever he could make of them. His soldiers and airmen did not train together and had framed no precise plan of action to meet an unlikely Japanese threat. In short, Brooke-Popham proved quite unable to handle a command for which he had neither the resources nor the essential experience of conditions in the Far East.

Automedon

The loss of the *Prince of Wales* and *Repulse* in December 1941 (to be described shortly) caused Australian Prime Minister John Curtin to send anxious cables to London and Churchill replied soothingly in January: 'Night and day I am labouring here to make the best arrangements possible in your interests and for your safety.'

Ever since August 1940 he had known that Britain could do nothing promptly in the event of a Japanese attack. For some unfathomable reason, he decided to send this news to Brooke-Popham by sea, aboard a Blue Funnel steamer *Automedon*. She sailed from Liverpool late in September 1940 and was captured by a German surface raider *Atlantis* (Captain Bernhard Rogge) in the Indian Ocean on 11 November, which took the mail bags to Japan. By the end of December, Churchill knew that the report was in Japanese hands. 'I do not take an alarmist view about the defence of Singapore', he wrote in January 1941, refusing to allow any significant reinforcement of its air strength. That resolution merely hardened after the German invasion of the Soviet Union in June. 'I must repeat my conviction,' he wrote a month later, 'that Japan will not declare war upon us at the present juncture,' and even if she did, that would become an American problem because 'the weight upon us would clearly be too great.'

'Britain's Strong Point in the East'

The RAF, fully supported by Churchill, chose to keep its main strength at home. Hindsight is always clear, but a few more Hurricanes in the Far East could have prevented Japanese bombers from driving the RAF away so easily from its Malayan airfields. Similarly, a couple of squadrons of the numerous Whitley or Hampden bombers in England, which were incapable of causing significant damage to German targets, would have given useful service in scattering troop transports and wrecking airfields around Saigon. But the Air Ministry was preoccupied in 1941 by Germany and Italy in the Mediterranean, the Middle East and the Atlantic. There was, everyone in Whitehall believed, a powerful fortress in Singapore and the Japanese would never be so unwise as to attack what *War Illustrated* in October 1940 considered 'Britain's strong point in the East'.

By 1941, 'the degree to which British policy-makers had relegated Singapore to the back of their minds and the bottom of their priorities does not seem to have become fully apparent' to Australians, New Zealanders, South Africans, Indians, Malayans or Chinese and 'neither Churchill nor the chiefs of staff ever candidly said so'. The Australian Prime Minister (now Robert Menzies) was in Britain from February to April 1941 and noted Churchill's love of 'the glittering phrase – so attractive to his mind that awkward facts may have to give way... He has aggression without knowledge.' To the fury of Churchill and most of his advisers, civilian or military, the Australians withdrew one division from the Middle East in 1941 and prevented two others from being sent to Rangoon. From their point of view, the defence of Australia was a priority. Churchill told Dudley Pound (chief of the Naval Staff) on 17 February that the United States 'would not base a battle-fleet on Singapore': we must get them into the war, but even if Singapore fell, we could use Australian ports.

Japan on the Attack

During August 1941 Japanese forces advanced through southern Indo-China to within 700 miles of Singapore. The plan to send out 'Force Z', a small British fleet, was revived. It comprised a new battleship, *Prince of Wales*, an elderly heavy cruiser, *Repulse*, and four destroyers, commanded by Admiral Sir Tom Phillips, vice-chief of the Naval Staff. It sailed without the support of *Indomitable*, an aircraft carrier that had run aground off Jamaica. Churchill, as well as his Admiralty advisers, still believed in the battleship, even though a dozen had already been sunk by submarines, gunfire or aircraft since the war began. A small aircraft carrier, *Hermes* (able to carry fifteen aircraft), arrived in Simonstown naval base shortly before Force Z sailed for Singapore, but Phillips felt no need to take her with him. Those aircraft, few as they were, supported by Singapore's Buffaloes, might well have saved the British capital ships from destruction by unescorted bombers.

In December 1941, Japan attacked American bases in Hawaii and the Philippines and intended to capture the Malay Peninsula and Singapore Island. Although the British had plenty of soldiers, they were not well trained and had no tanks. Brooke-Popham and Arthur Percival (the army commander), listened to the British Ambassador in Thailand, whose mind was still locked into the stately diplomatic procedures of peacetime, and they hesitated on 8 December to move swiftly against Japanese troops landing in a neutral state – southern Thailand – when they were briefly vulnerable. Thereafter British-led ground forces were committed to dogged resistance and constantly driven back.

Yamashita Tomoyuki, commanding the Japanese invaders, had fewer troops, but a Churchillian spirit: 'Do not stop; charge forward no matter what happens,' he told one battalion commander, 'and do not respond to fire from behind.' They suffered heavy casualties and were short of air support, ammunition, fuel and food, but were full of fight. Percival had failed to build defensive positions, morale was low and rivalries intense among his multi-national forces. He was also deeply concerned about the island's civilians, who were neither eager nor armed to resist ruthless invaders.

Into the Dragon's Mouth

On the afternoon of 6 December 1941, Tom Phillips (newly promoted to full admiral) learned – mainly from a US Navy radio unit in Honolulu – that many Japanese transports, strongly escorted, were heading for the Gulf of Siam. He knew also that the Japanese had bombers on bases around Saigon and submarines at sea. Although the odds against him were heavy and he had no air cover, he was exactly the kind of fighting man whom Churchill most admired. He decided to seek out and attack the Japanese invaders. News of Pearl Harbor, Clark Field and fighting in Malaya, convinced him that he should neither stay in Singapore, where aircraft could protect him, nor sail for safer waters and await events. He took Force Z out of Singapore at dusk on 8 December, without a word to either his army or RAF colleagues.

Phillips had no regard for aircraft, friendly or enemy. He received no advice from Pound, a personal friend who expressed, for no obvious reason, 'infinite faith' in the judgement of an officer who had last heard gunfire in 1915 and had very little sea experience. Force Z was spotted by a Japanese submarine on the afternoon of the 9th and then by three reconnaissance aircraft shortly before dusk, yet Phillips sailed on, hoping he might catch transports at sea or troops getting organised ashore. Finding nothing, he reluctantly decided to return to Singapore. Back in London on the evening of that day, 9 December, Churchill thought the fleet should 'vanish into the ocean wastes and exercise a vague menace', behaving as 'rogue elephants', or join the remnants of the American fleet at Pearl Harbor. Untypically, he did not order them to follow either course.

Left to exercise his own judgement, Phillips responded to a signal from Singapore reporting a rumour that Japanese troops might be landing at Kuantan, on the east coast of Malaya. He promptly turned Force Z at top speed in that direction. Buffalo fighters, standing by in Singapore, could have been sent to cover him, but he refused to break radio silence and call for them. During the morning of 10 December, Phillips learned that there were in fact no enemy forces in Kuantan, yet still he refused to sail for Singapore and wrongly believed his ships to be outside the range of Japanese bombers. The attack by eighty-five twin-engined Mitsubishi 'Betty' and 'Nell' aircraft (as the Allies named them), some armed with bombs, others with torpedoes, began just after 11 am. These bombers were not escorted by fighters and would therefore have been vulnerable to attack even by the inefficient Buffaloes. But Phillips still didn't radio for their help.

'Much to our surprise,' recalled one Japanese pilot, 'not a single enemy plane was in sight. This was all the more amazing since the scene of battle was well within the fighting range of the British fighters.' It would not be until nearly an hour later that the captain of *Repulse* (not Phillips) signalled urgently in plain English asking for help. The Buffaloes arrived within an hour. If they had been summoned at 11 am they would surely have disrupted the attack. But perhaps not, for Phillips had no idea how to handle ships in action and less still about what aircraft might do even to capital ships. Also, the defensive fire offered by both ships was inadequate and many allegedly quick-firing guns jammed repeatedly.

As the Japanese torpedo-bombers prepared to follow the work begun by the bombers, Phillips assured his torpedo specialist that 'there are no torpedo aircraft about'. When he at last realised his error and broke radio silence, it was to ask for destroyers to be sent, not fighters, and even for tugs. He chose to go down with his ship, one of 840 British lives lost that day, which at least prevented Pound from consoling him with another sea-going command.

As for the Japanese, only three aircraft were destroyed; twenty-eight suffered some damage, most of it minor. They circled the area where the ships had gone down, making no attempt to prevent the three surviving destroyers from rescuing more than 2,000 men struggling in the water, some injured and many covered in black oil. The Japanese only left when the Buffaloes arrived, leaving them to fly around, unable to help. Stalin told Churchill that Germans must have provided the aircraft and crews for a feat he supposed – as did most Europeans and Americans before December 1941 – to be far beyond Japanese capability. Harris, later head of Bomber Command, recalled his last words to Phillips: 'Tom, you've never believed in air. Never get out from under the air umbrella, if you do, you'll be for it.'

Disgracefully, Churchill refused to award honours or decorations to those members of Force Z who showed outstanding courage and resolution in a disaster for which he and his advisers were responsible. Two years later, twenty-four were reluctantly Mentioned in Despatches, the lowest recognition possible; thirteen of them posthumously. Shortly after the Force Z disaster, Brooke-Popham was recalled to England after thirteen unhappy months in Singapore. For no good reason, Churchill proposed to award him a baronetcy, but Sinclair for once objected to his master's voice and suggested waiting a while. In the event, Brooke-Popham got what he deserved, nothing.

'Britain's Worst Disaster'

By mid-January 1942, Churchill had finally realised that Singapore was not an impregnable fortress, yet large reinforcements of well-equipped British and Australian troops were landed, just in time to be killed or enslaved for the rest of the war. The final assault began on the night of 8/9 February and Churchill, in the manner so typical of a Victorian schoolboy, 'capped a series of grandiose cables' by insisting that every inch of ground be defended because 'the whole reputation of our country and our race is involved'. There must be no surrender and all principal officers 'are expected to perish at their posts'. Here we see Churchill at his worst. Wavell, recently appointed head of ABDA (American-British-Dutch-Australian) forces, with a headquarters in Java, added his own even less convincing blather, but it was no use. Percival surrendered in a scene never since forgotten on 15 February 1942.

'Our soldiers are not as good fighters as their fathers were', Churchill moaned to his old friend, Violet Bonham Carter. 'We had so many men in Singapore, so many men, they should have done better.' It was, he admitted, the 'worst disaster and largest capitulation in British history'. He had become resigned to the loss of the island, but longed for a glorious last stand by the people of Singapore, military and civilian, slaughtered in a bloodbath that he could later describe, heaving with emotion, if in fact Britain ended the war on the winning side.

Yamashita had 'accomplished a military feat in seventy days with three divisions that German generals had told him would probably take nearly a year-and-a-half with five divisions'. He captured numerous artillery pieces, thousands of vehicles, mountains of ammunition, food and fuel. Japanese casualties numbered only 15,000 killed or wounded. The British, as he later wrote, had been 'out-generalled, outwitted and outfought'.

A Strategic Illusion

Then and later, Arthur Percival made an ideal target for wrath and contempt. 'Long before historians had an opportunity to offer a researched evaluation,' wrote Clifford Kinvig, 'Percival was condemned by photography' because he happened to look like a frightened rabbit; a chinless wonder. Although he had a good record as a fighting soldier during the Great War and later as a staff officer, he lacked the personality and energy to command untrained troops in a theatre where the local population was unprepared for resistance.

He co-operated as well as possible with Conway Pulford, an able and experienced airman who arrived in Singapore in April 1941 to replace Babington, but it was not enough.

Archibald Wavell, as usual, was out of his depth. 'Personally, I should be most doubtful if the Japs ever tried to make an attack on Malaya,' he told Brooke-Popham as late as 13 November 1941, 'and I am sure they will get it in the neck if they do!' Shenton Thomas, the inept civilian governor, 'was a great drag on Percival's military effectiveness and examples of his indecision, obstructiveness, general bureaucratic approach and lack of a sense of urgency abound'. Airfields in Malaya were ill-equipped and unprotected by soldiers. The inadequate Buffaloes were further handicapped by the absence of a system of ground control. There was no civil defence or air raid warning system and the Royal Navy answered only to the Admiralty.

Although there are numerous accounts of the disaster, Ian Hamill got to the root of the matter as long ago as 1973: 'The Singapore naval base was an imperial symbol designed to give the appearance of reality to a strategic illusion: the illusion that a two-hemisphere empire could be defended by a one-hemisphere navy.'

Brooke-Popham is said to have told an American officer that the 'greatest value of Singapore is the misconception of impregnability built up in the Japanese mind'. Sadly, the Japanese were not deceived. Churchill claimed after the war that he could not understand how he failed to realise how vulnerable Singapore was, yet he had reassured Australia and New Zealand in 1939 that it was a fortress well able to withstand a siege for several months and both then and later he helped to delay reinforcement. Among senior officers and politicians in Singapore, Tedder (air commander, 1936-1938) understood most clearly the fragility of Britain's position and tried to inject a sense of urgency, but the will and resources needed to contemplate (let alone resist) serious defence were lacking.

The Italians of the Pacific

The fall of Singapore, wrote John Ferris, 'was a triumph of Japan over the United Kingdom in the air'. As long ago as 1920 Japanese naval officers had asked for British help in developing air power. Many authorities approved: 'diplomats to increase their influence, arms firms and the RAF to build a market,' and all Britons who wished to forestall intrusion by French, Italian or American interests. They were helped by the prestige Britain enjoyed for having helped to shape the Imperial Japanese Navy. Handley Page urged the RAF and his colleagues in the aviation industry to seize a golden opportunity for influence and profit.

The Japanese were regarded as the Italians of the Pacific, inferior socially and politically, inept on land and at sea, as all Britons, military or civilian, agreed. Consequently, in December 1941, as Ferris concluded, 'the RAF in

Malaya failed in every way: to stop invasion; detect the enemy; sink transports at sea; protect British warships and soldiers; or achieve air superiority. Mistaken faith in air power cascaded through every other British decision in the 1930s and during the first two years of the war.' A few obsolescent aircraft with inexperienced crews, it was supposed, would suffice to deter or resist Japanese attack, and ground forces would be needed only to defend airfields.

Mr Justice Bucknill conducted a strictly limited inquiry in March and April 1942 into the causes of the loss of the two capital ships and at a secret session of Parliament in April 1942 Churchill announced that a broad ranging inquiry would be held. This was never attempted. Other disasters, closer to home, filled Churchill's mind after the fall of Singapore. We will see in Chapter 22 how Allied forces fought on in the Far East and eventually turned defeat into a victory that Churchill barely noticed in his memoirs.

8

Will the Bomber Prevail?
Britain in the 1930s

An Invincible Weapon
Between the wars, the *idea* of air power, as much as any demonstrated *capability* dominated the minds of airmen and politicians, particularly in Britain and the United States, and won their support for strategic bombing as a potentially war-winning force. A swift 'knockout blow' from the air would prevent a repeat of the trench warfare so vividly remembered. Devoted airmen were sure that the bomber would dominate any future war. Defence would no longer prevail over offence and air power would matter more than either land or sea power.

·No one doubts that essential building blocks in Britain's air power appeared during Trenchard's years in office: flying schools to set and maintain standards; research and development facilities to encourage improvements; cadet colleges to train air crews; staff colleges to develop leaders and apprentice schemes to train mechanics. Despite Churchill's constant complaints, Britain had a well-capitalised, competitive, and research-intensive aviation industry between the wars. Churchill, however, revelled in numbers and never understood why many soldiers, sailors or airmen were not to be found in constant, direct contact with the enemy. The Air Ministry resisted, as well as it could, demands to build great numbers of machines that were either inadequate or would soon become obsolete.

In fact, the doctrine of 'quality over quantity' was often breached in response to pressure from the aviation industry and from politicians, while the threat of a sudden German assault was always in many minds. These were years of rapid change in airframes, engines and equipment and designers (like air commanders) had to learn from experience which types could perform adequately in wartime; with airfields, hangars and ground crews being built or trained as rapidly as possible in the late 1930s. There were, inevitably, serious misjudgements – especially in regard to transports and carrier-borne aircraft – but overall British air power outmatched that of its enemies.

The crucial step that airmen failed to take in the inter-war period, wrote Williamson Murray, was to learn from history. They failed even though by 1918 aircraft were already being used in every role that they would play in the Second World War: reconnaissance and direction of artillery fire; close support for soldiers advancing or retreating; bombing behind the battle lines; convoy escort and strategic bombing. In particular, it had been painfully learned during the Great War that most operations could only be carried out successfully if and when fighters had won aerial superiority.

Tragically, Trenchard and his acolytes chose to believe that the bomber (not even escorted by fighters) would prevail, if there were enough of them and their crews were sufficiently resolute. It was also believed that no other people could match the British for courage, either when pressing home their attacks or withstanding those made in retaliation. Many Americans were equally adamant, as one instructor at the Air Corps Tactical School asserted in the early 1930s: 'A well-planned and well-conducted bombardment, once launched, cannot be stopped.' By 1935, it was also asserted that 'escorting fighters will neither be provided nor requested unless experience proves that bombardment is unable to penetrate such resistance alone'.

Only after suffering intolerable losses over Schweinfurt in October 1943 did Ira Eaker – then commanding the US bomber force – urge that drop-tanks and long-range escort fighters be provided. As for the RAF, Arthur Harris was also obliged to recognise, after suffering equally unacceptable losses, that his bombers needed the support of night fighters.

'The only explanation,' that Murray could find was that, 'pre-war assumptions remained so strong that the real conditions of aerial warfare made relatively little impression.' The RAF took little interest in drop-tanks until 1943 and despite prodding from Hugh Dowding, head of Fighter Command, Sholto Douglas (assistant CAS) ruled in March 1940 that a long-range fighter must be inferior in performance to a short-range fighter. More than a year later, in June 1941, Portal (by then CAS) agreed and so informed Churchill, who replied that his apparently authoritative ruling closed 'many doors'. It was unlike Churchill to accept so meekly what were merely untested assertions.

Any Bomber Will Do
Many British airmen, politicians and journalists were convinced that the new German air force was being created not to support the army in land campaigns, but to bomb targets in Britain. The RAF therefore needed a bomber force to retaliate, if not deter, but it failed to consider the practical needs of a strategic bombing policy. In too many RAF minds it was not thought essential that bombs hit a particular target because the mere act of dropping them would have the desired effect of winning the war by undermining enemy morale.

What thought, for example, was given to the optimum size of a bomber? Where should it be armoured and what type and number of defensive weapons would it need? What was the ideal size of a bomb and what tests were undertaken to ensure that it actually exploded when dropped? What was done to develop accurate bomb sights? Was navigation seriously studied even over friendly territory, let alone that of a possible enemy? Would escort fighters be needed? Would bombing at night be possible? Would bad weather be a major problem? Was there an adequate air intelligence organisation set up to gather and assess information about how best to defend vulnerable industries and ports in Britain, how best to overcome enemy defences, on the ground and in the air? Not least – in the 1930s – how could military targets be hit without also hitting civilians working there or living nearby?

'A Matter of Faith'

Lazy and even dishonest assumptions were as widespread in all three services as they were in Whitehall and Westminster. When, for example, the Air Staff set up 'air exercises' in the 1930s, umpires ensured that offensive bombers always overcame defensive fighters. One serious experiment was attempted in 1937: thirty obsolete aircraft were placed within a large circle. For one week – at high and low levels, in daylight and in good weather, untroubled by flak or defensive fighters – bombers attacked these sitting ducks. They destroyed two, damaged eleven beyond repair, left six damaged but reparable and missed the other eleven entirely. The experiment was not repeated.

As for navigation, during a night exercise in 1937, two-thirds of a Bomber Command force was unable to find the fully-illuminated city of Birmingham and during the next two years nearly 500 bomber crews had to make forced-landings, having lost their way while flying within the British isles.

Slessor admitted in his memoirs that belief in the bomber was 'a matter of faith' between the wars, but faith is more fitting for a possible life after death than for preserving safety before then. Faith may move mountains, but it does not eliminate enemy air defences and yet Trenchardists virtually ignored these. Slessor also confessed that in the 1930s he too had subscribed to a spirit of traditional amateurism: an attitude that served well enough in dealing with unrest among poorly-armed and untrained 'natives', but would be swept aside by professional Germans, and later (to general surprise) by equally-professional Japanese opponents.

The RAF's Staff College discouraged independent thought in the 1920s and 1930s, serving as a disseminating station for approved doctrine, seasoned by essays on riding, hunting and how to cope with the bazaars of Baghdad. When war came in 1939, the bomber was quickly found to be wholly inadequate; so too were its crews, except in courage and determination. Without air supremacy, which only fighters could provide, enemy productive centres and communications could not be destroyed. In any case, as an Admiralty memorandum in 1932 declared, aerial bombing was 'revolting and un-English', whereas bombardment by land or sea, including blockade, were not.

Two years into a war in which Bomber Command was suffering heavily and achieving little, Slessor (then commanding a bomber group) was still preaching to Trenchard's text. By attacking widely different parts of Germany on successive nights, he told his crews: 'You spread the moral effect not only of the actual attacks but of the air-raid warnings in all districts over which you pass. You know Lord Trenchard's slogan: "Keep the Germans out of bed, keep the sirens blowing" and there is the devil of a lot in it.'

Precisely *what*, Slessor was unable to say. Another assumption was that Britons would prove more stout-hearted than Germans, if they were attacked from the air. Too many officers seemed unaware of the fact that an effective defence against bombers was not only possible, but had in fact been devised in Britain. They also assumed that the Germans could not conceive their own system of defence.

Consequently, numerous brave young men in Bomber Command found – as they died, were injured or captured – that their weapon and their training were alike inadequate. During the war, about half of all the men who flew with Bomber Command were killed. Their German opponents were not cowering sleepless, but fighting back effectively. All British bombers until 1942 were twin-engined machines poorly armed and armoured, able to carry only a light load from Britain to Germany. No truly heavy bomber, with four engines, large enough to carry a seriously destructive or fire-raising load was even nearly ready for service.

Bomber pilots had learned to fly mainly in daylight in good weather. Crews were not initially trained in such essential tasks as navigation, wireless operation and the use of guns. As for fighter pilots, they were very skilled at close-formation flying and crowd-pleasing aerobatics at air shows until 1938; moves that were entirely useless in wartime. Thereafter, they began to learn how best to use their excellent weapons as part of an ever-improving system of defence, at least in daylight.

The Air Staff observed the overseas wars of the 1930s in China and Spain, but drew no lessons from them. Civilians did. Whenever they went to a cinema, they saw newsreel clips of bombs falling, clouds of smoke rising, shattered buildings, women and children in distress. No-one in authority told them, as the years passed, that Japanese bombing was *not* overwhelming China or that the casualties from bombing in the Spanish Civil War were *not* decisive. They supposed, not unreasonably, that such destruction was definitive.

As for Spain, in September 1937, Wing Commander Victor Goddard (chairman of a Joint Intelligence Sub-Committee on Spain) reported that low-flying attacks had a severe impact on semi-organised and semi-disciplined ground forces, but he was sure that such attacks would not alarm British troops, if war came, because they had the discipline and fire power needed to resist effectively. Goddard clearly knew nothing about the actual state of the British Army in the late 1930s. He was able to visit Spain in February 1938, where he learned only what he already knew.

In September 1937, Air Ministry officials decided that British bombers were so fast and well-armed that they would not need fighter escorts. Close support of ground forces would be 'uneconomical' and, indeed, an improper use of air power. It would be years before the RAF recognised a need for aircraft designed for low-flying attack in support of British ground forces advancing or retreating. A few officers – among them Tedder, Coningham and (eventually) Slessor – understood the need for close co-operation with ground forces and their day would come, but only after unescorted bombers had suffered heavy losses in daylight raids.

Once More an Aviation Enthusiast

Until Germany invaded Poland in September 1939, Churchill was out of office and unlikely to return. For all the noise he made about the need to re-arm, he did not cast a single vote against the government on foreign or defence policy before the Munich Crisis; he denounced Gandhi in even stronger language than he applied to Hitler; he refused to condemn the atrocities committed by either Franco or Mussolini; and did not believe Japan posed a serious threat to British power in the Far East.

He had always devoted much of his enormous energy to writing and supervising the efforts of those paid to gather information for him. Out of all this emerged 'his story' of the Great War, a very long biography of his ancestor, the first Duke of Marlborough and plans for an even longer history of the English-speaking peoples. He also found time for frequent holidays far from Westminster. Late in 1937, he was still advocating the return to Germany of colonies confiscated after the Great War and when Eden resigned as Foreign Secretary in February 1938, Churchill was fourth quickest of 400 Conservative MPs to sign a round robin confirming their confidence in Chamberlain.

The navy used to be the 'sure shield' of Britain, Churchill declared. We cannot say that now because this 'cursed, hellish invention and development of war from the air' has weakened that shield. As early as March 1934 he said: 'I dread the day when the means of threatening the heart of the British Empire should pass into the hands of the present rulers of Germany.' True enough, but as Edward Ellington (a former head of the RAF) wrote after the war: 'When we resumed expansion in 1934, we had a much smaller basis on which to build than we should have had had Winston been as enthusiastic for expansion when Chancellor as he was when a critic.'

'Crying Wolf'

For the rest of the 1930s – when he gave his attention to airmen and air power – Churchill preached to the same text. 'With our great metropolis here, the greatest target in the world, a kind of tremendous, fat, valuable cow tied up to attract the beasts of prey, we are in a position in which no other country is at the present moment.' As usual, his purple prose was regarded with amusement, even contempt, by some fellow-politicians, but Rothermere (owner of the *Daily Mail*) was even more concerned than Churchill. My information, he told him as early as August 1934, is that the Germans will soon have a force approaching 20,000 aeroplanes, turning them out like sewing machines or motor cars.

Churchill, advised by his friend, Desmond Morton (head of the Industrial Intelligence Centre, 1930-1939, and close to him throughout the war) replied that that figure 'can have no reality', although the danger was serious enough to justify greater action. At this time, Churchill said that 'a bomb dropped on civilians is a good bomb wasted', and John Steel, head of Wessex Bombing Area agreed. In carrying out exercises, only military objectives were targeted, but presumably the civilians who worked in such places were fair game.

If another war came, Churchill said in November 1934, three or four million Britons would be driven out into the open country, confronting the government of the day with unprecedented problems in feeding and keeping order. By November 1937, the Luftwaffe would be nearly double the size of the RAF and Britain's air defences were no longer adequate to secure peace, safety and freedom. In no more than ten days, he said, London would suffer up to 40,000 casualties, even more, if incendiaries were used. Birmingham, Sheffield and other great manufacturing towns, as well as dockyards, oil storage depots other vital targets were just as vulnerable.

Few men, even politicians, have 'cried wolf!' as often and as eloquently as Churchill. Did he believe the figures he bandied about so freely? He certainly relished the money and publicity they earned him, from those who read what he wrote, listened to what he said and supposed that such a famous man must be well informed. He had no evidence that the Luftwaffe was poised to make any attack on Britain in the 1930s. Never at any time could it have caused such casualties as he claimed to fear and he took far too long to grasp the fact that good work was being done, from 1935 onwards, to prepare effective defences against aerial attack.

During the Great War, as First Lord of the Admiralty and later as Minister of Munitions, Churchill could, with some justification, think of airmen as 'his': he was in close touch with them, but despite the flow of information he received in the 1930s from some concerned airmen, this was no longer so.

In September 1938, Hastings Ismay (Secretary of the Committee of Imperial Defence) asserted that 'Germany's air defence was already perfect', which was by no means true, and that Britain's was 'singularly weak', which was incorrect also. Slessor would recall in his memoirs 'the shocking state of unpreparedness in the air' in September: like Churchill, he took no account of what was being done by officers and civilians under Dowding's direction at Fighter Command. He knew nothing about it. The RAF's ability to *defend* was improving rapidly, although its ability to offend remained feeble.

'It would be a great mistake,' Churchill asserted in August 1938, 'to imagine that the slaughter of the civilian population following upon air raids would prevent the British Empire from developing its full war power.' He repeated that opinion in September, with attacks on civilians in mind: 'So far from producing panic and a wish to surrender, they have aroused a spirit of furious and unyielding resistance among all classes. They have united whole communities otherwise sundered, in a common hatred of such base and barbarous methods.'

At that time, there had been no attacks on British civilians. However, Churchill was sure that if war came between states with equal air strength, the state which seeks the slaughter of the civil population is unlikely to succeed. He had changed his mind by the end of 1940, when British bombers were beginning their attempt to carry the war across the Channel.

Germany, he asserted, in September 1938, could already put into action simultaneously more than 1,500 aeroplanes and her industry is so organised that it can certainly produce, at full blast, 1,000 every month and increase that number as the months pass. As for casualties, Churchill's estimates grew wilder every time he had an audience or dictated a piece for the newspapers. On this occasion, he said 5,000 persons would be killed and 150,000 injured *in a single all-out raid* on London.

In his postwar memoirs he admitted to painting the picture even darker than it was. He actually painted it so black that his gross exaggerations, expressed so often and so vividly, helped to induce diplomatic paralysis. Chamberlain's government, full of men who loathed the very idea of another war, came to believe that only by yielding to all Hitler's demands could safety, at least for Britain, be ensured. In this loathing, most Britons – Conservative, Labour or Liberal – were at one.

Without a bomber force strong enough to deter Hitler, Chamberlain and the chiefs of staff were determined not to challenge him during the Czech crisis of September 1938. Only with the advent of radar and modern fighters in 1939 was Dowding able to feel a growing confidence in Britain's prospects of withstanding the Luftwaffe. As for destroying that air force and the state that had created it, that would surely call for a combination of all arms – land, sea and air – yet Churchill rejected peacetime conscription and had little interest in a strengthened British Army. When he spoke of a 'Grand Alliance', a slogan taken from his Marlborough biography, he meant the Royal Navy and the French army, supported by aircraft. We are in grave danger, he asserted, more dangerous than at the height of the U-boat campaign.

Preparing Defences
Mercifully, from a British point of view, some senior RAF officers guided by

Dowding – listening to civilian engineers, aircraft manufacturers and scientists – developed and produced modern fighters in the late 1930s that would match German fighters and prove markedly superior to German bombers. These bombers, like their British equivalents, were twin-engined, poorly armed for defence and carried too light a load to cause irreparable destruction of aerodromes, military depots, factories or ports. Numerous houses were wrecked, but many of their inhabitants survived. It took many raids for Churchill, other politicians and senior service officers to understand that the real bomber was far less deadly than the imagined bomber.

Of equal importance to the modern fighters was the development in Britain, by those same officers and civilians, of a system of control and reporting based on that devised during the Great War. In providing fighters with adequate early warning, it would be greatly helped – when serious attacks began – by information gathered in two chains of radar stations, one to detect high-flying raiders and the other to spot those approaching at low levels. Britain would be effectively defended against bombers in daylight in 1940, when it mattered most, and later (during 1941) in darkness as well.

Tragically, some influential voices in the Air Ministry hewed stubbornly to the Trenchardist line that only offence mattered. Aircraft production favoured bombers over fighters by a ratio of seven to three between 1936 and 1939. The RAF, wrote Alan Stephens, 'was extremely lucky that it had a number of dedicated and highly-perceptive people who insisted on developing the air defence system'. That system depended upon airfield construction. These airfields, both major bases and temporary landing strips, were designed and managed by a special Air Ministry unit although the actual work, including repairs and extensions, was carried out by Royal Engineer, RAF personnel and civilian contractors in Britain and overseas.

It became a very large business: in 1939, for example, the RAF had over 150 airfields, covering nearly 90,000 acres in Britain. By 1944, there were close to 500 RAF airfields and more than 130 assigned to Americans, covering more than 330,000 acres, and all needing ample storage space for fuel and weapons.

The Works Directorate of the Air Ministry employed nearly one-third of Britain's construction manpower. This was indeed, wrote Sebastian Cox, 'one of the great unsung achievements of the Second World War'. Some bright sparks in Whitehall understood an ancient truth – valid until the first nuclear explosion – that us humans will find an answer to every weapon and that weapon needs a great deal of back-up.

Malcolm Smith wrote: 'It is indeed a real measure of the failure of integration in the administration of British defence, the lack of cohesion between defence services, Treasury and Foreign Office that the RAF went to war and won its most famous victory with a policy that made nonsense of everything the Air Staff had been teaching for the last twenty years.' However it provided the essential airfields.

Churchill had begun to recognise in the mid-1930s the possibility of using science to help frame a defence. Although absolute immunity from air attack was impossible, Britain could guard herself against a mortal blow and perhaps even deter an attacker. Whoever had aerial superiority would enjoy a decisive advantage and Germany, he believed, was rapidly approaching that eminence. Aerial bombing, he declared, was 'the shame of the twentieth century'. Unlike rifles, machine guns, artillery fire and naval bombardment – not to mention swords, bows and arrows – he supposed bombing to be an exceptional means of terrorising a civilian population 'by the slaughter of non-combatants'. Given his life-long interest in military history, he could hardly have been unaware that 'non-combatants' always suffer in wartime.

If only some new method of assisting the defence could be devised, he mused, the whole of our affairs would be greatly simplified. By July 1939 he thought that if the aerial threat could be restricted or prevented, then the decision in wartime would remain as in the past with armies and navies. The matter was urgent, he added, because Germany might try to reduce Britain with a rapid 'violent aerial mass attack', employing 'psychological shock tactics'. This would be even more dangerous if Britain were not allied to France because Germany might then 'commence hostilities with the air arm alone'.

Churchill, Lindemann, Tizard

Churchill began to learn about radio and radar defences to assist British fighters against raiders approaching the coast. However they could give no help once raiders had crossed the coast and were flying over land. He saw no value in a growing Observer Corps that was training to monitor the progress of bombers over inland targets and advocated a curtain of mines, dropped by parachute, to intercept them. This impractical notion was foisted upon him by his scientific adviser, Frederick Lindemann, an Oxford physicist.

A 'poisonously unpleasant' man, he was shrewd enough to conceal this aspect of his character from Churchill. He had made his name during the Great War, working at Farnborough, where he learned to fly and bravely demonstrated what pilots should do to get out of a spin. Churchill, who was himself ignorant of all technical matters, greatly over-valued Lindemann's gift for explaining complex matters in simple words. He never realised that Lindemann was often mistaken. For instance, he assured Churchill in June 1939 that systematic day raiding of Britain was no longer possible, that night raiders could not reach military objectives, that aircraft were no threat to convoys and that the U-boat danger had been mastered. He was wrong on all these points. Nevertheless, as soon as Churchill became Prime Minister he found his favourite scientific adviser a sinecure in his government and had him elevated to the peerage as Viscount Cherwell.

Henry Tizard was a scientist of far superior merit. His 'greatest achievement,' wrote Solly Zuckerman, 'was the encouragement he gave to the development of the chain of radar stations which assured the RAF's victory in the Battle of Britain.' Chamberlain's decision to sack Lord Swinton (ablest of all Secretaries of State for Air) was a severe blow to Tizard, the RAF and to Britain.

In July 1940, however, Tedder, by now Director General for Research in the Air Ministry, supported Tizard's appointment as head of a vital mission to the United States. He was, thought Tedder, 'by far the best leader', a man 'who combines the wide scientific knowledge needed with the understanding of current operational requirements, and who has also an international standing as a scientist'. Churchill was persuaded. Tizard and his colleagues took with them to Canada and the United States a collection of information about anti-aircraft guns, gyroscopic gunsights, armour plates, jet propulsion, chemical weapons, self-sealing petrol tanks and especially the cavity magnetron, which delivered 10-cm radar into the hands of American industry. This collection gave a new dimension to the special relationship between Churchill and Roosevelt; it was, said one American scientist: 'The most valuable cargo ever brought to our shores.'

A Revived System
Many elements in Britain's air defence were the same in both wars – anti-aircraft guns, searchlights, balloons and aircraft – all eventually working together, aided by early warning from a network of coastal observers connected to control centres by wireless and telephone networks. Operations rooms, strikingly similar in layout and function, were used in both wars to co-ordinate the defenders' efforts and faced exactly the same problems.

Here are some examples. When will an attack be launched? Where will it come from? Which targets will it attempt to hit? How can the range and accuracy of guns and searchlights be improved? At what height should balloons be flown? Where should these 'static defences' be situated? How can aircraft get quickly enough into position to attack the enemy and with what weapons should they be armed?

It was soon learned in both wars that different aircraft, crews and methods of control were needed to deal with day and night raiders. It was also learned that the sight and sound of defences in action were necessary for civilian morale, however useless they might be from a military point of view. Airmen and politicians alike were obliged to swallow their exasperation and accept that people under attack needed to be cheered up and given hope.

One lesson the Air Ministry was reluctant to learn was the value of hard runways. As late as 1938, recalled Harold Balfour (later Under-Secretary of State for Air in Churchill's government), 'the Air Staff declared there was no need to plan for hard runways'. Nor did they; shortly before war actually began, in September 1939, there was not a single aerodrome in Fighter

Command with all-weather runways, as opposed to fields liable to be either muddy or dusty.

Will a War be Lost?

Churchill's sources regarding German air strength in the 1930s 'lacked authenticity,' wrote David MacIsaac, 'he juggled with hypothetical figures' and depended, as always, on a fluent pen and tongue. In fact, wrote Seaman, Churchill was 'taken in by Hitler's vauntings'; the Luftwaffe was not designed for strategic bombing against cities but for tactical support of armies in the field. Churchill's eloquent rants had grievous consequences when the war actually came: there was no immediate onslaught on Britain, for which 250,000 hospital beds had been assigned in London alone. Although he certainly painted a vivid picture of the German menace, Britain's intelligence services failed lamentably to modify that picture with a realistic assessment of the Luftwaffe's equipment and Hitler's likely intentions.

Senior officers in the Air Ministry seconded poorly-based fears. In another war, they calculated – for no good statistical reason – that bombing casualties would be fifty per ton. As it happened, the raids that actually struck at London in 1940-1941 caused, on average, three or four casualties per ton. Responding to widespread alarm at the prospect of massive casualties, in July 1936 Churchill urged a three-fold increase in RAF strength. He emphasised that it must also be made more professional – offering more permanent commissions – and laying a greater emphasis on training. However there was much disorganisation, with many squadrons only partly complete and the quality of servicing was low.

As a defence force, the RAF was neglible and its capacity for offence 'puerile'. In November 1936 he said 'Germany has specialised in long-distance bombing aeroplanes', which would have been news to most Luftwaffe officers then or later. A few weeks later, in January 1937, he again claimed that Germany already had an immense preponderance in heavy bombers. In fact, as British intelligence services should have known, German aircraft production, until 1937, was concentrated on training aircraft (more than half of the total) and less than one-fifth were bombers or fighters.

Despite his assertion that air power would be a major factor in another war, Churchill declared in January 1938: 'The air menace against properly-armed and protected ships of war will not be of a decisive character.' He agreed with most senior naval officers that aircraft could not destroy capital ships. He also underestimated the impact of air power on land forces: 'The whole course of the war in Spain,' he announced with his usual certainty, even about a subject he had not studied, 'has seemed to show the limitations rather than the strength of the air weapon... so far as the fighting troops are concerned, aircraft are an additional complication rather than a decisive weapon.'

Faith in the Turret Fighter

Churchill wrongly assumed in March 1938 that the RAF's focus on the forward-firing, fixed gun fighter was mistaken and a turret-armed fighter was essential. He had been assured by Lindemann that modern fighters met and flew past one another 'too quickly for human action' and pursuing from behind is open to deadly retort: how easy it would be, he thought, for our airmen to throw out aerial mines. Enemies following in the wake would therefore incur needless and possibly fatal risk. 'The only sure method is to swim along side by side and let him have it.'

In other words, Churchill knew nothing about the real problems airmen would face in modern combat and relied on whatever Lindemann told him, and *he* knew nothing either. Churchill recommended that Britain build, as quickly as possible and in the largest numbers feasible, 'fast, heavily-armed aeroplanes designed with turrets for fighting on the beam on parallel courses'. The matter was urgent because the Germans must know that 'we have banked upon the forward-shooting plunging "Spit-fire"'. For a man who had once shown an exceptional grasp of what aircraft might achieve in wartime, such opinions reveal that he was no longer up with the play. Fortunately, he was not Prime Minister in the critical years, 1935-1939, when effective fighters were designed and brought into service.

9

Preparing for War,
Britain in the 1930s

A Confident Prophet

By March 1939, Churchill had learned something of Fighter Command's work under Dowding's leadership. German bombing would fail, he now believed, because 'ninety-nine out of every 100 square miles of this island would be practically immune and safe from air attack'. He was, of course, entirely mistaken and neither Dowding nor any responsible person under his command would have made such a rash claim.

Churchill was on sounder ground when he said we have: 'the best machines' and our air defences were 'better armed' and 'constantly manned... Science has been brought powerfully to our aid against air attack.' By 1940 Britain will feel 'a great measure of confidence' because the progress of the German war machine 'will be more than overmatched by a year's improvement in the British Air Force.' This happened to be true, by a narrow margin helped by the Luftwaffe's misuse of its superior strength. Churchill's contribution to that 'improvement' was to help generate a sense of urgency in both the government and the service ministries.

During 1939 he published articles alleging that 'Bombs Don't Scare Us Now' and 'Air Bombardment is no Road to World Domination'. He also claimed, 'there is nothing in this problem of air attack which the British nation cannot confront'. At the same time, he warned that Hitler and Goering (head of the Luftwaffe) would not easily lay down 'the blackmailing squeeze of air terror', which argued for 'early action' by Britain and France. A German invasion, he said in August 1939, would require 'crossing the sea in relays for many hours', and would not be 'child's play' for the Germans. 'As daylight raiding will soon become too expensive, we have chiefly to deal with random night-bombing of the built-up areas.'

A Stream of Information: Rowley and Atcherley

From 1934 onwards, Churchill received a stream of information from civil servants, politicians and serving RAF officers about the state of Britain's defences, should there be another war with Germany. He did not solicit this information, which he used without disclosing his sources. Rothermere wrote to him on 30 April 1935 about his conversation with Norman Macmillan: 'As you know, he is one of the greatest test pilots this country has produced' and had assured Rothermere that German air power was already very great. Although he offered no evidence to support this claim.

A year later, in April 1936, Morton wrote to Churchill about information he had received from Wing Commander Peter Warburton, who claimed that the Air Ministry was 'too complacent' in its calculations and in May Lord Londonderry (Secretary of State for Air) wrote to him about his recent visit to Germany where Group Captain Francis Don (Air Attaché at the embassy in Berlin) gave him information about German air strength which came as 'a complete surprise'. According to Londonderry, there was a complete lack of knowledge in England about what was happening in Germany.

Actually, sufficient information about the growth of German air power was available to the Air Ministry, if it had been looking for it. One very important source was offered by two junior officers in October 1936. They were Squadron Leader Herbert Rowley (who had accompanied Arthur Coningham on the first east-west crossing of Africa in 1925 and was then serving at the Aeroplane and Armament Experimental Establishment, Martlesham Heath, near Ipswich in Suffolk) and Flight Lieutenant Dick Atcherley (a famous test, and stunt, pilot at the Royal Aircraft Establishment in Farnborough, Hampshire, where he developed a system of air-to-air re-fuelling which had been demonstrated at that year's Hendon Air Display).

Rowley and Atcherley took some leave, borrowed a Percival Gull three-seater monoplane from Robert Blackburn, chairman of Blackburn Aircraft, and flew from Martlesham Heath via Lympne in Kent and Amsterdam to Tempelhof aerodrome in Berlin. Just like that. German customs officials asked them no questions and they were charged only a nominal sum to house their aeroplane. They had timed their visit perfectly, for the German propaganda machine was geared to respectability in 1936 and so they got a friendly welcome. They were not deceived, however, for they shared Churchill's concern about the revival of German military strength, especially in the air.

Throughout the 1930s, the Air Staff consistently assumed a massive aerial assault would occur, if war broke out, but did little to examine this assumption. For example, what weight of bombs could any twin-engined aircraft (no four-engined bombers were yet in production) carry to a British target from bases in Germany, allowing for the weight of its crew, fuel, defensive weapons, ammunition and armour? The location and approximate size of all major German aircraft factories was known, probable production rates could be deduced and the scale of the threat realistically assessed.

Rowley and Atcherley had lunch in Berlin on 7 October with Colonel Friedrich Hanesse, of the air intelligence service, and frankly admitted that they were out to see as much as they could. Hanesse was 'most amused' and invited them to fly over to Rangsdorf (a civilian aerodrome, just south of Berlin) the next day and examine whatever interested them. They strolled into Tempelhof at 7.30 am on 8 October, wheeled their Gull out of its hangar, filled it with petrol, signed a receipt, and took off. No-one asked them who they were or where they were going. They flew all round Berlin – on their own, unchallenged – observing several large training bases and a new staff college.

On returning to Tempelhof, the Englishmen had lunch with a famous pilot, Ernst Udet, who had met Atcherley when both were performing at air shows in the United States. Rowley was privately astonished that Udet – great pilot, fine cartoonist and boon companion – should be in charge of Luftwaffe research and development. He was right to wonder, for during the next five years, until his suicide in November 1941, Udet grossly mismanaged his job. He told Rowley that he had recently condemned the Heinkel He 118 dive-bomber, preferring the Junkers Ju 87, which became the notorious 'Stuka'. This was good news for Britain in 1940 because the Heinkel was a superior design, faster and more agile. Fighter Command would have found it much more difficult to destroy than the Stuka. Udet also killed the Heinkel 112 fighter, later re-modelled into a potentially superb fighter, the 100, which was never put into production.

The Englishmen spent a day at Damm fighter station, home to one of the squadrons of the Luftwaffe's elite Richthofen group. They were shown everything: aircraft; cockpit equipment; re-fuelling methods and accommodation. This latter particularly impressed Rowley:

'The German Air Staff evidently realise that the skilled and intelligent airman deserves something better than the old-style barracks. The kitchen was well-run and clean and we sampled the dinner which was excellent. In the dining-room, each airman has his own chair instead of a bench. The sleeping quarters were equally well thought out, with airmen four to a room, having their own wardrobes and plenty of space. Each block has its own sitting-room with wireless and generally the airmen are very much more comfortable than in our own squadrons.'

Next day, Rowley and Atcherley returned to Tempelhof, where they were encouraged to crawl all over the civil version of Heinkel He 111 and Junkers Ju 86 bombers and agreed that they were at least as efficient as their British equivalents. They were flown to Rostock, Heinkel's factory, where they examined a brand-new Heinkel 111B-1 bomber and doubted if there was 'an airframe in England among all our latest bombers which looks better'. They noticed also that its armament consisted of three hand-held machine guns (very difficult to aim accurately) and calculated its likely speed, range and bomb load.

The Englishmen were then taken to Dessau, about seventy miles south-west of Berlin, to see an enormous Junkers factory. An American visitor assured them that 'the whole American aviation industry could be lost inside the Junkers organisation'. They left Dessau in rather a haze, stunned by its size and efficiency. They regretted that Wilfrid Freeman (head of Research and Development in the Air Ministry) had not also taken the opportunity to visit Germany.

Rowley and Atcherley spent ten days in Germany and Rowley's forty-four-page report, full of important information gathered by observant airmen who understood how air forces work, should have been a godsend to the Air Staff, but it was left unread. This negligence confirms the low opinion formed of the Air Ministry in the 1930s by Churchill, an opinion amply supported by subsequent historians. As one of them – I. B. Holley, Jr – wrote: 'One is left aghast at the extent to which unchallenged assumptions permeated RAF official thinking, given that the very survival of the nation almost certainly hinged on the soundness of its air power.' Rowley had taken the precaution of sending a summary of his report to Wing Commander Charles Torr Anderson – whom we shall meet presently – and he forwarded it to Churchill, arranging for him to meet Rowley.

In Rowley's opinion, the Germans understood that 'the power of an air force rests entirely on its striking force; that is the bombing aeroplane'. Army and navy co-operation, transports and even fighters were of far less importance. Here is the authentic Trenchard voice, but wiser Luftwaffe officers recognised the value of transport aircraft and paid close attention to the problems of using fighters and bombers in close support of ground forces. Dowding and Keith Park (his chief assistant) were also alert to the need for defensive fighters, but it would take years of effort by Tedder, Coningham and a handful of other officers to snap the RAF out of its Trenchardist fixation with strategic bombing and the war would be over before the RAF had its own fleet of modern transport aircraft. The Germans, Rowley believed, had grasped 'one simple and commonsense fact which has so far escaped our Air Staff': the need to concentrate on the mass production of a few proven weapons.

He had a point. 'By October 1936,' wrote Sebastian Ritchie, 'no fewer than fifty-five different experimental designs were in progress and six more were under consideration.' On the other hand, unless a net is cast widely, especially at a time of technical revolution, such big fish as the Avro Lancaster four-engined strategic bomber and the de Havilland Mosquito twin-engined all-purpose aircraft might not be caught. In later years, the Luftwaffe would suffer from a multitude of types, few of which were put into quantity production. Rowley would have been delighted to know that British manufacturers would soon leave Germany far behind.

In 1940 and 1941, the RAF received over 35,000 aircraft, the Luftwaffe just 22,000. In 1936, however, the RAF did not have 'a single aeroplane in service,' wrote Rowley, 'which has the slightest chance of reaching Germany, dropping bombs, and getting home again.' He was right to rate the Vickers Wellington highly, and right to regard the Armstrong Whitworth Whitley and the Handley Page Hampden as little more than 'death traps'. But he greatly over-rated the value of the Bristol Blenheim, brought into service in November 1936, as a bomber. For its day, it had value as a fast short-range reconnaissance aircraft, but it was never more than a marginally useful bomber and then only if escorted by fighters.

Maclean and Anderson

There would be further exchanges between RAF and Luftwaffe officers during 1937, but no more casual get-togethers over a drink or three, no more unsupervised flights over the Nazi capital, and certainly no more solos in a German bomber, such as Atcherley enjoyed. The 'Four-Year Plan', to be implemented under Goering, was announced in Germany on 18 October 1936, just three days after the departure of the English visitors. That plan would end what Richard Overy called 'the period of compromise' and lead inexorably to the world's most destructive war.

As a member of the Air Defence Research Sub-committee of the Committee of Imperial Defence since July 1935, Churchill had taken a close interest in every item of RAF equipment and the flow of detailed information to him from serving officers increased. Among them was Group Captain Lachlan MacLean, second in command of 3 (Bomber) Group, who sent him a long report in January 1937 on many RAF deficiencies, including inadequacies in aircraft, armament, pilot training, navigation and ground maintenance. 'In brief, if we have a war forced on us in the next three, possibly five years, we shall be powerless to retaliate, at any rate in the air. A fact which ought to provide food for thought.'

In October 1937 MacLean wrote to Anderson about a forthcoming visit to Britain by the German air minister, Erhard Milch. He would be accompanied by Hans-Jürgen Stumpff (chief of the Luftwaffe General Staff) and by Ernst Udet. 'How we have been let in for this visitation at the present moment,' wrote MacLean, 'is beyond imagination.' Anderson forwarded this letter to Churchill, together with a copy of comments by Edgar Ludlow-Hewitt (head of Bomber Command) on this visit: the RAF, he said, will 'have to comb the country in order to produce sufficient aircraft to get up any sort of show', and few of them – as the Germans would readily deduce – could reach even the German coast with a bomb load. Milch and his colleagues would be allowed to inspect on the ground one example of each modern aeroplane, none of them fully operational. 'This is a fair commentary,' wrote MacLean, 'on the state of equipment and the state of training!'

Churchill learned that fifty to sixty modern Gloster Gladiator fighters had been sent to China while RAF squadrons had to make do with older machines; that old anti-aircraft guns were being sold overseas before newer models were in production; and that fewer than twenty-odd anti-aircraft guns were all the defence available for Malta.

Roy Fedden, chief engineer of the Bristol Aeroplane Company, visited Germany twice in 1937 and wrote to Anderson in October: 'I am absolutely shattered at the tremendous progress of aircraft and engine production in Germany, not from the technical aspect so much as in quantity and organisation.' He sent a full report of what he had seen to the Air Ministry, where it was shelved, unread, just as Rowley's report had been a year earlier. Once again it was Anderson who ensured that it reached Churchill.

All this information was sent by Churchill to Maurice Hankey (Cabinet Secretary) in a private letter, not naming his informants and hoping to win his support. 'I remember how you played an essential part in saving the country over the convoy system,' he told him, 'and how when young officers came to you and told you the truth, against service rules, you saw that the seed did not fall on stony ground.' Hankey's eight-page reply, sent on 19 October 1937, reveals how deeply the spirit of Pangloss infused British governments during the 1930s: all is well, or if not, will be shortly. Critics may harm their careers, he wrote, and 'their reputations before posterity'. Also, 'there is almost invariably a perfectly sound explanation forthcoming' for any problems and so on. 'As a nation,' he told Churchill, 'we need "jollying" along rather than frightening.' Churchill curtly rejected this rebuke which, long as it is, was silent on the substance of the criticisms offered.

MacLean, commanding a bomber group at the time of Munich, told Churchill in December 1938 that he was leaving the service. He could no longer stand 'the methods of suppression and coercion' used to silence criticism and 'quench initiative or originality, should it in any degree run counter to orthodoxy'. Churchill forwarded this letter to Kingsley Wood (Secretary of State for Air), asking him to look into the affair because MacLean is 'one of the ablest men I have met in the air force'. McLean *did* resign, but was recalled in August 1939, promoted to air commodore and commanded a bomber group in the Middle East, 1940-2, before leaving to form an operational training group in Canada in 1943.

Anderson was perhaps the most important of those RAF officers who communicated regularly with Churchill late in the 1930s and visited Chartwell several times. By then, it was known in the Air Ministry that he was 'a frequent purveyor of information' to Churchill, but no disciplinary action was taken against him.

Most of Anderson's information concerned the lack of modern aircraft, failure to recruit men who were, or could become, skilled mechanics, wireless operators, etc., the need for more long-service officers, poor equipment (shortage of machine guns, bombs that failed to explode), inadequate training and sub-standard accommodation for officers and airmen. One point on which Anderson was most insistent was the shortage of skilled navigators: this lack would hit the RAF hard when war came. He also cited letters from Tedder (commanding in Singapore) about weaknesses there in training, organisation and the conduct of combined exercises.

In June 1937 Anderson had written to Churchill, confirming a report in *The Times* that the RAF's total strength was 124 squadrons, but Anderson believed that 100 of those squadrons were only equipped with obsolete aircraft and that some of the squadrons currently being formed had only training-type aircraft. In August 1937, he wrote again, referring to Churchill's comment on the 'power of personal example and inspiration' shown by the 1st Duke of Marlborough. 'It is just that influence which is so disastrously absent from the air force at this moment', but he named no names.

Anderson had been seriously wounded as a soldier during the Great War, but recovered and transferred to the RFC. He was granted a permanent RAF commission in 1919 and had a successful career, rising to the rank of group captain in 1940. He was personal assistant and air adviser to Beaverbrook, 1940-1942, 'where he helped to establish the Lancaster bomber on a proper production basis'. He was invalided out of the RAF in 1942. In April 1975 Martin Gilbert interviewed him. He recalled Churchill saying: 'I know what is troubling you. It is loyalty to the service and loyalty to the state. You must realise that loyalty to the state must come before loyalty to the service.'

Ralph Wigram

Churchill was also greatly helped by Ralph Wigram, a senior member of the Foreign Office, who told him on 19 December 1935 that 'it is idle' to get into arguments about aircraft with the Air Ministry. The real test 'is the capacity to manufacture machines and to train pilots in emergency', and in these regards we are behind Germany. Churchill was greatly impressed by Wigram, who died suddenly on New Year's Eve, 1937, aged only forty. 'He was a charming and fearless man,' he recalled, 'and his convictions, based upon profound knowledge and study, dominated his being... Like other officials of high rank, he spoke to me with complete confidence.'

It was not only RAF officers and civil servants who confided in Churchill. Major Gilbert Myers, formerly a gunnery instructor in the RFC and currently an employee of General Aircraft at Hanworth aerodrome, Feltham, told him in November 1936 that of a contract placed by the Air Ministry for eighty-nine Hawker Fury fighters only twenty-three had actually been delivered in more than twelve months.

Without the information provided by these men, Martin Gilbert (Churchill's official biographer) thought it would have been nearly impossible for him 'to have aroused public opinion' in opposition to the government's ceaseless determination to avoid or stifle public debate. This information helped to prepare him for high office when war came in September 1939. But did his exaggerations help to inhibit effective responses to Hitler's aggression?

What to do?
In September 1937, Churchill wrote to Lord Linlithgow (Viceroy of India) about how 'everyone is united in dealing with our deficiencies as fast as possible without interfering with the ordinary life of the country. This is a serious limitation.' The RAF, wrote Churchill, was 'but a fraction of the German, and I do not think we shall catch up. On the contrary, it would seem that 1938 will see Germany relatively stronger' in the air and more powerful on the ground than the French army.

In February 1938 Hankey wrote to Cyril Newall, recently appointed CAS, telling him about 'conversations' the government was to have with Italy and Germany. The prospects of doing a deal were strong, as long as we do not give 'parliamentary critics' any grounds for supposing that we are 'weakening' in foreign affairs.

Churchill alleged in March 1938 that the RAF lacked 'essential armament and equipment', meaning that many aircraft had 'no war value' and British production was only one-third of Germany's. He called for a debate, but Sir Horace Wilson advised Chamberlain on 10 March to refuse, which he did, 'flatly and firmly'. On 13 March, Anderson revealed to Churchill the 'rather misleading language' in the latest White Paper and Air Estimates: 'Both read well until one digs beneath the fine language.' For example, many 'pilots' were only partly trained; there were *not* eleven fully-functioning flying training schools; and Cranwell had *not* been extended to full capacity.

Thus encouraged, Churchill persisted in his campaign to strengthen and modernise the RAF. With adequate fighter defences, air raid shelters and vigorous reprisal bombing, he said in May 1938, the damage done by enemy bombers could be kept to 'manageable proportions'. In June he criticised 'the almost total absence of defence' for cities and 'vulnerable points' and declared that there were hardly any modern anti-aircraft weapons, whereas Germany had thousands. But the best defence against 'air murder, for such I must judge the bombing of civilian populations', was 'an air force so numerous and excellent that it will beat the enemy's air force in fair fight'.

The RAF's fighters must attack bombers so that if one in three were destroyed raiding would cease; it must also bomb enemy airfields, military depots, railway junctions and the like.

'I do not believe in reprisals upon the enemy civilian population. On the contrary, the more they try to kill our women and children, the more we should devote ourselves to killing their fighting men and smashing up the technical apparatus upon which the life of their armies depend.

This is the best way of defending London, and of defending the helpless masses from the bestialities of modern war.'

Like John Steel, former head of Wessex Bombing Area, he did not say how civilian casualties could be avoided. Both Treasury and Cabinet saw in air power a means of saving money on expensive land campaigns. They would have been happier still if they had known, as Richard Overy has written, that Germany's aircraft industry was 'appallingly inefficient in the first years of the war'. No surprise there, given what we now know of Goering and Udet as air force commanders.

Naval Aviation Neglected

On a different air problem, Churchill had emphasised in May 1936 that 'the integrity of operational command' over the sea 'is vital'. He therefore supported the Admiralty's demand for control of its own aircraft. The Fleet Air Arm, he said, 'is now vital' to the safety of warships at sea and necessary for every form of action. From 1918 to 1937, the FAA was part of the RAF, which trained its pilots and ground crews. The RAF was responsible for the design and production of its aircraft, but from 1930 onwards Dowding (then responsible in the Air Ministry for research and development) had assured the Admiralty – which paid for them – that it was getting exactly what it asked for.

Admiral Sir Caspar John later admitted: 'The Admiralty was not competent to say what it wanted and the Air Ministry was not competent to advise.' Neither service gave serious thought to the quality and number of naval aircraft produced and took little notice of what other nations, the United States and Japan in particular, were designing for use at sea.

In May 1936 Churchill advocated handing the FAA over to the navy, but nothing was done. In April 1937 he repeated his plea: 'All functions which require aircraft of any description... to be carried regularly in warships or in aircraft carriers naturally fall in the naval sphere.' It was the duty of the FAA to protect the fleet, reconnoitre for it and protect merchant shipping, if necessary. Consequently, the Admiralty should operate it.

It was different for army/air co-operation, which were both land-based. Two months later, in July 1937, Chamberlain decided to return the FAA to Admiralty control, but he rejected its bid for control of shore-based aircraft. These remained with the recently-formed Coastal Command, a decision which Churchill thought wise. So too did Edward Ellington (then CAS). Trenchard – although long retired – objected vehemently, but was then powerless.

Looking back in 1976, Stephen Roskill thought the Air Staff had been 'unjustifiably rigid in their indivisibility of air power argument' and the government ought to have settled the argument no later than 1935. Herbert Richmond, a retired admiral and life-long opponent of independent air power, complained publicly as late as November 1942 that the Air Ministry had supplied the FAA with ineffective types before the war. Hugh Dowding responded promptly: 'The Admiralty got precisely the types which they specified and demanded. They insisted on a plurality of roles for each type, and such hybrids as the torpedo-spotter-reconnaissance aircraft were foredoomed to inefficiency before pencil was laid to drawing board.' Most admirals, he concluded, 'were obsessed by the idea of *fleet action* and the role of naval aircraft was completely subordinated to this conception'.

Neither the FAA nor the Royal Navy nor Coastal Command were equipped or trained in joint operations to hunt or destroy U-boats in 1939. Thanks to the RAF's obsession with the bomber (which proved a totally inadequate weapon when put to the test until 1942), the RAF's contribution to the Battle of France, though gallant and determined, was of little value. It would be unable to cope effectively with U-boats until 1942. Fighter Command, under Dowding, successfully resisted Luftwaffe attack, but only when Tedder took command in the Middle East did the three services learn to co-operate with each other, and mercifully were never challenged there by more than a fraction of German power.

Inskip, not Churchill

Some people hoped, others feared, that after a General Election in November 1935, Baldwin would bring Churchill into the Cabinet. However, his victory was so complete that he had no need to employ a man whom he feared politically, although admiring his skill as a writer, speaker and painter. As Beaverbrook told Churchill, in his usual cheerful way, 'you're finished now'.

In February 1936, Philip Cunliffe-Lister, later Lord Swinton, the new Secretary of State for Air, expressed concern that the RAF was falling behind Germany and his proposal for rapid expansion was accepted by the Cabinet. Later that month, Hankey told Warren Fisher (head of the Treasury): we must not bring in Churchill who would 'upset the psychology of the whole machine'. He meant, presumably, that Churchill was not 'one of us' in backing Chamberlain.

To general surprise, Thomas Inskip, a lawyer, was appointed Minister of the Crown for the Co-ordination of Defence in March 1936. This cumbersome title was carefully chosen to pacify officers in all three services who feared that a Ministry of Defence would end their cherished independence. 'The chief qualification of the new minister for this new post,' wrote Geoffrey Smith (now editor of *Flight*), 'seems to be that he is completely without knowledge or experience of any of the three fighting services and therefore must of necessity be impartial in dealing with the problems of co-ordinating their needs and their contributions to the common object of defence.'

Morton told Churchill on 24 April 1936 that the appointment of Inskip was 'made in the hope that the international situation would so right itself that there would be no need for any hurry to re-arm, or perhaps even to re-arm at all'. He then made a point that weighed heavily with Churchill. The government, Morton wrote, were persisting in making Britain's weapons expensive 'works of art', rather than cheap and mass-produced as in Germany. Those unfortunate airmen who crewed Whitleys, Hampdens, Battles, Blenheims and Defiants would not have agreed that their aircraft were 'works of art' and they would soon learn that their German equivalents were superior. Like Churchill, Morton believed whatever suited him to believe.

Churchill seemed to some the man best qualified for Inskip's position, but his appointment 'might have been taken as a bellicose gesture', to be avoided at all costs. Baldwin admired his 'imagination, eloquence, industry, ability', but distrusted his judgement. Even so, Churchill offered Inskip sound advice on 3 June 1936. Your job, he said, will be to co-ordinate strategy, settle inter-service quarrels, ensure that goods ordered are actually delivered and create a structure for war industry and its organisation. 'It was my experience' during the Great War, Churchill concluded, 'that while people oppose all precautions in time of peace, the very same people turn round within a fortnight of war and are furious about every shortcoming. I hope it may not be yours.'

Among Churchill's keenest advocates was James Garvin, editor of the *Observer*. He wrote to him in October 1936 to say that as long ago as 1 June 1935 he had asked Baldwin in writing 'to make you Minister of Air and Goering's opposite number. He refused and the whole of his third premiership has been a calamity.'

Inskip faced ceaseless manoeuvres by all three service heads to exact funds from the Treasury at each other's expense. In January 1937 Churchill questioned the government's decision 'not to interfere with normal trade' while carrying out its re-armament policy. Yet part of this normal trade, he told Inskip, was to supply machine tools for military equipment to Germany. It should be stopped at once. On 26 March he suggested that Inskip draw up a list of everything an air squadron should have, from pilots to spare parts, and drop in on a randomly-chosen squadron without warning and see for himself whether in fact it had everything it was supposed to have. This was a practice which Churchill followed throughout his own career, untroubled about ruffling feathers, civilian or military.

In December 1937 Inskip produced a memorandum (drafted for him by Hankey) in which he argued that the RAF's role was not to *deliver* a knockout blow, but to resist it. This is 'one of the most important and influential statements on the RAF in the 1930s' because of the emphasis it gave to the need for more fighters: 'home defence is our primary object.'

German aircraft, thought Inskip, would more easily be destroyed over Britain by fighters than by bombers attacking their bases in Germany. He also asked what attention was being given to aircraft replacement and maintenance in the event of war. Britain's available resources, he argued, 'should be directed to an increase in war potential rather than to a further increase in our first-line strength'. That meant more 'shadow factories' (built by private firms prepared to embark on military projects). Fighters were cheaper to build than bombers and that is an important reason why his arguments prevailed.

Inskip failed, however, to recommend 'the compulsory drafting of labour and material from civil industry to those related to defence in order to accelerate the rearmament programme'. He won over the Cabinet, despite strenuous objections from the Air Ministry, which had not, at that time, a clear idea 'as to what was operationally possible' with the resources on hand: Trenchard and his successors had not done the homework necessary to give substance to years of easy generalisations. On 1 October 1938 fighter strength had been just over 400 aircraft, only seventy of which were Hurricanes; the rest were 'obsolete' or 'obsolescent' biplanes. Reserves were very low; factory output was quite unable to replace losses; there were too few airfields and operations rooms were as yet ill-equipped.

The unwelcome fact of weakness in the air would be driven home by Ludlow-Hewitt, appointed head of Bomber Command in September 1937. He reported to the Air Staff in November that his command was: 'entirely unprepared for war, unable to operate except in fair weather, and extremely vulnerable both in the air and on the ground.' The situation had not improved six months later in March 1938 when Anderson sent Churchill a copy of Bomber Command's training report for 1937. 'I cannot but regard the present low level of operational efficiency generally prevailing throughout the Command with concern and anxiety', wrote Ludlow-Hewitt. He felt it wise, however, to end on an optimistic note: once we are fully equipped with modern aircraft, he assured his Air Staff readers, all will be well.

Churchill wrote to Clementine in January 1938 to tell her, with glee as well as concern, that Chamberlain (now Prime Minister) had informed some French politicians visiting London that Britain was making 350 aircraft per month. He was misinformed: the true figure, which Churchill got from Morton, was only half that. Consequently, there is 'a certain reproaching' going on between Chamberlain and the Air Ministry.

'What happened was that poor Neville believed the lie that the Air Ministry circulated for public purposes and did not know the true figures. This gives you some idea of the looseness with which we are governed in these vital matters... It ought to make Neville think. He does not know the truth: and perhaps he does not want to.'

Newall, not Dowding

Hugh Dowding learned on 4 February 1937 that he had been passed over for the RAF's highest office, chief of the Air Staff, which would fall vacant in September when Ellington retired. He would then be fifty-five, and it may well be argued that the service needed young blood at the top: it was in the throes of a technical revolution and certain to be a major weapon (for defence or offence) should there be another war. The argument was given added force by those who observed Ellington in office. By no means 'young blood' (he turned sixty in 1937), he was widely regarded by senior officers in all three services and by those civil servants and politicians obliged to work with him as a liability.

'Uncle Ted' was apparently kindly and fair-minded, but he had seen active service only as a soldier, had never flown in combat, rarely in peacetime and seemed lost in the Whitehall jungle. Three of the RAF's most eminent officers – Trenchard, John Salmond and Freeman, all tigers at home there – openly despised him and a fourth, Slessor, would tell the head of the Air Historical Branch in 1975 that Ellington had been 'a disaster'.

The nod went to Cyril Newall: by no means youthful either, for he was less than four years younger than Dowding. A far abler officer was Edgar Ludlow-Hewitt: shrewd, experienced and widely-respected. Trenchard, Salmond and Freeman soon became as hotly opposed to 'poor old Cyril' as they had been to 'Uncle Ted'. One must note, however, that sweeping condemnation – except of each other – came easily to that particular trio.

Newall learned nothing from the Luftwaffe's effective conduct of operations during the Spanish Civil War. He even asserted that its adroit support of ground forces was a gross misuse of air power. The Luftwaffe used that war to gain priceless combat experience, but Newall resisted demands for similar support of British and French soldiers when Germans invaded Western Europe. When they occupied the Channel coast and prepared to attack targets in southern England, he still believed it necessary to employ bombers against what he called strategic targets (factories, oil tanks, railway junctions) far behind the front lines.

Not surprisingly, strenuous efforts were made from May 1940 onwards to get rid of Newall. A memorandum composed by an Australian-born officer, Wing Commander Edgar Kingston-McCloughry (a member of the Air Ministry's Directorate of War Organisation) and circulated anonymously, castigated him as 'a weak link in the nation's defence'; a man of 'inadequate mental ability, limited practical experience, weakness of character and personality, and lack of judgement and foresight'. Everyone who mattered read it and no-one leapt to his defence, although Slessor praised him in his postwar memoirs. Noble Frankland thought McCloughry 'a man of great ability, deep insights and ideas which were much in advance of his time', while admitting that he had 'a passion for intrigue or, as he would have put it, constructive criticism'. McCloughry remains one of very few RAF officers to have made a significant mark as an author, with four valuable studies of aviation history to his credit.

Chamberlain in Command

'Except possibly for Margaret Thatcher,' wrote Ernest May, 'no peacetime British Prime Minister has been so strong-willed, almost tyrannical', as Neville Chamberlain. He won for himself an influence over the media that 'if not quite on a par with that of Goebbels in Germany, exceeded that of any contemporary head of government in any other democratic nation'. Warren Fisher, his closest adviser, was Permanent Secretary of the Treasury and head of the Civil Service from 1919 to 1939. In his view, Britain's strategic priorities should firstly be the RAF (including civil defence), secondly the army, with naval precautions for Far Eastern defence a distant third.

From 1933, wrote Peden: 'Fisher had devoted himself to persuading his political masters to re-arm, and, down to 1938, his influence in this direction was more important than that of much more publicised advocates of rearmament, even Churchill.' Chamberlain, Fisher and the chiefs of staff all understood that the empire, although impressive in extent, offered little immediate support in opposing German aggression, although it might be a vital source of manpower and raw materials if Britain was not quickly conquered.

No British politician could match Chamberlain in the smooth conduct of business, but he detested criticism, expected admiration and as David Margesson (Chief Whip of the Conservative Party) wrote, he 'engendered personal dislike among his opponents to an extent almost unbelievable'. Chamberlain died in November 1940 and Churchill spoke eloquently in Parliament about his merits. On 22 June 1941, however, he revealed his true opinion to Jock Colville: 'The narrowest, most ignorant, most ungenerous of men.'

Chamberlain asked the chiefs of staff in March 1938, when Hitler united Germany and Austria, to report on the 'military implications' of going to war in defence of Czechoslovakia. The consequences, they replied, 'could well lead to an ultimate defeat'. The chiefs were 'most alarmed', wrote Peter Kemp, about Britain's weakness in the air: 'intensive propaganda in the years between the wars had raised an unholy fear of the bomber and its power of destruction.'

Edmund Ironside, head of the British Army, had already written late in 1937 that the Cabinet, 'are terrified now of a war being finished in a few weeks by the annihilation of Great Britain. They can see no other kind of danger than air attack and discount all other dangers.' At the height of the Munich Crisis, a year later, he wrote: 'We cannot expose ourselves now to a German attack. We simply commit suicide if we do... What a mess we are in.'

'Like Chatham,' wrote Chamberlain to his sister Ida on 12 March 1939, 'I know that I can save this country and I do not believe that anyone else can.' Three days later, the Germans occupied Prague and the rest of Czechoslovakia. From then on, Chamberlain began to realise that his triumph at Munich had been hollow, but he made a desperate situation far worse at the end of March by offering a guarantee that Britain could not possibly fulfill: to defend Poland if she were attacked by Germany. France immediately supported Britain. Romania and Greece were also guaranteed.

Admiral Chatfield (formerly First Sea Lord who succeeded Inskip as Minister for the Co-ordination of Defence in January 1939) told the Cabinet that these guarantees were merely words and all three chiefs of staff agreed, but none of them dared to contradict the Prime Minister, not even privately. By July, however, Churchill's day was coming. Reginald Barnes wrote to his 'dear old pal' on the 4th. 'Now, our rather slow movers in command, having gone rather more than the whole hog, and burnt their last remaining boat, seem to be realising at last that you might be of some help to them... I pray I shall see you in the Cabinet soon.'

In 1939 the army had only two divisions of fully-trained troops in Britain because government policies had concentrated on bombers and fighters for the RAF since 1934 and there was no tactical air arm trained and equipped to support ground forces. A weak Coastal Command remained part of the RAF even after the FAA was reluctantly returned to Admiralty control in 1937.

The Air Ministry remained responsible for the design and construction of naval aircraft and the Admiralty did not press hard enough to modernise or strengthen its air arm. Britain lacked the military strength in 1939 even to deter a far more rational enemy than Hitler. Chamberlain and his chiefs of staff recognised the severe limits imposed on Britain's actions: 'Far-flung interests and obligations to be defended against the threefold threat of Germany, Italy and Japan; the practical difficulties in responding to each specific initiative by the dictators; the slow pace of re-armament imposed by our fragile economic recovery; and the hindrance of anti-war opinion in the country.'

10

Miserable Jealousies and Divided Command: Norway, 1940

Hair-Raising and Hare-Brained Projects

'Jack had seen combined operations by the score, few of them a pleasant memory; and the likelihood of miserable jealousies between army and navy, the divided command, to say nothing of disconnected councils, were clear in his mind.' These thoughts expressed by Patrick O'Brian's fictional Captain Jack Aubrey accurately describe the actual situation of British and French forces before and throughout their campaign in Norway in April and May 1940.

Between January and early April 1940, wrote Brian Bond, 'Anglo-French discussions of strategic options focused to an astonishing extent on the possibility of armed intervention in Scandinavia', both to prevent German control of Swedish iron ore supplies and to distract Germany from an offensive on the Western Front. There was also 'the hair-raising possibility' that aid to Finland would add the Soviet Union to the enemies of France and Britain. Churchill, as ever, was impatient for action, 'anywhere but on the north-east frontiers of France', where the main German army might be encountered. Henry Pownall, then Gort's chief of staff, described the intention to aid Finland as 'the child of those master strategists Winston and Ironside. Of all the hare-brained projects I have heard of this is the most foolish; its inception smacks all too alarmingly of Gallipoli.'

Catherine Sinks

On 25 March 1939, in a paper sent to Chamberlain, Churchill argued that 'command of the Baltic is vital' to Germany. As soon as he was re-appointed First Lord of the Admiralty early in September, he began planning a Baltic operation. The Royal Navy would seize command of the entire sea, destroy the German navy en route, and sever German links with Scandinavia. Sweden's iron ore would be denied to Hitler and the effect on German industry, asserted Churchill, would be catastrophic. A vital source of raw materials for weapons of all kinds would be eliminated and the Soviet Union would be encouraged to act against a common enemy. For that reason he named the plan 'Catherine' in memory of that famous ruler: 'because Russia lay in the background of my thought.'

The plan looked well; on a map that took no account of geography, climate or the resources and level of training of Britain, her allies and enemies. As ever, Churchill desired action. He told Pound (an obedient First Sea Lord, kept in office long after he was obviously too ill to cope) on 5 December that he could never be responsible for a naval strategy excluding 'the offensive principle', adding on the 25th: 'The supreme strategy is to carry the war into a theatre where we can bring superior forces to bear, and where a decision can be obtained which rules all other theatres. We have to select from a host of dangers the one which can best be dealt with and which, if dealt with, causes the others to fall away.'

What mattered was offensive spirit: he believed that 'Britain could by boldness command the northern waters'. Under his direction, the Royal Navy showed an 'extraordinary willingness' to be offensive. It was 'spared the disaster which would surely have followed', concluded Gerhard Weinberg, had his 'pet project' in the Baltic been attempted. He was, wrote Correlli Barnett, 'a compulsive opportunist and an unrealistic strategist' and Catherine was only the first of many bold ventures which cost heavy casualties.

It was to have been led by four powerful battleships which would sweep aside any surface opposition, untroubled by aerial opposition. 'Battleships could be taken into the Baltic,' wrote William Manchester, 'but RAF fighters could not accompany them; the ships would be under constant, heavy attack from land-based enemy aircraft.' Churchill had the answer to that danger: a memorandum of 12 September 'to strengthen the armour deck so as to give exceptional protection against air attack'.

In spite of his long awareness of air power, he believed as strongly as any 'gun and battleship' sailor that the fleet's own anti-aircraft fire would be enough to protect it. As for mines, the construction of twelve 'mine bumpers' with a 'heavy fore end to take the shock of any exploding mine' would give adequate protection. Churchill had no evidence for what was merely an assertion. In any case, as he assured President Roosevelt on 16 October: 'We have not been at all impressed with the accuracy of the German air bombing of our warships. They seem to have no effective bomb sights.' That too was merely assertion.

Mercifully, Catherine 'shrivelled under scrutiny', as did several other proposed masterstrokes during the next six years. Pound emphasised the air threat and the fact that the operation would rely upon Sweden and the Soviet Union to provide naval bases: most unlikely in either case. For a host of practical problems, Catherine died. No responsible person, then or later, approved Catherine; except, as Churchill wrote in his memoirs, Admiral Tom

Phillips who later drowned in the South China Sea, convinced until almost his last breath that capital ships could resist aerial attack.

Catherine belonged, wrote Barnett, in the same 'cigar-butt strategy' as Churchill's plan to capture Borkum in 1915 or 'even the Dardanelles expedition itself: glibly attractive when arrowed broadly on a map of Europe, but a nonsense in terms of the technical means and military forces available, of the enemy's potential reaction, and of all the wider political and strategic probabilities'.

Can Wilfred Swim?

Thwarted over Catherine, Churchill now devised operation Wilfred. During the winter, the Swedish port of Lulea freezes over. The Germans, who usually shipped iron ore from that port, were therefore obliged to transport it overland by rail to the ice-free Norwegian port of Narvik and then by sea to Germany, keeping well within neutral Norway's territorial waters. On 19 September 1939 Churchill urged the mining of these waters in order to force the traffic away from the coast, into the open sea, where the Royal Navy could intercept it. Infringing the neutrality of Norway and Sweden did not trouble him.

'Small nations,' he told the War Cabinet in December, 'must not tie our hands when we are fighting for their rights and freedom.' Such was Wilfred's birth, but he grew up into the first major Allied offensive of the war, a plan to seize Narvik and even the ore fields. As with Catherine, Churchill's guiding thought was that Britain controlled the sea and Germany did not. He disregarded the fact that Germany controlled the air, had ample ground forces and sufficient naval strength.

With a campaign in France and the Low Countries pending, and his thoughts never far from an assault on the Soviet Union, Hitler had been prepared to see the Scandinavian countries remain neutral. Sweden was complaisant; Denmark too small to matter; and Norway could be left alone, for the time being. However, the British and French made so much noise during so many months and took so little action that Hitler's attention was drawn to Norway's strategic importance and he decided to strike first, which he did on 7 April 1940.

Chamberlain famously crowed to a Conservative Party meeting on the 5th that Hitler had 'missed the bus' and Churchill observed after the war that 'this proved an ill-judged utterance'. So it was, but Churchill was no wiser *at the time*. He supposed that the movement north of German ships was an attempt to bring on a sea battle to win control of the North Atlantic. Four cruisers and transport vessels, packed with troops, had been held in the Clyde, to meet the danger of an invasion of Norway, but Churchill had the troops put ashore so that the cruisers could put to sea at once to take part in what he hoped would be another Jutland, only this time ending in a crushing British victory.

In his memoirs, Churchill described 'a ramshackle campaign', one for which he bore major responsibility. Forces were hastily assembled with too few aircraft, anti-tank guns or transport. No thought was given to training men of different services to work closely together. The Allied command structure, wrote Weinberg, 'was chaotic and further hampered by examples of that gross incompetence on the part of British generals which would continue to bedevil the British Army at least until the summer of 1942'. The contrast with Hugh Dowding's Fighter Command could not be clearer.

Richard Peirse (deputy CAS) had written to Dowding on 4 April about plans to prevent ships carrying ore from Narvik to German ports by laying mines in Norwegian waters from the 8th onwards. The Germans may invade Norway, Peirse continued, and if they do we – the British and French – will send ships and men to resist them. Not much air support would be required, he airily supposed: one squadron of obsolete Gloster Gladiator biplanes and one flight of virtually defenceless Westland Lysanders for reconnaissance. Peirse, a Trenchardist, refused to consider seriously any use for aircraft other than as offensive bombers or defensive fighters, both types operating independently. Combined operations – between sailors, soldiers, airmen and allies – carefully planned in a single headquarters were not yet dreamt of.

'Amateurishness and Feebleness'

Consequently, from start to finish, wrote John Terraine, Anglo-French operations in Norway 'display an amateurishness and feebleness which to this day [1984] can make the reader alternately blush and shiver'. Weinberg, writing a decade later, agreed. British generals showed 'gross incompetence' then and up to the summer of 1942. True, but the other services, British and French, were no better. Jock Colville, one of Chamberlain's secretaries, who later served Churchill, noted in his diary on 27 April 1940: 'The plain truth of the matter is that we have inadvisedly landed an insufficient number of troops without adequate equipment or support from the air, and we have met or are meeting with a serious reverse.' Colville thought the chiefs of staff were much to blame, 'and also Winston who fusses but does nothing'.

A week later, on 3 May, Colville quoted some French officers who said: 'The British have planned this campaign on the lines of a punitive expedition against the Zulus, but unhappily we and the British are in the position of the Zulus, armed with bows and arrows against the onslaught of scientific warfare.' In his memoirs, Churchill – hard pressed by his co-authors – admitted that the British response to the German invasion of Norway had been a disaster, but as usual, and like Gallipoli he found scapegoats and wriggled adroitly to minimise his personal responsibility.

The loss of the aircraft carrier *Glorious* was worse than mere incompetence. Her captain, Guy D'Oyly-Hughes, was permitted to sail from Norwegian waters towards Britain on 8 June escorted by only two destroyers for no better reason than a desire to court-martial the officer in charge of flying as soon as he berthed. D'Oyly-Hughes failed to send up air patrols when he had ample time to do so. All three ships were caught and easily sunk by two German battlecruisers, *Gneisenau* and *Scharnhorst*. Only forty-five – not including D'Oyly-Hughes – of more than 1,000 men aboard the three ships survived. For forty years the Admiralty claimed that the carrier needed to sail virtually unattended because she was short of fuel, but this was not so.

The Allies had approved plans on 28 March 1940 for landing seven battalions in three different places, all without air cover, in a huge country with poor communications and still in the grip of winter. The navy began to roll mines into Norwegian waters on 9 April, but the Germans had moved first and fastest. Sea, land and air forces had swept into Denmark and Norway on the 7th. 'I consider Germans have made strategic error,' Churchill signalled Admiral Charles Forbes on 9 April, 'in incurring commitments on Norwegian coast which we can probably wipe out in a short time.' He repeated this opinion in the Commons two days later.

He seems to have quite forgotten the changes in warfare brought about by a weapon which he had done so much to foster before and during the Great War. The French were no help, in the first meeting between the army commander, Maurice Gamelin and Prime Minister Paul Reynaud, after Germany occupied Denmark and invaded Norway, Gamelin told Reynaud that a French brigade had been poised to go to Scandinavia. Reynaud asked where it was. In the Alps, Gamelin replied: to prevent its detection by German spies.

Another Dardanelles

The Luftwaffe used more than 1,000 aircraft in Norway, leapfrogging units north from one well-equipped airfield to another. Land-based RAF fighters were unable to challenge them and the navy's sea-borne fighters were few and of inferior performance. Churchill decided that Trondheim should be the main target and 'threw myself with increasing confidence into this daring adventure'. His disregard of the Luftwaffe was remarkable for a man of his past experience. Admiral Forbes told him: 'Shore batteries could no doubt be either destroyed or dominated by battleships in daylight' but the main task was 'an opposed landing, of which ample warning has been given, under continuous air attack'. The operation would cause heavy losses in men, weapons and ships. Churchill refused to accept Forbes's considered judgement. It is as if the Dardanelles disaster had never happened.

Failure in central Norway in no way lessened Churchill's enthusiasm for a crack at Narvik. Major-General Pierse Mackesy told the War Office on 20 April that a successful opposed landing there was impossible: 'A landing from open boats must be ruled out absolutely.' Admiral the Earl of Cork and Orrery agreed. Churchill's response was hysterical: 'If this officer appears to be spreading a bad spirit through the higher ranks of the land force,' he told Cork, 'do not hesitate to relieve him or place him under arrest.' Cork did neither and assured Churchill that nothing could be done without air cover. Major Millis Jefferis (who had been to Åndalsnes) reported to the War Cabinet that 'the moral effect' of seeing aircraft coming, unable to take cover, made it impossible for troops to withstand 'complete air superiority of the kind the Germans had enjoyed in Norway'. Churchill was unmoved, but agreed to Cork's request that he present on 6 May to Cabinet the unanimous objections of men on the spot. He stressed 'how very serious the repercussions of a defeat at Narvik would be', adding an argument that was always close to his heart: defeat would have 'a devastating effect on world opinion', wherever and by whomever that might be expressed.

German forces launched a devastating invasion of France on 10 May. Churchill became Prime Minister on that day and found time to complain to Cork on the 20th. 'I am increasingly disappointed by the stagnation which appears to rule in the military operations around Narvik, and delay in occupying the town itself.' As usual, he ignored the lack of air cover and, as usual, Cork reminded him. Although Narvik was taken a few days later, it was abandoned almost at once as a result of greater disasters in France. 'All the principles of combined operations', wrote Henry Pownall on 30 April, 'so carefully studied in peace, seem to have been thrown to the winds' and forces were 'expected to maintain themselves in the face of an absolute air supremacy'.

'Forlorn Endeavour in Remote Places'

The official historian of the campaign concluded that underrating air power was the most obvious lesson of the campaign. Churchill had been 'one of the most powerful guiding influences' in Norway, as he had been at Antwerp, the Dardanelles, against the Bolsheviks and at Chanak. His life-long enthusiasm for 'forlorn endeavour in remote places' cost many men their lives during his years as Prime Minister. Chamberlain – a man with no claim to be a war lord – had questioned Churchill's desire to invade Norway as early as 2 January 1940 on the obvious ground that British ships would be exposed to Luftwaffe attack, operating from bases in southern Norway, where 'they could develop a most serious air threat'. Churchill waved away his objection: a German invasion of Norway, he declared, 'would be vexatious but would in no way be decisive' and pressed on with a plan that was 'ill-considered, ill-founded and absurdly optimistic'.

A. J. P. Taylor commented on 'the curious contradiction in Churchill's nature as a strategist': for years he had emphasised the importance of air power – more so than any other politician – yet when it came to action, he could not resist the call of tradition and romance. He imagined that the Royal Navy could still assert its old supremacy unaided.

After the disaster, Churchill claimed, as usual, that it was not of his making. He had in fact disregarded the need for air power. German satisfaction in a complete victory was tempered by the fact that most of her small fleet of warships was sunk or disabled. Unless Hitler persuaded the British to make peace or his air force overcame the RAF in air battles over Britain, there could be no invasion. Perhaps there would have been merely a peaceful occupation. In the absence of Churchill, with all his faults, no other politician could have called upon the British people to resist any terms that seemed at all reasonable. Quite the reverse: most influential politicians would have 'behaved sensibly' in the wake of France's collapse. It was Churchill, he alone, who made it possible for Dowding's Fighter Command, greatly aided by the Royal Navy and by the brave, though inadequately equipped, crews of Bomber Command to stem, if not turn, the Nazi tide.

11

'The Greatest Victory in World History': Germany's Conquest of France, 1940

Britain Next?
Even before the German assault on Norway, the British assumed that they – rather than the Netherlands, Belgium and France – would be Hitler's next target after the conquest of Poland. British intelligence before 1939 failed dismally to offer the government reliable information about Hitler's obvious determination to use his powerful land and air forces to conquer the whole of Western Europe. It was scarcely less obvious that his Luftwaffe was unable to bomb British targets from bases in Germany. Neither Britain nor France realised that it was a *tactical* not a *strategic* air force. 'This misperception left the RAF over-committed to a defence and counter-strike strategy for the German attack in 1939 which never came,' wrote Richard Overy, 'and greatly inhibited what help it could give to French forces in 1940 when the German military finally did with its air force what it had intended.'

If Britain were to be next, General Joseph Vuillemin (head of the French air force) was asked in April 1940 if French fighters would be sent across the Channel to help. Vuillemin, 'an elderly bomber pilot not over-endowed with dynamism' thought not: an answer that did not help those who wished to see a stronger RAF presence in France. Vuillemin also opposed suggestions that industrial targets in the Ruhr be bombed if the Germans launched a western offensive. The Luftwaffe, he believed, would retaliate by hitting targets in France harder than the Anglo-French air forces could hit targets in Germany. Arthur Barratt told Vuillemin and Gamelin on 15 April that the Air Staff had 'certain knowledge' that Germany intended to attack the Netherlands alone and then begin 'an offensive on a very large scale against England'. This 'certain knowledge' was, of course, nothing of the sort.

A Half-Breed American
On 10 May 1940, most politicians recognised, many of them very reluctantly, that Churchill was the man needed to face a military crisis and so he became Prime Minister. 'A nation which found itself committed to a life-and-death

struggle against one of the most ruthless tyrannies in history was surely wise to entrust its leadership to a man eager to embrace the role', wrote Max Hastings, rather than Chamberlain, Halifax or Eden; men who 'who shrank from it'. Colville and some friends were among those 'shrankers' when they drank in champagne that evening the health of Chamberlain, whom they were pleased to regard as the 'King over the Water'.

Among those politicians – rightly regarded by Hitler as contemptible – who toasted the ex-king was one R. A. ('Rab') Butler, Under-Secretary of State for Foreign Affairs. He thought 'the good clean tradition of English politics, that of Pitt as opposed to Fox, had been sold to the greatest adventurer of modern political history'. He tried long and hard to persuade Halifax to accept the premiership and believed that the emergence of 'Winston and his rabble was a serious disaster' for Britain. Good men 'had weakly surrendered to a half-breed American whose main support was that of inefficient but talkative people of a similar type'.

Numerous influential persons thought as Butler did, and help us to be still more thankful for the 'half-breed American' – 'the chubby cuckoo', as Hastings called him, who did so much to save humanity from Hitler and thereby allow the likes of Butler to flourish: as thrive he did, only narrowly failing to become Prime Minister, but he ended his career as a noble lord and Master of Trinity College, Cambridge. Colville soon broke politically (though never socially) with Britain's Butlers and became devoted to the only man who had the will to resist Hitler's apparently inevitable victory.

A Protracted Pearl Harbor

Hitler had told his military advisers at the end of November 1939 that an attack would shortly be launched in the west, leading to 'the greatest victory in world history'. The assault, which began on 10 May 1940, was indeed a triumph, due mainly to air superiority and imaginative use of massed tanks, horse-drawn artillery and enthusiastic infantry over opponents who had, wrote Ernest May, 'more trained men, more guns, more and better tanks, more bombers and fighters'. But German field commanders proved too skilful, too well organised and above all too sure of themselves and their men for opponents who were always on the back foot, responding belatedly to enemy initiatives, at odds with each other and quite unpractised in making efficient use of their ample resources. For example, more than eighty reconnaissance sorties were flown over the Ardennes before the invasion without detecting the large-scale movement of German armour into that region.

Albert Seaton made the telling point that if Germany had not achieved a swift victory, she 'would have been plunged into a long war for which there was no equipment stocks or reserves'. And Ernest May argued that if Allied leaders 'had anticipated the German offensive through the Ardennes, even as a worrisome contingency, it is almost inconceivable that France would have been defeated when and where it was'. The German victory was 'the equivalent of a successful Pearl Harbor attack', a victory of the weak over the strong. It should give pause to those who like to believe that Britain, like France, had too many resources to suffer defeat in 1940. Could those resources have been harnessed by Halifax and the lackeys to whom he would have listened?

The Matador's Cloak

At dawn on 10 May German armed forces invaded Luxembourg, Belgium and the Netherlands. These attacks, wrote Liddell Hart, 'like a matador's cloak', waved at the British Expeditionary Forces and powerful French forces in Flanders, and lured them north-eastward. The main blow was then delivered just north of where the Maginot Line ended, through the densely-forested country of the Ardennes. The Germans knew that the region was only lightly defended because French commanders considered it impassable. Once a breakthrough was achieved, tanks burst into the flat plains of northern France and drove for the Channel coast, thereby splitting the Allied forces in two.

Britain's small army was unprepared for war against a European state in 1939. It eventually became very large, but desertion and absence without leave caused great anxiety throughout the war. It was entirely untrained, until 1942, in combined operations with seamen or airmen and depended heavily upon American tanks, aircraft and the support of US land, sea and air forces for its subsequent successes. Many men fought bravely and defended doggedly, but they never faced more than a fraction of the German army.

Man for man, neither British nor American soldiers were a match in skill or aggression for German or Japanese soldiers or those of the Soviet Union or Poland. The French army, although large, was poorly commanded and deployed, with no fewer than thirty divisions immobilised behind the Maginot Line. Alfred Sauvy, of the French ministry of finance, wrote in September 1939: 'The French are divided into two camps, those who do not want to make peace and those who do not want to make war.' The air force had few modern aircraft actually in service and its airmen were untrained in the task of supporting ground forces.

The invaders were never seriously troubled, on the ground – where they made efficient use of tanks, artillery and infantry – or in the air, where they had plenty of bombers, fighters, dive-bombers and transport aircraft, all skilled in supporting land operations. Hitler and his senior commanders, astonished by their success and fearing traps where none existed, troubled those doing the actual fighting more than their enemy.

Across the Channel, Churchill told his War Cabinet on 13 May that he expected a great battle to develop, as in the Great War. Once the Germans had achieved their swift crossing of the Meuse and broke out towards the Channel, however, 'the French High Command collapsed into panic, paralysis and defeatism whence the malaise spread downwards'. Only a few days into the invasion, the British began to think of saving themselves and Churchill's government was much less resolute than he claimed, then or later. If Hitler had been a wiser man, he could have made of France an anti-Bolshevik ally – an active ally, bearing in mind how hard many Vichy French supporters fought against Allied forces in the Middle East – and left Britain more isolated than ever.

What did Allied Aircraft do?

From 1939 onwards, the Air Ministry and the War Office argued over what help, if any, aircraft should give to armies in the field. The Air Ministry adamantly opposed close air support, believing that the RAF should be used either for home defence or for strategic bombing.

Portal and Slessor (with Trenchard using his privileged access to all and sundry) led the resistance to the development of aircraft designed and equipped to support armies, advancing or retreating, least of all if they were to come under the control of soldiers. Consequently, soldiers and sailors in Norway or in Western Europe in 1940 got little useful help. An Army Co-operation Command was formed late in 1940, but it was always a lame duck. Fortunately, the RAF in the Western Desert, under the command of Tedder and Coningham, learned from 1941 onwards that all three services must pull together and made of the fighter-bomber a vital weapon. Their success there obliged Churchill to back them, even though soldiers and seamen always had first call upon his emotions. Yet with every advantage on their side – in numbers and material – it still took the Allies until May 1943 to win control of the Mediterranean.

The RAF had sent two separate air forces to France in September 1939: ten squadrons of Fairey Battle light bombers, styled 'The Advanced Air Striking Force' and 'The Air Component of the Field Force' (four squadrons of Blenheim bombers, four of Westland Lysanders, useful only for reconnaissance and artillery spotting and four of Hurricane fighters). All came under Arthur Barratt, head of 'British Air Forces in France' from January 1940. He had few of the RAF's most effective aircraft under his command and his airfields were short of every kind of equipment. Far too little had been done during months of 'phoney war' to prepare realistic plans by soldiers or airmen. When invasion came, the RAF remained doggedly committed to planning and even occasionally carrying out so-called strategic raids on targets in Germany, rather than attacking German forces currently overwhelming French and British soldiers. Why? Many RAF commanders in 1940 had spent the best years of their lives telling each other so often that the battlefield was no place for bombers that they came to believe it.

General Marcel Têtu, French air commander in the north, ruled that attacks could only be made on the invaders in open country, not near urban areas. Barratt apologised for having authorised just such a raid and promised not to do it again. He was not offended: like many senior RAF officers, he regarded direct support of ground forces as an improper use of air power. So it was, when unescorted British and French bombers tried to destroy two bridges over the Albert Canal, west of Maastricht, on 13 May. The bombers were met by intense ground fire, suffered heavy losses and achieved nothing.

Charles (known to his intimates as Peter) Portal was the newly-appointed head of Bomber Command in place of Edgar Ludlow-Hewitt. Portal decreed that the notion of aircraft attacking German tanks, artillery or infantry was 'fundamentally unsound' and likely to have 'disastrous consequences on the future of war in the air'. The French fighter commander, General Astier de la Vigerie, agreed. He refused to provide escorts because he wished to keep his fighters available to resist Luftwaffe attacks on what he believed were 'strategic targets'. Têtu and Barratt then announced that Allied forces in Belgium must henceforth manage without air support.

On 14 May the Allies sent every available Battle to attack a German bridgehead over the Meuse. Their crews were brave and skilful, but their weapon was totally useless and they achieved nothing. Good men died and were injured or, if very lucky, captured. On that day, wrote Alistair Horne, 'the campaign was effectively decided'. Churchill visited France on the 15th and heard Gamelin, the French commander-in-chief, confess that he had no reserves and Prime Minister Reynaud already expected defeat.

Lord Rothermere had warned Churchill as early as December 1937 that the French air force was 'beneath contempt'. There were admirable pilots, but very few fine aeroplanes. 'Today nearly all the aeroplanes being delivered to the French air force are completely out of date. Moreover, the material used in their manufacture is of poor quality and not properly tried out before being utilised. Corruption in this vital branch of national defence reigns supreme.'

In the event of war, Rothermere predicted the fall of France 'in the first few weeks at most'. And yet when war came, Churchill expected the French army – with or without air support – to provide a staunch bulwark against German invaders. Churchill thought of the French army as it had been in 1914. His knowledge of France since 1918 did not extend beyond its casinos, holiday resorts and attendance at a few formal reviews.

The performance of the French air force in defence of its own homeland was surprisingly poor because throughout the Great War the French earned a high reputation in all aspects of aerial warfare. Inevitably, the large and powerful air force of 1918 disappeared in the 1920s, but even the goad of Hitler's aggression after 1933 failed to provoke an effective revival: one not helped by the appointment of nine different ministers of aviation in various governments between 1935 and 1939.

During the 1930s the French air force tried to follow the RAF's example of creating a strategic bomber force, but the result was even more of a muddle than in Britain. Worse still, the French were nowhere close to developing an efficient defence system, based on radar, radio, observer posts and modern fighters.

From 1937 onwards, the French designed a number of promising fighters and bombers, but they were neither produced in sufficient numbers nor located in the most likely battle areas. Many were evenly spread throughout France and its overseas colonies at the behest of local army or navy commanders. When the invasion began, no means could be found for gathering them to where they were most needed. Consequently, most of the available aircraft, air and ground crews contributed nothing to the defence of France.

From every point of view – doctrine, equipment, personnel, training, logistics, command and control arrangements, morale – the French air force was inadequate. Claims made by various commanders that France had 'a tactically formidable air force' and/or 'a truly formidable strategic striking force' were just that; claims. German soldiers and airmen were not supermen, led unerringly by brilliant commanders, although it suited many politicians and others in both countries after France's surrender to assert that they were. Most Germans were astonished, as well as delighted, by the speed and completeness of their victory, achieved in spite of the cock ups usual in conducting massive military enterprises.

Miracles and Lessons

The Germans reached the Channel near Abbeville on 19 May and by the 24th thousands of Allied soldiers had retreated into a vast pocket around Dunkirk. Hitler, who lost his nerve several times during both the Norwegian and West European campaigns, ordered his forces to halt. The order, much criticised in hindsight, was militarily sensible: it allowed recovery from the effects on men and machines of heavy fighting and gave time to bring up reinforcements and supplies. It was also politically astute, from Hitler's viewpoint, in offering Goering a chance to share in the army's glory.

No-one on either side of the Channel – at the time – expected the halt to make it possible for 340,000 trapped men (more than two-thirds of them British, the rest French or Belgian) to escape across the Channel. Numerous ships, small and large, naval and civilian, played their part, but the escape was only made possible by the courage of the French First Army: German records show that the French fought for every house and foot of ground. This fact has never been widely acknowledged in Britain.

Six British fighter squadrons were already in France on 10 May and Dowding was under constant pressure to send more. Then, on the 19th, the problem of the 'possible but unlikely evacuation of a very large force in hazardous circumstances' through Dunkirk, Calais and Boulogne was discussed in the War Office. A week later, Admiral Bertram Ramsay (commanding in Dover) was ordered to implement Operation Dynamo, an evacuation that was no longer unlikely.

Keith Park (commanding 11 Group in Fighter Command) had about 200 fighters at his disposal, but the area that had to be protected lay at least fifty miles from his nearest bases: a long way, there and back, for short-range fighters. Operating outside their planned defensive system, they could receive no help from radar and were obliged to rely on standing patrols that could last, at most, forty minutes, given the need to re-fuel and re-arm. Moreover, the area occupied by the soldiers had a perimeter extending for ten miles and the ships rescuing the soldiers were under enemy attack throughout their Channel crossings, both ways. To give continuous cover in strength would have required Dowding to concentrate virtually all of his Hurricane and Spitfires in the few airfields from which they could reach Dunkirk, and that would have exposed the rest of Britain to attack.

Fighter Command did what it could, but the losses of aircraft and experienced pilots over France before the evacuation began had been very heavy and Dowding was acutely aware of an even more serious challenge ahead if Britain chose to fight on after the fall of France. His losses showed that without a ground control organisation to help them, Dowding's fighters – intended for home defence – were only just a match for the Luftwaffe when fighting across the Channel. During three critical days (26-28 May), the War Cabinet met five times to consider what Britain should do if the Germans conquered France. Churchill concealed this debate in his postwar memoirs.

Halifax's suggestion on the 26th of approaching Mussolini was rejected, but Churchill admitted that 'if we could get out of this jam by giving up Malta and Gibraltar and some African colonies, I would jump at it'. The Cabinet decided to await the outcome of a Luftwaffe assault on Britain, believing that between them the RAF and the Royal Navy would successfully resist an invasion, but 'the whole debate,' as David Reynolds wrote, 'assumed an eventual negotiated peace rather than total victory... In the summer of 1940, it was inconceivable that Britain alone could enforce total victory on a Germany that now dominated continental Europe.'

Churchill's determination to fight on rested on at least three mistaken assumptions. One, that Germany's economy was already stretched to the limit; two, that the United States would soon enter the war; and three, that a newly-created special operations executive would 'set Europe ablaze' by encouraging citizens to organise 'a general uprising', sabotage factory production and wreck communications.

The Germans, presumably, would be unable to respond effectively. There was a fourth, which eventually had more substance: strategic bombing. 'The fighters are our salvation,' Churchill wrote on 3 September, 'but the bombers alone provide the means of victory.' His determination to fight on was glorious, and inspired many Britons to set aside the meek acceptance of aggression encouraged for so long by most politicians – right, left or centre – but in fact the rulers of Germany and Japan were destroyed mainly by the efforts of the Soviet Union and the United States.

Thanks to the courage of numerous seamen, amateur as well as professional, greatly helped by Dowding's fighters, the makings of a new army survived. Sadly, Ramsay was eager to nourish inter-service animosity and submitted to the Admiralty, as soon as he could, a report on Operation Dynamo that praised the navy and was unfair to the RAF. He failed to understand Fighter Command's obligation, like the navy's, would always be to regard protection of the homeland as the first charge on resources. Seven years later, in July 1947, when one might suppose such animosity had withered away, as a result of numerous campaigns ending in a total victory in which all services played a vital part, the Admiralty chose to publish Ramsay's report. By then, Ramsay was dead and some parts of his report were 'necessarily distorted', the Admiralty admitted, but it could not be corrected on the disheartening ground that it represented naval opinion at the time.

Paris fell, undefended, on 14 June and France surrendered on the 22nd, signing an armistice in the same railway carriage that had served for Germany's surrender in November 1918. French losses were estimated at nearly 300,000 killed or wounded and about 2,000,000 taken prisoner or missing in a campaign that lasted just six weeks. Victory cost Germany about 160,000 casualties, fewer than 30,000 of them fatal.

More than 68,000 British soldiers did not escape from Dunkirk (40,000 of them as prisoners) and some 200 ships of all sizes were sunk. These horrendous numbers have often been glossed over by postwar British writers. The RAF's losses were also appalling, especially for a service that had only expanded significantly in recent years: well over 900 aircraft, half of them fighters. Nearly 1,400 men, among them more than 530 pilots, were killed, wounded or captured. Many of them were experienced regulars or men trained in peacetime.

It is essential to have these grim figures in mind when exulting over the so-called 'miracle' of Dunkirk, and, even more, when evaluating the RAF's achievements during the rest of 1940. It is equally important to note the Luftwaffe's suffering, in a service barely five years old. By the end of June 1940, German airmen had fought their way through four campaigns (in Poland, Norway, the Low Countries and France) all victorious, but all costly in aircrews and aircraft, though 400 aircrew prisoners were released after the French surrender. These losses gravely impaired its performance during the rest of the war. During May, the Luftwaffe lost over 1,000 aircraft, a quarter of them fighters. 'The enemy has had air superiority', admitted the German 4th Army's war diary on 25 May. 'This is something new for us in this campaign.'

For some reason, Barratt chose to assure the Air Ministry on 4 June, just as the Dunkirk evacuation was ending, that all was not lost. France was rallying, he said, German losses were heavy and he agreed with Vuillemin that a great many more fighters should be sent across the Channel. But reality was beginning to break into the mind of Sholto Douglas, Newall's chief assistant in the Air Ministry. On 4 June he penned some splendid Whitehall nonsense for Portal: 'The strenuous and gallant efforts of your squadrons against objectives in collaboration with the land battle since 10 May have not always had results commensurate with the effort exerted.' He meant 'we've been beaten'.

Churchill signalled Reynaud next day: 'You don't seem to understand at all that British fighter aviation has been worn to a shred and frightfully mixed up [by the demands of Dunkirk].' Even so, on 8 June he still had some hope: 'We are giving you all the support we can in this great battle,' he told Reynaud, 'short of ruining the capacity of this country to continue the war.' But Dowding, ever a realist, told Barratt on the 12th that the game was up and it was time to get out. Nearly 200,000 soldiers and airmen (most of them British) were rescued by the Royal Navy from France's Atlantic ports by 18 June: a heartening achievement that has rarely attracted attention from writers focused upon Dunkirk. Churchill rightly said that 'wars are not won by evacuations', but they can be lost without them. Most of the British survivors of the disaster would serve in later, better-managed campaigns than those in Norway and France.

12

Before the Battle of Britain, 1923-1940

Ashmore and his Colleagues

The first serious postwar attempt to revive Britain's air defence system began as early as 1923. It was framed with France in mind. A cautious ally throughout the war, France was an imperial rival overseas. A committee formed in that year identified three requirements (all still of concern in 1940). First was the need for a chain of command designed to get full and swift co-operation between the service and civilian components of the system. Second was the need for early warning of approaching raiders. And third the need for rapid communication between those on the ground and those in the air.

An organisation entitled 'The Air Defence of Great Britain' was formed in January 1925, under the command of John Salmond. He had control of both bombers and fighters. Anti-aircraft gun zones and searchlight positions were marked out and an Observer Corps formed. Its headquarters moved out of the Air Ministry to Uxbridge, west of London, on 31 May 1926. Keith Park, then a squadron leader, was put in charge of 'Operations, Intelligence, Mobilisation and Combined Training' in August.

Ideas about air defence set down on paper in 1926-1927 were still valid when war came a dozen or so years later, although by then Germany – not France – was recognised as the likely attacker. The credit, in Park's opinion, lay chiefly with Edward Ashmore (in command of ground defences), Robert Brooke-Popham (first commander of 'Fighting Area', a subordinate formation, also set up in Uxbridge, which controlled all aircraft except bombers) and Felton Holt. He was Salmond's chief of staff and had commanded the Home Defence Force in 1916, an embryo of Fighter Command in 1936.

Ashmore and Holt drew upon their experience of defending London in the Great War. It was Holt who recruited Park and set him on the road to fame as 'the craftsman of Fighter Command' in the words of John Ferris. Fighter sectors, searchlight belts, anti-aircraft zones and balloon barrages were all devised, though only on paper. Holt was promoted to air vice-marshal in

January 1931 and appointed head of ADGB's Fighting Area on 1 April. Still only forty-four, it is likely that he, rather than Dowding, would have been appointed the first head of Fighter Command in July 1936, if he had not been killed in a flying accident in April 1931.

Dowding set up his headquarters in Bentley Priory, a village a few miles north of Uxbridge. Two years later, in July 1938, Park – now an air commodore – was appointed second in command, responsible for fighting efficiency. In later years, he rightly insisted that Fighter Command could not have been made ready for war in 1940 without the efforts of those who devised an air defence system in 1917 and revived it in the 1920s.

Enter the Scientists

The RAF's annual air exercise in August 1934, like those before it, was a fiasco. Three important consequences followed. Firstly, Dowding (at that time Air Member for Supply and Organisation) and a number of other senior officers were formed into a sub-committee of the Committee of Imperial Defence and ordered to study air defence. Next, Churchill focused his attention on air defence. And finally Albert Rowe, assistant to Harry Wimperis (Director of Scientific Research in the Air Ministry) wrote a memorandum, after reading the files on air defence, in which he concluded that unless science found some new weapon or method, then the next war would be lost if it started at any time in the next ten years.

Wimperis was convinced and on his initiative a Committee for the Scientific Study of Air Defence was set up under Tizard with Professors A. J. Hill (founder of operational research during the Great War), Patrick Blackett (a leading physicist), Wimperis and Rowe as members.

Its first meeting was held on 28 January 1935, by which time Wimperis had discussed the problems with Robert Watson-Watt of the National Physical Laboratory and his assistant, Arnold Wilkins. Dowding was asked to seek approval for spending serious money on trials. 'The sequel was one of the most influential scientific demonstrations ever held in Britain', at Weedon in Northamptonshire, late in February 1935. The pilot of a Handley Page Heyford bomber was instructed to fly back and forth keeping close to the centre of a continuous beam from a radio station at Daventry. Echoes from the transmission were discernible at ranges up to eight miles. 'We now have in embryo,' wrote Wimperis to Dowding on 4 March, 'a new and potent means of detecting the approach of hostile aircraft, one which will be independent of mist, cloud, fog or nightfall.'

Dowding pressed for money to finance further work and an experimental station was set up at Orfordness, near Bawdsey Manor, on the Suffolk coast: a suitable site because it was flat and isolated. The Air Ministry bought the manor, together with some land around it for the huge sum of £23,000, equivalent to more than £4,000,000 in the money of 2012. The Air Ministry, so often criticised in these years, deserves praise for this vital contribution to Britain's salvation in 1940. Swinton (Secretary of State for Air, 1935-1938) also played a vital part in helping this new device to be developed. Neither Churchill nor Lindemann had anything to do with it. Thanks to that money, and those who had the spending of it, radar became the catalyst of defence science.

During 1937 it was hoped that about twenty detecting stations would be built around the southern and eastern coasts of Britain. If the system worked properly, every aircraft approaching Britain would be detected by at least two stations. A means of collating their reports, identifying friendly aircraft and passing the information simultaneously to Fighter Command's operations rooms was being devised. Eventually, the controller in each of these rooms would be able to see at a glance plots of hostile raids, the movements of his own fighters, how much petrol and oxygen their pilots had left and even the state of the weather. If war came, a small group of scientists would move to the headquarters of Fighter Command in Bentley Priory.

Squadron Leader Raymond Hart, who began his long association with radar at Bawdsey, was responsible for creating a practical system out of scientific experiments. He advocated 'filtering', whereby information from a number of radar stations was compared and turned into a picture intelligible to controllers. Geoffrey Roberts, formerly a Post Office engineer, was sent by Rowe to Bentley Priory and invented an automatic plotting device, called 'the fruit machine', which converted range and direction into a grid reference quickly and accurately. Eric Williams, a young science graduate from Birmingham University, solved the problem of distinguishing between friendly and enemy aircraft. Known as 'pip squeak', it was easy to install and showed up clearly on radar screens. Harold Larnder, a radio engineer who had wide experience in communications work all over the world, joined the staff at Bawdsey in 1935 and was a godsend to Dowding, for he was able to get on equally well with civilian scientists and RAF officers and encourage them all to pull in the same direction. When war came, this collection of engineers, physicists and other scientists now working at Bentley Priory would be dignified in 1941 with the title Fighter Command Operational Research Section.

In September 1938, a new German airship – LZ 130, Graf Zeppelin – made its maiden flight. General Wolfgang Martini, head of the Luftwaffe's signals organisation, had it equipped as a flying radio laboratory and used it during 1939 to fly close to the British east coast in an attempt to discover what practical use, if any, the RAF was making of radio signals to get early warning of airborne intruders. The airship was closely monitored by Dowding's 'Chain Home' radar stations throughout its flight, but the Germans failed to detect their signals and Goering – who never had any patience with technical details – ordered the destruction of LZ 130.

Behind all these exciting breakthroughs, Dowding was constantly concerned to find and train personnel to use them. This was a problem never fully solved during 1940: there simply had not been enough time to recruit and train enough men (and women) to use equipment at the cutting edge and those who were responsible for training were themselves finding either that new devices appeared at irregular moments and unforeseen snags popped up all the time. By the end of a terrible war which ended with Britain among the victors, her military leaders in all services had enjoyed promotions, awards and public acclaim, but the backroom men and women who played an essential part were ignored. Not a single radar scientist was invited to participate in the Victory Parade. Watson-Watt and Tizard were knighted, but no marks of favour were bestowed at that time on such other heroes as Wimperis, Rowe, Larnder, Williams, Hill, Blackett and Wilkins.

Fighter Aircraft

Two new fighters, the Hawker Hurricane designed by Sydney Camm and the Supermarine Spitfire, designed by Reginald Mitchell, were strongly backed by Dowding, responsible for research and development. Ralph Sorley, serving in the Operational Requirements branch of the Air Staff, had seen a mock-up of both and praised them in a minute dated 1 May 1935. So confident was he in their promise that he asked for jigs and tools to be ordered at once. But a group called the 'Air Parity Committee' foresaw production difficulties. Although the Hurricane was based on Hawker's excellent Fury biplane, the Spitfire was totally new in construction as well as design and both posed tricky problems of wing armament and retractable undercarriages. By the end of 1937 no more than twenty-two Hurricanes were serving in two squadrons and only two Spitfires were on hand.

Dowding found himself lumbered with another fighter of no value whatsoever: the Boulton Paul Defiant, a two-seater single-engined machine whose sole armament was a four-gun turret firing to the rear. In June 1938 Douglas (assistant CAS) told Dowding that he must form nine squadrons of Defiants because 450 had been ordered in the belief that they would emulate the success of the two-seater Bristol Fighters during the Great War. This was to overlook the fact, well known to any sensible airmen, let alone senior Air Ministry officials and aircraft designers, that Bristol pilots had relied on their forward-firing guns; the rear gunner's main job was to protect his tail.

As late as June 1938, members of the Air Staff were asserting that the Hurricane and Spitfire were not the answer to Britain's air defence problems. The speed of modern bombers is so great, Donald Stevenson (responsible for 'Home Operations') believed, fighters can only attack them from the rear. A turret-fighter was therefore essential. Douglas supported this nonsense, as did Lindemann and therefore Churchill as well.

Worse still was the elementary fact that no successful fighter employed anywhere, at any time, has left the pilot weaponless, facing forward, and required to fly in such a way that a gunner, facing aft, might bring his guns to bear on a target which the pilot could not see. Despite the fact that the Defiant, carrying two men and a heavy turret, weighed at least half a ton more than the Hurricane, equipped with the same engine, Stevenson persuaded himself that the Defiant was 'slightly faster'. It was, in fact, markedly inferior at every point of comparison – as any competent test pilot could have told him and its inferiority to the Spitfire was even more pronounced.

A year later, with reality beginning to dawn in some official minds, the number of Defiant squadrons was reduced to six. Dowding was not appeased: he was 'faced with the necessity', he told Stevenson, 'of placing the Defiants where they will do the least harm'. In the event, only two squadrons were formed. They suffered appalling casualties as day fighters in the summer of 1940 and achieved nothing when tried as night fighters during the following winter. Nevertheless, Douglas and Stevenson survived and would play important parts in removing both Dowding and Park from Fighter Command before the end of 1940.

The Catalyst
Churchill's agitation from 1933 onwards about re-armament, even when based upon detailed information supplied by serving RAF officers, had little apparent effect upon Baldwin or Chamberlain. Party loyalty – reinforced by efficient managers – on both sides of the House easily overcame qualms, if any, felt by all but a handful of members. One can understand why. Churchill was an ageing maverick who had, it seemed, had his day. Fortunately, there were positive sources of energy and expertise in Britain beyond the closed world of Westminster: men of influence in industry, trade or commerce and officers in all three services as well as private citizens who heard what Churchill said, read what he wrote and – more importantly – had their own thoughts on the efficient use of air power. For them, he was a catalyst. Whether a tiny pebble or a massive boulder is a matter of opinion, but the fact is that an avalanche followed, meaning serious re-armament began in 1938.

Freeman and Tedder
Sebastian Ritchie has demonstrated that aircraft firms did not take excessive profits and prepared industrial expansion effectively. The Air Ministry oversaw these matters 'fairly well' and shortages of skilled labour did not impede air rearmament. German aircraft firms had more and better-trained technical staff than British ones, but whereas the British used their resources rationally, German firms 'spent theirs like drunken engineers in pursuit of prototypes, and ultimately performed worse than British firms in design and production'. Germany overtook Britain between 1933 and 1938, but Britain pulled ahead from 1939 onwards.

In June 1938, when he had already spent more than two years at the Air Ministry in charge of research and development, Wilfrid Freeman was made responsible for production as well. 'Everything in the way of re-equipping the RAF therefore hinged on Freeman', wrote Ritchie. 'No burden, except that of the Prime Minister, could have been greater.' A man notoriously difficult to please, he thought highly of Tedder and in July 1938 had him summoned to England (from Singapore) to take up the newly-created position of Director-General of Research and Development. During the next two years, Tedder recalled in the 1960s, Freeman created 'a team spirit of mutual confidence and understanding between the Air Ministry and Industry such as we never had before or since'. Tedder helped Freeman to manage 'one of the largest state-sponsored industrial enterprises in British history: the expansion of the military aircraft industry' from 1938 onwards.

An article by an anonymous 'production engineer' appeared in *Flight* in April 1938 critical of Air Ministry methods. Its insistence on design competition between firms, it argued, wasted scarce resources and was such a protracted business that aircraft were obsolete before they reached squadron service. The Air Ministry's production staff lacked practical knowledge of the aviation industry in matters of labour, plant, materials and equipment. There was also a lack of sufficiently close relations with other Air Ministry departments (technical, contracts, inspection) to avoid duplication and waste of time. In consequence of what *Flight* called 'the almost universal feeling throughout the country that all is not well with the RAF expansion', Freeman appointed Ernest Lemon, a railway engineer, to a new post, Director-General of Production, with a seat on the Air Council. The chairman of the Society of British Aircraft Constructors, Sir Charles Bruce-Gardner, was also found a seat on the Air Council. These changes, linking top airmen with top industry leaders, were of great value when war came, and owed nothing directly to agitation by either Churchill or Lindemann, although the noise they made certainly encouraged realistic preparations for war.

The Air Ministry suffered in the 1930s from a shortage of officers with technical qualifications. All were moved on to different posts every two or three years, ensuring that painfully-acquired expertise was lost and fruitful contacts broken. Nevertheless, much good work was done to transform a small air force into one capable of using vast numbers of aircraft that were increasingly complex. Most British firms were neither prepared for mass production nor to co-operate with each other. Several excellent fighter types appeared, but years passed before they were joined by efficient heavy bombers and the RAF lacked a transport type to compare with either the German Junkers Ju 52 or the American DC-3.

Air and ground crews were being recruited in huge numbers and these men needed intensive and prolonged training. Sites for airfields were being found, bought and equipped with hangars, workshops and offices, all of which needed power, water and drainage systems. Accommodation, including uniforms and bedding, was needed on a scale far beyond what the Air Ministry, or the government, could have envisaged as recently as 1935.

An Aviation Revolution

Until 1933, there were many small, intensely-competitive aviation firms, all under-funded and some ineptly managed. By that year, however, three firms (Vickers, A. V. Roe and Hawker) dominated the airframe market and two (Bristol and Rolls-Royce) for aero-engines. Firms were being pressed to abandon craft production for mass production, with all the problems of taking on and training workers, of finding adequate floor space for construction and storage and of arranging transport by road or rail on an unprecedented scale for inward goods and outward aircraft, complete or in parts. Manufacturers were naturally reluctant to move from making well-tested, metal-framed, fabric-covered biplanes to face up to a revolution: the alarming problems and greater expense of all-metal, stressed-skin monoplanes. These needed wing-mounted machine guns or cannons, retractable undercarriages and more powerful engines, their performance enhanced by the invention of variable-pitch propellers and the use of improved fuels.

At a time of rapid technological change, it made sense for the Air Ministry to be cautious about ordering new types of equipment into quantity production, because they might soon be superseded by better. But at a time of equally-rapid escalation in external threats to Britain, it also made sense to produce a great many aircraft as quickly as possible. The dilemma was real and not to be solved as easily as Churchill's orations in Parliament were composed and delivered.

A further complication, as Handley Page observed to Freeman in November 1938, was the fact that construction of truly 'heavy' (i.e., four-engined) bombers was very expensive and depended on orders that were certain and for which serious government money would not suddenly be cut off if or when Chamberlain got good news from across the Channel.

In 1935, Britain's aircraft industry had built nearly 900 aircraft for the RAF; a number that had increased to more than 20,000 in 1941. As for aero-engines, fewer than 3,000 were delivered in 1936, but twelve times as many in 1941. Aviation production overtook that of Germany during 1939 and was the highest in the world in 1940. Thereafter, Britain out-produced Germany by vast margins in numbers of airframes and engines, despite employing a smaller labour force and using less material. These were outstanding achievements and had the Luftwaffe been as well supplied – and as sensibly commanded at the top – the war would have lasted longer and been even bloodier.

Chamberlain, however, dismissed Swinton, an excellent Secretary of State for Air, in May 1938 for some political advantage. In his place, he appointed a London solicitor, one Kingsley Wood, who readily admitted that he knew nothing about aviation. He was, however, a competent organiser and broke the grip of the old 'family' firms of aircraft producers and insisted that they make full use of sub-contractors. He also combined these firms into four production groups that were to build designated types of bombers and fighters, and not waste time and resources on other projects. These reforms were unmatched in Germany, where Goering and Udet presided over a most pleasing chaos, from a British point of view. Although some serious mistakes were made, aviation production in Britain far outstripped Germany in quality and quantity.

Airfield construction really began in 1934. It cost a fortune and employed thousands of engineers, builders and labourers from then on. To support these airfields, there were 300 major structures to store bombs, fuel and spare parts. 'The civil engineering achievements of the Air Ministry in conjunction with the UK civil engineering industry', including thousands of balloon sites, were outstanding and repeated throughout the Middle East and on the Continent. Perhaps the best tribute to their efforts is the fact that most historians have simply assumed that such essential facilities would be there when needed.

Noel Birch, a director of Vickers with special responsibility for foreign sales, argued that the company should be wary of building military aircraft: it might well find, if or when the risk of war abated, that it would be: 'competing for work that would not keep a cat, and our foreign sales gone!' Although designers and managers recognised that risk, 'they produced long-range or high-speed aircraft before the Air Staff had finally decided it needed them'. During 1936, the Air Ministry trimmed the procedures by which a design moved into production. Dowding – when responsible for research and development – agreed and some excellent machines appeared far sooner than they would under the old system. Apart from the immortal Hurricane and Spitfire, the RAF acquired the Wellington, Mosquito and Beaufighter. Such duds as the Battle, Whitley and Hampden also appeared, partly in response to political demands for 'parity' in numbers with Germany.

Another problem was the reluctance of companies to farm out designs to sub-contractors and thereby allow competitors to exploit their own hard-earned expertise. Although the Wellington proved to be an outstanding success, its geodetic construction was so labour intensive that it had no successor. One type was not fostered as it should have been: Frank Whittle's jet-powered monoplane first flew as early as May 1941, but British jets played no significant part in a war that lasted for another four years.

Beaverbrook's Year
The first person Churchill turned to when he became Prime Minister was his old crony, Max Aitken, Lord Beaverbrook, who would remain close to him

throughout the war. Max often irritated him, but he was one of very few men or women with whom Churchill could be at ease, wallowing in memories of old friends and enemies. He had been a convinced appeaser until the last moment, his advice was often mistaken, he loved to make mischief, but he was immensely rich and Churchill found him fun to be with. In May 1940, the two spent the best part of three days alone together, choosing the members of a new government. Churchill put Beaverbrook in charge of a 'Ministry of Aircraft Production'. He knew nothing about aircraft design, testing or production, but he did know how to keep employees on their toes and win over important people. Decisions were made on the spur of the moment and midnight telephone calls were usual. He brought with him several *Daily Express* secretaries and men such as Patrick Hennessey (from Ford Motors), Charles Craven and Trevor Westbrook (both from Vickers-Armstrong), who regarded most senior airmen and civil servants as obstacles to the new regime.

Freeman and Tedder found themselves under Beaverbrook's authority and in constant argument with a host of business men, trying in vain to resist a total focus on the immediate crisis. No-one queried a need to build Hurricanes, Spitfires and Wellingtons, but two other types – the Blenheim and the Whitley on which Beaverbrook also insisted – were already known (at least to airmen who had to use them) to be of limited value. Unfortunately, output enchanted Beaverbrook, as it did Churchill: never mind the quality, count the numbers.

Speaking of quality, Geoffrey de Havilland's twin-engined, wooden-framed Mosquito had been designed late in 1938, and at Christmas 1939 Freeman ordered fifty, but Beaverbrook rejected it until Freeman persuaded Hennessey to allow what became one of the war's most effective aircraft to be built. The Air Ministry was not blameless: officials there objected to the Mosquito being fitted with Merlin engines until March 1941.

'We have to win the war as well as this battle', Tedder told Freeman as early as 21 May 1940, who agreed entirely. 'We must keep on looking to the future', continued Tedder. 'We must keep working on new equipment and if we break up technical teams now it will be difficult to get them together again.'

In Downing Street on the evening of 18 June Beaverbrook told Colville that 'the Air Ministry was rotten and Sinclair a thoroughly bad minister who was hoodwinked by his subordinates'. Years later, Tedder told Air Marshal Sir Theodore McEvoy that 'the Beaver' was amusing to read about, but not to work for. 'Like Winston, he was a bully, a flatterer and absolutely unreliable. Both were at their best in crises, but unlike Winston, Beaverbrook was quite incapable of non-crisis routine work, of plodding through dull stuff, hour after hour, and most of what had to be done at MAP was *dull*, believe you me!'

On 30 April 1941, Churchill accepted his friend's fourteenth offer to resign and then in June, in one of his perverse moods, chose to appoint him Minister of Supply. Brendan Bracken, a wheeler and dealer always at Churchill's side, said Beaverbrook 'takes up more of the PM's time than Hitler'. John Moore-Brabazon, who succeeded 'the Beaver' at the MAP, told Hankey in October that he had still not caught up with the chaos he left. As many as 1,400 aircraft were currently grounded for lack of spare parts, thanks to the ministry's insistence on front-line production. Hankey, who regarded Beaverbrook as a 'first-rate muddler', was not surprised.

During 1940, Beaverbrook's personality and actions had bitten deeply into the souls of both Freeman and Tedder, who monitored his erratic course during 1941 with fearful fascination. In January 1941, for example, Tedder met Tony Phillpotts, private secretary to General Auchinleck, but a Beaver journalist in civilian life. Phillpotts was quite certain, he told Tedder, that Beaverbrook knew that the duties of an ever-growing wartime ministry were beyond him and would have resigned after a couple of months, 'but Labour is afraid of his getting any other job, which might be a stage towards the premiership, if Churchill departed'. Tedder was vastly amused by John Steel's quip, relayed by his wife, in May: 'Churchill resigns and Beaverbrook sends for the king.'

Early in November 1940 Freeman left the Beaver's ministry to become chief assistant to Portal, newly-appointed head of the RAF. Freeman wanted to leave because Beaverbrook was urging the formation of an army air force. 'I disagree with you on so many other points of policy,' he said, and 'I am gravely disturbed at the quarrels which seem to take place incessantly between the MAP and the Air Ministry. I do not understand your policy of non-co-operation with the Air Ministry.' Beaverbrook, quite unabashed, replied blandly.

On 4 November, however, the eve of his departure, Freeman wrote fulsomely to Beaverbrook, praising:

> 'The energy, courage and decision with which you tackled the difficult problem of aircraft production. Without the ever-increasing flow of aircraft from the storage units, for which you have been entirely responsible, our pilots could never have won such resounding victories. It has been a great privilege and an abiding lesson to serve under you and if at any future date I can serve you again in any capacity, I shall indeed be grateful for the opportunity.'

Beaverbrook replied at once. You, 'more than any other man, gave the RAF the machines whose superior quality won the vital battles of this summer'.

Tedder wrote more calmly on 19 November. Beaverbrook had offered to ask the Air Ministry to appoint him to a command. Tedder replied that he would take whatever was offered, made no apology for having spoken very frankly and bluntly on two or three occasions, and was ready to leave the ministry at any time. Churchill, advised by Beaverbrook, refused to allow Tedder's appointment as deputy to Arthur Longmore, head of RAF Middle East.

At this critical moment, however, fate lent Tedder a helping hand. On 24 November, Owen Boyd, en route by air to Cairo as Longmore's deputy, was carelessly landed in Sicily instead of Malta for a re-fuelling stop and captured. Tedder was the next most senior officer in the RAF, Portal renewed his proposal and Churchill relented, thereby making one of his most valuable contributions to the Allied cause. Wiser than Longmore, Tedder knew how to milk the Air Ministry cow: gently, making pleased noises when he got a bucket half full, rather than roughly complaining that the bucket was half empty.

Meanwhile, on 25 November 1940, Tedder had sent an astonishingly frank report to Sinclair on his service under Beaverbrook. His methods were 'so grave as to threaten the efficiency of the service and consequently the safety of the country'. Wholesale withdrawal of development aircraft and pilots from experimental stations was justifiable to meet Britain's desperate situation in May and June, but not later. 'The present administration of the Ministry of Aircraft Production is based on force and fear,' wrote Tedder, and 'threats are the very essence of its direction.' Only Churchill himself spoke so bluntly to Sinclair, who found to his surprise that Portal agreed with Tedder. He therefore silently accepted the report.

During months of desperate crisis in the summer of 1940, Beaverbrook proved to be an inspired appointment, sweeping away the glumly persevering atmosphere of the Chamberlain regime. Of equal importance was the fact that Beaverbrook and Dowding (head of Fighter Command) quickly became firm allies. They were an unlikely combination, one so reserved, the other so exuberant. Dowding agreed with Churchill that the new ministry 'made a surprising improvement in the supply and repair of aeroplanes... clearing up the muddle and scandal of the aircraft production branch', as Churchill told Sinclair on 3 June. For his part, Beaverbrook respected Dowding and never numbered him among 'the bloody air marshals' whom he regarded with contempt.

One Little Man

In August 1941 Dowding praised Beaverbrook in his despatch on the Battle of Britain and did so again in a letter to *The Times* published on 1 June 1945. 'We had the organisation, we had the men, and we had the spirit which could bring us victory in the air', but not the machines needed to withstand the drain of continuous battle. Dowding honoured 'the indomitable spirit of one little man', who achieved what 'no other man in England' could have done.

The 'little man' responded on 5 June. 'You know of my faith in the commander of the Battle of Britain... the greatest event in the war.' Rod Banks, an outstanding engineer who was made Director General of Engine Production and then of Research and Development in the new ministry, agreed with Dowding. Beaverbrook, he said, 'did a great service in getting the contracts procedure cleaned up so that firms could go ahead with the minimum of delay and paperwork'. His other great service 'was when he got the repair facilities further removed from RAF control and distributed more widely among industry'.

A Civilian Repair Organisation, created in October 1939, was taken out of Air Ministry control and transferred to the MAP in May 1940. Thanks to that organisation, more than one-third of the fighters serving during the Battle of Britain were repaired machines. Harold Balfour, Under-Secretary of State for Air, was also well placed to assess 'the Beaver's' impact. He later wrote, 'from my first-hand knowledge, even though on the Air Ministry side of the fence', the narrow margin between defeat and survival in 1940 would not 'have been tipped in our favour' without Beaverbrook. He created a vital sense of 'urgency and enthusiasm' that woke up many dozy persons in and out of uniform who had not realised that Britain was facing a desperate crisis. Churchill, Beaverbrook and Dowding were foremost among those who in the summer of 1940 killed off the lingering 'business as usual' attitude of Chamberlain's government and his supporters.

Practice Months

The months of the so-called 'phoney war' (September 1939 to April 1940) were vital to Fighter Command. It was during those months, *after* Hitler's invasion of Poland, that essential experience was gained, by those serving on the ground as well as in the air, that was far more intense and realistic than in any peacetime exercises. Dowding, Park and those who worked with them, military or civilian, began to learn what their fighters could do by themselves and with help from ground controllers and a chain of coastal radar ('RDF stations').

As explained earlier, radar had been developed before the war by scientists working with airmen and during the 'practice months', operators of these new-fangled gadgets gradually learned to use them, in spotting and tracking intruders at both high and low levels. There was also an Observer Corps, mostly civilians, who formed a network throughout Britain. From April 1936, it was commanded by a regular RAF officer, Air Commodore Alfred Warrington-Morris, until his retirement in 1944. Given that RDF, even when it worked properly, gave Dowding and Park no help once intruders had crossed the coast, these observers – who manned their posts non-stop until the end of the war – were an invaluable help. Neither Churchill nor Lindemann contributed anything *practical* to Fighter Command's efforts in the critical years, 1936-1940.

As soon as the war began, Dowding had been anxious about the employment of his precious fighters across the Channel to meet the threat of a German invasion of Western Europe. He knew that bad weather and the need to re-fuel and re-arm made a maintenance base in France necessary and recognised the thin end of a wedge. If the Germans *did* invade, it was possible that all his fighters would be sent to resist them and resources would be drained away, as through a running tap, on the Continent. This would leave Britain dangerously, if not fatally, exposed. As a result of his efforts to co-ordinate British and French fighter cover over Channel convoys, Dowding was dismayed to learn how weak the French air force was: in aircraft (numbers and quality), organisation on the ground as well as in the air and in leadership.

The Ugly Sisters

John Salmond, head of the RAF in the years 1930 to 1933, was recalled to active service in May 1940 in his sixtieth year. He went to Harrogate, in the West Riding of Yorkshire, to take charge of armament production in Beaverbrook's new ministry. Although he had reached the top of what was then a small service, he had never been 'an especially studious man, even by the unexacting standards of the RAF', thought David Omissi, and had declined since his retirement. For example, he wrote to Trenchard on 11 May: 'Will the government now make up its mind that it is essential to bomb the sources of supply of German aircraft *in Germany*?' Hitler will bomb anything and everything in Britain when it suits him: 'and if we don't bomb his sources of supply now, when we are in a favourable position to do so and he is not, being immersed in operations in Belgium and Holland [not to mention France], then it may be too late.'

Salmond was clearly unaware of the capabilities of either the British bombers then in service or the German fighters which would oppose them as they flew unescorted to and from their targets. His 'great hope', he added, was that Trenchard would be rescued from his long retirement and be appointed Secretary of State for Air. This wish would be dashed, though he and Trenchard, conniving together, like the Ugly Sisters, played an important part in getting Dowding – admittedly, an unlikely Cinderella, but at least as worthy of memory – out of Bentley Priory. Mercifully, they did not succeed until late in November 1940. They also opposed Newall, who earned their displeasure by wavering from the true faith of a bomber offensive, ignoring the fact – as they had done throughout their careers – that British bombers were inadequate in every measurable way: number of machines; navigational skill of crews; range; altitude; speed; weight and quality of bombs carried; defensive armour and armament.

Salmond then outlined his thoughts on Germany's likely approach to the problem of conquering Britain. The Germans will use troop-carriers and parachutists. He believed that they 'are prepared to sacrifice machines to any extent so long as they effect a landing, and will land even in places where great risk is entailed to the personnel they are carrying'. All Britain's open spaces must therefore be 'under suspicion' because parachutists 'land on a concerted plan and frequently in large numbers. They are very highly trained in self-concealment before attacking their objective. They are normally dropped at night.'

Let us pause here to reflect that these 'troop-carriers' would be virtually defenceless Junkers Ju 52s. See them trundling slowly across the Channel, in daylight or darkness, each with a maximum of sixteen lightly-armed soldiers aboard. The British did not know how many had been lost during the campaigns in Norway and the Netherlands, but they did know that losses had been heavy: actually, more than 300, all with well-trained crews in addition to soldiers aboard. If used in operations against an unconquered Britain, escort would be more difficult, air and ground defences would offer a far stronger challenge than those available in Norway or the Netherlands and it does seem as if losses would have been catastrophic.

In any case, how serious would be the threat to Britain posed by widely-scattered, lightly-armed troops, without supporting tanks, artillery or trucks, who could not be reinforced with replacements, weapons, ammunition, food, water and medical services unless resistance had collapsed? Salmond, who knew little about Fighter Command's defensive system, understood that an Observer Corps network covered the whole country, but 'the difficulty of seeing parachutists, etc., at night is always very great'.

It followed therefore, in Salmond's mind, that use must be made of 'an enormous untapped reserve of watchers in the youth of the country of non-military age, e.g., boy scouts, National Cadet Organisation, Air Defence Cadets, etc.' These stout lads could quickly be made into a force of 'first-class protective value'. As for the defence of aerodromes, Salmond admitted that he was 'not in the picture', but he doubted whether army units would arrive quickly enough in the event of enemy landings. Satellite airfields not actually in use should be obstructed. Were there 'crows nests' on hangar roofs, where men could watch for approaching enemy bombers and shoot them down – presumably with rifle or machine-gun fire – as they attempted to land or passed overhead?

There is more of this nonsense, which nowhere mentions either Fighter Command or Dowding. Yet Salmond would later be selected to chair an enquiry into Dowding's conduct of night defence, about which he knew nothing. Salmond resigned from his position with the Ministry of Production in March 1941 and played no further part in important affairs. Nor did Trenchard, although he spent the rest of the war milking his reputation within the RAF to invite himself to wherever there was interesting action, holding busy men 'with his glittering eye', rather like a more amiable Ancient Mariner. Foolish as the Ugly Sisters may now seem, even in June 1941 – with German forces fully engaged by an invasion of the Soviet Union – Churchill offered the War Office an opinion equally foolish, given the information available to him about German and British aviation resources: 'We have to contemplate the descent, from the air, of perhaps 250,000 parachutists, glider-borne or crash-landed aeroplane troops.'

An Immortal Letter

The Norwegian fiasco had an important effect on Dowding. If the Royal Navy could fail so dismally to prevent the Germans from mounting a successful seaborne invasion of Norway, how much easier would be an invasion of Britain across the Channel, if Fighter Command were defeated? The evidence of crass incompetence in the management of military affairs was very much in Dowding's mind when the German assault on Western Europe began. What reliance could a prudent commander place on soldiers, sailors or politicians, British or French? Dowding therefore resisted demands to allow his precious fighters, especially his few Spitfires, to cross the Channel in an attempt to stem the assault. Even so, six squadrons of Hurricanes were in France on the first day of the assault and within a week he had lost the equivalent of six more. Another four were fighting over France each day and returning, if they could, to England each evening.

The pressure for yet more assistance was 'relentless and inexorable', in Dowding's words, so on the morning of 15 May he attended a Cabinet meeting at which Newall spoke up, resisting the sending of any more fighters to France. Dowding did not confront Churchill on that occasion. Following Newall, he spoke calmly and lucidly, making a case for retaining all his fighters for home defence. At that time, however, the British ground forces were still in position near Brussels and could not be denied aerial support. Next day, 16 May, the Air Ministry ordered Dowding to prepare eight half-squadrons for service in France. He then had only thirty-six on hand. In his postwar memoirs, Churchill mistakenly claimed that Dowding had told him that only twenty-five squadrons were needed for home defence, not fifty-two. After the war, when the mistake was pointed out to him, he simply refused to correct it.

Dowding wrote to the Air Ministry on 16 May. We must face the possibility, he penned, that the Allied armies might be defeated. In that case, he assumed that Britain would fight on, so did Churchill, but by no means all Britons in high places agreed and the Prime Minister had to use his immense skill in passionate argument to outface them. If Britain did fight on, Dowding continued, he was sure that Britain would be able 'to carry on the war single-handed for some time', if not indefinitely, if 'an adequate fighter force' survived, and the fleet remained in being while home forces were 'suitably organised'. But if the air defence force was drained away in an attempt to prevent defeat in France, the result 'will involve the final, complete and irremediable defeat of this country'.

This letter has become the most famous written by an airman at any time in any country to any recipient. The framed original now hangs in an honoured place in the RAF College at Cranwell in Lincolnshire, a better resting-place for it than any office of the now defunct Air Ministry or even than the National Archives at Kew in London. It has been quoted in countless books, articles, radio and television documentaries, films, websites, lectures, essays and conversations on the Battle of Britain. It is less well known that Newall attached this letter to a clear statement on air defence weakness circulated to his fellow chiefs of staff that same day.

Churchill flew to France on 16 May and telegraphed to London asking for six more squadrons to be sent, as well as the eight half-squadrons. They would give the French army a last chance 'to rally its bravery and strength'. He then made a point that always weighed heavily with him: 'It would not be good historically if their request were denied and their ruin resulted.' It would look a whole lot worse, 'historically', if Britain's ruin followed.

He then added, in his airy way, 'night bombardment by a strong force of heavy bombers can no doubt be arranged'. Every fighter in Britain (or in France) could not prevent France's 'ruin' in May-June 1940 and as for 'heavy bombers', there were none. British and French medium bombers could not hit German targets hard or accurately in daylight, let alone in darkness. This was the payoff for years of talk and little action, as Churchill himself had said and written so eloquently often.

The War Cabinet met at 11 pm on 16 May and agreed, in its supine way, to Churchill's request. He returned to England the next day, declaring that this was 'the gravest decision that a British Cabinet ever had to make'. At this critical moment, Newall told the Cabinet that there were not enough airfields in France for the extra squadrons, so they remained in Kent and crossed the Channel each day. Churchill at last saw the light on 19 May and ruled that no more fighters were to leave Britain no matter how serious the situation became in France. All but three squadrons returned home on the 24th and Dowding told the Air Ministry that their return had 'converted a desperate situation into a serious one'.

Churchill asked the chiefs of staff on the 27th to report on Britain's prospects of continuing the war 'alone against Germany and probably Italy'. They replied that as long as Fighter Command remained 'in being', the RAF and the Royal Navy together should be able to prevent a German invasion. But if Germany obtained air superiority, the navy could only prevent an invasion 'for a time'; not for 'an indefinite period'.

Harold Larnder, head of the Research Section at Bentley Priory, was asked by Dowding on 2 June to prepare a simple graph showing the balance of Hurricane 'wastage' against replacements. By then, Dowding had lost over 400 fighters and as many of his, even more precious, peacetime trained pilots in just three weeks since the German invasion began. He therefore sought and obtained permission to attend another Cabinet meeting on 3 June. He showed the graph to Churchill: 'If the present rate of wastage continues for another fortnight,' he said, 'we shall not have a single Hurricane left in France or in this country.' Once again, Newall supported him.

BATTLE OF BRITAIN: AIR DEFENCE SECTORS

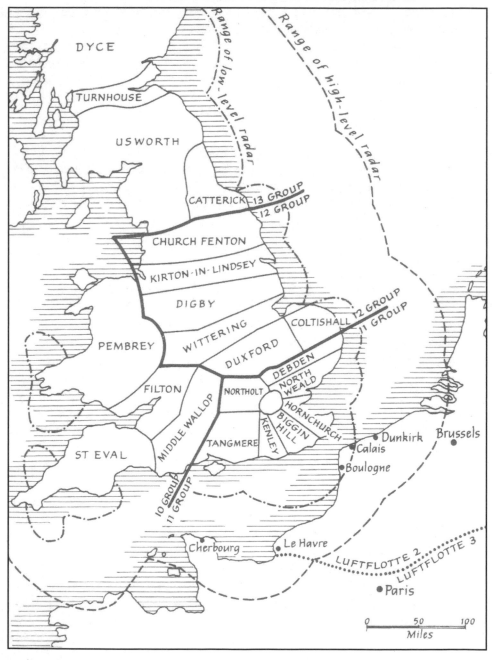

13

The Battle of Britain and After,
1940-2010

Avoiding Defeat

Then came what we know as the Battle of Britain: 'A contest like no other in human experience, witnessed by millions of people continuing humdrum daily lives,' as Max Hastings wrote, 'newspapers were delivered and honey was served for tea a few thousand feet beneath one of the decisive battlefields of history.' After the European war ended, Churchill was asked what had been for him the worst moment. Two of them, he replied, 'when everything was at stake': the Battle of Britain and the Battle of the Atlantic.

Dowding's task, although vital, was strategically simple. He was well aware that he could not achieve *victory*, but he could *avoid defeat* until bad weather made an invasion impossible in 1940. When good weather returned, six months later, the British Army should be greatly enlarged, re-organised and re-equipped; coastal defences improved, and the whole air force – not only Fighter Command – would be stronger.

There would have been time for intensive training, more and better aircraft would be on hand, and the Royal Navy would remain on full alert. As Colville, one of Churchill's secretaries, wrote in his diary for 14 June: 'If we can hold on until November, we shall have won the war. The holding-on is going to be a grim business, a chance for the whale to prove his superiority to the elephant.' Grimmer than Colville thought, because he expected Roosevelt to be re-elected President of the United States in that month and to declare war on Germany immediately. Colville was unaware of American military weakness at that time. 'When the Germans struck in the West,' wrote Weinberg, 'the United States army could field fewer than a third the number of divisions Belgium put in the field; there were all of 150 fighters and fifty heavy bombers in the army air force.'

'Well! Now it is England [meaning, 'Britain and her empire'] against Germany,' wrote Dowding to Churchill on 17 June, 'and I don't envy them their job.' In fact, Fighter Command was greatly helped by non-British pilots and ground crews: men from New Zealand, Australia, the United States,

France and, not least, from Poland and Czechoslovakia. Many of them were experienced and all of them highly motivated to fight Germans and (for those who did not speak English) eager to overcome language and cultural difficulties. It took some time for Dowding to accept eastern Europeans as readily as he accepted those from France or Belgium. But he did, and after the battle was full of praise for their 'unsurpassed gallantry'. Hitler would get nothing like the same intensity of support from any of his actual allies or those so-called neutrals who backed him while he seemed to be a winner.

Churchill said on 18 June that the Battle of France was over and the Battle of Britain was about to begin. 'Upon this battle depends the survival of Christian civilisation... Let us act so that future generations will say, "This was their finest hour".' Stirring words, even after so many years of repetition and parody, but neither Churchill nor Dowding, nor indeed the brave airmen and devoted ground crews on both sides of the Channel knew that Hitler had no idea what to do next, at this glorious moment for the Nazi regime.

'We are Very Close to the End of the War'

His forces had triumphed everywhere and many unconquered states were eagerly offering benevolent neutrality, if not active alliance. Hitler had good reason to suppose that a peace with Britain on his terms was likely because Chamberlain and his numerous supporters remained influential. Had Hitler taken no action against Britain during the rest of that summer, 'sensible' men would soon have raised their heads again to resume their pleas for an armistice. Churchill, who remained unpopular with most of Whitehall and Westminster, would have had no outlet for the inspiring rhetoric that swayed popular opinion in favour of fighting on, regardless of Germany's superior power.

If the British fought on, Hitler had several options in addition to aerial attack: a blockade of imports, using U-boats and aircraft; an alliance with Spain, Portugal and Eire, permitting use of key points in the Mediterranean, the Atlantic islands and the west coast of Ireland; overthrowing Stalin's rotten regime in the Soviet Union; encouragement of anti-British sentiment in the Middle East and Asia, pleasing his admirers in Japan; or strengthening isolationist sentiment in the United States.

On 23 June, Josef Goebbels (Hitler's propaganda minister) had good reason to declare: 'We are very close to the end of the war.' Churchill would soon fall, Goebbels thought, and the British people would then set up a 'compromise government'. In March 1939, Goering had assured Count Galeazzo Ciano, the Italian foreign minister, 'rearmament had not progressed very far in Britain and France'. His intelligence experts calculated British air production at 300 aircraft a month by the autumn of 1939 (when the true figure was more than double this and rising fast) and also regarded British air defences as markedly inferior to German. The world, in those happy days, was Hitler's oyster.

Eagle Day

There must be a German writer who has said something akin to Shakespeare's words about fortune following upon taking a tide at the flood, but if so Hitler and his courtiers had not read him. There are, of course, always reasons for missing an opportunity: reasons that only hindsight can clearly reveal. In this case, the Luftwaffe had suffered heavy losses and needed time to set up a ground organisation near the French coast to stock up on fuel, weapons and spares. It was not until 21 July that Goering called a meeting of his senior commanders to consider how to get air superiority in preparation for Operation Sealion, a proposed invasion of Britain. Ten days later, Hitler directed that a major air assault – Eagle Day – be launched from 5 August onwards, and 15 September be considered the target date for Sealion to go ashore.

The British, inspired by Churchill, made good use of the relatively quiet summer weeks between the fall of France and the decision to attempt an invasion of England. On 30 June, for instance, Dowding had fewer than 600 fighters and twice as many pilots available for operations. The early warning system was still 'a work in progress'. By Eagle Day, however, his fighter strength had increased by a quarter and he had another 200 pilots available in addition to those Polish and Czechoslovak pilots who had escaped from Germany and needed no motivation. Everyone on the ground and in the air was becoming more skilful at his or her job every day. They got a further bonus when bad weather delayed the offensive until 13 August. Even then it got off to a muddled start. As Telford Taylor wrote, 'the eagle did not swoop to the kill; rather, he fell off the perch'.

Churchill and Dowding

The Battle of Britain was, in fact, a campaign, and lasted for at least four months, from July to October. The challenges posed were varied and unprecedented. It was fought, moreover, on the British side by a force that had had little opportunity for realistic combat training in peacetime and suffered the loss of many experienced airmen in France. Their replacements were not merely green in combat, they were less competent as pilots.

By July, Luftwaffe bases lay within close range of many British targets and could spread or concentrate attacks to suit itself during long hours of daylight. Dowding, however, was untroubled. He had lunch with Churchill at Chequers on 13 July and: 'the only thing that worried him in life was the ridiculous dreams he had every night; last night he dreamt that there was only one man in England who could use a Bofors gun and his name was William Shakespeare. It was, he said, most disturbing.' Churchill, for once, was lost for words.

In July 1940, Churchill learned that Dowding – a RAF officer whom he had grown to respect – was fending off a fifth attempt to winkle him out of

Bentley Priory: this at a time when a critical air battle was just beginning. Churchill sent a well-merited rebuke on the 10th to Archibald Sinclair, an old friend who was leader of what was left of the Liberal Party whom he had made Secretary of State for Air.

Sinclair was an amiable Scottish aristocrat with pleasant manners, easily overawed by senior officers and officials. Churchill had been 'very much taken aback' to learn that Sinclair intended to remove Dowding from Fighter Command at the end of October. Dowding is 'one of the very best men you have got', Churchill told him, 'and I say this after having been in contact with him for about two years'. He had 'greatly admired the whole of his work', especially in 'resisting immense pressure to dissipate the fighter strength during the great French battle'. Much of that pressure had come, of course, from Churchill himself, who was big enough – on the very eve of the Battle of Britain – to admit that Dowding had been right to resist.

Churchill thought Dowding should remain in office for the rest of the war and might very well be promoted to replace Newall. Sinclair reluctantly agreed to leave Dowding in office. On 10 August, however – at the height of the battle – he wobbled again and Churchill reminded him forcibly of his wishes. By November, however, although the Luftwaffe's daytime offensive had been rebuffed, Fighter Command was unable to prevent its offensive in darkness from causing great harm and demand for changes at the top now became intense. Newall had already gone (replaced by Portal of Bomber Command), Douglas (deputy CAS) replaced Dowding and Leigh-Mallory (head of 12 Group in Fighter Command) replaced Park.

'One of the Greatest Days in History'

The effective resistance offered in south-eastern England led Goering to believe that there could be few fighters available elsewhere. Accordingly, large formations were sent from bases in Norway and Denmark towards north-eastern England on 15 August. Thanks to Dowding's prudence and radar's early warning, 13 Group had enough fighters on hand to challenge them and the Luftwaffe suffered heavy losses. That victory was vital for Dowding. Had the attack succeeded, his defences would have been dangerously stretched from then on. When the crisis came in September, there was no attack on the north-east. Churchill spent part of that day at Bentley Priory and told Colville to give the good news to Chamberlain, then recovering from an operation, who was delighted to hear it.

'So he ought to be,' replied Churchill, 'this is one of the greatest days in history,' he added, with typical exaggeration. Dowding's foresight, he continued in more measured terms, 'deserves high praise, but even more remarkable has been the restraint and the exact measurement of formidable stresses which had reserved a fighter force in the north through all these long weeks of mortal conflict in the south. We must regard the generalship here shown as an example of genius in the art of war.' It was on leaving Park's headquarters at Uxbridge next evening, 16 August, that Churchill uttered his immortal words: 'Never in the field of human conflict has so much been owed by so many to so few.'

On 31 August Churchill invited Dowding and Portal (soon to succeed Newall as CAS) to dine with him at Chequers. Colville was present and noted in his diary:

> 'Dowding is splendid, he stands up to the PM: refuses to be particularly unpleasant about the Germans, and is the very antithesis of the complacency with which so many Englishmen are infected. He told me that he could not understand why the Germans kept on coming in waves instead of concentrating on one mass raid a day which could not be effectively parried.'

These 'scattergun' tactics would not have been followed had Dowding been in command on the other side of the Channel. It seemed obvious to him, and Churchill agreed, that one should use maximum force against targets of the greatest value, as well-led European armies had so often done in the past.

Churchill and Park

On the morning of 15 September, a day later designated 'Battle of Britain Day', Churchill visited Keith Park at Uxbridge. Dowding had chosen him as senior air staff officer in July 1938 and made him responsible for the Command's fighting efficiency. He had excelled as Dowding's right-hand man at Bentley Priory and was sent in April 1940 to command 11 Group, which would become, during that immortal summer, the most vital position in Britain's front-line defence following the German conquest of Western Europe.

If nothing much was happening, Churchill said, 'I'll just sit in the car and do my homework'. Park welcomed him, his wife and a secretary and escorted them down to his bomb-proof operations room, fifty feet below ground level. Churchill had a high regard for Park. Although Dowding exercised supreme command, 'the actual handling of the directions of the squadrons', wrote Churchill after the war, 'was wisely left to 11 Group'. Park's was the group 'on which our fate largely depended. From the beginning of Dunkirk, all the daylight actions in the south of England had already been conducted by him, and all his arrangements and apparatus had been brought to the highest perfection.'

No sooner had the visitors been seated in the 'dress circle' than Park received a radar report that enemy aircraft were massing over Dieppe. Churchill later recalled Park walking up and down behind the map table (on which all aircraft movements, friendly and enemy, were plotted as accurately as possible) 'watching with a vigilant eye every move in the game'. Everyone was working quietly. Churchill said: 'There appear to be many aircraft coming in.' Park replied calmly: 'There'll be someone there to meet them.'

That was the day when the Luftwaffe made its greatest bid for victory in daylight. The effort failed and two days later Hitler postponed an invasion 'until further notice'. 15 September was set aside in 1942 and for every year since as Battle of Britain Day. That battle, wrote Noble Frankland, 'must rank directly with Drake's defeat of the Armada and, though less directly, with Nelson's victory at Trafalgar, as being among the handful of decisive battles in British history'.

Trenchard, however, was displeased. He argued that it was 'wrong to commemorate a battle that had come to be so closely associated with one command'. A curious point of view, even for Trenchard, whose faith in the bomber and low regard for the fighter (or any other type of aircraft) never wavered. Consequently, 'he found it difficult to accept that the RAF's greatest achievement was a *defensive* victory'.

Boyle claimed in his biography of Trenchard that he was the man who prepared the victory in the Battle of Britain. 'This is not so', replied A. J. P. Taylor. 'The Battle of Britain was won by Fighter Command and radar. Trenchard had despised one and knew nothing of the other. What Trenchard prepared was the strategic air offensive of 1940-1941, which was a total failure... Like Haig, his hero, Trenchard was an extremely resolute and dogged commander', but the bombers upon which he pinned his faith proved to be inadequate and their crews were under-trained. Men who were wiser and had a surer grasp of aviation problems would be hard pressed to turn Bomber Command into an effective weapon.

Over the whole campaign, Fighter Command suffered more than 1,000 casualties (over half of them killed) out of nearly 3,000 pilots or air gunners who made at least one sortie. A number of British writers have asserted that Fighter Command was not in danger of defeat at any time in the summer of 1940. Even if the Luftwaffe had overwhelmed Britain's air defences, they believe, it lacked aircraft equipped with armour-piercing bombs or torpedoes, and crews trained in their use that were needed to sink the heavy units of the Royal Navy. If the Luftwaffe had gained control of the air over the Channel and southern England, wrote Hastings: 'Mediterranean experience soon showed that in a hostile air environment, the Royal Navy would have found itself in deep trouble.'

We will never know, of course, what impact a new daylight offensive would have had, beginning perhaps as early as March 1941, following the serious material and morale damage done to Britain during months of night bombing. A renewed offensive would surely be better planned; it would last much longer; Fighter Command's casualties would be heavier; and American reluctance to get involved would have been strengthened. Writers can as easily argue that the Germans could not possibly conquer France, Belgium and the Netherlands in a few weeks in May and June 1940, but they did. 'By great good fortune,' wrote Terraine, 'rational military judgement did not decide the issue. Hitler took the astonishing and lunatic course of attacking the Soviet Union while Britain remained undefeated at his back. So Britain was saved by the folly of her enemies.'

Ultra

Throughout the war, Churchill – and later the Americans – made ever-increasing use of a marvellous source of information about German plans. They did not disclose the secret in their postwar memoirs and it was only revealed in 1974. Churchill had a particular enthusiasm for intelligence information, but he never revealed the source to confound his critics or justify his actions.

In July 1939, Polish code-breaking experts gave duplicates of the German enigma machine to the French and British. Men and women working on 'Ultra' at Bletchley Park in Buckinghamshire intercepted and translated German wireless signals that had been enciphered by that machine, which the Germans believed was invulnerable. That information began to reach the government during the Norwegian campaign, but British armed forces lacked the weapons and skill to make good use of it, as would often be the case until late in 1942.

Ultra provided Dowding with valuable information about the Luftwaffe's organisation, order of battle and equipment. But its information about the timing, size and proposed targets for particular raids usually arrived in Dowding's hands (for handing on to Park and his other group commanders) too late to be of help in meeting raids that had already been and gone. Also, it could not tell if the Germans made last-minute changes of plan as weather worsened or improved, or units were found to have more or fewer aircraft immediately available than had been supposed.

Ultra was unable to tell whether Fighter Command would outlast the Luftwaffe because it was silent on the losses and effective strength of German units and the size of reserves, nor could it forecast changes in methods and objectives because such communications went between Berlin and formations in France by landline. 'For all his major decisions,' concluded the official historians of British intelligence during the Second World War, Dowding 'depended on his own strategic judgement, with no direct assistance from the Enigma.' On 13 October 1940 Churchill was 'astounded' to learn of 'the vast congregation' allowed into the secret. 'The Air Ministry is the worst offender', he said, ordering several recipients to be struck off, and adding Dowding. Until then, perhaps not surprisingly, he had not been on the Air Ministry list.

The Blitz

At about 5 pm on 7 September 1940 the Luftwaffe launched a massive attack on London. During the next hour-and-a-half, nearly 350 bombers (escorted by more than 600 fighters) set fire to docks, oil tanks and warehouses along both banks of the Thames east of the city. They also blasted numerous densely-populated streets. It was by far the most powerful attack yet launched by any air force against any target. For the next seven hours, wave after wave of bombers flew over London, finding fresh targets in the light of fires started earlier. They bombed at leisure, unhindered either by anti-aircraft fire (of which there was little and that ill-directed) or by night fighters (of which there were few and those ill-equipped). Dowding lost twenty-four pilots killed or injured and more than sixty enemy aircraft were destroyed or damaged. During the sixty-eight nights between 7 September and 12 November, there were only ten on which the Luftwaffe did not mount what it regarded as a 'major' raid (one that dropped at least 100 tons of bombs).

At that time, Britain's night defences were not nearly as effective as the day defences. Few heavy anti-aircraft guns were available and all lacked radar assistance to direct fire accurately. Like the barrage balloons and searchlights, they served mainly to keep bombers high. Radio counter-measures effectively upset German guidance beams, but London was an easy target to find without them and it was not too difficult to find other cities in such a small island. As for night fighters, there were, in September, eight squadrons assigned to that duty – six of Blenheims, two of Defiants – all close to useless.

A fighter, specially designed for night work, had begun life as long ago as November 1938, but it would not be until the end of March 1941 that the Bristol Beaufighter, a twin-engined, two-seater, was in regular service. It was very fast, had a long endurance and was powerfully armed. Better still, it benefitted from work done to bridge the gap between scientific research and the solution of the vital practical problem of building a radar set small enough to fit into an aircraft and finding companies capable of mass production. This work was still in progress during the winter of 1940-1941.

Overwhelmed by alarm at the success of German night bombers and anxious to be seen by Whitehall's other authorities, civilian as well as military, to be taking positive action, the Air Ministry chose Salmond on 14 September to chair a meeting of senior officers, among them Douglas, Freeman and Tedder. After two days of deliberation they produced a list of recommendations. Only then was Dowding asked to comment. He rejected most of the recommendations coming from officers who knew nothing about the difficulties of devising an effective system of night defence.

Salmond felt so hotly opposed to Dowding that he considered making his way to Buckingham Palace and demanding that the king sack him personally. Presumably wiser heads informed him that it was now some years since British sovereigns lost the power to act like that. Still raging, he wrote to Trenchard on 25 September: 'As you and I know,' Dowding 'has not got the qualifications of a commander in the field, as he lacks humanity and imagination.' Newall should also be sacked because 'his strategic judgement is completely at fault'. Although Trenchard – the other Ugly Sister – agreed wholeheartedly, he preferred more devious methods of working. 'I never mention that you and I are working in agreement on the matter,' he told Salmond on 4 October, 'as I feel it is more use our apparently being independent, but working for the same cause.' Historians rightly make much of the inept management of the Luftwaffe by Goering and Udet. Given the opportunity, which they so ardently desired, Trenchard and Salmond would have caused as much harm to the RAF.

Salmond wrote to Churchill next day, 5 October. It was 'imperative', he thought, that Dowding go and that was also the opinion of 'most, if not all, service members of the Air Council'. Churchill, however, was not ready to sacrifice a 'genius in the art of war', as he had described Dowding after the Luftwaffe's attack on northern England. He understood more clearly than a couple of retired air marshals, becoming more eccentric by the month, that the difficulties facing Dowding had no easy solution. On 13 October Churchill again had him and Portal as guests at Chequers. He told them that he was sure Britain would win the war, although just at the moment he could not quite see how.

Vice-Admiral Tom Phillips (vice-chief of the Naval Staff) poked in his oar on 16 October. Knowing even less about the problems than Salmond and Trenchard, Phillips recommended to Churchill that day fighters be used on patrol over London in darkness. Churchill invited Dowding to respond, which he did the same day. German bombers flew too high and too fast to be picked up by searchlights, he said. Only reliable airborne radar sets linked to ground radars would serve in a purpose-built fighter with crews helped by blind-flying apparatus and well practiced in taking off and landing in darkness and bad weather.

'You will note,' Dowding ended, 'that Admiral Phillips suggests no method of employment of fighters, but would merely revert to a Micawber-like method of ordering them to fly about and wait for something to turn up.' It was an attitude only too common in the Admiralty, which for years advocated sending out 'hunting groups' of destroyers to look for U-boats in the vastness of the open seas. Only reluctantly and after a great deal of wasted effort did it turn to more intelligent use of its resources.

Dowding wrote several long and detailed letters in October and November, which he circulated widely, about the problems and solutions being sought. True enough, but dull stuff for men in Whitehall in and out of uniform who felt that something dramatic must be done. During September, the Luftwaffe flew about 6,000 sorties over Britain in darkness and lost only four bombers. They killed or seriously injured more than 50,000 civilians in London and other parts of Britain during the last four months of 1940 and who could say what further disasters in darkness and daylight the new year would bring?

Defeat usually costs commanders their jobs, so out they go. Only gradually would the scale of achievement by Dowding and his colleagues before the Blitz be recognised. Britain had not been obliged to make a deal with Hitler, nor had she been invaded and conquered, but how would she fare in 1941? Dowding and Park were replaced by Douglas and Trafford Leigh-Mallory (formerly head of 12 Group) who claimed to have the answers. In fact, another 40,000 civilians were killed or seriously injured by aerial attack during 1941, most of them before mid-year, when the German assault on the Soviet Union began.

The failure of the Luftwaffe to eliminate Fighter Command in the summer of 1940 meant that its forces available to attack the Soviet Union in June 1941 were actually weaker than in the attack on Western Europe in May 1940. Belief in German invincibility was shaken; resistance began in occupied territories and some influential Americans thought Britain might survive. Neither Spain nor Portugal joined the Axis, therefore the Atlantic islands, Gibraltar and Malta did not fall into enemy hands. Churchill 'conducted the nearest-run campaign of the summer against the peace lobby', a large group that adroitly ducked for cover only after the day battle made it clear to everyone – friend, enemy, neutral – that Britain would fight on. But it was Park who wielded the weapon that Dowding created and Churchill decided to use. Had he failed, as he could have done, the efforts of all the others would have come to nought.

Jealousies and Cliquism

The transition of Dowding and Park from Fighter Command in November and December 1940 'to quieter spheres,' wrote Denis Richards in an officially-sanctioned history of the RAF in 1953, 'though doubtless wise in itself, was not perhaps the most impressive immediate reward that might have been devised for the victors of one of the world's decisive battles.' Sir Humphrey Appleby, immortal master of words used to conceal meaning in BBC television's 'Yes Minister' could not have put it better. Sir Humphrey would also have approved of the Air Ministry's best-selling pamphlet on the battle. Written anonymously by one Hilary St George Saunders, a librarian in the House of Commons, it carefully avoided even mentioning the names 'Dowding' and 'Park'.

Churchill was angered by the Air Ministry's conduct and in April 1941 asked Sinclair to explain. Although it was a time of serious crises in the progress of the war, Churchill found time to condemn an attempt to make 'unpersons' of two outstanding officers. These actions, he told Sinclair, 'are a discredit to the Air Ministry'. Sinclair waffled away in the best Sir Humphrey tradition: we wanted 'to tell a simple story of the fighting from the human side and present it rather as the "soldiers' battle", which it very largely was'. This is nonsense, as everyone who had anything to do with

Fighter Command knew perfectly well. It is difficult to think of any other campaign in recorded history more closely directed from the top, often hour by hour, for months.

Churchill was not impressed and eventually, in August 1943, Sinclair admitted that his petty attitude would not do and saw to the production of an illustrated edition of the pamphlet that not only named Dowding and Park, but even used photographs of them. Tedder, who held a vital office in England throughout 1940 and was well aware of Park's work in that critical year, spoke much more warmly of him than either Sinclair or Richards. 'If ever any one man won the Battle of Britain,' said Tedder (by then CAS, in February 1947), 'he did. I don't believe it is realised how much that one man, with his leadership, his calm judgement and his skill, did to save not only this country, but the world.'

For years senior officers of the navy and army, civil servants and politicians had been exasperated by the muddle, indecision and conflicting statements regularly emerging from the Air Ministry's various offices. In Churchill's opinion, based on years of close observation, an opinion supplemented by a steady stream of information coming from intelligent, but exasperated RAF officers, 'jealousies and cliquism' were rampant in 'a most cumbrous and ill-working administrative machine'.

As long ago as July 1934, a retired air commodore, Peregrine Fellowes, had complained to Churchill about the serious lack of 'practical knowledge of flying' among the Air Ministry's senior officers. Many of them, he said, 'seldom flew even as passengers'. The Air Ministry's top brass – under Salmond, Ellington or Newall, with the 'retired' Trenchard constantly prowling various corridors – amply justify Churchill's contempt. He had formed a low opinion of the ministry in 1935 and only a few officers earned his respect during the next decade.

New Men in Charge

There was a strong belief in the Air Ministry that Fighter Command could have acted more aggressively even during the day battle, and that it must do so in 1941. It was not unreasonable for Churchill and Beaverbrook, such staunch allies of Dowding throughout the summer of 1940, to accept that new men, so strongly backed inside and outside the Air Ministry, could do better. If, however, there had been a second daylight battle in 1941 – as was widely expected by Britons, Germans, conquered Europeans, hesitant allies and apprehensive neutrals – it might well have been lost because Douglas and Leigh-Mallory were far less skilled as operational commanders than Dowding and Park.

On 29 December 1940 came one of the most destructive of all German raids on London. The night-fighter force, admitted Douglas after the war, 'had no success'. It was not until effective radar equipment, on the ground and in the air, came into service that a significant number of interceptions were achieved. In April 150 German bombers were withdrawn from France for a campaign in the Balkans and more left in May to prepare for the assault on the Soviet Union. Even with greatly-reduced forces, the Luftwaffe was able to carry out the most damaging attack London suffered throughout the war during the night of 10-11 May. The defences claimed twenty-eight bombers destroyed and Douglas considered this 'eminently satisfactory'.

In fact, only seven of the 550 bombers employed were actually brought down by British defences on the ground or in the air. That raid indicated what a maximum effort, prolonged for months, could have achieved during the summer of 1941. No-one in Britain could know, on the morning of 11 May 1941, that the worst was over. From a German point of view, the worst should just have been beginning.

Trenchard, Salmond and Freeman did not call for the dismissal of Douglas and Leigh-Mallory for their failure. Several senior army officers in the Middle East, abruptly sacked by Churchill, must have wondered why the great man's beady eye did not fix upon these two. The level of training in Fighter Command during 1941, when there was time for it (unlike 1940) was very low, but Douglas was fixated on ceaseless offensive operations even with pilots not ready for combat. Those airmen who fought in the campaigns of 1940 caused serious damage to the Luftwaffe and significant political damage to the Nazi regime, but those who carried out forays across the Channel in 1941 achieved nothing comparable. They were as brave and determined as the men of 1940, but they should not have been fighting there.

As early as 19 January 1941 Churchill was concerned about the management of Fighter Command. He asked Portal why that command had many more crews than aircraft when 700 aircraft were available in storage units. Portal had no answer. At this time, British forces in the Mediterranean and in the Far East were desperately short of modern aircraft and crews for them. The words 'advance' and 'morale' never ceased to thrill Trenchardists. As Portal, a devout disciple of the master, said on 13 February 1941: 'I regard the exercise of the initiative as in itself an extremely important factor in morale, and I would willingly accept equal loss or even more in order to throw the enemy onto the defensive.' It may be that many of the pilots so 'willingly' sacrificed by Portal should have spent more time in training in 1941, pending posting to theatres overseas where their services were really needed, than in attempting pin pricks across the Channel.

The failure of these pin pricks, that kept very few German fighter pilots from either the Eastern Front or the Mediterranean was disguised by extravagant victory claims. In the second half of 1941, the RAF claimed the destruction of more than 700 enemy aircraft over France and the Low Countries. Actually, the Germans lost barely 100 fighters in combat during the whole year (another fifty were lost in accidents or on training flights), but nearly 470 airmen in British service were killed between November 1940 and the end of 1941 for no strategic or political advantage.

They died on two kinds of operation, known as 'Rhubarb' (fighters only) and 'Circus' (when bombers were present). Crews were not given specific targets and were not firmly discouraged from blazing away at random. Consequently, they killed French civilians and their livestock and made it that much easier for the Germans to rule them. Even at the end of 1941, when most of the Luftwaffe had left for the Eastern Front, Douglas was allowed by Churchill to keep no fewer than seventy-five squadrons of day fighters in Britain, against thirty-four assigned for the whole of the Middle East. It was a misjudgement that helped to delay Allied victory over much weaker forces in that theatre.

American Interlude

While Dowding was still at Bentley Priory, Sinclair told him of the government's need to strengthen Britain's organisation in the United States (still neutral) for selecting, modifying and purchasing aircraft and weapons. The appointment of an airman with both professional knowledge and recent experience of combat needs lay within Beaverbrook's control. He wanted Dowding to have it and Sinclair agreed. Dowding was reluctant, but next day, 14 November, Churchill explained to him the importance of getting American war aviation to develop along the right lines, in step with that of Britain, adding that the 'public interest, of which I am the judge', required his consent. Dowding had no answer to that and later Churchill told Sinclair: 'I think he will perform the task very well, and I will give him a letter for the President.'

Churchill pointed out to Sinclair, who needed constant reminding, that 'I have a very great regard for this officer and admiration for his qualities and achievements'. Henry Tizard (who had been sent to the United States in August as head of a mission to exchange secret information with American authorities) sent Dowding some notes on 21 November about what he had learned. 'All members of my mission,' he wrote, 'including particularly the service members, were quite definitely of the opinion that even in those directions where the Americans were technically efficient, they had not thought out operational problems, and it is on that side that you may be able to help them most.'

Dowding arrived in Washington early in January 1941 and was warmly welcomed by everyone who mattered, civilian or military. This was partly because he represented Britain at a time when many Americans were becoming convinced that with their help Hitler might be defeated, but mostly because he was the first commander who had withstood a German assault. The press liked him because he was no smiling smoothy, a type – both British and American – with which they were only too familiar. Also, he praised aspects of the American aircraft industry, especially its navigational instruments and bomb sights. He pressed for the urgent production in both the United States and Britain of airborne radar sets. This was done, a decision that proved of great value to both countries.

Having guarded against the danger of losing the war and having, he hoped, made the base secure, Dowding now felt able to consider how it could be won. He thought it could be done by a combination of bombing and blockade, without a massive invasion of the Continent. Here he was mistaken, but he was right to say that U-boats would soon prove to be a greater menace to Britain than bombers, day or night.

On 20 April Dowding set out for Beaverbrook his impression of aircraft plants which he had visited in the United States and Canada. Construction, design and equipment were all, he thought, excellent. But the Americans, naturally enough, knew little about 'actual war requirements', especially in armour and the effects on airframes and engines of gunfire. Although the aircraft industry was not suffering from strikes (so far), the pace at which manufacturers got government permission to proceed with orders was as slow as it had been in Britain before the war. As for the Atlantic Ferry Organisation (ATFERO), whereby American-built aircraft were flown to England, 'the muddle, lack of planning and complete unpreparedness' were shameful.

When Lord Lothian, British Ambassador to the United States, had died in December 1940, Churchill had taken the opportunity to despatch Halifax to Washington as his replacement. He had arrived, most reluctantly, in January and at once backed a campaign urging Americans to subscribe to the RAF Benevolent Fund. Dowding was a member of the fund-raising committee, but he thought it 'wrong and humiliating' to press Americans for help and said so, publicly. Halifax rebuked him, but Dowding was unrepentant: 'My position on the committee entitled me to object to this barefaced panhandling.'

To accuse a noble lord – ex-Viceroy of India, ex-Foreign Secretary, nearly a Prime Minister – of 'panhandling', behaving like a dropout, begging in the street, was a dreadful insult. Protected against unkindness all his life, deeply infected by Victorian 'high-mindedness and humbug', Halifax was very aggrieved. Dowding, a man of integrity as well as outstanding ability, would not bow to a man who was notable, as his biographer wrote, for no quality higher than a 'puzzled rectitude'. General Sir Hugh Tudor, who had known Churchill since their days in South Africa, wrote to him in September 1938 dismissing Halifax as 'a pious rabbit'. But let us never forget that this lightweight, to put it kindly, could so easily have been appointed Prime Minister in May 1940.

Jack Slessor, Director of Plans in the Air Ministry, had been sent to Washington in November 1940 to set out the RAF's needs and do what he could to get American help. An able officer, but only too ready to regard most other senior airmen with contempt, he could not believe that Dowding's presence in the United States would benefit Britain. A man of limitless confidence in his own opinions, Slessor took it upon himself to advise Portal to see that Dowding was provided with detailed instructions and a minder from the embassy to vet all his statements. Portal, wiser than Slessor, took no action and soon learned – especially from Beaverbrook – that most Americans liked what Dowding had to say. Halifax, however, asked Churchill on 25 March to summon him home, on the grounds that his personal opinions contradicted official thoughts, as Halifax understood them. Beaverbrook stood up for Dowding, but he himself had no wish to make a new career in the United States and Churchill eventually agreed that he should come home, which he did early in May 1941.

Halifax remained in Washington, publicly supported but privately bypassed, for the rest of the war. He was allowed no significant role in the constant and vitally important questions arising between Churchill, Roosevelt and their principal advisers. To General George C. Marshall, head of the US Army, Field Marshal Sir John Dill, head of the British Joint Staff Mission in Washington, was the Briton who mattered. Insofar as there was a 'special relationship' between Britain and the United States it was effectively represented by Dill and Marshall from August 1941 until Dill's death in November 1944. It was at Marshall's insistence that he was accorded the rare honour for a non-American of burial in Arlington cemetery, Washington. They had become friends, as well as allies, unofficially sharing their opinions and the information that came before them. They were far closer than Roosevelt and Churchill.

Dowding was one of the few Britons of indisputable military quality and personal merit whom Americans had met in recent years: a refreshing contrast to the aloof nonentity Halifax and those of similar stamp who found comfortable lurks in Washington. His stay was brief, but it did help American leaders, civilian and military, to learn that Churchill was not alone in his determination to resist Hitler. From then until the end of the European war, Americans would meet many other exceptional Britons. Dowding, in this sense, was among 'the first of the few'.

An Official Despatch

Churchill recommended that Dowding succeed Longmore, sacked in May 1941 as head of Middle East Air Command, but Sinclair and Portal both objected, wisely preferring to promote Tedder, Longmore's deputy. Early in June Churchill wanted Dowding to take over Army Co-operation Command from Barratt, but Sinclair, backed by Portal, refused. In September Tedder fell out of favour with Churchill, who again urged the appointment of Dowding. Sinclair and Portal, strongly supported by Freeman (Portal's deputy) objected – even more wisely this time, because Tedder was already proving to be an outstanding commander.

Although the Air Ministry was right to reject Dowding for these commands, Churchill's advocacy shows the strength of his regard. The fact that Churchill accepted his rebuffs shows also a critical difference between his use of power and Hitler's.

On 29 June 1941 Dowding was asked to take on a job he could not refuse and no-one in the Air Ministry could deny his right to do it. This was to write a despatch on the Battle of Britain. He would have to work quickly because he was to be retired, for no good reason, as from 1 October. This date was nearly seven months before his sixtieth birthday – 24 April 1942 – the date on which he had earlier been told he must retire. No doubt that piece of information had been misfiled or lost somewhere in the Air Minstry's bowels. As one would expect, he submitted his report well ahead of the deadline, on 20 August. He had no hand in the production of what was officially regarded as the Air Ministry's 'admirable' pamphlet on the battle and was not even consulted by its anonymous author.

He did, however, review it for the *Sunday Chronicle* on 26 October 1941, observing that it tended 'to exaggerate the ease with which the most dangerous assault which has ever been made on this country was beaten off'. Park's contribution, he added, should be more widely known. 'His initiative and resource in countering each new move on the part of the enemy, and his leadership of the gallant men whom he commanded, were beyond all praise.' Heart-warming words from a man not given to praising lightly. Dowding also wrote that the Hurricane was a good thirty miles an hour slower than the pamphlet stated, and Fighter Command was by no means stronger at the end of the battle than before it, as its author (reflecting the opinion of Douglas) asserted.

Numerous experienced pilots had been killed, injured or posted overseas and their replacements were far less skilled as pilots and therefore more vulnerable in combat. Neither Douglas nor Leigh-Mallory ever accepted that one well-trained pilot was worth two under-trained men, however gallant.

The battle, in Dowding's opinion, really began on the outbreak of war in September 1939. His report is lucid, perceptive and the tone throughout is temperate. His arguments and those of others are calmly summarised. He repeats what was for him the 'fundamental principle' of national defence: 'An adequate and efficient fighter force ensures the security of the base, without which continuous operations are impossible.' He made the point for the umpteenth time in a letter to the eminent military historian Basil Liddell Hart on 27 February 1942: 'You can't win a war with fighters, but you can't do anything at all without them.' He outlined the difficulties of defence in darkness: bringing into service an effective night-fighter; getting airborne radar to work adequately; training personnel on the ground and in the air and – not least – trying to do all this in bad weather when German raids were constant. 'I had to leave the development of night interception at a very

Count Ferdinand von Zeppelin. Churchill's aviation interests began at the age of thirty-three in 1908, with reports of the flight tests carried out by Zeppelin's airships in Germany.

Top: Zeppelin LZ224, first flown in June 1908.

Left: Captain Gilbert Wildman Lushington. One of the pilots who tried to teach Churchill to fly. Sadly, Lushington was killed, only two days after his first flight with Churchill, in a flying accident.

Above: Churchill, after flying – with a pilot – over the fleet, 1914.

Top: Churchill, after a flight with a pilot in 1915.

Middle left: A German LVG biplane, one of which made the first raid on London, 28 November 1916. According to *The Times*, in July 1917, the raid by this frail biplane was: 'the event of last year [that] has been of most significance to the future of humanity.'

Middle right: Charles Samson: Churchill greatly admired his skill and courage as a pilot during the Great War.

Left: Felixstowe F2A flying boat.

Above: Curtiss H12 'Large America' flying boat.

Left: Damage caused by a Zeppelin, Baytree Road, Brixton, 1916.

Below: A non-rigid airship (SSZ) on patrol over the North Sea.

Above: Marshal of the RAF Lord Trenchard. He had a powerful influence on the development of military aviation – and the careers of favoured officers – in Britain during, and after, the Great War.

Right: Air Vice-Marshal Sir John Salmond, chief of the Air Staff from 1930 to 1933, and a devout Trenchardist.

Below: Two Handley Page 0/400 bombers at Dunkirk on 20 April 1918. Such machines began the RAF's strategic bombing campaign against Germany, which became of great importance during the Second World War.

Top left: De Havilland 9A of 30 Squadron on patrol over the desert in the 1920s. It was a key weapon in justifying the continued independence of the RAF in policing and controlling the British Empire in the Middle East.

Top right: Marshal of the RAF Sir Edward Ellington. He served as chief of the Air Staff during the years 1933-1937.

Middle left: Marshal of the RAF Lord Newall. He was chief of the Air Staff from 1937-1940 and, like Ellington before him, was an officer of limited ability.

Middle right: Vickers Vernon troop-carrier, 1920s. It was a poorly-designed machine. The RAF would fail to match such excellent transport aircraft as the American Douglas DC2 and 3 or the German Junkers Ju 52, which first appeared in the 1930s. The Bristol Bombay was comparable, but only a few were built and Arthur Tedder regretted that fact throughout his time in the Middle East, 1941-1943.

Bottom: Sir Philip Cunliffe-Lister, later Lord Swinton. An outstanding Secretary of State for Air, who should have served for longer in that important role.

Signal reradiated
by aircraft

Direct signal from
BBC to Travelling Laboratory

Top left: Sir Thomas Inskip, Minister for the Co-ordination of Defence, 1936: another man appointed to a vital position who had neither the background nor the influence required in those dangerous days.

Top right: Marshal of the RAF Lord Tedder with Lord Trenchard. Tedder was among the greatest commanders, on any side, during the Second World War and Eisenhower's right-hand man from 1943 to 1945.

Middle: The Daventry radar experiment, February 1935: a critical moment in Britain's decision to develop a chain of radar stations around her eastern and southern coasts.

Bottom: Sir Robert Watson-Watt, one of the essential founding fathers of Britain's system of aerial defence in the 1930s.

"BRING HIM BACK—IT'S YOUR LAST CHANCE"

Top left: Sir Henry Tizard: another of the fathers of an effective British system of aerial defence in the 1930s and 1940s. He was insufficiently valued by Churchill.

Top centre: Frederick Lindemann, later Viscount Cherwell: greatly over-valued by Churchill as his scientific adviser. Far too many of Cherwell's opinions proved to be mistaken.

Top right: Air Chief Marshal Sir Edgar Ludlow-Hewitt, head of Bomber Command, 1937-1940

Bottom: 'Bring him back – it's your last chance!' TAC in *Sunday Pictorial*, 23 April 1939. Ever since the disastrous conference in Munich late in 1938, Prime Minister Neville Chamberlain was under pressure to find a place in his government for Churchill.

Left: Barrage balloon over Tower Bridge: these passive defences effectively deterred low-level attackers.

Below: 'Goering over the Cockney Heart', *Evening Standard*, 11 September 1940. It is indeed fortunate for Britain and her allies that Goering, in 1940 and later, proved to be such an inept military commander.

Top: Focke-Wulf Fw 200C-4 Condor: a converted civil airliner, it caused great harm to Britain's merchant shipping, but there were always too few of them to prevent supplies reaching or departing Britain and they were too fragile for hard service.

Bottom left: Air Chief Marshal Hugh Dowding looks on while King George VI decorates Flight

Lieutenant Alan Deere with a Distinguished Flying Cross at Hornchurch, Essex, on 27 June 1940.

Bottom right: Major General Sir Hastings Ismay: a wise, intelligent officer, who was well able to speak bluntly to the Great Man and in return received his consistent, if sometimes reluctant, support throughout the Second World War.

Above: Sir Archibald Sinclair and Air Chief Marshal Sir Charles Portal, January 1941: for several years, both these officers directed the RAF with great skill and determination.

Above right: Marshal of the RAF Lord Sholto Douglas: a senior officer whose ambitions never matched his abilities. He was most fortunate to rise so high in the RAF.

Right: Air Chief Marshal Sir Robert Brooke-Popham with Field Marshal Archibald Wavell in 1941.

Below: Mitsubishi G3M bomber, known to the Allies as 'Nell'.

Top left: Mitsubishi G4M bomber, known to the Allies as 'Betty'.

Top right: Sketch of General Jan Christian Smuts by Tedder: Smuts was among the very few men, at any time in his long career, who could silence Churchill. Tedder had the highest regard for him.

Bottom left: Douglas and Sir Archibald Sinclair, Secretary of State for Air, 1940-1945. Sinclair admired Douglas and fostered his career.

Middle right: Sketch of Churchill by Tedder: Churchill never regarded Tedder as one of his favourites, but – unlike Hitler – he could be persuaded to recognise outstanding ability and support an officer with whom he was not in sympathy.

Bottom right: Tedder where he was most at ease: sitting on the sand, surrounded by pilots with 'Mary' Coningham to his left.

Left: Park and Coningham at Castel Benito, Tripoli, in February 1943.

Middle: Consolidated B-24 Liberator bomber: a vital weapon in the Allies' need to 'close the gap' in the Atlantic where U-boats could lurk undisturbed.

Bottom left: Churchill and Tedder in the Western Desert, August 1942: this was the time when major changes were made in the British leadership – Auchinleck was relieved and Montgomery appeared.

Bottom right: Air Marshal Sir John Slessor and Captain D. V. Peyton-Ward, RN, at Coastal Command Headquarters in 1943: by that time, the RAF and the RN were working together effectively to defeat the U-boat danger.

Top: 'The Magnificent Seven': Overlord's commanders (less Harris and Spaatz). At the front, Tedder, Eisenhower and Montgomery; behind, Bradley, Ramsay, Leigh-Mallory and Bedell Smith, in Norfolk House, London, on 1 February 1944.

Bottom: V-2 rocket ready for launching: fortunately, for the Allies, the Germans devoted enormous resources to this weapon, which never posed anything like the threat from the V-1.

Inset: V-1 flying bomb on the ground: this relatively cheap and highly effective weapon could have been produced in greater numbers early in 1944 and caused severe disruption to the preparations for D-Day.

Left: Brooke, Ike and Churchill in positive mood towards the end of the war in Europe.

Middle left: Tedder, Marshal Georgi Zhukov and Carl Spaatz in Berlin on 8 May 1945: Eisenhower chose Tedder to represent the Western Allies in formally ending the campaign against Germany.

Middle right: Coningham and General Lewis H. Brereton: he commanded the American tactical air forces and they worked well together in 1944 and 1945.

Bottom: General Sir William Slim, Air Chief Marshal Sir Keith Park and Admiral Sir Arthur Power in Singapore on 12 September 1945: now the campaign against Japan was over.

Top: A Douglas DC-3 dropping supplies to ground troops of the 14th Army in central Burma by parachute early in 1945.

Middle left: Unloading supplies for the Berlin Airlift from an Avro York on 17 September 1948 by jeep headlights because the Russians had cut the electricity supply to Gatow.

Middle right: The 14th Army memorial stone, near the entrance to the Commonwealth War Graves Commission Cemetery at Kohima, India.

Bottom: Churchill and his wife Clementine with Baron Tedder of Glenguin, at the founding of Churchill College, Cambridge on 15 October 1961.

interesting stage', he wrote, but he believed that 'the back of the problem had been broken'.

In August 1942, a year after he submitted his despatch to the Air Ministry, Dowding told Churchill that it had been withheld even from commanders-in-chief and service members of the Air Council. Churchill asked Portal to explain. He at once assured the Prime Minister that Dowding must be mistaken, but on 12 September was obliged to admit that Dowding had been right: due to 'an oversight', wrote Portal, the despatch had not been circulated to all concerned. The oversight was probably not deliberate, merely yet another example of the chronic inability of Air Ministry officials to manage simple routines.

Dowding's Last Task

Dowding's departure from active service was, naturally, a muddle. Although his retirement was duly gazetted and reported in the press, it did not take effect. At least, not for long. He had only been retired for a month when Beaverbrook wrote to tell him on 31 October that Churchill required him for another important job, from which 'immeasurable benefits will flow'. Churchill had instructed Hastings Ismay on 22 October to inform Sinclair that he could not agree to the retirement, without prior consultation, of such an important officer. 'This principle is fully recognised,' said Churchill, 'by the other service departments.'

Sinclair, suitably abashed yet again, invited Dowding to examine the RAF's establishments and suggest reductions: a task, Sinclair told Dowding, of 'extreme delicacy as well as urgency', given the immense strain on human and material resources in a war that, at the time, Britain was not winning.

Dowding refused, but Churchill again told him that he had a right to demand his service. He went on to say that he had only learned of Dowding's retirement from the newspapers, and said it again when Dowding expressed astonishment. Dowding replied that he was very reluctant to work with Sinclair because he disliked and distrusted him. Churchill protested that his old friend 'had never said a word against you, though others may have'. Dowding spent the night of 14-15 November at Chequers, ostensibly to discuss possible methods of saving manpower in the RAF. But Churchill was nicely relaxed with the help of a drink or three and gave Dowding the benefit of his reflections on various subjects, breaking off now and then to join in the chorus of songs from Victorian musicals, issuing from a phonograph. In short, the abstemious (though pipe-smoker) Dowding was no fit companion for an off-duty Churchill. As he later recalled, the evening 'was not suitable for serious conversation'.

Nevertheless, Dowding took on the task. Portal had already assured Churchill that he ran a lean machine and cuts in RAF manpower were impossible. As long ago as November 1940, when Harris moved from 5

Group to the Air Ministry, he had observed that its staffs were 'fantastically bloated' and did what he could to begin 'an enormous and very suitable clear-out'. However it was no use. Dowding tried hard, travelling widely throughout Britain and enquiring closely into manning levels, but he was handicapped by a lack of expert assistance; a deficiency that Portal and Freeman would not remedy.

By the middle of June 1942 he had had enough and made a typically rude message from Freeman, 'an excuse for a show of injured dignity' and resigned on the 18th. Despite crafty opposition, he had found more than 700 officers and 24,000 other ranks tucked quietly away, without real jobs. Sinclair was not pleased and told Dowding that it was 'an act of disloyalty' to bring Air Ministry 'defects' to the Prime Minister's attention. Dowding had no answer to such disgraceful words and returned, this time permanently, to the retired list with effect from 15 July 1942. It amused him to reflect that he had served for eighty-one days beyond his sixtieth birthday.

Unpromotable
On 17 July 1942 Alexander Hardinge (King George VI's private secretary) suggested to the Air Ministry, at the king's request, that Dowding be promoted to the rank of marshal of the RAF. Sinclair certainly consulted Portal and Freeman, probably Trenchard and Salmond and they all agreed, expressing sincere regret, that it could not be done. Only a CAS could hold that rank and the rule could not be broken (although it would be, twice, as we shall see, in 1945). The king was obliged to accept his rebuff.

In May 1943, however, Churchill wrote to Dowding to offer him elevation to the peerage as a baron (not as a viscount) in recognition of 'your ever-memorable services to this country during the Battle of Britain'. This honour – the first such elevation since Trenchard was made a viscount in 1919 – was in the gift of the king and the prime minister and therefore could not be resisted by the Air Ministry.

Two years passed, the war in Europe ended, and Sinclair wrote to Dowding on 9 May 1945 commending his 'inspiring leadership' that helped to save 'our island citadel... The whole nation, indeed freedom-loving men and women the world over will always gratefully remember you and the gallant "few" who fought and flew under your command.' Three weeks later, Sinclair wrote more honestly to Douglas: 'I felt as though I had won a battle when I got Fighter Command into your hands and, looking back, how right I was.' Hundreds of pilots killed on pointless raids over France in 1941-1942 may not have agreed.

Not even in the glow of victory could Dowding be promoted because he had never served as CAS, but that alleged rule was later waived in the case of two officers whose undoubted merits may be considered to fall below those of Dowding. These were Arthur Harris, whose conduct of Bomber

Command during the years 1942 to 1945 has attracted, with good reason, severe criticism as well as high praise, and Sholto Douglas, who held several commands but none at a critical time.

On 20 October 1988, when his particular opponents were all dead or moribund, a statue of Dowding was unveiled by Queen Elizabeth, the Queen Mother, outside St Clement Dane's church in London. The initiative came not from the Ministry of Defence, into which the Air Ministry had by then been buried, but from survivors of those who actually fought in the battle, on the ground as well as in the air. That honour came late enough, but another twenty-one years would pass before a statue of Sir Keith Park was unveiled in Trafalgar Square. Neither statue is an official tribute. Both were made possible by the efforts of countless private individuals. Park's statue stood in Trafalgar Square for six months (November 2009 to May 2010) and is now in the RAF Museum at Hendon. Another statue of him now stands, permanently, in Waterloo Place, near New Zealand House, and was unveiled on 15 September 2010, the seventieth anniversary of Battle of Britain Day.

14

Disunity and Defeat in the Middle East, 1940-1941

An Unsinkable Aircraft Carrier

In January 1942, Keith Park was pulled out of Flying Training Command and sent to Egypt at a time of acute crisis for the British Empire, the Soviet Union and the United States. He was to be Air Defence Commander of the Delta Area, a position similar to that he had held at 11 Group: handling fighters (in darkness as well as daylight), anti-aircraft guns and searchlights, supported by a radar chain and ground observers. After six months there he was sent to Malta. Between Gibraltar and the incomplete defences at El Alamein – a distance of over 2,000 miles – Malta was the sole British base. This 'unsinkable aircraft carrier', anchored a mere sixty miles south of Axis aerodromes in Sicily, had already suffered heavy air attack. On 2 July, the eve of Park's transfer there, Churchill told Parliament that there was, at that moment, 'a recession of our hopes and prospects in the Middle East and in the Mediterranean unequalled since the fall of France'.

Yet the very success of Rommel's offensive averted Operation Hercules, a planned invasion of Malta. At Rommel's request, it was postponed on 23 June and during the next few days he reached out for what seemed the available prizes of the Nile Delta and the Suez Canal. Had they fallen, the surrender of Malta would have followed without the need for a costly invasion. Hitler's agreement to Rommel's request proved to be one of the war's most fateful decisions because Rommel was still outflanked along his lines of communication by naval and air power based on Malta. The failure to conquer that island led directly to Rommel's defeat because half his supplies were destroyed by attacks launched from Malta.

Park's conduct of offensive operations during the rest of 1942 earned him high praise from Portal who told him in November that he was to be knighted (KBE, personally invested by King George in June 1943). Soldiers also praised him. Archibald Nye (second in command of the British Army) wrote to Ronald Scobie (commanding Malta's soldiers) in December: 'If you read the English newspapers, you rather get the impression that Rommel was beaten solely by the brilliance of our generals. That, of course, is very good publicity, but it is very bad history!'

An American general, Dwight D. Eisenhower, was equally impressed by the efforts of Park and his men. In a telegram to Churchill on 5 December he wrote: 'Daily reports show that Malta is straining every nerve to help us, and I have nothing but praise for the work Park has done.'

'A Man of Nuts and Bolts'

Middle East Air Command was a vast, almost square territory: from Gibraltar south to Takoradi on the coast of Ghana is nearly 2,000 miles, from Takoradi east to Aden in Yemen about 3,000, from Aden north to Habbaniya in Iraq 1,400 miles and from Habbaniya west to Gibraltar twice that distance.

Churchill had rejected Portal's initial recommendation that Tedder be sent there as Longmore's deputy, believing him to be a mere technician, 'a man of nuts and bolts'; useful, but not for operational command, and unlikely to provide inspirational leadership in a war currently being lost. 'It was not true,' Churchill told Tedder in August 1942, making one of his rare apologies, 'and I was not told the truth. I am sorry.'

Yet Tedder's record up to December 1940 suggests that he was a man of pen and ink, if not of nuts and bolts, and Churchill therefore had good reason for rejecting him as a commander of fighting men. Opportunity, however, is the mother of greatness and 26 November 1940 (the day on which Tedder was appointed) marks the moment when an exceptional national and allied commander began to emerge. In Terraine's opinion, he was 'the outstanding airman of the war, with the largest view of its conduct'.

Sideshows

The war in the Mediterranean deeply concerned Churchill. It mattered a great deal to the men and women who served and suffered there under British command. Their defeats and victories have been the focus of intense attention by many postwar writers, especially in Britain, and yet they were sideshows in this most terrible of wars. Until 1942, only four British divisions – amply provided with American tanks and aircraft – fought against four of Germany's 170 divisions. As for Italy, Mussolini believed, wrote Denis Mack Smith: 'that British troops would be unable to fight in the heat of North Africa and hence there would be no difficulty about his conquest of Egypt. Tunisia would be another easy victim.'

He was mistaken. If Italy had remained neutral, the British would have had no opportunity to fight against a beatable enemy and like Franco and Salazar, Mussolini would probably have lived out his days in comfort and died in his bed. For Americans, despite the huge resources of men and material they eventually poured into the Mediterranean campaign, it was always an exasperating prelude to a direct assault on occupied Europe, one that mattered less to most of them than the war against Japan. As for Stalin, the Mediterranean campaigns were a distraction from the real war on the Eastern Front.

Although Allied efforts in the Mediterranean never came close to winning the war, Britons were elated in November 1940, at the height of the Blitz, to learn that torpedo bombers had sunk three of Italy's six battleships. They had been anchored in Taranto, a major port in the Heel: safe, the Italians believed, from attack by sea or air. It was Britain's first naval/air victory of the war and greatly eased the problems faced by her Mediterranean forces because next day all the seaworthy vessels left for Italy's west coast, thereby reducing the threat to British convoys in the Mediterranean.

Britons, encouraged by Churchill, loved the sideshows. 'Special forces absorbed a dismayingly high proportion of Britain's most ardent warriors, volunteers attracted by the prospect of early independent action.' They reflected Churchill's belief, as Hastings wrote, that 'war should, as far as possible, entertain its participants and showcase feats of daring to inspire the populace'. These 'private armies', eager to butcher and bolt, sometimes earned dramatic newspaper headlines (which always mattered to Churchill) and have left us entertaining memoirs, but the regular army was always short of good infantrymen in vital battles against well-trained and highly-motivated enemies. He was an amateur meddler saved from worse disasters primarily by Soviet and American resources in men and commanders, aided by those exceptional commanders in all three services who emerged during this cruel war. They had, in common, ways to resist, restrain or simply work round Churchill. At the same time, they benefitted hugely from the labours of civilian scientists and technicians whose names are barely known.

From Takoradi to Cairo

Meanwhile, in December 1940 Tedder took up his new command. Wiser than Boyd, he chose to examine a newly-established aircraft assembly base at Takoradi (on the coast of modern Ghana) en route to Cairo. He flew there at his ease, aboard a civilian flying boat. The flow of crated aircraft to Takoradi from Britain and from the United States was already important for all operations in the Middle East. These aircraft, assembled in Takoradi, then flew via several staging-posts across equatorial Africa to Khartoum and finally down the Nile to Cairo, a total distance of nearly 4,000 miles.

Tedder's decision to visit Takoradi en route to Cairo was helpful to Portal, who was frequently quizzed by Churchill on the time it took to get these aircraft into combat. As always, problems seemed easy to solve in Churchill's office, where he complained of 'frightful congestion' in North Africa, but Tedder was able to convince Portal – one of those necessary men capable of outfacing Churchill – that everything possible was being done with the limited resources available. The flow from Takoradi would become vital after Germany entered what had hitherto been an Italian preserve in February 1941 and made it more dangerous to send aircraft through the Mediterranean. It increased still further after Hitler declared war on the United States in December 1941 and American ships were permitted to carry aircraft across the Atlantic to Takoradi.

'The Greatest Man I Have Ever Met'

In a letter to his wife Rosalinde in February 1941, Tedder reflected on the *purpose* for which he was asking men to risk their lives. 'The Nazi regime has literally inspired their younger generation with a creed – an incredibly evil one – but it is an inspiration.' No-one on our side is saying anything more than we are fighting to win the war. This was because, he thought, 'our noble leaders, our Winstons and our Beavers, are unadulterated materialists'. Churchill had no interest in the postwar world, Tedder believed, and took it for granted that the British Empire would be restored to its prewar grandeur. 'Martial glory' and 'superb honours' were what mattered to him: 'it was not in his nature,' as Hastings wrote, 'to understand that most men cared more about their prospects in a future beyond war than about ribbons and laurels to be acquired during the fighting of it.'

Tedder found his own inspiration in Jan Christian Smuts, whom he met in March 1941 and from then until the day he died gave the same uncritical worship that so many of his British contemporaries lavished on Churchill during and after 1940. Smuts was a man of such overwhelming personality that he could silence even Churchill. He had helped to found the RAF and was now Prime Minister and head of South Africa's armed forces. Reflecting on Smuts in the 1960s, Tedder wrote: 'I thought him then, and still think him, incomparably the greatest man I have ever met, possessing Churchill's versatility and vision without his vices.'

As Colville wrote, Smuts was highly regarded by all who knew him, service or civilian. If Churchill died during the war, Colville thought it would be a great 'imperial idea' if Smuts succeeded him as Prime Minister and put this idea to his mother (a close friend of Queen Mary's) with the idea of it 'filtering through' to the king, who 'can send for whomsoever he wishes'. So thought Colville, but in fact it seems likely that Anthony Eden (Foreign Secretary) would have succeeded.

A Fatal Diversion

In March 1941, Smuts supported the opinion of Eden, Dill (head of the British Army) and all three Middle East commanders that an attempt should be made to fulfill a promise made by Chamberlain in April 1939 to help Greece if Germany invaded. Churchill agreed, though claiming in his postwar memoirs that he did so only because he believed Wavell's desert flank to be secure. Actually, he was eager to revive a desire formed during the Great War to form 'a Balkan front' against Germany that combined the powers of Greece, Yugoslavia and Turkey.

Wishful thinking about this front, as many British historians have written, animated Churchill in both world wars. His 'Balkan front' fantasy was strongly supported by Portal, even though they both knew that Britain lacked the aircraft, soldiers or seamen to resist German power in 1941 and they both knew from intelligence interception that the Germans were planning an assault.

Portal persuaded himself that the RAF could deter Soviet aggression in Romania by threatening to bomb her oil wells from Turkish bases. Francis de Guingand (then a senior planner at Wavell's headquarters in Cairo) published his memoirs as early as January 1947 in which he revealed his opinion that the operation never had a chance of success.

By intervening in Greece, he wrote, 'we brought about disaster in the Western Desert and threw away a chance of clearing up as far as Tripoli'. Cyril Falls, a thoughtful military historian, agreed. He published an account in 1948 of 'a sorry tale of political and strategic frivolity'. Maurice Dean agreed. From an air point of view, the move to Greece made little sense because neither soldiers nor sailors could survive without air support. There were a few RAF squadrons in Greece, but their main logistic support was more than 400 miles away. Airfields in Greece or Crete were few or non-existent. Communications by road, landline, radio or wireless were minimal. Viewed coldly, Dean concluded, 'the operation was just not on'.

Many subsequent historians concur, some in even stronger language: such as John Terraine ('a definite touch of madness'), Stephen Roskill ('little short of lunacy') and Tuvia Ben-Moshe ('another Churchillian disaster'). Despite his early enthusiasm for air power, Churchill 'counted unthinkingly,' as A. J. P. Taylor wrote, 'on the ability of British sea power to hold Crete' and Donald Macintyre agreed: the fleet, thought Churchill, could operate 'without air support in waters dominated by an enemy air force'; this after the disasters in Norway!

Eden claimed in a signal to Churchill on 7 March 1941 that if Longmore 'can hold his own', then 'most of the dangers and difficulties of this enterprise [in Greece] will disappear'. But Longmore's resources were entirely inadequate and no amount of exhortation in London or courage in Greece could increase them.

From a military point of view, Churchill's decision exchanged one certainty for another: victory in North Africa became defeat in Greece, followed by defeat in Crete and in North Africa. Tripoli had been there for the taking in February. 'With Tripoli gone,' wrote Klaus Schmider (a German historian) in 1997, 'an Axis return to the African continent would have required either a major amphibious operation or a *détente* of a fundamental nature between Germany and Vichy France.' Both were unrealistic. The decision to halt the

British advance at El Agheila on 12 February 'must therefore rank as the most gratuitous and incomprehensible error of omission of the whole Second World War'.

Wavell was an enthusiastic advocate of the Greek adventure, but Bernard Freyberg, commander of the garrison, failed to set up a secure base and especially to keep a tight grip on Maleme airfield, in Crete. Driven out of Greece, the British forces were soon driven out of Crete as well. Wavell had Churchill understand that he had set up a strong defensive flank in the Western Desert when he had not. Crete became a costly disaster. Freyberg, chosen to command in Crete, was just the sort of brave warrior whom Churchill most admired, but more is required of high command than bravery. He had no understanding of the impact that aircraft had upon surface operations.

Like Churchill he had a high regard for his own reputation and 'persuaded Churchill to assert in his postwar memoirs that the campaign had cost the Germans 15,000 casualties. The true figure, well known by that time, was 6,000, including 2,000 dead.' From a German point of view, Malta would have been a far more useful conquest, from which to impede British operations in the Mediterranean.

After the war, Tedder was among those who argued that moral and political arguments justified what turned into a disastrous military campaign, one that lengthened the North African campaign by two years and left the Far East open to Japanese aggression. He thought that if Britain had failed to resist the German invasion, the United States might lose their faith in us and cut off supplies of munitions and aircraft.

It seems likely, however, that American opinion would have been more impressed by victory in North Africa than by defeat in Greece and Crete. Churchill told Colville on 28 September 1941: 'So far the government had only made one error of judgment: Greece.' His instinct, he then said, had been against the diversion: 'We could and should have defended Crete and advised the Greek government to make the best terms it could.' Colville was not convinced. 'I seem to remember his influencing the decision in favour of an expedition and Dill being against it,' but Churchill was adept at revising the past to suit current needs.

Thorold and Dawson

On 1 May 1941 Longmore was abruptly summoned to London. He had annoyed Portal and Churchill by complaining too often and at too great a length about his problems and shown too little gratitude for the efforts made to help him. He was replaced on the 4th by Tedder, who well understood that the Air Ministry had no magic wand. A month later, he got someone close to a magician when Air Vice-Marshal Grahame Dawson arrived in Cairo, charged to see what was actually being done behind the battle fronts.

Dawson knew Cairo: he had been chief technical officer there from 1920 to 1925 and was used to managing somehow with insufficient materials. He could improvise and knew about engines, airframes and supply lines; a tireless as well as highly-skilled man, he was just what Tedder needed for 'receiving, modifying, distributing, salvaging, and repairing aircraft and supplies' for the whole command.

Group Captain Henry Thorold's men, recalled Tedder, achieved much in Takoradi, assembling and testing aircraft for the long haul to Egypt, 'and Dawson's men worked wonders in the Middle East. Without them I do not see how we could have mustered sufficient air strength to hold the Germans and Italians in 1941 and to defeat them in 1942 and 1943.'

Ernest Hives, responsible for the production of the Rolls-Royce Merlin engine, said that Dawson always took the 'route one' approach to problems, whether with aircraft or persons and made it work when it mattered most. Yet most accounts of the Desert War barely mention him or Thorold.

The Mokattam hills, outside Cairo, were honeycombed with caves left over from the builders of tombs, palaces and pyramids for the Pharaohs. Dawson had many of them turned into workshops and storage areas. Floors were cemented, walls whitewashed, power and water were laid on; not least, they were cool enough to permit working throughout the day. Air Ministry officials resisted this splendid initiative, but Portal backed Tedder and so Dawson got his way. Fully mobile and self-supporting salvage units were essential, given the time taken to ship out any materials from Britain or the United States. Thanks to Thorold, 'my thorough Thorold', said Tedder, numerous aircraft (with experienced crews) reached Cairo and thanks to Dawson, many of those that crashed in subsequent combat or training flights were collected from the desert, repaired, and flown again, or used as vital spares.

The Old Man of the Sea

Unfortunately, discussion – let alone co-operation – with the naval commander (Admiral Sir Andrew Cunningham) was difficult because he would rarely move from Alexandria, except to go to sea. In November 1938 he had declared that the Royal Navy 'could not visualise any particular combined operation taking place and they were therefore not prepared to devote any considerable sum to equipment for combined training'. He was gradually weaned from such nonsense, but always remained a ship commander who disliked staff work and co-operated reluctantly with other services. He was by no means alone among senior officers in his disregard for services other than his own and Tedder was unusual in his emphasis on all three working together.

Tedder regarded Cunningham as 'our old man of the sea... even more of an anachronism than Wavell'. As he told Freeman on 29 May 1941, it was 'sheer lunacy' that vital decisions concerning all three services had to be made at places more than 100 miles apart. Cunningham urged Churchill to increase the RAF's strength in the Middle East, rightly believing that Fighter Command retained too much strength in Britain, especially after Hitler's invasion of the Soviet Union in June 1941, but he wanted naval control of any reinforcements. He never accepted the argument that it was the air commander's responsibility to decide between army and navy appeals for support, still less the corollary: that the air commander's judgement might be superior to his own.

Near Cape Matapan (Tainaron, the southernmost tip of mainland Greece) in March 1941, Ultra intelligence had enabled twenty-one Fairey Swordfish torpedo-armed biplanes of the Fleet Air Arm, launched by the carrier *Illustrious*, to strike three Italian cruisers and two destroyers. These losses gravely weakened Mussolini's fleet and confirmed German disdain for their Italian allies. But Cunningham's judgement in aviation matters was 'beyond comprehension' for Tedder. His aircraft carrier, *Formidable*, was put out of service for nine critical months as a result of aerial attacks suffered during an ill-conceived and ineptly-executed venture into the Aegean on 26 May 1941. Her absence enabled the Italians to recover control of the central Mediterranean and tied Cunningham to the east of that sea, within shore-based fighter cover.

Defeat can be an effective teacher. Gradually, during 1942, having suffered the loss of many ships, Cunningham's mind broadened, or he learned to listen to his more intelligent staff officers. He accepted a need to co-operate with airmen, especially under the overall command of Eisenhower, an American soldier with a particular gift for persuading officers of all services, British and American, to work together. Another important reason for Cunningham's improving relations with Tedder was their growing exasperation with Churchill, who they saw as a gifted politician, author and orator, who had in abundance the personality and energy to lead a nation in wartime, but who wrongly believed himself to be an authority in all military matters.

A Turning Point?

An opportunity to end British power in the Middle East and capture Iraqi oil fields was missed in April 1941 because Hitler, with his mind fully occupied by plans for Barbarossa, failed to give Rashid Ali of Iraq and his fellow thugs (the so-called 'Golden Square') strong enough backing when they attacked the RAF's main base at Habbaniya, about fifty miles west of Baghdad. Only a handful of obsolete training aircraft stood in their way, but somehow they were hastily converted into bombers and fighters. Some modern aircraft and soldiers arrived to help, together with an absurd signal from Churchill: 'If you have to strike, strike hard.'

These ramshackle forces overcame both Iraqis and a small German air force during April and May in the war's most bizarre conflict. Yet it was a very important conflict, as both Tedder and Churchill recognised. 'If the school had been overcome,' wrote Tedder, 'the Germans would have got a foothold in Iraq. If they had then created a bridgehead behind us, through Vichy-controlled Syria from Greece, our Middle East base could have been nipped out with German forces both to its east and west. We might then well have lost the war.' Who can say? It does, however, seem that the Germans failed to take advantage of a clear opportunity to seize sources of precious oil in Iraq.

A Blunt Battleaxe

Operation Battleaxe, a hastily-planned assault by inexperienced British-led troops, poorly trained and equipped, began on 15 June 1941. They were sent against the carefully-prepared defences of General Erwin Rommel at Halfaya Pass, guarding access from Egypt into eastern Cyrenaica, where Australians held the besieged fortress of Tobruk. Wavell was worried, 'because he is repeatedly told from home that we have strong numerical air superiority', but Tedder told him that this was not so. The available fighter force should, however, be enough to secure and maintain 'a reasonable degree' of superiority.

Portal warned Tedder on the 11th that 'political circles' in London would be watching the RAF's performance closely. Tedder replied at once: he quite understood that if Battleaxe failed, the army would blame the RAF, if possible. Battleaxe did fail. The fighting lasted for three terrible days, ending in a thorough defeat for British forces on the ground and in the air: thirty-six fighters and bombers were lost in exchange for only ten enemy aircraft.

'Every single one of our plans has failed', lamented Churchill on 21 June. As an enthusiast for military affairs, he should have understood that this particular battleaxe was blunt before it was swung: amateurs, no matter how bravely they fight, usually lose to professionals. Churchill – prince of amateurs – refused to accept that the precise knowledge he derived from Ultra about Rommel's strategic situation was more than offset by his superiority on the battlefield.

British information about German dispositions and intentions was inadequate, whereas Rommel's ground and air patrols, aided by intercepted wireless messages, gave an accurate picture of British dispositions and intentions. The Axis victory was not, however, properly exploited because Hitler began a massive invasion of the Soviet Union on 22 June. Meanwhile, Wavell was at last sacked and Claude Auchinleck, an altogether superior soldier and commander, arrived from India to replace him in the struggle against Rommel, now regarded by friend and foe alike as a desert wizard.

Harriman and Lyttelton

Two high-powered civilians – one American, one British – reached Cairo in mid-1941 and began to bring inter-service squabbling under control. First was Averell Harriman, President Roosevelt's special envoy, to sort out problems with the use and storage of American supplies. Two weeks later, on 5 July, Oliver Lyttelton arrived to take up a new appointment as Minister of State, with direct access to the War Cabinet. Both men gave excellent service to their masters in Washington and London, and to the commanders of the armed services.

Before he left England, Portal gave Lyttelton his written opinions on the situation in the Middle East and invited him to show them to Harriman. The great problem, wrote Portal (echoing the reports he received from Tedder), was to get all three services to recognise that 'the war in the Mediterranean is one great combined operation in which constant collaboration and give-and-take between the Cs-in-C is indispensable'. There was an acute need for a combined headquarters, but as long as the general and the admiral 'merely go their independent ways expecting air support to be given automatically on demand, we clearly cannot expect very good results'. Lyttelton duly formed a Middle East Defence Committee, comprising all three Cs-in-C, plus Ambassador Miles Lampson and an army officer in charge of supplies and administration behind the fighting areas.

15

Unity and Victory in the Middle East, 1941-1943

Architect of Victory

Auchinleck was summoned home at the end of July 1941 to discuss prospects for a renewed offensive in the Western Desert and Tedder decided to go with him. Churchill was anxious that 'brisk action' be undertaken to show support for the Soviet Union's desperate resistance to Hitler's forces and, if possible, divert some of them southward. The two commanders met Churchill and the chiefs of staff on 31 July. Next morning, they appeared before the Defence Committee. As always, Churchill was impressed by numbers (airmen, soldiers, sailors and their various weapons) and declared that he could not understand why more of them were not actually engaging the enemy. Tedder explained that he had a frontline strength of no more than 560 modern aircraft of which only three quarters were serviceable at any one time. As for pilots, 200 (including many of the most experienced) were employed on the essential Takoradi-Cairo route, others served as instructors in training units in Kenya, Egypt and the Sudan, units that were no less essential.

Tedder assured Churchill that he was actually *short* of combat-ready pilots. If the Middle East were to become a decisive theatre of operations he would require many more bombers, and crews for them. He pointed out to Churchill and to Air Ministry officials that most aircraft reaching the Middle East had to be unloaded from ships and erected before they could be flown, all of which took time. They operated far from supply and repair depots in a harsh climate and the vastness of the theatre obliged him to maintain several basic ground organisations. Outside the Delta, telephone facilities were so poor that everyone had to rely upon wireless communications and he emphasised that it was always necessary to allow for a higher sickness rate in the tropics than in Britain.

For the moment, Churchill fell silent, though he was never convinced – then or later – that airmen, soldiers or sailors could be properly employed away from the sound of shot and shell, or that weapons, ammunition, transport, food and water did not simply appear at need or that men might sometimes be faced with better-armed and more skilful enemies or be too ill to fight. Worse still, Churchill never agreed that any fighters or bombers currently serving in Britain could be spared for the Middle East, still less for the Far East.

On the morning of his return to Cairo, 12 August, Tedder had the intense pleasure of again meeting Smuts, who had come to visit South African forces and meet Lyttelton and Auchinleck. Shortly before boarding his aircraft to return home on the 16th, Smuts took Tedder by the arm and said: 'The air, the organiser of victory. My heart goes out to you.' Tedder cherished these words, but in a letter to his wife (and in many speeches, lectures and ultimately in his memoirs) he changed 'organiser' to a more elevated word, 'architect'.

Intelligence
Ultra was beginning 'to hit its stride late in 1941 and blossomed magnificently in the summer of 1942', wrote Harold Deutsch. Churchill issued a decisive order on 22 October 1941 that gave Bletchley Park 'extreme priority' in the allocation of personnel. After his heroic leadership in the summer of 1940, this was 'assuredly Churchill's greatest service to Britain and the Allied cause'. Intelligence – not only derived from Ultra – became a vital factor in every Anglo-American campaign. Although Ultra was of great value to victory in the Mediterranean, the Germans had sufficient evidence to doubt the absolute security of their communications and, indeed, 'could, in fact, have prevented the Allied success completely if they had only used the Enigma coding machine correctly'. Here, as in every other war theatre, the Germans contributed to their own downfall.

Getting Together
In July 1941 Tedder replaced Raymond Collishaw, as his field commander, with Arthur Coningham (head of 4 Group in Bomber Command), whom he hoped would manage scarce resources more wisely. Coningham was always known as 'Mary', a version of 'Maori', which he was not, having been born in Brisbane. He was brought up in New Zealand, but his parents had no Maori blood. He would become, in Liddell Hart's words, 'the real hero' of the Desert War.

Ludlow-Hewitt, one of the RAF's shrewdest officers, had told Portal as long ago as April 1940 that Coningham was the pick of his five group commanders as a leader in wartime. Personally, Coningham was everything Tedder was not: famous and much decorated for his feats as a combat, air-display and long-distance pilot, pioneering most of the Takoradi-Cairo route as long ago as 1925. He had also served in Khartoum and knew Egypt. He was a man of style, presence and wide experience, long regarded as a high flier (in several senses of that word).

Tedder told him to 'get together' with the army commander as his first task. This order, recalled Coningham, was of 'fundamental importance and had a direct bearing on the combined fighting of the two services until the end of the war'. The army responded to Coningham's initiative and agreed to set up a joint headquarters when the 8th Army was formed in September 1941. Until then, Churchill had been led to believe that the army's 'grievances and complaints' had not been met by the RAF. In particular, the failure to develop a dive-bomber. By September 1941, however, it was clear to Tedder and Coningham, if not to all soldiers and sailors, that the dive-bomber was of little value without fighter cover and a far more useful weapon was the fighter-bomber.

It was in September that Churchill ruled (in response to Tedder's arguments, relayed by Portal) that ground forces must not expect, 'as a matter of course', to be protected against aerial attack. 'Above all,' he wrote, 'the idea of keeping standing patrols of aircraft over our moving columns should be abandoned.' Any hope of winning and retaining air superiority would be undermined by this 'mischievous practice'. Whenever a battle was in prospect, Churchill concluded, the army commander was to 'specify' to the air commander the tasks he wanted performed, both before and after the battle. But it was the duty of the air commander to decide how best to carry them out.

These fundamental rulings were to be widely publicised and vigorously enforced by Tedder, as far as he was able, during the rest of the war and must rank high among Churchill's most useful contributions to Britain's part in the Allied victory. He was often 'difficult', and became more so the longer the war lasted, but – unlike Hitler – he could be persuaded to understand other points of view.

During 1942, however, tension between Portal and Alan Brooke over air support for the army was constant. Churchill sought a middle ground and Army Co-operation Command was created in response to army pressure, but the Air Ministry never gave it full backing. The extravagant assertions by Harris (and others) about Bomber Command's ability to win the war on its own did not help. Brooke demanded an army air force, but Churchill ruled in October that whenever the army has a foothold in occupied Europe, 'the system of organisation and employment of the Royal Air Force should conform to that which proved so successful in the Western Desert'. This was the work of Tedder and Coningham.

Churchill's doctor, Sir Charles Wilson (later Lord Moran) observed the RAF's self-confidence at this time. Someone had told Wilson that Tedder's father was 'a rough diamond' (which is by no means true) who had fought his way to the top, which is. 'In the son the facets have been polished, but the hard stone is left.' Tedder was quite unlike any other officer whom Wilson had met: 'a quick mind and a sharp tongue. He admires Smuts, thinks he is a greater man than the Prime Minister, and says so.'

The Arrival of the Americans

Tedder had learned during his long experience of research and development in the Air Ministry that neither Britain's aircraft industry nor her merchant fleet would be able to supply the modern fighters, bombers and – of no less importance – the transport aircraft needed to survive, let alone end up on the winning side in this war. An alliance with the United States as close as a marriage would be essential. He therefore welcomed Roosevelt's announcement in August 1941 of the creation of a military supply line, to be operated by Pan American Airways as a practical means of moving desperately-needed aircraft and other equipment across the Atlantic and on to Cairo. Alas, PAA proved so eager both to pursue its own profit and to exclude British civilian competition that serious harm was done to the conduct of military operations. During 1942, it would be Americans rather than Britons who won this battle. They cancelled PAA's African contracts, 'militarised' its bases and set up an Air Transport Command.

Major-General George H. Brett, representing Lieutenant-General Henry H. Arnold (head of the US Army Air Forces) arrived in Cairo on 10 September in a huge four-engined bomber, a Consolidated B-24 Liberator. It was the first Tedder had seen. In size, clean lines and capacity to carry a heavy load a long way, it was far ahead of anything in RAF service. Tedder was very much taken with Brett, first of a long line of American airmen with whom he would work for the rest of his career. For his part, Brett was equally impressed by Tedder and then by Coningham, whom he was sent to meet on the 14th. Brett proposed to take over the port of Massawa in Eritrea, on the south-west coast of the Red Sea, and set up a complete maintenance organisation there and at Asmara, thirty miles inland, with a forward base at El Faiyum, fifty miles south of Cairo.

Tedder agreed with Brett that an 'outpost office' was needed in Washington, headed by a senior RAF officer able to speak for Tedder, as well as a senior American officer resident in Cairo, able to speak for Arnold. It was in the Mediterranean, wrote Williamson Murray, where British and American air forces proved 'adaptive and innovative'. They worked out a realistic approach to air warfare and recognised a need to co-operate with other services. It was Tedder who 'fashioned an air instrument that was responsive' to their needs. The Desert Air Force, under his guidance, developed a system that maximised the potential of air power within a framework of overall co-operation with ground forces.

'Calm Courage in the Midst of Tumult'

During October, planning was in full swing for Operation Crusader. Its chief aim was to drive Rommel out of Cyrenaica and thereby relieve Tobruk, which hitherto had absorbed so much naval and air effort. No fewer than twenty-five ships had been sunk and nine seriously damaged while attempting to supply the fortress, relieve its garrison or carry away sick and wounded. Also, the passage of British shipping through the Mediterranean would be eased by capturing ports and airfields along the Libyan coast. Every apparently well-informed person, civilian or military, in London or Cairo, scented victory.

Numerous troops, armour, trucks and aircraft arrived from Britain or from the United States. All three services, putting past quarrels behind them, were resolved to pull together as never before. There was even excited talk about what to do *after* Rommel's defeat. Should Tunisia be occupied? Should Sicily be invaded? Or, most thrilling of all prospects, should there be a massive expedition to the Caucasus to help the Soviet Union?

At this precise moment, Tedder suddenly found himself on the very edge of the sack. Portal had asked him on 8 October to compare British and Axis air strengths and his views on how he intended to exploit air superiority. He replied on the 13th: 'We shall be definitely superior in mechanised forces but numerically inferior in the air.' These were the words, 'numerically inferior', that infuriated Churchill, who had a lifelong obsession with numbers and was desperate for a victory that would impress Britain's allies.

Portal sent Tedder a signal on the 14th that was 'obviously pure and almost unadulterated Winston', as he told his wife; one of those signals written 'for the record', a practice with which Tedder was already familiar. Churchill told him, through Portal, that no commander should expect to go into a major battle at full strength and units must not be omitted 'merely' because of a shortage of transport when 'improvisation' can supply the remedy. Everything must be thrown forward, even unescorted bombers, and heavy losses would be 'fully justified'. This gung-ho language was driven by political, rather than military, considerations because Peter Fraser (Prime Minister of New Zealand) had asked for an assurance that the British forces would have air superiority, a sensitive point, given the heavy casualties New Zealand had recently suffered in Greece and Crete. These were avoidable disasters for which Churchill was responsible, but he always loved the idea of charging full tilt at any enemy and was most adroit – by dint of long practice – at finding someone else to blame if failure followed.

As German forces rolled eastward into the Soviet Union during October and the Americans remained determined to avoid an open alliance with Britain, Churchill worked himself into a lather, and decided to sack Tedder. His martial spirit had for some time found the calm, practical tone of Tedder's signals deflating. Tedder, ironically, had a quality that Voltaire attributed to the 1st Duke of Marlborough: 'That calm courage in the midst of tumult, that serenity of soul in danger, which the English call a cool head.'

In the absence of dramatic appeals and uplifting slogans without which he himself could not function, Churchill wrongly concluded that the air aspect of Crusader would be conducted timidly. But Portal, Freeman, Auchinleck,

Lyttelton and even Sinclair said they would resign if Churchill insisted on sacking Tedder. 'Figures can be made to prove anything', Auchinleck gently reminded a politician who had so often used those that suited his purpose. Churchill gracelessly gave way and sent Tedder a curt signal of support on 24 October, to which Tedder replied almost as brusquely.

As David Reynolds wrote, Churchill's impatience with military commanders 'reflected his real yet limited experience of war'. As a young man, he certainly showed himself brave in combat, but he never commanded any formation larger than a battalion, never attended a staff college, never learned to plan operations and had no interest in logistics. He did not understand 'large-scale, resource-intensive operations involving the mobilising and deployment of complex formations and different arms'. He was a man for whom boldness and aggression were the answer to all military problems: 'fighting, gnawing and tearing', so that 'the weaker or more frail gets life clawed out of him by this method'. Such rants, fortunately, were increasingly ignored by commanders who were learning how to conduct massive military operations against opponents who were not only brave, but skilful, carefully trained and equipped with effective weapons.

A Failed Crusade

On 16 November 1941, with Operation Crusader set to begin on the 18th, Churchill signalled Auchinleck in what Tedder called a 'very Marlburian' attempt at inspiring prose: 'The Desert Army may add a page to history which will rank with Blenheim and with Waterloo,' he wrote. 'The eyes of all nations are upon you. All our hearts are with you. May God uphold the right.'

Tedder, an educated man who despised such rodomontade, contented himself with a two-word message to all air units: 'Good hunting'. In his opinion, men at the front needed no ponderous exhortation from an elderly politician sitting snug in England. 'This is the first time,' Churchill announced in the House of Commons, 'that we have met the Germans at least equally well-armed and equipped.' He knew from Ultra that Auchinleck had more than 600 tanks to set against Rommel's 160 and that Tedder had 660 aircraft to oppose the Luftwaffe's 640.

The operation began with torrents of rain and violent thunderstorms. After five days, Auchinleck received an urgent request from his field commander, Alan Cunningham (brother of the admiral), asking permission to break off the offensive. Auchinleck ordered him to get on with it, but Rommel launched a surprise counter-offensive on 24 November which broke through at once. The shambles was too much for the Auk, who sacked Cunningham on the 25th. Churchill and Brooke (who would be appointed head of the army on Christmas Day) urged Auchinleck to be his own field commander.

Had he done so, the course of events during the rest of the Mediterranean war would have been drastically altered, probably to Britain's advantage.

Instead, he appointed his deputy chief of staff, Neil Ritchie, a desk officer who had no experience of desert operations and no noticeable capacity for leadership. As Crusader faltered, Churchill worked himself into another rage and for no good reason pressed Portal to get rid of Tedder (not Ritchie) but Auchinleck again supported the airman: 'He has been absolutely splendid in this show, full of resolution and courage and most helpful with suggestions.' He would be 'most distressed' if Tedder went, and 'for the good of the army' he hoped that Churchill would not insist; and he did not.

News of the Japanese attack on Pearl Harbor reached Tedder on 8 December. 'The Japs have gone mad dog with a vengeance', he wrote to his wife that evening. Lyttelton thought it would shorten the war, but Tedder thought Vichy France and Spain would now join Hitler openly. Hitler's declaration of war on the United States was excellent news for Britain, sweeping away all remaining awkwardness about co-operating with a 'neutral' power. On the other hand, as Freeman told Tedder on 14 December, Japan's entry into the war 'will hit you very hard' because the Americans will now cut off your aircraft supplies while their minds turn to resisting the Japanese and helping the Soviet Union.

Meanwhile, Crusader came to a lame end on 6 January 1942 with many casualties on both sides. The Germans and Italians lost more than 8,000 men killed, wounded or captured and the British over 10,000 in seven weeks of bitter conflict. Rommel lay safely at El Agheila even though the 8th Army 'had enjoyed an enormous numerical superiority in tanks (four British to each German),' wrote Strange, 'and the RAF's Desert Air Force had virtually swept the few opposing Luftwaffe squadrons from the skies.' A week later, Tedder reported to Freeman. 'There is no doubt that one or two opportunities of putting the Hun in the bag have been lost, mostly, I think, through an excess of bravery and shortage of brains.'

It was necessary to press on westward to Tripoli before anything could be done to help the Soviet Union, and both options would be hampered by an almost total lack of capacious transport aircraft to get supplies forward. Only the Bristol Bombay was much use and Tedder had only a handful of them. Air Ministry officials, thinking only of bombers and fighters, had overlooked the need for a large fleet of modern transport aircraft in the 1930s.

Rommel Strikes Back
On 21 January 1942 Rommel began an astonishing offensive, helped by gales, rain and sandstorms hindering reconnaissance on the ground as well as in the air. It was an offensive that had profound strategic consequences for both sides. Within a week, the Germans were back in Benghazi, which had been lavishly stocked with food, fuel, ammunition, vehicles and clothing for the proposed advance to Tripoli. The 8th Army was in full retreat to a defensive line stretching from Gazala (thirty-five miles west of Tobruk)

southward to Bir Hacheim. Coningham's main fighter force received no warning of the army's retreat and only just escaped in time. At the end of January, after three months of almost constant endeavour, Middle East Command had lost about 530 aircraft, an average of nearly six every day. The Axis lost 460, nearly five every day.

Auchinleck told Arthur Smith (his chief of staff) on 30 January 1942 that co-operation between tanks, infantry, and artillery was poor and we need 'more original leadership' in the field. He had already told Churchill, not for the first time, that 'it is no good just counting tanks or regiments and pretending that ours are individually as good as the Germans because they are not'. As Tedder told Portal, the army had several 'first-rate, intelligent, forceful leaders', including Auchinleck, but for many years social position, good horsemanship and hunting skill had mattered more to those who ran the army's staff college than systematic study of modern military problems. There were hundreds of officers 'lacking skill, energy and imagination', wrote Hastings. 'Their courage was seldom in doubt, but much else was.'

Tedder's own problems included the fact that many aircraft had been sent to the Far East since December 1941, in a last-minute effort to stave off disaster there, and Coningham had no Spitfires, the only fighter that could match the best German machines. Hundreds remained in England under the command of Douglas to guard against the consequences of a Soviet collapse and a renewed threat of invasion. Nor did Coningham have any long-range heavy bombers because such weapons were only just beginning to be produced in vast quantities in Britain and would all be assigned to Bomber Command, under the instruction of Harris, from February 1942.

Between mid-December 1941 and the end of May 1942 Malta was unable to interfere with convoys sailing to North Africa, even though secret intelligence provided Tedder and his colleagues with accurate information about their timing and routes. Axis hopes of linking an assault on Egypt with a larger offensive from the north against Arab oil lands were clearly realistic. Rommel attacked on 26 May and within a month had driven the British to El Alamein, on an excellent natural defence line some sixty miles west of Alexandria, which the navy rapidly and silently left.

The famous fortress and port of Tobruk fell into Rommel's hands on 21 June, together with enormous stocks of petrol, ammunition and provisions, as well as 2,000 vehicles and more than 30,000 soldiers, one-third of them South African. On the 23rd Tedder found time to write to Portal. 'I have never openly admitted it', he wrote, but if he had had some heavy bombers and more fighters to escort them he might have prevented 'the present fiasco'. Perhaps he should have 'openly admitted' his opinion and demanded that Churchill and his chiefs of staff decide between the needs of the Middle East and those of the home commands. Portal, however, would have been immovable: in August 1942 he assured Tedder that he was 'absolutely opposed to diverting more heavies from the attack on Germany', which he (and Harris) mistakenly believed was 'really beginning to have great results'.

Ritchie was sacked on 29 June and at last Auchinleck took personal command. Both Tedder and Coningham were pleased 'that passive bewilderment was being replaced by active command'. Rommel advanced over 350 miles in six weeks to the last line of defence before the Nile valley, inflicting heavy casualties on both the 8th Army and the Desert Air Force. The force of 125,000 men confronting Rommel at Gazala on 26 May had been reduced by the end of June to half that size.

Coningham's losses were equally grave: at least 600 fighters and more than 100 medium bombers, but the loss of pilots, air and ground crews hurt the Desert Air Force even more. Panic in Egypt followed a triumphant announcement on German radio that Rommel would be in Alexandria on 6 July and in Cairo three days later. Orders were given for secret documents to be burnt and for days ashes and tiny scraps of paper filled the streets.

Auchinleck was undermined in part by his poor choices as field commanders and in part by the reports of an American colonel, Bonner Frank Fellers, to Washington which were intercepted by the Germans. On 10 July 1942, however, Rommel's excellent wireless intelligence company, under Captain Alfred Seebohm, was captured and the source of the leak discovered. Auchinleck appointed Francis de Guingand as his Director of Military Intelligence. This was a good move, but the Gazala battles were lost, thanks to incompetent corps commanders and Ritchie's inability to direct them. Auchinleck took over personally, but it was too late: his victory at First Alamein was a 'little appreciated masterpiece', but he had to go.

'Drastic and Immediate Changes'

On a forty-mile front, from El Alamein in the north to the edge of the virtually impassable Qattara Depression in the south, Auchinleck stopped the rout. 'Our air forces,' he wrote later, 'could not have done more than they did to help and sustain the 8th Army in its struggle. Their effort was continuous by day and night and the effect on the enemy was tremendous.' Without their 'devoted and exceptional efforts, we should not have been able to stop the enemy on the El Alamein position'. They were also helped by Rommel's over-extended lines of supply and communication, and by the ease with which Auchinleck could be reinforced, now that he lay so close to a large, undamaged supply-base. Of great value to the Allies was the fact that from now on Rommel would be fighting virtually blind, once his excellent radio intercept company was captured on 10 July and in the same month he was no longer able to read detailed signals sent to Washington by the US military attaché in Cairo.

Terraine regarded Tedder as 'the outstanding British airman of the war, with the largest view of its conduct'. He presided over an air force that had every type of aircraft and frequently told Admiral Cunningham that 'sea, land and air operations in the Middle East Theatre are now so closely inter-related that effective co-ordination will only be possible if the campaign is considered and controlled as a combined operation'. The message had by now got through to Cunningham, but neither to Portal nor Harris. Rommel came close to victory in July 1942. Had he been given more support, thought Alan Levine, 'he could almost certainly have overrun Egypt'.

Forces were available in Western Europe: no fewer than twenty-nine divisions were lying idle to meet the threat of an Allied invasion that was not yet realistic. As Rommel later complained, 'after Alamein and the Allied invasion of North Africa his masters suddenly found it possible to throw considerable forces into the futile defence of Tunisia'.

On 26 July Tedder wrote to Portal. He rightly suspected that 'people at home' were losing confidence in Auchinleck, who had made several poor appointments. Churchill was then at his lowest ebb and in July an MP seriously suggested that he be replaced by Henry, Duke of Gloucester, third son of King George V and Queen Mary, a man of no distinction, military or civilian.

'If ever a change at the top becomes unavoidable,' Tedder concluded, 'for heaven's sake let them choose someone who is alive and young, someone with fire. Surely the army has men like that amongst its galaxy of generals?' Portal showed this letter to Churchill, who asked him to show it to Eden (Foreign Secretary) and Lyttelton (now Minister of Production and a member of the War Cabinet). They agreed with Tedder's assessment. So Churchill, accompanied by Brooke (head of the British Army), decided to go to Cairo and see for himself. He arrived on 3 August, wearing the uniform of an air commodore.

On the 8th, after five eventful days, Tedder reported to Portal that Churchill was 'bubbling over with vitality and cheerfulness' and spent more than an hour alone with Tedder. 'I told him frankly what my views were... the last failure in particular has shaken the faith of the troops in their leadership and in the armour, not without cause.' Smuts had also arrived in Cairo and Tedder told him: 'Selection, promotion and removal of staffs and commanders must be entirely based on results, not on seniority, personal friendships, old school ties, etc. Failures must be analysed and exposed, not, as invariably in the past, buried under many coats of whitewash.'

Having listened to Tedder, Smuts and a host of lesser lights, Churchill decided that 'drastic and immediate' changes were needed. Harold Alexander, summoned from Burma, became C-in-C of a command shorn of Iraq and Persia. Bernard Montgomery was summoned from England to be Alexander's field commander (after William Gott, the first choice, was killed on 7 August) and three generals were dismissed. Auchinleck after learning, by letter, of his fall on the 8th, politely refused Churchill's offer of the new Iraq-Persia Command, and returned to India.

'A Strategic Failure of the First Order'

By the end of July 1942, Lord Gort, governor and commander-in-chief of Malta, and Admiral Sir Henry Harwood, commander of the Mediterranean Fleet, were deeply concerned about Malta's fuel shortage. They resisted Park's determination to strike at Axis aerodromes in Sicily and southern Italy and ships supplying Rommel in North Africa. Malta's aircraft and fuel, they argued, should be reserved to meet a direct threat to the island.

Yet Ultra kept all the British commanders accurately informed about the timing of Axis shipping movements and even details of the loads they were carrying. Park had been the very apostle of defence in the summer of 1940, but now he believed, and Tedder agreed with him, that offence was essential. Unless his aircraft seriously impeded the build-up of Rommel's forces, the 8th Army might well be defeated again and the fall of Malta would follow that of Egypt, no matter how prudently its fuel, ammunition and food stocks had been conserved.

An Allied convoy, named Operation Pedestal, entered the Mediterranean during the night of 10-11 August. It consisted of fourteen merchant vessels, escorted by thirty-six warships. The Germans prepared to attack it with all the strength they could muster – more than 500 bombers and fighters – against which Park could oppose at most 150 aircraft. By the time the severely damaged tanker *Ohio* was hauled into Malta's Grand Harbour, nine of the merchant vessels had been sunk and seven of the escort sunk or damaged. Had the Italian fleet shown the same determination as the Luftwaffe, Operation Pedestal would have been a total disaster for the Allies.

The arrival of five merchantmen represented, for the Axis, 'a strategic failure of the first order'. The island's fuel reserves were extended, thanks to the *Ohio*, from four weeks to three months. Park's handling of his outnumbered force earned him high praise in London and he passed the appreciation on to his air and ground crews. 'The RAF here are grand,' wrote Major-General Ronald Scobie (commander of Malta's ground forces) to Lieutenant-General Archibald Nye (deputy head of the army) 'with a fine commander in Park. They have their opposite number in Sicily completely down at the moment... Relations between the services are very good and co-operation is excellent.'

The arrival in Malta of those five merchant ships, including the oil tanker, on 15 August had enabled the island to join in systematic attacks, guided by accurate intelligence information, on Rommel's supply lines. These attacks, aimed at ships sailing for his African ports and at trucks carrying such supplies as reached those ports towards his front line, fatally weakened him.

Moscow Interlude

Hot upon the heels of these great events came Churchill's unprecedented journey to Moscow, 'one of the most courageous things he did', thought

Tedder. Less than a month after Hitler, Stalin's ally, turned on him, Stalin was demanding that Britain come to his aid. Churchill did his best, but that help was long limited to strengthening the bomber offensive and sending – at heavy cost – supplies by sea to Murmansk, while struggling to contain the U-boat threat in the Atlantic as well as fighting against Germany and Italy in the Mediterranean and North Africa. This despite obvious dangers from German forces and extreme weather conditions: a decision, as Peter Kemp wrote, that 'was a triumph of political expediency over military reality'. These convoys eventually delivered nearly a quarter of all Allied aid to the Soviet Union, including 5,000 tanks and 7,000 aircraft, at a cost of 122 war and merchant ships and the lives of more than 800 seamen.

Two B-24 Liberators left Cairo about midnight on 10 August 1942, bound for Teheran and then, after re-fuelling, the Soviet capital. Churchill and his personal staff travelled in one; with Tedder, Brooke, Wavell (now C-in-C India) and Alexander Cadogan of the Foreign Office in the other. Churchill intended to inform Stalin personally that there would be no 'second front' in Western Europe in 1942. He also wished to convince him that a successful campaign in North Africa would draw German forces away from the Eastern Front and that a bomber offensive, growing more powerful by the day, would absorb German resources and undermine morale. Both Liberators reached Teheran safely, but two hours out of that city the pilot of Tedder's Liberator told him an engine was faulty: should he press on or turn back? Tedder reminded him that the decision lay solely with the pilot no matter how important the passengers were. So back to Teheran they went, a decision that saved their lives because the fault was likely to have resulted in a fire that would soon have reached a petrol tank.

Tedder and his companions reached Moscow on 13 August, almost a day after Churchill. It had been a bad day for Cadogan in particular. He was 'scared stiff', Tedder observed, that Churchill might say or do something without advice. Which, of course, he had always been prone to do, no matter how many minders clustered around him. A state villa outside Moscow had been assigned to Churchill and he was joined there by the second planeload for a cheerful lunch. In the absence of minders, Churchill had enjoyed a very late evening with the Soviet ruler. 'Unfortunately,' wrote Tedder, 'in his account of it all to us he rather let himself go, speaking of Stalin as just a peasant whom he, Winston, knew exactly how to handle. Being fairly certain that the whole villa was a network of microphones, I scribbled *mefiez vous* [beware], and passed it to him. He gave me a glare which I shall never forget, but I am afraid it was too late. The damage was done.'

It is clear from Cadogan's diaries (published in 1972) 'that both Churchill and Brooke were surprisingly naive about the dangers of bugging'; it is likely, thought Reynolds, that Stalin was well informed about all Churchill's 'private' conversations when in the Soviet Union.

When the first official meeting began, Stalin expressed 'utter contempt' for Allied military efforts and Tedder had to admit that from a Soviet point of view those efforts were: 'very much small beer, and rather flat beer at that!'

Tedder was keenly aware that a great opportunity to assist Stalin at a time when he was in dire peril had been missed as a result of the failure of Operation Crusader late in 1941. That opportunity never recurred, although Tedder and his staff spent countless hours during 1942 on plans to send as many as twenty squadrons to southern Russia – but they all depended on defeating Rommel first – however the 'Desert Fox' was still running free in August.

While Stalin and Churchill wrangled over grand strategy, Tedder and Brooke had long meetings on 15 August with three Soviet commanders (not one an airman) to discuss two possibilities: an assault on occupied France and combined operations in the Caucasus. They got nowhere. But the atmosphere at a farewell banquet on the 15th was moderately cordial because Stalin had been told about the proposed Anglo-American invasion of North West Africa (Operation Torch) and had been assured that the bombing of German cities was already causing destruction and would cause more in coming months. Stalin's toast to the British Army 'was perfunctory, to say the least,' recalled Tedder, 'whereas he walked the full length of the table and back', to toast the RAF: 'I think with the deliberate intention of baiting the Prime Minister and Alan Brooke.'

Victory at Last
Back in Cairo on 18 August, Tedder learned that Montgomery's abundant energy, self-assurance, skill as a trainer of troops and insistence that armour and infantry work together were already lifting the morale of the uniformed civilians under his command. In Coningham's opinion, expressed to Tommy Elmhirst (in charge of everything that he did not wish to be bothered with) as early as 16 August 'we now have a man, a great soldier if I am any judge, and we will go all the way with him'. And so they did, but they did not then know that Montgomery's self-assurance would rapidly degenerate into an arrogance that angered all his fellow-commanders nor that he would deliberately isolate himself from them.

His arrogance was fed by Brooke, by the BBC, Britain's newspapers and even by Churchill. They all resented the fact that victory over Germany and Japan would be achieved mainly by the abundant resources of the Soviet Union and the United States. Only Eisenhower, the Supreme Allied Commander, was able – with great difficulty – to restrain Montgomery. In this task, he did not get the support he should have from Churchill or Brooke, while Alexander was but an indolent straw man, easily manipulated by men with stronger personalities and more energy.

None of Montgomery's predecessors enjoyed either the intelligence or resources made available to him. Montgomery knew nothing about Ultra before his appointment and then, typically, protested strongly (but vainly) against anyone except himself having access to it. He regarded himself as a military genius and refused to acknowledge essential help from the Y service, monitoring the battlefield conversations of German commanders. He had a massive superiority in men and equipment in opposing the Germans in the desert and Tunisia, but always refused to act quickly. Even more than his subordinates, he had fallen under the spell of a German commander who had a positive genius – matched only by Bill Slim in the Far East – for achieving maximum results with minimum resources.

To his credit, Montgomery repudiated the notion that the army commander should control his supporting air forces. Tedder made this point to Portal in February 1943. The outcome was large-scale support on a mobile basis for the army, but it did not get operational command. Although the RAF retained that command, substantial resources were now dedicated to army support for a Tactical Air Force to be used in north-west Europe, just as Tedder and Coningham had done in North Africa.

Rommel's attempt to conquer Egypt began during the night of 30-31 August, just as the worst sandstorms for many weeks swept Coningham's airfields. The attempt was ill-conceived because he lacked secure supply lines, reinforcements, air superiority and reliable information about his enemy's location and resources, whereas the British had precise information about his intentions, strength and weakness.

The attack was a long right hook, aimed at the Alam el Halfa Ridge, a key point some fourteen miles behind the centre of the British line. Held up by unexpected minefields and air raids on an unprecedented scale which caused him heavy casualties the attack was called off on 6 September. Montgomery had achieved his first and most significant victory. Until then, the army had lacked confidence as a result of headlong retreats *to* Gazala in January and then *from* Gazala in May. But Montgomery's careful disposition of his forces, helped by accurate information about enemy intentions would enable him to win a decisive victory. He was determined to follow Rommel warily and give him no opportunity to strike back yet again at over-confident enemies.

The difference between this land battle and previous ones, Tedder signalled Portal on 7 September, 'is that in this one soldiers have refused to play the enemy game and send tanks against guns. Enemy has been forced to send his tanks against our guns.' Tedder also observed intensive, realistic training going ahead everywhere in Egypt, on the ground and in the air. The growing expertise of a small American air force, under the able command of Major-General Lewis H. Brereton, was particularly gratifying. 'They are learning from us and we are learning from them, I was glad to hear this from both sides.' Victory in the desert was at last looming.

When the battle of El Alamein began, Allied airmen had achieved air superiority and Montgomery was therefore able to assemble and deploy infantry and armour as he saw fit, untroubled by worries about aerial attack or even reconnaissance. Nevertheless, as numerous historians have observed, the land battle did not go according to plan. By insisting that it had, Montgomery founded a reputation for infallibility among the undiscerning, but lost the credit he deserved among his fellow commanders for the skill, determination and rapidity of decision with which he re-shaped his forces.

This he was able to do because the resources available to him were vastly superior to those of the Axis: nearly 200,000 British-led troops with more than 1,000 tanks (many of them American) against barely 100,000 Germans and Italians with fewer than 500 tanks. In artillery, Montgomery had nearly twice as many guns of all calibres and also enjoyed excellent communications and ample supplies, whereas Rommel was short of everything. Even so, the initial assault (Operation Lightfoot, launched on 23 October) had failed by the 26th, obliging Montgomery to re-organise battered forces and hastily devise a fresh assault (Operation Supercharge) for 1 November.

Portal, obsessed with bombing Germany, had refused to provide Tedder with a strong enough bomber force to ensure the destruction of Rommel's forces at El Alamein. Had that happened, the 8th Army would have been able to advance so rapidly westward to support Operation Torch (Allied landings on 8 November in Morocco and Algeria, led by Eisenhower) that the enemy could have been defeated in North Africa before Christmas.

It seems likely that heavy bombers could have helped to bring about a decisive victory enabling Anglo-American troops to force the surrender of Italy and then to engage Germany's main strength much sooner. A strenuous effort would have been required to shift sufficient ground resources in addition to the bombers themselves to Tedder's command, but the consequences of ending the European war even six months sooner are immeasurable. On the other hand, the Anglo-American armies were inexperienced and several commanders were found to be inadequate; nor did they expect either French or German forces to resist so stoutly.

The campaign saw the rise of American ascendancy in the alliance, but it proved beyond question that neither ally was yet ready to take on the Germans in Western Europe. None of this is discussed in Churchill's memoirs, nor is there any analysis of the shambles of Anglo-American airborne operations. It was enough for Churchill to exult over the long-awaited victory in Egypt of a British general. As a bonus, when his account was published, reviewers naturally assumed, as with the other volumes, that it was Churchill's own work, which was not the case. Henry Pownall was the 'master of English' who described the battle of El Alamein.

Montgomery's cautious pursuit of Rommel after El Alamein is easy to understand. He had no experience of desert fighting; he had never commanded a corps, let alone an army, in battle; but he did understand that

Churchill – and still more, the British public – needed to believe, after so many defeats, that a smashing victory had been achieved. In fact, it was easier said than done to pursue even a fatally-weakened Rommel westward with any rapidity.

Tunis, the ultimate goal, lay 2,000 miles beyond Alexandria and almost the whole of that immense journey had to be made along a single metal road, one inadequately maintained in peacetime and since then regularly mined, blown up, bombed and shelled by both sides. Countless mines made movement off the road hazardous and both ground and air forces lacked adequate transport.

16

From Algiers to Italy, 1943-1945

Douglas for Tedder?

Archibald Sinclair, who loved nothing better than to shuffle senior air commanders from pillar to post, wished Tedder to replace Wilfrid Freeman as vice-CAS about the end of November 1942 and appoint Sholto Douglas – an officer whom he strongly favoured – as head of RAF Middle East. Tedder resisted this move, with the help of Richard Casey (an Australian appointed Minister of State in Cairo) and Churchill agreed to leave well alone. Awards were then handed out to recognise victory in The Battle of Egypt. A GCB for Alexander, whom Churchill admired inordinately for his Great War record, his command of the rearguard at Dunkirk and his cheerful personality; a KCB for Montgomery and promotion to full general; and a KCB for Coningham, but no promotion. However, Churchill spoke of him in the House of Commons as 'no mere technician, but a redoubtable warrior', and the British press thereupon praised him warmly.

Sinclair recommended Tedder for a GCB, but Churchill, at his pettiest, insisted that the award be made to mark his two years of 'distinguished service' in North Africa and must not be linked to any part he played in the battle of El Alamein.

More than two years later, on 21 February 1945, Harris wrote to Trenchard. 'Tedder and his RAF saved the rout in North Africa and made the subsequent victory virtually a walkover for the army.' This is too sweeping a claim, but Churchill's action was certainly mean-spirited. It was Harris, never a man to step back, who had badgered Churchill at his own dinner table to get Tedder 'a grudging and belated GCB, after the public have forgotten'. Since then, although he had gone on to yet greater achievements, growled Harris, 'it has never, of course, entered the Air Ministry's head to make Tedder a marshal'. As it happened, Tedder *did* reach that rank, but only automatically on elevation to CAS; he was then made a baron, but not, as Alexander and Montgomery (or Churchill's friend Lindemann) a viscount. One doubts if the slight cost Tedder any sleepless nights.

Eisenhower, Supreme Commander of all Allied forces in North Africa, signalled the combined chiefs of staff (British and American) on 26 November to say that Tedder, Park (Malta's air commander) and Brereton (commanding the 9th Air Force, embracing all US units in the Middle East) had arrived in Algiers to discuss air operations. The ground advance, he said, had been supported 'in fine fashion' by airmen, despite 'difficulties encountered in rain-soaked landing fields, poor supply and lack of maintenance facilities'. Tedder emphasised these and other 'difficulties' in a long signal to Portal on the 28th. In particular, the most forward fighter airfield lay about 100 miles behind the most forward troops. Eisenhower had not yet recognised the importance of a combined headquarters and commanders, his ground and air troops, were widely scattered.

Tunisia: Another Stalingrad

On the positive side, Admiral Andrew Cunningham (having escaped from Washington) was the overall naval commander and agreed with Tedder that there should be a single air commander. Although there was a great deal of muddle and inexperience among the Allies, they were greatly helped by Hitler's foolish decision to pour strong forces into Tunisia. These forces naturally took full advantage of Allied muddle and inexperience, but only for a few months.

Overall, the Axis powers lost 506 ships and 2,257 aircraft during the Tunisian campaign. Given their control of the sea and the air, the Allies could only get stronger as they learned from experience, whereas the Axis forces were trapped as completely as their comrades at Stalingrad. Taken together, these enormous losses ensured that Hitler could no longer win the war. However stoutly his remaining forces resisted, they must eventually be beaten.

They had not been beaten in November 1942, however, and Churchill told the over-busy Sinclair on the 30th:

'It seems to me quite impossible to remove Tedder from the Middle East at this time. No-one has his knowledge, connections or influence. In my opinion, he should act like Kesselring [commanding all Axis forces in the Middle East], combining the air effort both in the Libyan and Tunisian spheres.'

These were the words that not only saved Tedder from being returned, most unwillingly, to the Air Ministry as Portal's vice-CAS in succession to Freeman, but also made it possible for him to become an outstanding Allied commander, in partnership with Eisenhower, for the rest of the war.

A New Hub in Algiers

Portal signalled Tedder on 1 December to say that he and his fellow chiefs were about to suggest to Eisenhower that 'you assume command of all air forces in Mediterranean forthwith'. Churchill was 'favourably inclined' and if Eisenhower agreed, would ask the combined chiefs and Roosevelt to approve. Portal again signalled Tedder: 'Would you be prepared to move your Advanced HQ to Algiers immediately and take personal command?'

To no-one's surprise, Tedder agreed at once. One of his first decisions was to bring Grahame Dawson (with some of his key assistants) to Algiers from Cairo to take charge of maintenance and supply for the whole command. As in Egypt, so now: Dawson insisted on damaged aircraft being collected, if at all possible, from wherever they had come down and repaired immediately. Wrecks were a prime source of spare parts and Dawson made it clear to everyone that these were times of crisis and therefore 'managing somehow' was the motto. Tedder thought he was 'as vital an architect of victory as any commander in the desert'. One RAF officer recalled Montgomery saying 'he had brought his army 2,000 miles; he wouldn't have got 2,000 yards without Dawson's aircraft, always ready in any number, serviceable for battle and that was what really counted'.

Sadly, Dawson would be killed on 14 November 1944 when a Liberator in which he was a passenger en route from Algiers to Paris crashed in very bad weather near Autun, about fifty miles south-west of Dijon in eastern France. It was the same storm which destroyed Leigh-Mallory's York, at about the same time (noon), some fifteen miles east of Grenoble.

Seeking Another Unified Air Command

On 16 December Tedder told Portal that Eisenhower understood the need for a unified air command, but was uncertain about Washington's reaction to putting Americans under British command. On the same day, Eisenhower told the British chiefs that Tedder greatly impressed him: 'He is a top-flight soldier and has helped us immeasurably,' but he preferred an American, Major-General Carl A. Spaatz, as air commander and wanted him to command air forces in both the Mediterranean and England. He had brought Spaatz to Algiers from England, where he was creating a bomber force that would one day cause immense destruction in Germany.

Spaatz was a most able officer, as he later proved, but at that time he was not ready for such elevation. He knew little enough about mounting operations in England and nothing whatsoever about the Mediterranean. In both theatres he would be opposed by enemy troops who were battle-hardened and he had yet to learn how to combine his efforts with those of other services.

Eisenhower nevertheless pressed for Spaatz to be appointed commander, Allied Air Force, and though both Churchill and Portal disapproved they agreed that any system of unified command was better than none, pending a final decision at a conference in Casablanca held between 13 and 24 January

1943. That conference, headed by Roosevelt, Churchill and a galaxy of civilian and military chiefs, was intended to work out a strategy for winning the war; no easy task, in the absence of Stalin, whose armies were doing most of the fighting. He had been invited, but refused to leave the Soviet Union.

As Tedder had long desired, it was decided at Casablanca that he would leave Cairo for Algiers and command everything with wings between Gibraltar and Palestine. He would be under the overall direction of Eisenhower, who signalled General Arnold in Washington to say that he and Spaatz were both 'delighted with the prospect of getting Tedder into this headquarters, where we may profit constantly from his great experience and soldierly qualities'.

Churchill remained impressed by Coningham: 'I saw Coningham's hand in recent operations', he wrote to Portal on 27 February. 'No doubt his control and Tedder's general organisation will bring about an improvement, but here is the place where we want to fight the Hun and where the Hun has to fight us *in the air* and every effort should be made by us, apart from the Americans, to bring the strongest forces constantly into action.' Hitherto, he continued, Allied air operations in Tunisia had failed, but 'I am counting on you to retrieve it, now that you have the best men on the spot and in the right places'.

Tenacious Axis resistance in Tunisia ended on 13 May and 250,000 Germans and Italians were captured. 'All the shouting about the Tunisian campaign leaves me utterly cold', wrote Eisenhower to the head of the US Army, General George C. Marshall, on that day. The Allies should have taken Tunis by mid-December, allowing Sicily to be conquered and the Italian mainland invaded months sooner. 'Another error,' thought Eisenhower, 'was the initial decision not to unify our air forces under a single command.' That mistake was remedied by Tedder and Spaatz, who 'accomplished a practical perfection in the co-ordinated employment of the air forces of the two nations'.

Tedder and Zuckerman

Churchill arrived in Algiers at the end of May 1943 to discuss with British and American commanders plans for Operation Husky, the invasion of Sicily. The air forces, said Tedder, 'had been blasting Italian communications for weeks' in an attempt to weaken Sicily, but now it was necessary to seize Pantelleria, 'the Italian Gibraltar' (according to Fascist rhetoric), a small island about sixty miles from the nearest Sicilian coast, provided with radar stations, observation posts, a submarine and torpedo-boat base, fuel and munitions dumps and a large airfield with an underground hangar. It was also a sitting duck, given Allied air superiority, and after twelve days of systematic bombardment the garrison of more than 11,000 men surrendered.

Pantelleria's chief importance was that it introduced Tedder to Solly Zuckerman, with whom he would work closely for the rest of the war.

Zuckerman was an eminent zoologist who got into war work by studying the effects of exploding bombs on humans and structures. He had arrived in Algiers on 15 March 1943 and his research immediately impressed both British and American air commanders and they promised to improve bombing performance. Tedder appointed him chief scientific officer and graded him as of group captain rank.

'The Most Momentous Enterprise of the War'
Operation Husky began on 10 July. 'It is easy now', recalled Tedder in his memoirs, to forget the scale of this enterprise: 160,000 men in the initial assault, with 14,000 vehicles, six hundred tanks and nearly 2,000 guns. They were transported to Sicily by an Allied armada of 2,600 vessels, under the command of Andrew Cunningham, who described Husky as 'the most momentous enterprise of the war' to that date.

Excluding coastal and transport aircraft, Tedder had, under his command, 2,500 serviceable fighters and bombers and the Axis – having sacrificed so much strength in Tunisia and Stalingrad – could muster fewer than 900 serviceable fighters and bombers in the whole of Sardinia, Sicily and Italy. Air superiority was therefore achieved and maintained, much to Cunningham's relief. It seemed to him 'almost magical that great fleets of ships could remain anchored on the enemy's coast'. By 1943, Anglo-American air forces in the Mediterranean alone, as Alan Levine emphasised, outnumbered the whole Luftwaffe.

Portal, pressed by Churchill, asked Tedder on 23 July for a full report on the airborne operations. Distressing casualties had been suffered by American and British airborne troops by a lethal combination of inexperienced pilots (either carrying troops or towing gliders), poor navigation, high winds, darkness, enemy flak and searchlights, smokescreens and, not least, indiscriminate fire from Allied sailors and soldiers ashore. The result, wrote Sebastian Ritchie, was 'one of the most depressing chapters in the troubled history of Second World War airborne operations'. Should there be a next time, Tedder reported, he advised prolonged prior training, the use of experienced pathfinders, greater concentration of flights and routes directed well away from 'friendly' ground forces or naval units. Gliders, he thought, were a better bet than parachute drops because troops could be landed close together with more and heavier weapons, ammunition, radios, food and even transport. Tragically, as Ritchie's careful analysis of this and subsequent operations demonstrates only too clearly, airborne forces were costly, in resources and manpower, and achieved little.

On 22 July, with the Allies safely ashore in Sicily, Tedder arranged for Zuckerman to take technical assistants there and gather information about what bombing had actually achieved and which targets, in subsequent campaigns, should be aimed at. He concluded that attempting to destroy key points in a railway system – junctions, marshalling yards, repair facilities – and bombing airfields would greatly help ground forces. Enemy movement of troops, heavy weapons and supplies would be seriously impeded and air cover interrupted. Hitting trains on the move and breaking bridges had obvious value, but were more difficult targets. Together, Tedder and Zuckerman devised a bombing strategy of cutting enemy communications that proved highly successful during the rest of the European war, and yet it generated opposition of such intensity that neither man ever forgot or forgave those responsible.

Tedder was concerned that ground commanders were now expecting more than air support for their operations in Sicily, they wanted bombers to lead the way in blasting holes in enemy defences. Tedder and other airmen would increasingly demand that soldiers be readier to use their own weapons, but why should they, if bombers could do all that their over-vocal champions claimed? Both American and British generals were acutely aware that most of their soldiers were amateurs, quite without the resolution, discipline and aggression that were normal in German, Soviet and Japanese armies. Tedder was as reluctant as other air commanders, British or American, to admit that even so-called heavy or strategic bombers simply lacked the weight and accuracy to offer an effective substitute for ground troops and their weapons.

Harold Alexander, who had a gift for presenting any situation in the best possible light, signalled Churchill on 17 August that after only thirty-eight days of fighting the last enemy soldier had been 'flung out' of Sicily. Although more than half the Axis forces had escaped, Tedder was right to emphasise the fact that the Allies took over 160,000 prisoners and killed more than 3,000 German and Italian troops during the campaign. The much-trumpeted Axis was broken when the Italian king dismissed Mussolini on 25 July. It then seemed likely that Hitler, having already suffered heavy losses on the Eastern Front, in Tunisia and now in Sicily, might focus his attention on resisting a Soviet advance in the east and preparing to meet an Allied landing in the west.

In later years, it has been argued by some historians – sitting at their ease and overlooking the fact that most Anglo-American soldiers were by no means hardened warriors – that the Allies ought to have prevented the evacuation of 40,000 Germans, 10,000 vehicles (including guns and tanks) and 15,000 tons of equipment to the mainland. However, the official historians of British intelligence, with ample evidence before them and plenty of time to consider it, pronounced it still an 'open question' whether an evacuation could have been prevented. It has to be remembered that in August 1943, except on the Eastern Front, the sight of Germans moving backwards was still rare enough to exhilarate all Britons and Americans who had personal experience of their fierce and skilful resistance. However, one doubts whether, from a German point of view, a long and costly resistance in Italy was wise when the men and resources spent there were needed closer to home. As Dowding had argued in 1940: 'What matters most?' For him, the answer was 'the British Isles'; for Hitler, it should have been 'Germany and Austria'.

On to Italy

After Sicily, Italy was an obvious target. In Churchill's opinion, it was 'the soft underbelly' of Axis power in Europe: not an opinion shared by anyone who actually fought in that long, hard campaign, as opposed to studying maps many miles away. Churchill, the military enthusiast, had overlooked Napoleon's opinion: 'Italy is like a boot. You must, like Hannibal, enter it from the top.'

Although the Calabrian toe was easier to occupy, Salerno Bay (in the shin) offered greater strategic value. That bay lay a long way from Sicily for troop transports and naval escorts, but just within the range of shore-based fighters. Should aircraft carriers – so useful, but so vulnerable – be risked within comfortable range of enemy airfields? Would Italy fight on without Mussolini? Would the Germans abandon their ally?

Tedder advised Portal on 26 July that Operation Avalanche (a landing at Salerno) was 'practical' from an air point of view, given a concentrated attack on Axis air forces for three weeks prior to the landings and a maximum effort, once ashore, to secure airfields. Montgomery (and therefore Alexander) preferred a safe, steady drive from the Calabrian toe. Operation Baytown (an unopposed crossing from Messina to Reggio) began on 3 September. It encouraged Italy's post-Mussolini group of leaders to sign a secret surrender that day, publicly revealed by Eisenhower on the 8th.

Operation Avalanche began next morning and was stoutly opposed by the Germans. As a consequence of the decision to mount Baytown, the Avalanche forces were smaller and less experienced than they need have been. Disaster was only narrowly avoided during four critical days, 12-15 September. By the 18th, the British 8th Army and the Anglo-American 5th Army (under Mark Clark) had joined up and two weeks later the prime tasks of Baytown and Avalanche had been achieved. Three excellent ports – Naples, Bari and Taranto – were in Allied hands, together with well-equipped airfields around Foggia and Naples.

During ten days of savage fighting (9-18 September) the Germans suffered some 3,000 casualties (killed, wounded or missing), but the Allies lost more than twice as many. Consequently, Hitler backed the strategy advocated by Albert Kesselring (now commanding German forces in Italy) that every inch of ground should be contested. A 'Gustav Line' was constructed across the peninsula south of Rome.

During the last four months of 1943, everyone who fought on either side or studied the course of events in those months became acutely aware that an invasion of France would cost countless lives. George Marshall, wisest of the Allied strategists, thought Hitler made a great mistake in ordering Albert Kesselring to defend Italy. The men and materials lost in that campaign should have been reserved for the defence of Germany. The mistake was all the greater because Kesselring was an outstanding commander, much abler than any of the commanders on the Allied side in Italy.

Slessor, Park, Churchill

During December 1943, it was decided that Lieutenant-General Ira C. Eaker be made first head of the newly-formed Mediterranean Allied Air Forces with his rear headquarters in Algiers and his advanced headquarters at La Marsa in Tunisia. Jack Slessor (late of Coastal Command) was appointed Eaker's deputy and head of all RAF forces in the Mediterranean from a headquarters in Caserta Palace, near Naples. Park, strongly recommended by Portal, was promoted to air marshal and sent to Cairo in January 1944 as head of the RAF in the Middle East, under Slessor's overall supervision. His responsibilities could not have been more widespread: combat operations in the eastern Mediterranean and in the Indian Ocean, and operational training in Egypt, Cyprus, Palestine and South Africa.

Slessor, however, immediately decided that Park was out of his depth in coping with the 'semi-political problems' of so vast a command, problems which he himself relished, as a man who was heart and soul a 'Whitehall Warrior'. In particular, he complained to Portal, he feared 'we shall lose our position in the Middle East and the control of policy will drift increasingly into the hands of the army', because Park was 'a very stupid man'. Fortunately, both Portal and Tedder were well aware of Slessor's arrogant disdain for most officers in all services and his itch to meddle outside his service duties in sensitive regions which he knew only slightly and could rarely visit.

Portal and Tedder knew that Park would get to know the units under his command and co-operate willingly with other services and with allies wherever they could be found in the Middle East, South Africa and especially with the essential Americans. He had already done so in Malta and Sicily and would do so in Egypt during 1944 and later in the Far East.

As for Churchill, he – like Portal and Tedder – had taken the measure of both Park and Slessor. Brevity, which Churchill required of subordinates in their dealings with him, was not a word in Slessor's vocabulary, written or spoken, and he was too free with advice on non-aviation matters. Churchill had confidence in Park and so too had men to whom Churchill listened (quite apart from Portal and Tedder): Smuts; Beaverbrook; Eisenhower and Eaker. Smuts expressed great pleasure at Park's appointment to Cairo: 'It is a most fitting honour and recognition for his great work in Malta.'

Despite his best efforts, Slessor found himself obliged, during 1944, to recognise Park's authority. In the 1945 New Year's Honours List this 'very stupid man', already knighted once (KBE), received the more prestigious KCB. Group Captain Tom Gleave, an official British historian of the Mediterranean campaigns in 1943-1944, summed up: 'Keith Park was a first-rate candidate for Jack Slessor's attention. Keith hated bumff. Jack Slessor revelled in it.'

Another Avoidable Disaster

As early as September 1942 Tedder and his fellow commanders in Cairo had considered whether it would be possible to recapture Crete and perhaps seize the Dodecanese Islands, especially Samos, Leros, Cos and the much larger Rhodes. They concluded that the attempt would consume men, materials and time required to make a success of Husky, that the islands would have little value once the Cyrenaican airfields were recovered and that garrisons there would be unable to resist a German attack mounted from Greece. Had these sensible conclusions continued to govern action in 1943, recorded Tedder in his memoirs, 'we should have been spared much unnecessary loss and heart-burning'.

Unfortunately, Churchill's authority over British – as opposed to Allied – actions remained strong. He urged the Middle East commanders on 27 July to plan an assault on Rhodes: 'as I need this place as part of the diplomatic approach to Turkey'. Long after the war Tedder confided to Theodore McEvoy 'with a vehemence surprising in so temperate a man' that Churchill's obsession with Turkey angered him deeply. His own service in Constantinople throughout the Chanak affair (1922-1923) and careful study of the Dardanelles campaign while at Staff College (1929-1931) gave him the knowledge to regard a third Aegean adventure in which Churchill had a hyperactive hand with grave suspicion.

Churchill hoped to generate a major campaign, Operation Accolade, in the Aegean, despite American objections that it would delay the assault on occupied France, Operation Overlord. Tedder's unwavering support for American resistance to Accolade, condemned by an official British historian as 'this rash experiment', helped to ensure him a high place in Overlord. That would become the greatest campaign mounted by the Western Allies during the war, one in which American voices prevailed as never before; and those voices flatly refused to increase Mediterranean commitments.

Sholto Douglas, Tedder's successor as air commander in Cairo, agreed wholeheartedly with Churchill about the possible advantages of an Aegean adventure. Although Alexander and Cunningham agreed with Tedder, Churchill had his way. In September, Samos, Leros and Cos were seized, but not Rhodes, and the escalation desired by Churchill began: 'glittering prizes', he declared, await those who 'improvise and dare'. 'This is a time to think of Clive and Peterborough,' he wrote to Maitland Wilson, C-in-C Middle East in September, 'and of Rooke's men taking Gibraltar.' Such silliness rolled off his tongue as readily as ever, but his influence on the conduct of operations had been waning since Casablanca in January 1943 and this disastrous Aegean adventure hastened its decline.

German reaction was prompt and severe. Churchill told Tedder on 3 October that 'Cos is highly important and a reverse there would be most vexatious. I am sure I can rely upon you to turn on all your heat from every quarter, especially during this lull in Italy.' Tedder, aware that Eisenhower's opinions now mattered more than Churchill's, replied coolly the next day: 'You have no doubt heard from CAS that we are putting maximum effort against enemy in Greece. Anything further I find possible will be done.' The Germans were recovering Cos as he wrote, the garrisons on Samos and Leros faced a bleak future and the German grip on Rhodes remained secure. Our main purpose, as Eisenhower, Tedder and all their sensible colleagues agreed, was to defeat the Germans in Italy.

Tedder warned Portal on 8 October that a proposed visit by Churchill to Tunis 'would be most dangerous and might have a disastrous effect on Anglo-American relations'. Brooke, head of the British Army – who usually regarded Eisenhower and Tedder with contempt – noted in his diary on the 8th that:

'Churchill has worked himself into a frenzy of excitement about the Rhodes attack, and has magnified its importance so that he can no longer see anything else. He has set his heart on capturing this one island even at the expense of endangering his relations with the President and the Americans and the future of the Italian campaign.'

On that same day, 8 October, Roosevelt replied sensibly to Churchill's plea for his personal intervention. 'Strategically, if we get the Aegean Islands, I ask myself where do we go from there? And, vice versa, where would the Germans go if for some time they retained possession of the islands?' Churchill asked that a conference of high commanders be held at La Marsa to assess Accolade's merits, but he himself was dissuaded from attending and the commanders rejected it. Douglas, however, clung to Churchill's opinion and even Portal, usually the most level headed of men, told Tedder on 12 November that Leros was 'more important at the moment than strategic objectives in southern France or north Italy'. Churchill added his voice to Portal's on the 16th: 'This is much the most important thing that is happening in the Mediterranean in the next few days.' The days when his voice was decisive were over, but he would not give in.

In Cairo, on 24 November, he grabbed Marshall's lapels and uttered one of his most foolish remarks: 'Muskets must flame.' Marshall was not impressed. The Leros garrison had already surrendered and British losses, in a campaign that achieved nothing, were heavy: twenty-six naval vessels, more than 100 aircraft and nearly 5,000 men killed, wounded or captured.

Thousands of Italians, who had supported the British or failed to resist them, were murdered. Such a complete rout strengthened Turkey's resolve, which had never weakened, to stay neutral.

This Aegean adventure, making no military and little political sense, puzzled Eisenhower. Six years after the war ended, he asked his friend, Sir Hastings Ismay (Churchill's chief staff officer at the time) if he could explain it. Churchill, replied Ismay on 11 October 1951, 'placed a wholly disproportionate emphasis in his memoirs on the importance of the islands in the Eastern Mediterranean'. There is, naturally, no admittance in those memoirs that his insistence achieved nothing except unnecessary casualties.

The 'Cold War' Begins in Warsaw

Slessor was closely involved in the first clash of what became the Cold War, born in Warsaw during August and September 1944. As one of Britain's pre-war planners, he felt 'a sense of obligation' to Poland, as well he might, for Britain gave a guarantee of independence to her 'first ally' that proved to be the deadest of dead letters as soon as the Germans invaded in September 1939. Later, he saw at first-hand how brave and skilful many Polish airmen and soldiers were and he also knew what an essential help Polish mathematicians had been, on the eve of war, in revealing Germany's Ultra secrets to the French and British.

'I was still guileless enough to believe' in the middle of 1944, he wrote, that the Soviet Union would welcome Polish assistance in the overthrow of Hitler's Germany. Most leaders of the poorly-armed Polish Home Army (AK, Armia Krajowa) agreed that they could only recover Warsaw with the help of the Red Army, rapidly approaching from the east.

On 1 August General Tadeusz Bór-Komorowski, head of the AK, ordered a rising in the capital. But Soviet forces did not join in and even refused landing rights to British and American aircraft attempting to bring in weapons, ammunition, medical supplies and food. What was left of the AK surrendered on 2 October. About 150,000 Polish men, women and children had been killed and most of the survivors were used as slave labour in Germany. Warsaw was systematically destroyed by the departing Germans, who suffered about 10,000 dead and 16,000 wounded: well-armed and experienced soldiers who would not be available for the defence of their homeland. Despite protests from Roosevelt and Churchill, Stalin imposed a long-lasting Communist regime on Poland.

A Great Unsung Saga

The months of August and September, Slessor recalled, were the worst of his career. His airmen – Polish, British and South African – were faced with 'the blackest-hearted, coldest-blooded treachery' on the part of the Russians and some 200 of his most gallant airmen lost their lives while trying to supply the Poles fighting in Warsaw. Their 'compassionate and selfless devotion to duty', wrote Neil Orpen, has never since been forgotten. It was indeed one of the RAF's many 'finest hours' in that terrible war. The dropping-zones lay up to 900 miles from Allied bases in Italy, a very long way over rugged country, with no help from ground radio stations and no weather information; country that was still held by a well-armed enemy.

Portal, narrowly focused as ever, was reluctant to help. In his mind, the bomber offensive over Germany 'might prove decisive if we did not allow ourselves to be drawn away by less essential calls on our resources'. As for the special operations executive (SOE), just 150 tons of supplies were dropped on Poland during the critical months of 1944, while more than 3,400 tons were delivered to Yugoslavia. According to Norman Davies, the effort to help Warsaw is 'one of the great unsung sagas of the Second World War', although it failed. Very much more could have been done, but Soviet refusal to help was decisive. Churchill and Roosevelt did not insist on relief being given top priority and Slessor failed to explore these questions of strategy, politics and morality in his long, shallow memoirs.

For ruling circles (and many citizens) in Britain and the United States, 'Uncle Joe' was still a hero in 1944 because they were acutely aware that neither British nor American forces could destroy Hitler's regime by their own efforts. Churchill and Roosevelt recognised that Poland lay within a Soviet 'sphere of influence' and they could do nothing to ensure her independence.

The last of Slessor's many letters to *The Times* would be about the Poles. On 18 September 1976, he wrote: 'A memorial is to be unveiled in London to some 14,000 Polish officers killed or missing in Russia during the Second World War, including over 4,000 murdered at Katyn.' The British government refused to be officially involved in this tribute and Slessor raged in vain.

17

The Battle of the Atlantic, 1939-1945

A Decisive Campaign

What Churchill called 'The Battle of the Atlantic' was, like the so-called Battle of Britain, one of the war's decisive campaigns and lasted for as long as Hitler's war. Without command of the sea, the Anglo-American land and air campaigns could not have been mounted or sustained. Without pressure on the Germans from the west and seaborne aid, Soviet successes in the east would have been harder to achieve. Yet in November 1940 Churchill told the Defence Committee (Operations) that, in his view, the Admiralty was making 'extravagant demands' for aircraft at a time when it was essential to strengthen Bomber Command. He thought the navy was not making the best use of its Fleet Air Arm (FAA). The whole matter of assignment of forces must be considered jointly by the Admiralty, the Air Ministry and the Ministry of Aircraft Production. He then recalled, wrongly, that the RNAS had expanded so greatly during the Great War that the Royal Flying Corps was left dangerously short of men and materials.

The demise of the RNAS in 1918 had long-lasting consequences. Even after the FAA returned to the Royal Navy in 1937, naval aviation remained 'tactically and technologically backward' compared with the United States and Japan. This was because the loss of the RNAS cleared a path to the top for single-minded sea dogs such as Dudley Pound and Tom Phillips. As assistant chief of Naval Staff in 1928, Pound suggested that 'convoy would be the wrong strategy to adopt in another war because it exposed shipping to attack from surface raiders, which he saw as the primary threat'. He had forgotten the important role aircraft and airships had performed in the Great War. So too had his close friend Tom Phillips, who 'simply refused to comprehend the potential of air power over the sea'.

Between the wars, as Phillip Meilinger wrote, Coastal Command was an 'unwanted stepchild' of the Royal Navy. As a result, it was years before its Sunderlands and Beaufighters were supported by such efficient American types as the Hudson, Catalina and above all the Liberator. Not until 1943 did naval airmen have the aircraft, the equipment and the tactics needed to overcome the U-boat menace.

The British only began to use Ultra to help route convoys in June 1941, but they used it effectively until February 1942. Karl Doenitz suspected that the Allies were reading his radio messages to U-boats, but his experts assured him that that was impossible. A blackout of U-boat cyphers that began in February 1942 lasted for ten months and pacified his doubts. Fortunately, he lacked sufficient U-boats in 1939-1941 to achieve a decisive victory. The crisis in March 1943 is well known, but the 'air gap' was the main problem, wrote Marc Milner, and the 'singularly decisive influence of air power on the Battle of the Atlantic was well understood at the time, at least by sailors'. Long-range aircraft were essential. 'Submerged U-boats, driven down by aircraft, lacked the speed, range, endurance and tactical effectiveness to tackle convoys in the broad ocean.'

Slessor and Churchill

In October 1942, Jack Slessor, assistant CAS (Policy) in the Air Ministry, was told that he was soon to take over Coastal Command, even though he knew nothing about the war at sea and the difficulties in combining British, American and Canadian resources in the air or in the water. He was, however, well served by his staff and in December 1942 code-breakers at Bletchley Park broke into the latest version of the Enigma machine, so that by the time Slessor took command in February 1943 he and his colleagues were being accurately and promptly informed about Doenitz's intentions and the location of his U-boats.

As for Churchill, so fulsomely praised by Slessor, he had little to say about Coastal Command. Its achievements were not dramatic enough for his boyish taste. 'I could not rest content with the policy of "convoy and blockade"', he admitted in his memoirs, when in fact the escorted convoy proved to be the most effective means of overcoming the U-boat in both world wars. After the war, it was supposed that the so-called 'hunter-killer' groups of aircraft carriers and surface vessels had been the U-boat's deadliest foe. In fact, of the 770 German and Italian boats sunk at sea by Allied action, only twenty were destroyed by those groups as compared to more than 250 by aircraft alone. Yet Slessor, devoted to what he thought of as offensive action, constantly pressed for more and stronger hunting groups in the Bay of Biscay. However, he did co-operate fully with Admiral Sir Max Horton, at 'Western Approaches', based in Liverpool, who was responsible for all North Atlantic convoys.

The Atlantic campaign, waged by two services (the RAF and the Royal Navy) and three nations (Britain, the United States and Canada) was one enormous battlefield, stretching from the Hebrides to Halifax in Nova Scotia and from Casablanca to the Caribbean. 'One shudders to think,' wrote

Slessor, if the Germans had built up 'their really decisive arm, the U-boat service,' before the war, instead of wasting resources – human and material – on a 'third-rate heavy ship force'. Churchill thought so too. 'It would have been wise for the Germans to stake all upon it.' Even in the last two months of the war, U-boats sank no fewer than forty-four Allied ships.

Inter-Service Rivalry

After Pearl Harbor, the Americans suffered unnecessarily heavy losses to U-boats along the east coast as a result of poor equipment, strained relations between the navy and the army and civilian reluctance to accept that 'business as usual' must be interrupted. 'The violence of inter-service rivalry in the United States in those days had to be seen to be believed,' wrote Slessor, 'and was an appreciable handicap to their war effort.' John Buckley agreed. Anglo-American air co-operation over the Atlantic in the years 1942-1943 was 'a catalogue of mistrust and suspicion'; logical procedures were passed over simply because they would have required a degree of co-operation that not even the influence of Roosevelt and Churchill could impose.

On the British side, Slessor resisted strengthening Coastal Command at the expense of Bomber Command, but it was the acquisition of a small number of very long-range B-24 Liberators that would close the 'Atlantic Gap' and prevent the U-boat from cutting supplies to Britain and troops from the United States and Canada to prepare for Operation Overlord.

Closing the Gap

Churchill and Portal supported Harris for too long in his reluctance to regard the Battle of the Atlantic as vital. The 'slavish adherence' (in Buckley's words) of Churchill and the Air Staff 'to the principles of the strategic bombing offensive seemingly blinded them to the harsh realities of the Battle of the Atlantic'. They opposed the allocation of long-range aircraft to Coastal Command, even though Pound had rightly said in March 1942: 'If we lose the war at sea, we lose the war.'

The failure of the Allies to close the Air Gap before 1943 'remains one of the great unsolved historical problems of the war'. The answer lies in the fact that most B-24 Liberators (by far the most effective weapon) were assigned either to the American bomber offensive over Europe or patrol in the Pacific. Yet only about forty to fifty Liberators were needed to close the gap permanently. 'For many historians of the Atlantic war the myopia of the airmen who drove the strategic bomber offensive seems incredible', and yet that offensive depended upon securing the Atlantic.

The Atlantic victory, wrote Slessor in May 1943, meant that 'many of us could be spared to take part in the more direct offensive against objectives in German and Italian soil'. To tell men who had just achieved a decisive victory that they might now 'be lucky enough to take part in the real work of the war' confirms Terraine's opinion that Slessor simply did not understand what was at stake in the Atlantic. A committed bomber believer, he regarded the proposed Overlord operation with deep suspicion, convinced that Harris was conducting 'true air warfare', that would bring victory without an invasion.

It would not be until March 2004, nearly sixty years after the end of the war in Europe, that Coastal Command received its first national monument, unveiled by the Queen in Westminster Abbey, to commemorate nearly 11,000 men who lost their lives in some 2,000 aircraft. But they accounted for nearly 200 U-boats and another twenty-four in joint action with surface vessels. 'Constant Endeavour' was indeed a fitting motto for that command.

At the end of the Great War, the RAF had more than 600 aircraft in home waters engaged in opposing U-boats, but it would not be until the third year of the next war that the Air Ministry assigned enough aircraft to mount a serious challenge to a renewed U-boat threat.

Harris had assured Churchill in June 1942 that Coastal Command was 'merely an obstacle to victory': a foolish remark even by Harris's standards and one that Churchill did not contradict. Harris, wrote Sebastian Cox, 'did not explain how the population, including his aircrews, were to be fed, or his aircraft fuelled, if the U-boat war was lost'. Here, as so often, Harris 'would have done better to eschew hyperbole'. Until 1941, that command had been virtually powerless, with neither the aircraft nor the weapons needed to challenge U-boats.

By 1943, wrote Slessor, the decisive air weapon was the Mark XI Torpex-filled depth charge, dropped in sticks of four to eight at very low levels. By mid-1941, possession of fuelling bases in Iceland made continuous surface escort across the Atlantic possible, but Liberators were needed to close the gap in air cover. A three-cornered struggle between the US Army and navy air forces and Bomber Command went on until 1943 when at last Coastal Command's claim was admitted: 'It surprised everyone to see how few of these splendid machines were sufficient to tip the scale. In mid-May, an attack by thirty-three U-boats failed to sink a single merchant ship and at the end of that month Doenitz admitted that the battle was lost. But Slessor, among others, regarded it as a *defensive* victory. As devout Trenchardists, they pined for what they regarded as *offensive* action, quite overlooking the fact that overcoming U-boats was an essential task: unless that were done, there could have been no landings in Normandy.

The Leigh Light

Twin-engined Vickers Wellington bombers, equipped with what became known as the 'Leigh Light', played a significant part in the battle from June 1942 onwards. Inventor Wing Commander H. de V. Leigh had flown anti-U-boat patrols in 1917 and 1918. He returned to the RAF in 1939 and served at Coastal Command HQ under Frederick Bowhill, who had been his squadron commander in 1917. In September 1940, Bowhill asked his staff for 'bright ideas' about how to destroy U-boats at night. Air-to-surface vessel (ASV) radar was no help at night, which was when U-boats surfaced to re-charge their batteries. At Leigh's suggestion, a searchlight was installed in the mid-upper turret of a Wellington in March 1941, but it was not until June 1942 that the device became effective over the Bay of Biscay.

Inadequate Co-operation

Early in 1939, Doenitz had said he would need 300 U-boats to isolate the British Isles. At that time, he believed: 'Aircraft can no more eliminate the U-boat than a crow can fight a mole.' He was proven wrong. Luckily for Britain and the United States, he had always 'lacked eyes': reliable long-range aircraft.

The four-engined Focke-Wulf Fw 200 Condor, a converted airliner, had been pressed into service in 1940, but it was not robust enough for hard service over the sea. In any case, there were few of them: only 252 were built between 1940 and 1944. Had the Germans developed a more effective machine for co-operation with U-boats – an aircraft as robust as, for example, the Short Sunderland – and built them in far greater numbers, their impact would have been even graver on Atlantic shipping. But Goering, the war's most inept air commander, had no grasp of what modern aircraft might achieve and refused, in any case, to co-operate with the navy. Hitler took little interest in the war at sea and never pressed him.

Unwise Faith in ASDIC

In 1937, the British Admiralty decided that the U-boat would never again threaten shipping, thanks to ASDIC, a sonar device. These so-called experts quite overlooked the fact that ASDIC could not detect U-boats on the surface, where they spent most of their time. Using their diesel engines, they were faster than most merchant ships and usually attacked during hours of darkness. Using their electric motors, when submerged, they could move only slowly and not for long.

The Admiralty, forgetting its Great War experience, decreed that U-boats should be hunted; a satisfyingly offensive task, even though few were caught. In fact, they were usually to be found close to convoys of merchant ships. Not until 1943 did Coastal Command get the equipment it needed: long-range aircraft; bombs; depth charges and air-to-surface vessel radar. At every step of the way it had to fight the Admiralty for effective air-sea co-operation. It was also bitterly opposed by Bomber Command and most members of the Air Staff who remained fixated on the bomber as a war-winning weapon. Victory, far too long delayed, came only in May 1943, when no fewer than forty-one U-boats were sunk and Admiral Karl Doenitz admitted defeat.

Portal's Failure

In February 1941, Portal complained to Richard Peirse (his successor as head of Bomber Command) that the RAF was 'on the defensive with a vengeance owing to the situation in the Atlantic', adding that 'a very high proportion of bomber effort will inevitably be required to pull the Admiralty out of the mess they have got into'. These were astonishing words from an airman with such a high reputation.

It is generally agreed that Hitler caused the 'mess', helped along by British and French politicians, and that British bombers only began to harm Germany in 1942. It is not easy to understand how Portal could regard the war at sea as an annoying distraction from what he thought of as 'the real war' in the skies over Germany. The Admiralty was largely responsible for the weakness of its FAA, but Portal certainly knew how poorly equipped Coastal Command was. Early in March 1941, Churchill – not Portal – directed Bomber Command to devote its attention to 'defeating the attempt of the enemy to strangle our food supplies and our connection with the United States' by attacking U-boats at sea, in docks and in building yards and by attacking German bombers used against shipping.

The most dangerous failure in Churchill's conduct of the naval war was his refusal to back the navy's demand (supported by Coastal Command) that long-range aircraft be diverted from Bomber Command in 1942. The pigheadedness of Portal, combined with Harris's tunnel vision came close to losing the Battle of the Atlantic. The U-boat threatened to bring British industry to a standstill, ground Bomber Command for lack of fuel and prevent the possibility of an Anglo-American liberation of the Continent. 'Here was the absolute crux,' wrote Barnett, 'of Britain's war against Germany.' Harris never understood this and Portal accepted it, only reluctantly.

The Channel Dash

In February 1942, Hitler decided that three powerful warships, accompanied by destroyers, mine-sweepers and torpedo-boats, must leave Brest, on France's Atlantic coast (where they had been regularly attacked), and sail through the English Channel to greater safety at Wilhelmshaven in Germany. They would have ample air cover for most of their journey. This 'Channel Dash', as the British called it, like many German operations, 'was a tactical success but a strategic failure': at Brest, the ships were a standing threat to trans-Atlantic convoys; at Wilhelmshaven, they could more easily be contained and did nothing useful before they were destroyed.

At the time, however, on the eve of the surrender of Singapore, and with Operation Crusader having failed in North Africa, it was a severe blow to all Hitler's opponents. The three services had not worked together, and performed poorly separately, failing to use reliable intelligence for fourteen hours after the Germans had left Brest. There was plenty of courage, as so often in these early years of the war, but efficient use of ample resources was sadly lacking. While Germany rejoiced, in Britain 'the sense of national shame was profound... Churchill was taken aback by the scale of popular anger; it seemed that by this stage of the war, while the British public was inured to a seemingly unbroken run of defeats on land, it was not prepared to accept humiliation in a domain that it considered to be its birthright.'

Overcoming the U-boat

March 1943 saw 'the rock bottom of Allied fortunes; a twenty-day period in which ninety-seven ships (over 500,000 tons) were lost': it was the period in which Germany came closest to severing links between Britain and the United States. As so often in the Second World War, the Allies were greatly helped by their enemies. For example, the commanders of the German navy had preferred battleships to U-boats and consequently not enough of these far more dangerous weapons were built.

Goering used his immense influence to prevent the development of long-range patrol aircraft, capable of working with U-boats; in 1941 and 1942 Hitler diverted too many U-boats to the Arctic and the Mediterranean, where their successes were less valuable than they would have been in the Atlantic. As in other theatres, the Germans were too confident in the security of their wireless communications.

Yet by the end of May 1943, the Allies had achieved a decisive victory over the U-boats. A turning point came with the successful defence during four days, 4-7 April, of Convoy HX 231, sailing from Newfoundland for Britain. Warships under Commander Peter Gretton, aided by long-range B-24 Liberator bombers, all of them helped by code-breakers and radio direction findings were responsible.

Only three of the sixty-one merchant ships making up the convoy were lost and Liberators sank two of the twenty U-boats that attempted to attack them. Gretton later reported that 'air cover again showed itself to be the key to this problem'. Time and time again, Liberators intercepted U-boats at a distance from the convoy, causing them to dive and so lose contact with their targets. Ultra information was of great value, but not in itself decisive.

In September 1941 – three months before Hitler's declaration of war – Roosevelt had publicly ordered the US Navy to attack German vessels on sight. The D-Day landings and the Battle of Normandy were, in Terraine's opinion, 'the supreme offensive action of the Western Allies in the war, their great contribution to the defeat of Germany'. The victory in the West could not have taken place without the victory in the Atlantic.

John Ferris argued that Ultra has been over-praised in the years since the secret was revealed for its part in the Allied victory in the Battle of the Atlantic. That battle, in fact, was won by Allied shipyards, 'not by steel-eyed naval captains', brave and skilful as they were, but by 'four-eyed cost accountants'. The U-boat never came close to sinking enough merchant ships to prevent American men and materials from crossing the Atlantic. Ultra certainly helped greatly in enabling shipping to avoid U-boats, but other sources of intelligence, notably direction-finding, were important. Long-range aircraft and centimetric radar aboard convoy escorts were equally vital.

BATTLE OF THE ATLANTIC, 1941

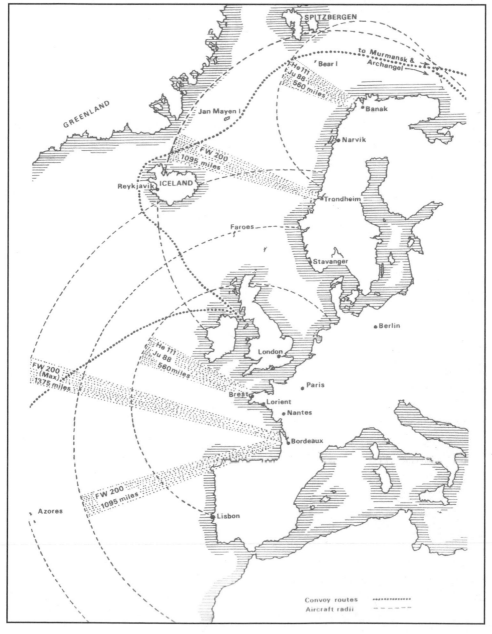

18

Was the Bomber a Decisive Weapon?
1939-1945

Bold Untested Claims

By 1918, bombing had its place in the armoury of all the nations involved in the Great War, but after the Armistice, questions were asked about the RAF's purpose. How much should be spent on it at the expense of the other services? What should be the balance between offensive bombers and defensive fighters? If war threatened again, what strength should be devoted to a bomber offensive, what to winning control of the seas and what to close support for armies advancing or retreating?

Later, there were intense disputes about targets: industrial plants; military bases; aircraft manufacturers; civilian morale; transport systems; oil resources? Bold untested claims had helped to preserve the RAF's independence (and attract a disproportionate share of government funding), while contributing to deep public anxiety about the destruction bombers would cause. The claims were merely assertions and not backed by analysis of either the damage that could be done with the means at hand or the defence that the enemy might offer. Exercises were indeed carried out, but with rules tailored to suit prevailing assumptions.

Unready for War

The result was that when threatened by Hitler's aggression, Britain's bomber force caused him no alarm. Early in 1936 the Air Staff made plans for four-engined long-range bombers, but progress was slow: partly for technical and labour reasons and partly because the rapid development, in 1936 and 1937, in the performance of fighters and the quality of anti-aircraft defences raised strong objections to such a costly project. Would not a greater number of cheaper twin-engined bombers serve Britain better? The Germans, it seemed, had abandoned the idea of building a few truly heavy bombers in favour of a greater number of twin-engined types. Nevertheless, the Air Staff planned in 1938 for what it called an 'Ideal Bomber', to be available by the end of 1941. These were the decisions that paved the way for the immense force of heavy bombers that came into service from 1942 onwards.

For no good reason and despite ample evidence to the contrary, the Air Staff assumed that the Luftwaffe was intended as a long-range bomber force aimed at Britain when in fact it was designed and equipped to give close support to armies in operations against Poland, France and ultimately the Soviet Union. Consequently, the Air Staff was persuading itself in 1938 that a handful of Whitley bombers could destroy Germany's war-making capacity. 'The bomber chiefs seem to have been existing in some mysterious climate,' wrote John Terraine, 'unrelated to geographical, mechanical or numerical reality.' Edgar Ludlow-Hewitt, who became head of Bomber Command in September 1937, soon told his Air Ministry masters that his command was a virtually useless weapon of war. Two years later, his bombers attacked naval targets in daylight (suffering heavy losses for no reward) and dropped leaflets in darkness (which had no impact whatsoever).

Ludlow-Hewitt was sacked in April 1940 in an attempt by Cyril Newall and his supporters among the Air Staff to silence an articulate, well-informed critic. Hugh Dowding, head of Fighter Command, would have suffered the same fate in June 1939 if his designated successor – who knew nothing about Fighter Command – had not suffered an accident. On the other hand, as John Ferris has written, the government had required Bomber Command to be ready for war in 1942, not 1939: 'how far did the spadework of the 1930s produce its strength of 1942; a million-man force able to scrape together 1,000 bombers, to flatten small cities at a single bound, to expand despite heavy casualties?

In 1935, Hitler had told Sir John Simon (Britain's unusually-gullible Foreign Secretary) that Germany had already achieved 'air parity' with the RAF. 'This was totally untrue', wrote Herbert Dinerstein. 'Hitler wanted to frighten the British and scare them he did. He frightened them into building an adequate air force.' Hitler scoffed in one of his speeches at the notion that they had done so in August 1939. 'Where can they attack me?' he asked. 'In the air?' Here he was interrupted by hysterical laughter to which he cheerfully responded.

One Sure Path

Only a few minutes after Britain declared war on Germany, air raid sirens sounded over London. It was a false alarm and a fitting comment, wrote Malcolm Smith, on 'inflated contemporary estimates of the potential of air power'. It would be nearly a year before Britain came under sustained attack; almost two years before she began her own attack on Germany; and three before that attack began to cause serious damage. As early as July 1940, Churchill had in mind 'only one sure path' to victory, as he told Beaverbrook on the 8th:

'That is an absolutely devastating, exterminating attack by very heavy bombers from this country upon the Nazi homeland. We must be able to overwhelm them by this means without which I do not see a way through.'

In September, in a memorandum for the Cabinet, he added: 'The navy can lose the war, but only the air force can win it.'

This 'belligerent enunciation', as Ralph Bennett called it, of the Trenchard doctrine, to which many in the Air Ministry remained committed throughout the war, was intended to bolster spirits, but at that time there were no British heavy bombers and few twin-engined machines that could damage Germany. Then and later, aerial photographs were able to show damaged buildings but not whether the machinery inside was wrecked and the British had no means of knowing how long repairs took or whether workers had been killed, injured or frightened away. They simply made assumptions, including that Hitler had placed German industry on a war footing, but he did not do so until July 1943, when catastrophic defeats on the Eastern Front and in North Africa already made it clear that Germany must be defeated.

Speaking at the Mansion House on 14 July 1941, Churchill said: 'We will mete out to the Germans the measure, and more than the measure, they have meted out to us.' Everyone cheered and he offered Hitler a direct challenge: 'You do your worst, and we will do our best.'

There could be no 'second front' in 1942 (major Anglo-American landings in France) as the Soviet Union and many of its supporters in Britain demanded: the essential landing-craft, ground forces, heavy weapons and aircraft simply did not yet exist. In its place, Churchill told Portal in March, that the bombing of German cities must remain the main offensive action. 'It is not decisive, but better than doing nothing, and indeed a formidable method of injuring the enemy.' As Michael Carver wrote long after the war, 'it is indisputable that between the evacuation from Dunkirk in 1940 and the return to France on D-Day, 1944, Britain had to find some way of fighting Germany. Running up and down the desert coast of North Africa was not enough. The bombing campaign was a necessity for national morale if for nothing else.'

Sinclair always asserted that any injury to German civilians was purely incidental. The government 'never quite had the courage to come clean' and admit that *all* Germans were in danger. 'Had it done so,' Sinclair believed, 'I think it would have received overwhelming popular support. The morale of the Germans was exactly what we were trying to destroy: our adversaries called it "terror bombing", which it was.'

It also generated hatred of the enemy, always good for morale, and Anglo-American bombers were attacked until the last days of the war. But from the end of 1942, the Luftwaffe was driven onto the defensive. The Allies thereafter gained almost complete control of the air, a mastery that permitted landings at Sicily, Salerno, Anzio and Normandy. They bombed wherever they liked and invaded Germany without aerial opposition. As a result, eighty per cent of all the bombs dropped on Germany in the whole war were dropped between July 1944 and May 1945, causing irreparable damage. There could be no let up: Arnhem and the Ardennes showed only too clearly that German ground forces remained tenacious enemies. The bombing offensive was of great value in easing the westward advance of Soviet forces in 1944-1945.

Trenchard's Memorandum
In May 1941, the long-retired but ever-active Trenchard had sent Churchill a memorandum, which he forwarded to the chiefs of staff. 'Using his peculiar mathematics', as Tami Biddle wrote, he declared that ninety-nine per cent of the bombs dropped on cities contributed directly to the destruction of German morale. The attacks should be made every night, even by single bombers, and heavy losses – such as were suffered under his direction in the Great War – must be endured. On the other hand, asserted Trenchard: 'If you are bombing a target at sea, then ninety-nine per cent of your bombs are wasted.'

Early in June, he assured Portal that everything turned on 'the difference between the German and British mentality': unlike Britons, German civilians were 'very badly' affected by repeated bombing attacks. Damage to essential services caused by 'indiscriminate bombing in a town was far greater than that caused by the aimed bombing of factories'. Portal was a diligent administrator, a career airman with a formidable personality, and yet he did not dismiss this nonsense out of hand. He did acknowledge, however, that bombing was not the RAF's only obligation, but his fellow-chiefs (Pound and Dill) chose to believe, for no obvious reason, that 'the most vulnerable point in the German nation' was civilian morale under air attack.

The Butt Report
David Bensusan-Butt was a civil servant in the War Office secretariat, assigned to assist Lindemann, now elevated to the peerage as Viscount Cherwell. He produced a report in August 1941 that was the first serious examination, based on analysis of photographs and claims made by bomber crews. He found, to the surprise and dismay of many RAF officers, that on any given night only about one in five crews dropped bombs within five miles of their targets. Peirse, head of the command, refused to accept Butt's evidence, preferring to rely on crew reports and his own untested opinions. It is 'an awful thought,' wrote Churchill, that 'perhaps three-quarters of our bombs go astray. If we could make it half and half we should virtually have doubled our bombing power.'

He had just received an absurd paper from Portal, calling for 4,000 heavy bombers to use in a massive air offensive that would, he believed, break German civilian morale. It was irrational because British industry could not possibly build so many heavy bombers and also provide modern weapons for ground and sea forces. Churchill was not impressed. 'The most we can say' about Bomber Command, he replied, 'is that it will be a heavy and I trust a seriously increasing annoyance' to Germany. Portal explicitly linked the attack on German morale and interwar air control: admittedly, the scale of the former has been 'greatly magnified', but it remains an extension of a policy which proved 'outstandingly successful' between the wars. He quite overlooked the fact that the Germans had a somewhat greater capacity to defend themselves than the virtually-unarmed people of the Middle East.

In his better moments, Portal was one of a handful of officers emerging to meet desperate crises in all three services who had the professional knowledge and personal character to challenge Churchill. Hitherto, replied Portal, Churchill had spoken of heavy bombers as a means of winning the war or at least making it possible for British soldiers to return to the Continent. If that was no longer government policy, he asked the Prime Minister to inform the chiefs of staff at once. We would 'require an air force composed quite differently from that which we are now creating'.

Meanwhile, Portal was at last moved to seek some elementary improvements in Bomber Command's performance: there were to be trained navigators and gunners, marker bombs, 'expert fire-raising crews' and more careful thought given to targeting. But he remained convinced that keeping Germans awake in widely-scattered areas would undermine their morale. Churchill admitted that Bomber Command had a major role to play, but warned Portal against 'placing unbounded confidence in this means of attack'.

Churchill then made a point that had never been properly examined by the prewar RAF. 'Even if all the towns of Germany were rendered largely uninhabitable, it does not follow that the military control would be weakened or even that war industry could not be carried on.' He then recalled the RAF's claims concerning the impact of bombing and the fears aroused in Britain before and especially during the Munich Crisis; claims and fears that he himself, of course, had so eloquently underlined for years. This picture of aerial destruction, he told Portal, 'was so exaggerated that it depressed the statesmen responsible for the prewar policy, and played a part in the desertion of Czechoslovakia in August 1938'.

When Churchill became Prime Minister, he found to his surprise and relief that in Fighter Command he had an effective weapon, if only of defence. By September 1941, however, after reading the Butt Report, he realised that British bombers were failing over Germany even more completely than German bombers had failed over Britain. By the end of that year, fortunately, the German crusade against the Soviet Union was faltering, Japan had attacked the United States and Hitler chose to declare war in support of his Asian ally.

Tizard and Churchill

Early in 1942, now that the United States was in the war and the Soviet Union had not collapsed, doubts were expressed in British ruling circles about the wisdom of continuing with an expensive bombing offensive that was costing the RAF many lives and causing little obvious harm to the German war effort. Dudley Pound was not alone in asking for more bombers to be diverted to support the navy in a campaign against U-boats. That was an assault which must be won if vital imports of food and raw materials were to continue and if Britain were to be a base for massive American reinforcements.

The future of 'area bombing' seemed to be in the balance until Lord Cherwell made a 'crucial intervention'. He sent a minute to Churchill on 30 March 1942 in which he calculated, on the basis of damage inflicted upon Birmingham and Hull that '10,000 bombers blitzing main cities could destroy the homes of one-third of the German population by mid-1943. This would break German war will.'

Henry Tizard, Chief Scientific Adviser at the Air Ministry, disagreed. Churchill, however, preferred to rely on the opinions of his old friend. Cherwell advocated a bomber offensive with 'characteristic intensity', and his biographer (Lord Birkenhead) explained that he was 'determined to thwart the claims of the army, the navy, Coastal and Fighter Commands for more resources, and bent every effort to maximising Bomber Command' because he wanted Germans to share the suffering they had inflicted upon others.

Tizard did not oppose bombing Germany, but he argued that Cherwell's calculations were grossly exaggerated and urged the Air Ministry to take a broader view of its responsibilities, especially in the Atlantic and the Mediterranean. But he was obliged to leave London. Patrick Blackett, an outstanding physicist, had backed Tizard, but he too was ignored because of his work for the Admiralty.

Tizard had sent Freeman (vice-chief of the Air Staff and Portal's alter ego) a memo on 20 February 1942 in which he lamented the alarming losses suffered by Bomber Command – more than 700 aircraft in eight months – costing probably as many casualties in air crew as the number of Germans killed. Freeman's response was: 'My first reaction is that you have been seeing too much of Professor Blackett.' He made no attempt to refute Tizard's figures.

A New Bomber Champion
Early in 1942, Arthur Harris was appointed head of Bomber Command and with the Butt Report in mind realised that some spectacular achievements were needed. His bombers made a bad start, hitting a Renault truck plant in Paris which killed more than 400 French civilians. He then turned his attention to Lübeck and Rostock, lightly-defended, wooden-built towns on the Baltic coast, easy to find and likely to burn well. Urban workers and their families would be killed, injured or so demoralised that war production would be seriously reduced and Nazi rule undermined. This was the theory.

In fact, Harris had only fourteen squadrons of heavy bombers on hand in March 1942: two of them were of Lancasters (neither yet operational) and the rest were Stirlings, Manchesters – neither of which were efficient weapons – and Halifaxes. He depended on three twin-engined types: the useful Wellington and the useless Whitleys and Hampdens. He and Portal needed all the RAF's traditional faith in the bomber to persuade themselves, the navy and the army, that it was a war-winning weapon.

Portal assured his fellow-chiefs of staff in November 1942 that it would be possible, from 1943, to drop one and three-quarter million tons of bombs during the next two years: twenty-five million Germans would be made homeless, and nearly two million would be killed or seriously injured. Neither he nor Harris had any patience with those who doubted these figures or flinched from accepting such a fearful loss of life.

Harris had a long correspondence about casualties with Sir Arthur Street, Under-Secretary of State at the Air Ministry, late in 1943. Street was among those who flinched, but Harris swept his reservations aside. The German economic system, which he had been instructed to destroy, included workers, houses and public utilities and they must therefore suffer injury and death, if the war was ever to be won. Harris realised that the Air Ministry wished to avert public controversy and avoid conflict with religious and humanitarian opinion, but he would not allow his crews to be sacrificed in a cause which authorities were reluctant to avow publicly.

The Butt Report convinced Harris that an Operational Research Section (ORS) must be set up in his HQ. He gave it full support and during the rest of the war hundreds of valuable reports were produced. The ORS, wrote Wakelam, 'contributed to the establishment of a near-precision capability, one regularly as accurate' as that claimed by the Americans for their daylight attacks. But neither Harris nor the Air Ministry nor the Ministry of Economic Warfare grasped the simple fact that unroofed factories had not necessarily ceased production or that production was not continuing elsewhere. The failure to understand this, together with the assumption that Germans lacked the resolution of the British under attack upset all calculations on the subject dearest to Harris's heart.

The responsibility for ensuring that lessons were drawn from other theatres, where intelligence was taken more seriously, lay with Portal, but he rarely pressed Harris. 'The Mediterranean,' wrote Bennett, 'was the obvious source of lessons.' By mid-1942, Tedder had acquired a great deal of information about the Luftwaffe from intelligence sources and had learned that co-operation with other services, 'rather than scorn for them', benefitted all three. In 1944, Tedder advocated the co-ordination of all arms; a policy which he 'was to make so peculiarly his own' between April and September when Bomber Command was effectively under his control.

The Air Ministry refused to permit publication, after the war, of Harris's

Despatch on War Operations, alleging that it contained information of value to a future enemy. However, he used it in his book, *Bomber Offensive*, published in 1947. Not until 1996 did the despatch itself appear, with a thoughtful introduction and commentary by Sebastian Cox. Harris regarded Bomber Command as a weapon that could, by 'area attacks', so weaken German morale and industrial capacity that an Allied invasion of occupied Europe would be unnecessary.

He opposed the creation of a Pathfinder Force, intended to help bombers find actual targets, rather than simply blast urban areas. He supposed that attacks on the Ruhr had severely damaged war production, when in fact vital factories had already been moved elsewhere.

Harris refused to focus attacks on German fighter production in 1943, believing that the destruction of Berlin would bring victory, one that his bombers failed to achieve at very heavy cost to themselves. He took credit for the effectiveness of attacks on communications in 1944, but continued to believe that they had been a distraction from his main task.

On the other hand, his massive attack on Cologne in May 1942 probably ensured that the bombing offensive would be continued. As Brian Bond wrote, 'Germany was waging a barbaric "total war" on the Eastern Front, and the Holocaust was beginning: in these circumstances, it is not clear why her cities should have been immune to attack from the West' and few people – at the time – thought they should be.

As for the attack on oil targets in the last winter of the war, there were in fact few nights when Harris's bombers could have done more. About half of the command's tonnage was dropped on transportation targets. The direct impact of the bombing offensive was very great and the indirect effects may have been equally important: large numbers of German airmen, soldiers and weapons were used solely on defence, and many civilians were needed to repair railways, factories and power supplies or simply to clear away rubble.

Harris allowed that Dowding and Fighter Command had done well to resist a Luftwaffe offensive in 1940 that might have cleared a path, if not for invasion, then for those in Britain who thought peace should be made with Hitler. Now that those dangers had receded, he believed that all Britain's aviation resources should be devoted to strengthening the bomber force and regarded any support for armies or navies as wasteful diversions. Harris chose to believe, as did many American air commanders, that the German economy was tightly stretched from 1940 onwards, and the morale of Germans under aerial attack was fragile, that photographs taken by bomber crews indicated unsustainable destruction and, in the American case, that day bombers hit their targets precisely and shot down many defensive fighters.

As early as mid-June 1942 Harris told Churchill that he did not wish to see 'Britain's youth slaughtered once again in the mud of Flanders'. In fact, more than 55,000 of them were 'slaughtered', though not in Flanders mud.

About half of all the aircrew who served in Bomber Command were killed and thousands more were injured on operations or on training flights; many were imprisoned by the Germans.

'No other Western Allied combatants, except for their American daylight counterparts,' wrote Mark Wells, 'suffered the same huge casualties, nor faced the mathematical certainty of their own deaths so routinely and so unflinchingly.' The Americans lost 35,000 men in their bombing operations. Harris, like his American colleagues, believed that these casualties must be accepted, if Hitler were to be overthrown.

All objections to a total focus on Bomber Command were dismissed by Harris and yet, as Tami Biddle pointed out: 'Virtually the whole of the Western war effort – including Bomber Command's own fuel supply – depended on sea lines of communication.' Harris's tunnel-vision contrasted sharply with the broad understanding of Tedder, who came to prominence in the Middle East and quickly learned that only inter-service co-operation would avoid defeat, let alone bring victory. A much more intelligent man than Harris, he saw the war 'as a single problem in which the strategy, tactics, and the technique of sea, land and air warfare respectively are inevitably and closely interlocked'.

Disaster at Dieppe

While Churchill was in Moscow in August 1942, reports of the massive raid over Cologne at the end of May and news that Bomber Command was growing stronger by the day impressed Stalin. Churchill therefore seized the opportunity to tell him that there would soon be a 'serious raid' on Dieppe by some 8,000 men with fifty tanks, who would stay a night, 'kill as many Germans as possible', and then withdraw. This raid marked the low point of Churchill's 'butcher and bolt' approach to undermining German power. As he said, it would be like 'a bath in which you feel with your hand to see if the water is hot'.

The result, on 19 August, was that thousands of men under British command were fatally scalded. Planned for months, it was the largest amphibious attack mounted under British control since Gallipoli. It was also, in proportion to the forces used, the worst defeat the Allies suffered throughout the war. The air battle was the largest in which RAF fighters were involved: more squadrons than at the height of the Battle of Britain.

Everything went wrong: the chosen target; intelligence information about the strength of German defences; the provision of naval and bombing support; the timing of the assault; and the failure to achieve surprise. Churchill had demanded action in an attempt to impress Stalin. Most of the troops employed were Canadian and two-thirds of them were killed, wounded or captured. Fighters did their best to cover both the soldiers and the ships, but over 100 were lost.

Typically, Churchill skated lightly over this disaster in his memoirs, taking refuge in the claim that 'lessons learned' at Dieppe paved the way for success on D-Day nearly two years later. They were actually ancient truths: incompetent planning usually leads to disaster.

Here is where we meet Louis Mountbatten, son of Prince Louis of Battenberg, married to a granddaughter of Queen Victoria, whom Churchill had appointed First Lord of the Admiralty in December 1912. Battenberg, German-born, was forced out of office soon after the Great War began, but Churchill – a devout royalist – had always kept an eye on Battenberg's son, now known as 'Mountbatten', and eagerly elevated him to chief of combined operations in April 1942.

Mountbatten submitted a report on the Dieppe raid that laid overall responsibility on Bernard Montgomery, then in charge of South Eastern Command. Churchill accepted the report at the time, but there had been two plans: one, for which Montgomery was responsible (code-named Rutter) was ready in early July, but abandoned because of bad weather and signs that the Germans were ready for it. Montgomery had nothing to do with its revival – now named Jubilee – which was pressed by Mountbatten.

When working on his postwar memoirs, Churchill learned that Mountbatten was in fact responsible and sent him a draft of his proposed account. Mountbatten, seriously alarmed, re-wrote his version and Churchill let the matter drop because it was 'thanks to him that this egregious social climber had been so absurdly over-promoted'. Churchill always found it difficult to resist an officer with 'dash' (in whatever direction and for whatever purpose) and when dash was combined with royal blood he was dazzled. The disaster scars the reputations of both Churchill and Mountbatten, and is no credit to Hastings Ismay, who had been instructed by Churchill to find out what happened at Dieppe and why.

The chiefs of staff share the blame for giving in to Churchill's pressure to mount the raid. 'Brooke kept quiet,' wrote Hew Strachan, 'because the raid would ward off Soviet pressure for a second front'; Pound wanted an alternative to Russian convoys; and Portal still believed that defensive fighters could allow bombers an easy run to and from German targets. The raid lacked bomber or battleship support and soldiers were expected, as in the Great War, to make a frontal assault on prepared positions.

The Battle of Berlin

Harris's headquarters at High Wycombe were only a short drive away from Chequers and he frequently visited Churchill there in attempts to convince him that the bomber was the key to victory. During the winter of 1943-1944, he was given every chance to make good his claims. Early in November 1943, he sent Churchill a list of forty-seven German towns: nineteen were already 'virtually destroyed', he believed, and another nineteen 'seriously damaged'. He proposed Berlin and eight other cities as the remaining priorities. He went on, in typical 'bomber baron' language: 'We have not far to go. But we must get the USAAF to wade in with greater force... We can wreck Berlin from end to end if the USAAF will come in on it. It will cost between us 400-500 aircraft. It will cost Germany the war.' By December, he had convinced himself that British bombers, supported by twin-engined Mosquito night fighters, could have the European war won by 1 April 1944.

Carl Spaatz agreed. In November 1943, he had assured Harry Hopkins (Roosevelt's special adviser) that once the winter was over, Anglo-American bombers would oblige Germany to surrender in three months. There would be no need for an Allied invasion by soldiers with naval support. In fact, the diversion of these bombers from the Ruhr to Berlin was one of the major strategic errors of the RAF's war: it was heavily defended; far from British bases; usually covered in cloud or smoke and the diversion permitted the Ruhr's industries to recover.

'One of Harris's major mistakes,' thought Max Hastings, 'was failure to grasp the importance of repeating blows against damaged targets.' He paid too much attention to dramatic photographs.

Wiser heads among the Allied commanders were less ready than Harris's staff officers to nod in agreement with whatever their formidable boss asserted and so preparations for an invasion went ahead. Bomber Command suffered appalling losses throughout the winter of 1943-1944, culminating in a raid on Nuremberg at the end of March when ninety-five of nearly 800 bombers despatched were lost. Many of the survivors were damaged and carried home injured crewmen. It was the command's worst night of the war and caused little damage. About 120 of the bombers actually attacked Schweinfurt, fifty miles north-west of Nuremberg. That disaster marked the end of Harris's bid to win the war with British bombers.

As Brian Bond wrote, the Air Staff made a fair case for strategic bombing before the war, but 'the single-minded persistence' with which it acted until the Nuremberg raid 'and the resulting marked reluctance to take heed of unfavourable intelligence or adapt to other types of operations' before that disaster caused heavy and unnecessary losses. Throughout his campaign focused on Berlin, between 18 November 1943 and 31 March 1944, more than 1,000 bombers and nearly 8,000 airmen were lost; many more damaged bombers got back to Britain with dead or wounded men aboard.

Fortunately for the Western Allies, Ronnie Harker (a test pilot with Rolls-Royce engines in Derby) reported in April 1942 that the North American's P-51 fighter (the Mustang) 'was aerodynamically superb. It had far less "drag" than any comparable fighter, it never stalled, and it was astonishingly fuel-efficient,' but its Allison engine was inadequate. At Harker's suggestion, a Rolls-Royce Merlin 61 engine was fitted instead of the Allison at Duxford and the result was a fighter that had the range (when fitted with drop fuel tanks), speed, high-level performance and agility to accompany American bombers to any German target and shoot down any German fighter.

Wilfrid Freeman had five more Mustangs converted, gave two to Spaatz and the Packard company was asked to build Merlin engines in the United States. Resistance to fitting an American fighter with a British engine was eventually overcome, but only by the combined efforts of such Anglo-American heavyweights as Freeman – 'the principal matchmaker', in Sebastian Ritchie's opinion – helped by Spaatz, Tedder, Hopkins, Churchill, Roosevelt and Robert Lovett (Arnold's chief deputy). The essential catalyst was the shattering losses suffered by American bombers late in 1943: so appalling that resistance in Washington to using a British engine was overcome. During a 'Big Week' in February 1944 these fighters, produced at an astonishing rate, fatally weakened the Luftwaffe's fighter defences.

What Targets?

A Combined Strategic Targets Committee was formed in October 1944, shortly after Eisenhower (in effect, Tedder) was obliged to relinquish control of the heavy bombers to Portal and Arnold, with Norman Bottomley (Portal's deputy) and Spaatz, commanding American heavy bombers, as their agents. Harris regretted the change: the months when Eisenhower was his 'admiral' and Tedder 'captain on the bridge' were, he recalled, the most positive of his long service in Bomber Command.

Tedder chaired the Allied Air Commanders' conferences at which target priorities were decided and advocated 'a balanced offensive against Germany's synthetic petroleum and transportation sectors. Unlike many of his colleagues, Tedder saw these target systems as complementary, not alternatives. A co-ordinated attack on the Reich's railways and inland waterways would damage both the war economy and the armed forces. All types of aircraft could be used: heavy bombers to hit marshalling yards; medium bombers and fighter-bombers to hit junctions, bridges, trains and barges.

The CSTC was formed to sort out the immense amount of information available, allowing members to pick and choose whatever suited their opinions. The chief pickers were Sidney Bufton (Air Ministry), Oliver Lawrence (Ministry of Economic Warfare) and two Americans, Alfred R. Maxwell (heavy bomber operations) and Henry Pincus (Enemy Objectives Unit). They were convinced that destroying oil targets would see an end to the war in 1944. In fact, they failed to realise that over ninety per cent of Germany's energy was derived from coal. 'To chase the phantom of quick, cheap victory' the CSTC opposed Tedder's proposal.

The German economy depended on coal and railways to move it. Many American analysts wrongly assumed that road transport played the same role in Germany as it did in the United States. Until mid-February 1945, Lawrence ignored all intelligence information relating to industry and transport. He was then obliged to admit that as many as 20,000 commercial intercepts made weekly were unencrypted because he considered them worthless. His actions 'prevented the full fury of Allied air capabilities from destroying the German transportation network before winter began, and thus they may have extended the war by several months'.

During the winter of 1944-1945, Churchill was abandoning his self-appointed role as a 'war lord' and returning to those in which he had always been most comfortable: writer, orator and politician. He distanced himself from Harris and Bomber Command's failure to win the war on its own. Even in the middle of June 1943, Churchill had begun to have doubts. After Nuremberg, Bomber Command made a major contribution to the transportation plan, to support the Allied armies stuck in Normandy and attacks on oil and chemical plants. Targets were never neatly separated, of course: traffic moved through towns full of soldiers and past oil and chemical plants.

Writing in 1985, Zuckerman still found it difficult to understand why the Air Staff and Harris refused to accept Tedder's argument that communications were a 'common denominator', affecting all possible targets. Yet both the British and American strategic air forces resisted. Harris always preferred 'area attacks' and Spaatz was happiest with oil targets. In fact, Germany's transport system was the most vital target. An exchange of written opinions between Portal and Harris on targetting priorities has become famous. They wrote at such length that subsequent historians have been easily able to pick out and emphasise whatever points best please them, and set aside those that do not.

On 28 March 1945, Churchill sent a minute to the chiefs of staff in which he declared that 'the destruction of Dresden remains a serious query against the conduct of Allied bombing'. He maundered on, with his postwar reputation in mind, about the need for 'more precise concentration on military objectives... rather than on mere acts of terror and wanton destruction, however impressive'. Portal refused to allow him to get away with what Biddle called his 'sanctimonious turnabout', to stand in 'harsh after-the-fact judgment of a raid he had urged and was fully informed of ahead of time'.

Churchill was obliged to back down and rewrite his minute, but he refused to grant Bomber Command its own campaign medal and in his postwar memoirs he (and his writing partners) ducked the issues raised by strategic bombing. These partners were a 'syndicate' of cosmetic surgeons determined to shape Churchill into the wisest, most heroic of men, with his wholehearted co-operation. He was indeed, at his best, wise and heroic, but there were – as with all of us – flaws.

Harris, who had always resented the Air Ministry's attempt to 'prettify' the language used to publicise strategic bombing, agreed entirely with Portal's anger at Churchill's dishonesty. Throughout the war, Churchill had backed bombers as pointing 'the one sure path' to victory. Sinclair (always echoing Churchill) claimed in the House of Commons that any injury done to civilians was 'purely collateral, a by-product of attacks on legitimate economic targets'.

By May 1950, however, when Charles Webster and Noble Frankland (historians of Bomber Command) sought Churchill's views on Dresden, he simply lied: 'I thought the Americans did it.' As a politician and author, enjoying peacetime fame and fortune, he was 'concerned about the potential for postwar backlash against Bomber Command's methods' once the vile regimes in Germany and Japan were no more.

Since 1945, as Malcolm Smith wrote, Harris's reputation has suffered almost as much as Haig's. 'The decisive breakthrough in the air for which Harris worked always seemed, like Haig's, to be just around the corner' and would be achieved if more manpower and material were provided and not dissipated on other operations.

American airmen had long shared the belief of British airmen that the bomber was a war-winning weapon. Both air forces would suffer grievous losses in trying to make good that belief, but from early 1944 the Americans had at last achieved mastery in the air. During the last year of the war, Anglo-American bombers caused immense destruction and loss of life in both Germany and Japan. Britons and Americans had learned that victory in a fiercely-fought world war required the combined efforts of all three services: bombers could not do it alone. Even so, it is unlikely that those efforts would have prevailed without the astounding capacity of the Soviet Union to sustain appalling casualties and create a war machine that played, by far, the greater role in destroying Hitler's Germany.

No Need for American Armies

Churchill made a broadcast on 9 February 1941 in which he said: 'In the last war the United States sent 2,000,000 men across the Atlantic. But this is not a war of vast armies... We do not need the gallant armies which are forming throughout the American Union. We do not need them this year, nor next year, nor any year that I can foresee.' What Britain needed, he said, was 'an immense and continuous' supply of war materials. This was an opinion he had picked up from Trenchard. Until 1944, it was all that Britain could offer, and even then massive land armies (British, American and Canadian) would be required to overcome German forces gravely weakened by losses on the Eastern Front and in North Africa.

In his memoirs, Churchill passed swiftly over this vital aspect of the Allied war effort, barely mentioning even his close relations with Harris, head of

Bomber Command from February 1942 until the end of the war: as Henry V said to Falstaff, when it suited him to re-invent himself: 'I know thee not, old man.'

What did the Offensive Achieve?

Encouraged by Zuckerman, Tedder was trying to create a Bombing Research Mission from September 1944 onwards. He had hoped for a joint survey with the Americans, but they were determined to go it alone. Academic pundits flocked to Germany on the heels of the Allied armies, desperate to confirm their faith in precision attacks by day bombers and equally desperate to denounce the heresy of area attacks by night bombers. But John Kenneth Galbraith (later to become one of the most distinguished economic gurus of the age) upset many pundits by finding that 'the attack on transportation, beginning in September 1944, was the most important single cause of Germany's ultimate economic collapse'.

Although disappointed, Tedder agreed that Tizard should head a team of British graduate-level research students and officials with experience in communications, civil engineering and urban management. The question of testing weapons and assessing their performance had concerned Tedder since at least 1932 and with Portal's backing he formed a small RAF team to study past performance and offer guidance for future decisions.

On 3 January 1945, however, Churchill refused to sanction a British Bombing Research Mission, a refusal that Tedder regarded as 'scandalous, perverse, personal and political', but sadly typical of much of Churchill's conduct in the last year of the war. He had always been at heart a politician and a man obsessed with his reputation. He sensed that 'the one true path' to victory (aerial bombing) which he had so vehemently advocated would be criticised once Germany had surrendered. He was advised to duck for cover by his old friend, Cherwell.

Despite Churchill's opposition, Zuckerman set up a Bombing Analysis Unit (BAU). But it was stuck, as he told Tedder on 27 February 1945, between American isolationists and Air Ministry neglect. Tedder asked for Portal's support on 22 March for a field research team, based on the BAU. Portal agreed. He had already told his fellow chiefs that without such research 'we shall face the grave danger of government opinion on the lessons of this war being based largely on propaganda, personal recollection, or on the results of investigation by other nations'. Brooke and Cunningham agreed, Churchill, far from his best by 1945, remained opposed, but Tedder and Zuckerman created a British Bombing Survey Unit (BBSU) by joining Bomber Command's Operation Research Section to their BAU.

Unfortunately, it lacked civilian experts and depended largely on statistics gathered by the Americans. It also reflected too closely the opinions of Tedder and Zuckerman, advocates of communications attack ahead of either oil or 'area' attacks. Carefully reasoned though these opinions were, they would have carried more weight had they been subjected to independent analysis. The main conclusions of the official history of the *Strategic Air Offensive against Germany* were that Anglo-American bombers made 'an important and ultimately decisive' contribution to the defeat of Germany; that command of the air was achieved mainly by the USAF; and that victory proved far more difficult to achieve than most airmen, British or American, had expected.

It was also found that German production of weapons, including radar and signals equipment, was reduced by more than one-third and numerous Germans were diverted from war service in uniform or factories during the last two years of the war to deal with damage and casualties and prevented from moving rapidly to battle fronts. Men and women no longer went readily to work and got less done when they were there. Postwar surveys found that ninety-one per cent of German civilians regarded bombing as the worst burden of the war. The price paid by airmen was high and deserved to be fully honoured by Churchill and his writers in the massive account of 'his story' that they jointly produced, but it was not.

19

'Preparing a Great and Noble Undertaking', 1944-1945

Anzio: What Overlord was Spared

During October 1943, Churchill expressed his fears to the British chiefs of staff that a landing in north-west Europe might give Hitler 'the opportunity to concentrate, by reason of his excellent roads and rail communications, an overwhelming force against us and to inflict on us a military disaster greater than that of Dunkirk'. The chiefs agreed that as an alternative to Operation Overlord Britain should strengthen her forces in Italy, capture islands in the Aegean and advance into the Balkans. But in November, when the 'Big Three' (Roosevelt, Stalin and Churchill), met in Teheran, Stalin insisted that Overlord begin in May and Churchill was obliged to agree.

However, in January 1944 Churchill persuaded the Americans to join British forces in Operation Shingle, under the command of an unusually-incompetent American general, John Lucas. Shingle was an amphibious landing at Anzio, on the Italian west coast, about thirty-five miles south of Rome, intended to get behind the formidable German 'Gustav Line'. It was the last Anglo-American operation Churchill inspired and a costly failure. Shingle, wrote the British official historian, 'was given an extraordinary degree of importance. It was fathered by wishful strategical thinking and was not made the subject of a searching tactical analysis.'

Slessor offered no criticism of Churchill's part in the 'unsound conception', although the great man himself admitted that 'Anzio was my worst moment of the war. I had most to do with it. I didn't want two Suvla Bays in one lifetime.' That is exactly what he got. 'Churchill's vision of a cheap, quick victory at Anzio was wishful thinking and counter to everything he had been told regarding the practicality of a linkup between the Shingle force and the 5th Army.' But the entire Allied high command – Eisenhower, Brooke, and Alexander in particular – shares in the blame for allowing a loquacious politician to impose his mistaken notions.

The Germans were defending the town of Cassino and Monastery Hill overlooking it as a vital part of their Gustav Line, barring Clark's army from advancing on Rome and also preventing relief of the Allied forces at Anzio. Attempts to break through in January and February failed and the ground force commanders, Freyberg in particular, demanded the destruction of a famous Benedictine abbey on top of the hill, believing that the Germans were using it as an observation point. They weren't, until Allied bombers wrecked it on 15 February and the ruins offered them excellent defensive positions.

Slessor was delighted at the time, but later claimed that he had opposed 'a shocking miscalculation' and the historian Carlo D'Este found that most of the bombs had missed the abbey and it was largely destroyed by artillery fire. The destruction 'was the crowning example of the failure of Allied strategy in Italy in 1944'. It brought no military advantage and the only people killed were Italians. The lesson, not followed three months later in Normandy, 'was that heavies were not suitable for close support of ground action': they were far too inaccurate, and the bombing was not immediately followed up by ground forces.

Slessor and Lauris Norstad (MAAF's Director of Operations) gave attention to systematic attacks on communications, especially bridges, using Martin Marauder B-26 medium bombers and fighter-bombers in Operation Strangle. Between 15 March and 11 May (when Operation Diadem, the ground attack on Rome began), MAAF was constantly on the attack. Casualties on both sides were heavy. Clark was set on reaching Rome and allowed strong German forces to retreat in good order and fight on for another ten months.

Although the Allies were not driven away from Anzio, they suffered heavy casualties: 40,000 dead, wounded or captured, and perhaps as many again sick or deserted out of a force of 110,000. Carlo D'Este described it as 'one of the bloodiest campaigns of World War II', and one man who fought there prayed: 'God help us. You come yourself. Don't send Jesus, this is no place for children.'

Anzio, in fact, leaves as big a blot as Gallipoli and the Dodecanese campaign on Churchill's reputation. He fulfilled 'a lifelong fantasy', thought D'Este, by playing the part of a commanding general. It never occurred to him that he lacked the skills needed for such a part.

'The planning was a masterpiece of incompetence', wrote Shelford Bidwell, made worse by its commanders: Mark Clark, 'avid for glory as the liberator of Rome', and Harold Alexander, a Churchill favourite who was, wrote Michael Howard, 'charming, personally courageous, but ineffectual; like Ian Hamilton at Gallipoli, a gallant gentleman, far out of his depth'.

Years later, Slessor told Auchinleck: 'I became convinced, as a result of serving alongside [Alexander] for a year in Italy, that he is quite the stupidest man who has ever commanded anything more than a division... he owes his position entirely to Churchill's occasional gross misjudgement of men.'

The hope was that victory over strong German forces in Italy would permit an advance through Austria into Germany as an alternative to landings in

Normandy. By March, however, it was clear that Rome and all of Italy north of the capital would remain in German hands for months to come. Operation Strangle, in April 1944, revealed again to Slessor (and other bomber enthusiasts) that German soldiers remained effective despite Allied air superiority: bad weather, inaccurate target-finding and reluctance among some Allied soldiers to engage closely helped them.

Both Slessor and American bomber enthusiasts found it difficult to understand that ground forces could fight effectively even when the Allies controlled the air. Slessor consoled himself, in writing to Portal, with the opinion that 'the Hun is undoubtedly the world's finest ground soldier'. Men who fought against either Japanese or Soviet soldiers, including historians who (unlike Slessor) have studied their efforts may not agree.

The Anzio disaster weakened further the confidence of Churchill and Brooke in the proposed Normandy landings, but mercifully the commanders responsible proved to be far more competent than Alexander, Clark, Freyberg or Lucas in Italy.

Eisenhower and Tedder

In October 1943 Eisenhower expected George Marshall to be appointed Supreme Allied Commander for Overlord. He told his chief of staff (Walter Bedell Smith) who was about to visit Washington to discuss air matters with Marshall that he would need an airman with a good understanding of both strategic bombing and the problems of supporting ground forces. Marshall should therefore insist on Tedder for this appointment. It will be a 'bitter blow for me to lose him', Eisenhower continued, but Tedder was an expert who also had the full confidence of Portal and would therefore be able to use, 'during critical junctions of the land campaign, every last airplane in England'.

By the end of 1943, Tedder's support for American views on Italy as a strategic bomber base and his resistance to the Aegean adventure had drawn him away from Portal and towards all his American colleagues, not only Eisenhower. His opinion of Spaatz was improving and he welcomed the part he played in creating the 15th Air Force, which attacked German targets from its Italian bases. However, Tedder believed that Spaatz – just like Harris – exaggerated the bomber's capacity for destruction. Spaatz never wavered from his belief that bombers alone could win the war and there was no need to land men on the shores of occupied Europe.

This opinion was seconded by Harris in even more extravagant language: 'To divert Bomber Command from its true function,' he declared, 'would lead directly to disaster.' In order to win a measure of co-operation from such narrowly-focused men, Tedder would need all those qualities that Zuckerman saw in him of 'patience, tact, cunning and political sense', together with Eisenhower's backing, who trusted him.

Eisenhower learned on 6 December 1943 that he, not Marshall, would command Overlord. Tedder was to be 'my chief airman' with Coningham co-ordinating the tactical air forces and Spaatz commanding the bombers. Tedder wrote to his daughter on the 15th, telling her that he had seen a lot of Smuts at recent meetings. 'One feels he is in a different class from Winston, Roosevelt, Uncle Joe [Stalin] etc., he's a bigger man all round; just as good and astute a politician, just as good a leader of men, a better judge of strategy, and a more far-seeing statesman.'

A comparison between Churchill and Smuts was very much in Tedder's mind at that time. Churchill had asked him to place fifteen fighter squadrons at Turkish disposal between mid-February and the end of March 1944. Tedder reminded him, not for the first time, that his resources did not allow such a dispersion, least of all for no good military reason. He sent this signal with a fervent prayer – answered, for once – that Churchill might never again try to involve him with Turkey.

Churchill had arrived in Tunis on 11 December and remained there, suffering from pneumonia and a heart attack until the 27th. Tedder and his second wife Marie (usually known as 'Toppy') dined with him on the 14th and Toppy told her mother that 'a lot of the fire had gone out of his eyes, this I suppose due to dope... He *does* look ill, as if the engine is running down'. She wrote again on the 18th to say that Clementine Churchill had arrived: 'which made all the difference to the old devil! We are lunching there today. I have been keeping him supplied with invalid food – which he adores – and dug up a supply of thirty-five-year-old brandy!'

On that day Churchill formally proposed Tedder to Roosevelt as deputy Supreme Allied Commander, 'on account of the great part the air will play in this operation [Overlord], and this is most agreeable to Eisenhower'. Montgomery was proposed as ground commander, despite Eisenhower's preference for Alexander, because, said Churchill, 'Montgomery is a public hero and will give confidence among our people, not unshared by yours'. This may have been true for British ground forces, but would become very much less so for American ground forces during the rest of the European war. Spaatz also returned to England, taking with him James H. Doolittle as head of American bombers in place of Ira Eaker, who went – most unwillingly – to Italy as Tedder's successor. Harris would remain in command of British bombers. Slessor became Eaker's deputy, Sholto Douglas returned to England as head of Coastal Command and was succeeded in Cairo by Keith Park.

Eisenhower repeated his preference for Tedder and Spaatz as his principal airmen for the proposed liberation of occupied Europe in a letter to Marshall written on Christmas Day, 1943.

'I am anxious to have there a few senior individuals who are experienced in the air support of ground troops. The technique is one that is not (repeat not) widely understood and it takes men of some vision and broad understanding to do the job right. Otherwise, a commander is forever fighting with those air officers who, regardless of the ground situation, want to send big bombers on missions that have nothing to do with the critical effort.'

Tedder played a significant supporting role to Eisenhower by insisting on stressing intelligence for all decisions of the Supreme Command. Like Eisenhower, recalled Kenneth Strong, 'he invariably turned to his intelligence advisers for facts about the enemy'.

'Mary' Coningham, appointed to command a tactical air force in the Overlord operation, wrote to Tedder on 30 December. He and Alexander had flown that morning to Montgomery's headquarters at Vasto on the Adriatic coast, some fifteen miles south of the Gustav Line to bid him farewell. 'I mentioned your appointment, but he brushed it aside and said that you were merely the air adviser to the Supreme Commander. The cheek of the blighter! He then told me that he considered that my proposed appointment to tactical was wrong.'

By Montgomery's standards these insults were mild, bearing in mind his genius for causing lasting offence and Coningham reminded Tedder – who needed no reminding – that Montgomery believed himself invincible and would attempt to command all American as well as British armies.

An Officer by the Name of Mallory

Walter Bedell Smith wrote to Eisenhower from London on 30 December. 'We all believe that Tedder should be the real air commander and your adviser in air matters', but an officer by the name of 'Mallory' was claiming that position. 'Mallory' was Air Marshal Sir Trafford Leigh-Mallory. By December 1943 he had spent six years in Fighter Command, five as a group commander and one as its head. His professional judgement during those years has often been criticised by combat pilots, other commanders and historians. Nevertheless, backed by Portal and therefore by Sinclair, he had been confirmed in November by the combined chiefs of staff as head of the proposed Allied Expeditionary Air Force (AEAF) to support Overlord; promotion to air chief marshal followed in January 1944.

To paraphrase what his brother George (who had not added 'Leigh' to his name) said about Mount Everest, Leigh-Mallory was appointed because he was there. The head of Fighter Command could hardly be overlooked for a senior place in a massive combined services operation launched from southern England, but months of ill-will and confusion would have been avoided if Portal had made it clear to Leigh-Mallory, as he should have done, that he was subordinate to Tedder and Coningham. When British and American air commanders assembled in London during January, they were unwilling to accept Leigh-Mallory into their close-knit team even before they discovered that he was unimpressive: personally and professionally.

A Lousy Organisation

In January 1944 there was a strong belief in Whitehall and among many Britons, thanks to fervently patriotic reporting by the BBC and in their newspapers, that Eisenhower was merely a figurehead for an operation to be conducted by Montgomery, a British hero since the battle of El Alamein. As Eisenhower confided to his diary on 7 February, he was tired of being regarded as a friendly front for British generals who made all the important decisions. 'The truth,' he wrote, 'is that the bold British commanders in the Mediterranean were Sir Andrew Cunningham and Tedder', not Montgomery and still less Alexander, much as Eisenhower admired the latter. Backed by Marshall and Roosevelt, Eisenhower had made all the critical decisions in 1943 and would do so, even more confidently, in 1944 and 1945. In air matters, they would be the ones Tedder wanted.

After Germany's defeat, Spaatz was asked by an American historian about the air organisation. He replied that he had wanted the same organisation as had worked so well, after trial and error, in the Mediterranean. Eisenhower, Tedder and Spaatz himself 'kept in such close touch' from 1944 onwards that the system was made to work well enough, but he hated to think what would have happened if any one of the three had been struck down.

Portal ought to have remembered what Anglo-American tactical air forces had achieved in the Mediterranean under commanders well versed both in co-operation with each other and with ground forces, operating a wide variety of aircraft: fighters, fighter-bombers and transports. Leigh-Mallory was experienced only in handling British fighter operations across the Channel, revealing no particular merit in selecting targets or disrupting German control of France and Belgium.

Harris and Spaatz (aided by Doolittle) commanded British night and American day bombers and were to continue with Operation Pointblank, the Anglo-American air offensive against German targets. Coningham and Brereton were the obvious choices for command of tactical air forces and there was simply no place for Leigh-Mallory at the top level, except in the minds of Portal and Sinclair. 'In other words,' said Spaatz, 'it was a lousy organisation.'

Churchill raised with Sinclair and the three British chiefs of staff, on 6 January, the 'anxiety' expressed to him by Eisenhower and Bedell Smith about the air organisation for Overlord. 'They disliked the powers granted to Leigh-Mallory, who has, apparently, let it be known that he intends to be a real C-in-C in the air', but Tedder, thought Churchill, 'with his unique experience and close relation as deputy to the Supreme Commander, ought to be, in fact, and form the complete master of all the air operations'.

However, Sinclair – ever ready to meddle on behalf of his favourites – wanted a more prominent role for Leigh-Mallory. He suggested to Churchill on 7 January that Coningham and Brereton be placed under his 'active command'; so too should all airborne forces, a photo-reconnaissance wing and, not least, all heavy bombers assigned by the combined chiefs to Overlord. Tedder, in Sinclair's opinion and that of the British chiefs, should be politely kicked upstairs to make room for Leigh-Mallory.

'There is a fundamental difference,' the chiefs pontificated on 8 January, 'between command arrangements in the Mediterranean and those in the United Kingdom.' In the Mediterranean, Tedder controlled all air forces, but in Britain that position was held by Portal with Harris and Leigh-Mallory under him. Tedder was asked for by the Americans 'not as a substitute for Leigh-Mallory but as a deputy to Eisenhower', the mouth through which the Supreme Commander speaks, the ear through which he listens and no longer a mere airman. As for Eisenhower, he was 'in effect, a task force commander with certain forces allotted to him for re-entry onto the Continent and the subsequent invasion of Germany'.

These foolish words emanated from Brooke, head of the British Army. Known (behind his back) as 'Colonel Shrapnel', he had found that blunt opinions, rudely expressed, but based on professional knowledge of the army far beyond that of most officers, won arguments.

Montgomery was another totally committed army man, even curter. Both believed that British soldiers would lead the way to victory over German soldiers and that the other services, British or American, especially in the air, were no more than useful allies. The unwavering confidence of Brooke and Montgomery in their own opinions and their belief in the superiority of British to American soldiers lie at the heart of all the problems faced by Eisenhower, Tedder and their colleagues during the rest of the European war. Canadians were also undervalued.

Brooke and Montgomery did their best to ignore the fact that American forces far outnumbered those of Britain the longer the war lasted, and that the Americans had more and better weapons, medical facilities and 'comfort zones' behind the fighting lines. Nor did they willingly accept the fact that the Soviet Union was largely responsible for the defeat of Germany.

Eisenhower in Command
Eisenhower decided to form his headquarters as far as possible from the differing distractions of Whitehall and the West End. Leigh-Mallory expected him to move to his own headquarters at Bentley Priory in north-west London, where communications were excellent. But Bedell Smith was aware that the Mediterranean team – all of whom had sand in their boots – would be swamped there by British officers who had none. He therefore set up shop for Eisenhower some fifteen miles south of Bentley Priory, at 'Widewing' in

Bushy Park, near Kingston-on-Thames. Leigh-Mallory was furious, but helplessly so, as he would so often be during the coming months.

Tedder and Spaatz had lunch together on 22 January and agreed that a set-up similar to that in the Mediterranean should be created, 'presided over by Tedder', and include representatives from both strategic and tactical air forces. They confirmed their agreement on the 24th: 'operations must be conducted the same as in the Mediterranean area, no matter what type of organisation was directed by topside.' So much for the British chiefs of staff and Sinclair.

Tedder told Portal on 22 February that the air organisation was still shaky. 'Spaatz has made it abundantly clear that he will not accept orders, or even co-ordination, from Leigh-Mallory', and Harris's representatives were concerned only to adjust their bombing statistics to demonstrate that 'they are quite unequipped and untrained to do anything except mass fire-raising on very large targets'. Both could be brought to heel, but it had to be both.

One of the main lessons of the Mediterranean campaign, Tedder reminded Portal, was the need for unified control of air forces. If Churchill and the British chiefs concocted a formula to exempt Harris from Eisenhower's control, 'very serious issues will arise'. Eisenhower had a long talk with Churchill late on 28 February and summarised their conclusions for Tedder next morning. Eisenhower was determined to have the final say, through Tedder, about all air operations during Overlord. He therefore warned Churchill that unless he got full co-operation from the British, he would 'simply have to go home'. Churchill had no answer to such blunt words.

Despite his postwar protestations, Churchill always had doubts about Overlord. He never got over his 'enthusiasm for dashes, raids, skirmishes, diversions, sallies more appropriate – as officers who worked with him often remarked – to a Victorian cavalry subaltern than to the direction of a vast industrial war effort', wrote Max Hastings. War, like life, was for Churchill, exhilarating, even fun. During the early months of 1944, he still wanted to keep Italy, the Greek islands, the Balkans and Turkey in the forefront of Anglo-American ambitions. As alternatives, he hankered for an assault on Norway or Bordeaux, even Sumatra (a rare expression of interest in the war against Japan): anything, in other words, appealed more strongly than a direct engagement across the Channel.

As Liddell Hart wrote in 1960, Churchill and Brooke were 'half-hearted about Britain's promised commitment to the invasion of Normandy'; they were only whole-hearted about campaigns in the Mediterranean and the Balkans, where they could evade those German armies not already engaging the forces of the Soviet Union.

The Americans, however, like the Russians, had had more than enough of what Hastings described as Churchill's 'butterfly strategy-making', ardently seconded by Brooke, who had 'a sublime, and exaggerated, conceit about his own strategic wisdom'. Faced with the inevitable however, Churchill rightly recognised that he must back Eisenhower and his chosen deputy. Tedder was 'the aviation lobe' of Eisenhower's brain, Churchill told the British chiefs on 29 February, and must be allowed 'to use all air forces permanently or temporarily assigned to Overlord' as he thinks best.

Bomber Command could not be entirely handed over to Eisenhower – because of the demands of Pointblank – but Overlord, said Churchill, 'must be the chief issue of all concerned and great risks must be run in every other sphere and theatre in order that nothing should be withheld which could contribute to its success'. Portal accepted, on 2 March, that Tedder was to be regarded as an *operational* commander as well as Eisenhower's deputy. After a long meeting of the chiefs next day, Brooke noted that Tedder 'is now to assume more direct command', which could only be done 'by chucking out Leigh-Mallory', who should never have been chucked in.

Tedder thought Leigh-Mallory could be found a vacancy in the Far East, but this suggestion – which would have spared him and many others much anguish – was not followed through. The strategic air forces were to be placed at Eisenhower's disposal when he asked for them. They would remain under the command of Harris and Spaatz, but receive their 'general directives' from Tedder. This 'passage of responsibility' was to come on 14 April. According to the British historians of the strategic offensive, this was 'an historic event by which a Supreme Air Command was at last created', even if only for a time.

Controlling the Channel

By the end of 1942, Coastal Command had devised 'strike wings' to destroy or at least disrupt shipping to and from German ports and, above all, to win control of the Channel. These wings became a necessary part of Overlord's success, as Christina Goulter wrote. The excellent twin-engined Bristol Beaufighter used its powerful cannon and rocket armament against German shipping and ports; Beaufighters also attacked U-boats with torpedoes. These operations, from 1943 until the end of the war, were greatly assisted by reliable intelligence information.

The strike wings are of 'historical importance', recorded Stephen Roskill, because they represented, from April 1943, a joint enterprise by Bomber, Fighter and Coastal Commands. How many of the disasters during more than three years of war could have been avoided, he wrote, if inter-service co-operation had been a priority for the RAF and Royal Navy in 1939? More than 500 vessels were sunk or damaged, Germany's steel production fell by ten per cent in the last year of the war and substantial resources – including 150,000 men – were tied up in resisting strike wing attacks. Were they in blunt terms 'cost effective?'

Between April 1940 and May 1945, mines dropped by Bomber and Coastal Command during nearly 20,000 sorties, at a cost of 450 aircraft, sank more than 630 vessels in the Channel and the North Sea; direct attacks during nearly 38,000 sorties, at a cost of more than 850 aircraft, sank 366 vessels. These are appallingly heavy casualties on both sides: an average of twenty-two aircraft and seventeen ships down in every month for five years.

This aspect of the war at sea was no mere sideshow in comparison with the well-known campaign against the U-boat, but it was scarcely mentioned by Churchill in his memoirs. For all that he proclaimed a 'Battle of the Atlantic', long after it was actually in full swing, he remained far more concerned to increase the strength of Bomber Command and regarded Coastal Command as merely a defensive necessity. Yet when the war was won, Bomber Command was lightly passed over in those memoirs.

The Transportation Plan

There were bitter disputes over how best to use Allied air superiority in 1944 and 1945. Advised by Zuckerman, Tedder proposed what became known as the 'transportation plan': a systematic attack on the numerous marshalling yards and railways serving the invasion area. It should go on for as long as possible, to exhaust repair squads and force them to use up essential materials. The Germans must not be allowed to move reinforcements of heavy weapons (tanks, artillery) or ammunition, fuel, food and water quickly and easily to the landing areas. The plan was so arranged that Calais, rather than Normandy, seemed to be its focus.

Apart from destruction, Tedder hoped to canalise surviving traffic and therefore make it more vulnerable to subsequent attack. Later studies of attacks in Sicily and Italy showed that bridges were not as difficult to hit, if low-flying medium bombers were used, as Tedder and Zuckerman thought. Although the plan was sensible, it was hotly opposed by alleged experts, British and American: many of them academics, over-stimulated by their first brush with the real world, especially in wartime. Although ignorant of the actual workings of transport systems (to say nothing of military operations), they persuaded themselves that the railway system in Western Europe had large reserves of spare capacity and what really mattered was destruction of oil sources.

Spaatz was foremost in advocating an 'oil plan', overlooking the difficulty lightly-loaded day bombers, operating far from their bases in England or Italy, would face in destroying widely dispersed, well-defended oil targets. For no good reason – as ample aerial photographs revealed only too clearly – he believed that American bombers hit targets with 'precision' and had advised Arnold on 10 January to speak in press handouts of 'overcast bombing technique' or 'bombing with navigational devices over cloud'; at all costs he was to avoid the term 'blind bombing' which was in fact what day bombers usually did. Ramsay Potts, an American bomber pilot who ended the European war as Director of Bombing Operations, admitted that the Allies did 'area bombing of precision targets'.

As Sebastian Cox wrote, the Americans described all their attacks as 'precision' attacks, when in fact they were nothing of the sort: 'more than seventy per cent of the bomb tonnage dropped by the 8th Air Force between September 1944 and April 1945 was dropped non-visually, i.e. blind-bombing.' Max Lambert commented that 'the Americans dropped their bombs when the formation leader did, rather than individually. It follows that if the formation covered ten acres, you would get a ten-acre bomb plot, so the idea of each bomb going "into the pickle barrel" is plainly nonsense.'

They faced long journeys out and home, dependent on imperfect navigation in weather that was often bad and always unreliable whatever forecasters had predicted. These handicaps remained, even when at heavy cost the enemy day-fighter force had been gravely weakened late in February during what Americans called 'Big Week': a hard-earned triumph that cost 2,600 aircrew killed, wounded or captured. But experienced German flak gunners remained a threat until the last days of the war.

Harris's opposition to Tedder's plan had been partly based on his belief – again for no good reason – that his crews were unable, even in 1944, to find and hit any target smaller than a city centre. But he always obeyed specific orders and respected Tedder. British night bombers were far more destructive than American day bombers (because they carried heavier loads) and were becoming, as aerial photographs revealed, more accurate as well. The transportation plan could not have succeeded without the co-operation of Harris, who privately realised that the breathing space thereby given to German targets was also a rest for Bomber Command, which had taken a terrible hammering during the winter of 1943-1944.

The transportation plan, as Spaatz admitted to Arnold on 14 June, 'opened the door for the invasion'. The Germans were unable to move reinforcements towards Normandy quickly enough or on a sufficiently large scale to prevent the Allies from securing a bridgehead. Since Eisenhower the soldier had learned his wartime trade in North Africa, he knew what he owed to airmen. His son John, a lieutenant in the US Army, said to him on 24 June: 'You'd never get away with this if you didn't have air supremacy.' Eisenhower replied: 'If I didn't have air supremacy, I wouldn't be here.'

As well as communications, attacks on electric power plants – where they could be located – were obviously profitable. After 1945, several writers in Britain and the United States argued that a more sustained effort should have been made to identify and target these plants.

Portal summoned everyone who mattered to a meeting on 25 March, where Spaatz admitted that his oil plan could have no *immediate* effect on helping soldiers to get established in Normandy. That was the decisive point, as Eisenhower ruled. When Portal asked him if the plan would not handicap Allied movement *after* the bridgehead was secure, he got a dusty answer: that was not a matter of immediate concern and in any case the Germans could be expected to smash everything in reach as they retreated. Spaatz was satisfied because British night bombers would be doing most of the work while his bombers continued to aim at oil targets in daylight.

'Smearing the RAF's Good Name'

After the meeting on 25 March, Portal informed Churchill that 'very heavy' civilian casualties would be 'unavoidable'. Churchill was rarely at his best by 1944 and refused to recognise the obvious consequences of *any* plan to liberate occupied Europe. Members of his War Cabinet, who knew little about military realities, expressed alarm and asked for the matter to be reconsidered. Cherwell was invited to do this and in his usual easy way asserted that as many as 40,000 civilians might be killed, a further 120,000 would be seriously injured and the plan would fail anyway. Churchill, accustomed to accepting Cherwell's pronouncements on practical matters as gospel, worked himself into a frenzy. On several occasions in April – while raids were actually being carried out – he had the arguments endlessly rehearsed at his 'midnight follies', as Zuckerman described them.

Although it quickly became clear that Cherwell had been mistaken and that French and Belgian civilians recognised that their communication networks (road and canal, as well as railways) were essential targets and had been warned to avoid them, Churchill blathered on endlessly. 'There is no better plan', Tedder assured him. 'I'll show you a better plan', came the confident reply. Zuckerman saw Tedder's knuckles whiten as he gripped the edge of the table, but he refused to quarrel. 'You are piling up an awful lot of hatred', Churchill snapped at him on 3 May. 'You will smear the good name of the Royal Air Force across the world.'

He claimed not to understand, let alone accept, arguments in favour of the plan. Fuel and arms dumps and troop barracks, were better targets he said, ignoring the fact that such targets were usually found in or near towns, put civilians at greater risk (because specific warnings could not be given) and were of marginal value. He was well aware by 1944 that the Germans did not spare civilians anywhere in occupied Europe who showed even signs of resistance.

How tired he looked, recalled Tedder: 'the rush of events since 1940 had undermined even his strength', he had been very ill as recently as December 1943 and every senior commander who had to deal with him from then until the end of the war was familiar with his tedious, endless, alcohol-fuelled ramblings, usually far into the night.

Whatever his merits as a national symbol, Churchill never showed any understanding of the skills and sheer hard labour needed to get large formations – on land, at sea or in the air – into effective combat with powerful opponents. Inspiring words, individual courage and ignorance of battlefield realities were never enough. Tedder knew that he had Eisenhower's support, backed by Marshall and Roosevelt: men with whom Churchill could not argue and win. Portal backed the plan and so too, for what it mattered, did Sinclair. Harris did his best to wriggle out of any contribution to the transportation plan, but was obliged to do so. To his surprise (which reveals how little he knew about the capabilities of his force), bombers caused significant damage to communications in France and the Low Countries.

Roosevelt, Koenig, Lockhart

Tedder visited his hero Smuts at his London hotel on 2 May, who supported him fully. Sadly, Churchill did not consult Smuts before writing to Roosevelt on the 7th to invite him to order Eisenhower to cancel the plan. Churchill's letter used the word 'slaughter' (of French civilians) four times and quoted casualty estimates that he then knew to be false. Roosevelt, neither impressed nor deceived, replied coldly on the 11th and Churchill grudgingly accepted defeat on 16 May.

Eisenhower sent Bedell Smith to tell General Marie-Pierre Koenig (head of Free French forces in Britain) about the plan on that day. 'We would take twice the anticipated loss,' Koenig assured Bedell Smith, 'to be rid of the Germans.' Civilian casualties in France and Belgium before and after D-Day were indeed horrendous, so too was the destruction of livestock, homes, public buildings, pasture and woodland. Antony Beevor, writing in 2009 and making use of French sources, estimated that over 34,000 civilians were killed during the Normandy campaign by Allied and German forces.

Tedder had lunch in London on 6 May with Sir Robert Bruce Lockhart, Director-General of the Political Warfare Executive. Lockhart thought Tedder 'the most naturally and mentally best-equipped commander I have ever met'. And he had met many, during a long career spent among powerful people. They discussed Cherwell, whom Tedder described as 'a bad man, a really bad man. Yet the PM listens to him.' As for Churchill himself, his 'brilliance was still visible', even to Tedder's unenchanted eyes, 'but now his peaks were fewer and shorter, and his slumps deeper and longer'. Yet Tedder feared his collapse, because the Cabinet comprised men whose abilities did not include a firm grasp of military matters.

Freeman's Folly

On 25 May, Freeman (now chief executive of the Ministry of Aircraft Production) wrote to Portal about the choice of a new Air Member for Personnel (AMP). He proposed that Tedder be appointed and advised Portal to summon Slessor from Italy to take over as Eisenhower's deputy: this on the very eve of D-Day. Portal wisely ignored this grotesquely mistimed proposal. The old friendship between Freeman and Tedder had been withering since 1943 and was now dead. Tedder had grown with the ever-increasing demands of total war, understanding that Britain was a vital, but junior, member of a coalition in which he had a key command role.

When to Go?

Starting on 1 June, the commanders met daily to consider weather reports, but only Eisenhower could give the order to launch Overlord. They met in Admiral Ramsay's headquarters at Southwick House, north of Portsmouth. Early on the 4th, Montgomery asserted his willingness to launch what Terry Copp has rightly emphasised was an *Anglo-Canadian* army next day even if bad weather prevented the air forces from giving their support.

Mercifully, wiser heads agreed that air superiority was essential, together with a naval bombardment aimed at beach defences. Next day, 6 June, taking advantage of a brief break in the weather, Eisenhower made his heroic decision to begin what he called 'this great and noble undertaking'. Years later, when Tedder was writing his own account of Eisenhower's decision, he recalled these words spoken by Marshal Joffre in 1914: 'I see they are trying to decide which of my generals won the battle of the Marne. If it had gone the other way, I know who would have lost it.'

20

From Normandy to Arnhem, 1944

Invisible Assets: (1) Fortitude and Patton

'We must trust in our invisible assets', noted Admiral Bertram Ramsay in his diary: Operation Fortitude and the continuous stream of information derived ever since 1940 from the reading of German signals at Bletchley Park. Fortitude, an elaborate deception plan, persuaded the Germans that the Normandy landings were a feint, and that the main assault was still to come in the Pas de Calais.

Fortitude was commanded by an American, Lieutenant General George S. Patton, whose spectacular deeds in the Mediterranean had made him well known as a dynamic commander to allies and enemies alike. He was therefore awaited by a large, fully-equipped army. The deception was never rumbled and that army, which might well have overwhelmed the Allied bridgehead in Normandy, did not move until the bridgehead was secure.

These 'assets', as Ramsay called them, would have been of no value without air superiority – close to *supremacy* – won by the courage and skill of Allied airmen at appalling cost: 2,000 aircraft and more than 12,000 men were lost between 1 April and D-Day. Between that day and the end of August a further 4,000 aircraft were lost, together with nearly 17,000 men. Well over half of these losses were suffered by American airmen.

The casualty rate for the Allied armies in Normandy, wrote Gary Sheffield, 'was higher than for the British Army (including the Royal Flying Corps) at Passchendaele in 1917'. In fact, over half of all deaths suffered by British armed forces during the Second World War came in the last eighteen months. Normandy was indeed 'a hard-fought battle', one which some recent historians argue the Allies could not have lost. No doubt it seemed more closely-run at the time, by men who were actually there.

Invisible Assets: (2) Hitler and his Missiles

As in every theatre of combat, from June 1941 onwards, it is now clear that Hitler, ably seconded by Goering, was the most valuable 'invisible asset' enjoyed by the Allies. Hitler was convinced that the British would try to re-capture Norway and ordered strong fortifications to be built in the Narvik-Harstad region. Even less realistically, he had the Channel Islands heavily fortified. The men and weapons tied up there, quite apart from the severe defeats suffered on the Eastern Front, in North Africa and Italy, gravely weakened the German army and air force.

The German High Command was persuaded – by its own thinking as well as Allied deception plans – that the main attack would come across the Straits of Dover and for too long refused to believe that Normandy was the target and not a diversion. Worse still, Gerd von Rundstedt, the principal German commander, refused to accept Erwin Rommel's advice – based on experience in the Mediterranean – that the invaders must be challenged on the beaches, as soon as they landed. He ignored the fact that Allied air supremacy would impede, if not prevent, movement towards those beaches once the Allies were ashore.

Hitler had missed great opportunities to disrupt an Allied return to Europe long before the Normandy landings. One was the failure to focus on the flying-bomb (the V-1) and to waste precious resources on a rocket (V-2). The British had been aware of German work on these weapons since late in 1942. Cherwell, confidently mistaken yet again, announced in October 1943 that 'at the end of the war, when we knew the full story, we should find that the rocket was a mare's nest', i.e. something that did not exist.

Luckily for the Allies, the Germans chose not to concentrate on developing and producing cheap and effective unpiloted flying bombs, launched either from the ground or an aircraft. Many could have been ready by early 1944, in good time to destroy or disperse the numerous soldiers, trucks and tanks packing into roads and fields near England's south-eastern coasts. Although flying straight and level, the V-1 was fast and small and could only be picked off with difficulty by defending fighters or ground gunners, who were further handicapped by darkness, cloud or rain. During the months before D-Day, the Allies dumped heavy bomb loads on real, suspected or abandoned launch sites (in an arc from Cherbourg to St Omer) to little effect.

A few hours after the Normandy landings, Hitler ordered the V-1 offensive to begin on 12 June. All told, about 10,000 flying bombs were launched against England and about 3,500 eluded the defences, killing or injuring about 24,000 people, mostly in or near London. Grievous as these losses were, at a time when most Britons believed that victory was in sight, they could have been much heavier. On 18 June, with the agreement of Churchill and the British chiefs, Eisenhower decided that the attack on missiles – Operation Crossbow – should have priority for the air forces over everything except a battlefield emergency.

The first German rocket, the V-2, struck England on 8 September, but two months passed before Churchill allowed publication of what many

Londoners already knew: that the Germans had a new weapon to supplement their flying-bomb attacks. The last of more than 1,000 rockets, travelling at five times the speed of sound, was fired from Holland at England on 27 March 1945. In all, more than 9,000 people were killed or seriously injured, in and around London.

Defence against the V-1 was difficult, and impossible against the V-2. Yet it was the V-1 that could have disrupted Allied plans for landings in Normandy because the V-2 was far more difficult and costly to build but still carried the same warhead. As well as these muddles, James Corum wrote, Hitler chose 'to throw away his last reserve of bombers in meaningless attacks on British morale' early in 1944. More than 300 bombers were lost over England that could have caused havoc among the shipping supplying the Normandy beachheads on and after D-Day.

The Germans did, however, cause Allied airborne forces severe losses, despite 'the lessons' allegedly learned in North Africa and Sicily. But too many German commanders had one eye on an increasingly unpredictable Hitler and the other (as was essential in the Third Reich) on each other. Resistance to the invaders was therefore unco-ordinated. Too few mines and stakes (intended to impede landing craft) were laid in the approaches to Normandy.

The Luftwaffe, except when resisting Allied bombing of Germany, was by then negligible; the U-boat had been defeated and surface naval forces were weak. Hitler chose to make all decisions, from a remote location, and usually insisted on stubbornly clinging to every position, boasting that the V-1 offensive would prove decisive, and dismissing several commanders. Rommel was seriously injured on 17 July and then came the attempt to kill Hitler on the 20th, which ended whatever military judgement he had ever had and led to a widespread and prolonged purge of enemies, real or imaginary.

Hitler's 'sea wall' strategy was a disaster: no fewer than 200,000 troops were locked into coastal fortresses that were simply bypassed. Rommel had warned that the invaders must be fought *on the beaches*, but German forces that were better armed, better equipped and better trained than those of the Allies remained inland, preparing counter-attacks. When they moved, they found that Allied air supremacy had cut bridges and railways in the rear, impeding reinforcements and supplies, and disrupting those forces that did move.

The chief tormentors were heavily-armed British Typhoons and American Thunderbolts, which gave constant close tactical support without any fear of Luftwaffe fighters: those that still remained were needed closer to home, fending off Allied strategic bombers. Not as dramatic, but equally valuable, were the numerous unarmed artillery reconnaissance aircraft which pinpointed targets far inland for warships in the Channel. Once beachheads were established, the Allies poured in numerous soldiers and tanks. Although individually outmatched, sheer numbers made eventual victory likely.

The last bonus was Hitler's order that men facing local defeat must hang on instead of retreating and living to fight another day. Whatever problems the Allies faced, as strong personalities clashed and feared the test of battle with a powerful enemy, their problems were minor compared with those faced by German commanders, all subject to Hitler's personal decisions.

Perhaps the Allies benefitted most from Hitler's decision, on the night of 9-10 June, to stand and fight in Normandy whatever the cost. He thus played into the hands of Anglo-American soldiers, who proved much more adept at hanging on grimly than they would have been at pursuing a skilful enemy, able to mix a measured withdrawal with savage counter-attacks at times and places of his own choosing. As Pete Quesada, an outstanding American tactical air commander, later reflected: 'One's imagination boggled at what the German army might have done to us without Hitler working so effectively for our side.' After the Allied breakout at the end of July, Hitler no longer had the option of a fighting withdrawal because all his strength had been spent in Normandy. 'We are gaining ground rapidly,' remarked one German soldier in a letter home, 'but in the wrong direction.'

Allied Air Supremacy

From D-Day onwards, British and American fighter-bombers claimed to be inflicting heavy losses upon German armour and mechanised transport: claims based on fleeting glimpses of smoke and flames. Allied Operational Research Sections (ORS) enquired closely into these claims by Thunderbolt and Typhoon pilots. Severe damage was certainly caused to soft-skinned motor transport, often carrying petrol, but not to tanks, armoured vehicles and flak batteries. Although the air forces did not destroy these, they did scatter formations, although these often fought back and brought down many attackers. Even so, the Germans found daytime movement dangerous and some soldiers were just as demoralised as the British and French had been by the Luftwaffe in 1940.

Failure at Caen

In mid-June, Tedder planned a re-organisation of the air forces intended to get rid of Leigh-Mallory and his HQ at Bentley Priory. Coningham had disturbed the 'complacency' of a meeting there on the 14th by bluntly stating that his information about the ground situation did not agree with that put forward by Montgomery's representative: the army had suffered 'a severe setback' and the situation was 'near crisis'. Tedder decided upon 'a terrific punch' – using Coningham's medium bombers and fighter-bombers – and went with him to a meeting in Normandy with Miles Dempsey (head of the British Second Army).

Tedder learned that Leigh-Mallory had a plan to 'unstick' the army, but had not discussed it with Spaatz or Coningham. Tedder reminded

Montgomery that Coningham was his opposite number, not Leigh-Mallory, but it had now become almost impossible to get through to the man they contemptuously referred to as Britain's 'Napoleon'.

Caen was heavily defended by the Germans because it gave access through open country to the Seine and on to Paris, essential for the rapid shaping of airfields and ideal for tank movement. The western end of the beachhead, by contrast, was a land of small fields, thick hedges, stone walls, solid farmhouses, broad streams and steep valleys: a land easy to defend. From the start of 1944, Montgomery had made it clear to everyone concerned in all three services that Caen was his prime target. Tedder therefore expected a major effort to take it on the first or second day of the invasion, before the Germans gathered their strength. Having shown insufficient urgency on that first day, British (and Canadian) soldiers were forced into bitter and costly actions that lasted for six weeks.

According to Christopher Dawney, Montgomery's 'Military Assistant', he deliberately gave the RAF 'a totally false impression... as to when he was going to get those airfields, south of Caen'. Once in Normandy, Dawney recalled, we realised that the master: 'didn't care a damn about those airfields, as long as he could draw all the German armour on to that [eastern] side and give a chance for his right swing to break out!'

In fact, as D'Este argued in 1983, Montgomery *did* intend to take Caen on or soon after D-Day, but for him – as indeed for Churchill – the past existed only to serve the convenience of the present. He had – as Hastings wrote, echoing many other historians – a certain 'lack of concern for truth in his make-up'.

An exceptional storm, during 19-22 June, was a major factor in preventing Caen's capture before the end of that month because the artificial harbours were wrecked or badly damaged and few supplies or reinforcements could be landed for four critical days. During those days, the Allies were vulnerable to a fatal counter-attack, but it did not come, in Tedder's opinion, thanks to the success of airmen in isolating the battlefield. Montgomery, making a virtue of necessity, gradually settled for attracting yet more German armour to the Caen front, thus easing the way for an eventual breakout elsewhere. But he failed to make his change of plan clear to Eisenhower or Tedder, with whom – as in Mediterranean days – he avoided regular contact.

Mustard Gas?

Churchill raised the idea of reprisal raids for V-1 attacks with his chiefs of staff on 1 July. He suggested that the British announce their intention to destroy a host of small German towns if the attacks continued. Churchill won the support of Bedell Smith, but Tedder thought the idea ineffective and 'wickedly uneconomical'. Portal agreed with Tedder on 3 July, but Churchill persisted. Portal suggested adding V-1 attacks to the list of war crimes with which

Germany would be charged after the war, but feared that the reprisals proposed might cause the Germans to murder air crew prisoners. Churchill then urged the use of mustard gas, 'from which nearly everyone recovers... to drench the cities of the Ruhr and many other cities in Germany in such a way that most of the population would be requiring constant medical attention'. He wanted the matter studied, 'in cold blood by sensible people, and not by that particular set of psalm-singing uniformed defeatists which one runs across, now here, now there'. The Air Ministry had in fact made plans for one-fifth of Britain's bomber force to be used, if ordered, to make gas attacks.

Thunderclap

Meanwhile, the Americans were preparing an attack on civilian morale, code-named 'Thunderclap': 2,000 bombers would drop 5,000 tons in daylight upon a small area of central Berlin. Bomber Command could follow up in darkness. American commanders were vocally opposed to attacking German civilians *directly*, asserting that they attacked only 'military' targets. Actually, they usually bombed through cloud and persuaded themselves that any civilian casualties were incidental, not intentional. What if such attacks had been launched just after 20 July, when for a short while Hitler's regime was faltering? In January 1945, however, after the Battle of the Bulge and after the Soviet Union had resumed its westward advance, the 'Thunderclap' plan was revived. On 25 January, Tedder asked if the time had come to stage this operation and Spaatz agreed: it would be delayed, however, until the Russians were on or across the Oder.

On that very day, 25 January, Churchill read an intelligence report suggesting that the Germans might hold out until September, if they could prevent Soviet forces from conquering Silesia. He therefore asked Sinclair what plans the RAF had made for: 'blasting the Germans in their retreat from Breslau?' Portal replied on Sinclair's behalf. The Allies could use the 'available effort in one big attack on Berlin and attacks on Dresden, Leipzig, Chemnitz or any other cities where a severe blitz will not only cause confusion in the evacuation from the East but will hamper the movement of troops from the West'. Portal recommended, however, that the combined chiefs of staff, Spaatz and Tedder, be consulted before anything was done. Churchill insisted on immediate action, although Tedder and the commanders of both bomber forces were reluctant to change from their preferred targets: the Americans, as always, wished it to be known that they aimed only at 'military targets' and were acting in support of their Soviet allies.

Charnwood

'The principle which worked in the Mediterranean – of the army and air commanders living together – has been allowed to lapse', wrote Leslie Scarman (Tedder's senior staff officer) on 22 June. This was partly because poor communications in Normandy prevented Coningham from operating in a joint headquarters with Montgomery and partly because the Allies still lacked airfields across the Channel. Tedder put these points to Eisenhower, who replied on the 25th that he wanted Tedder to make it his 'special province' to keep in close touch with Montgomery. Tedder tried, but Montgomery was offended by Coningham's criticism of the army's failure to take Caen and wanted him sacked. Tedder assured Eisenhower on 1 July that Coningham's removal would be 'a disaster' and his frankness was entirely justified.

At Leigh-Mallory's request – supported by Eisenhower – 450 British heavy bombers tried to break the stalemate at Caen on 7 July as their contribution to Operation Charnwood. They dropped over 2,000 tons of bombs on the town's northern outskirts, but British soldiers failed to take prompt advantage of the bombing and most of the casualties were later found to have been French civilians. Charnwood's failure generated widespread frustration. Even if Montgomery was fireproof, surely it was time for Eisenhower to assume direct command?

At this desperate moment, 10 July, a vile minute from Churchill arrived on Tedder's desk: 'How many Frenchmen did you kill', he asked, during the transportation attacks before D-Day? Tedder was never among those high British commanders who wilted when Churchill sounded off, and by 1944 was as fireproof as Montgomery. He replied calmly: probably not more than 10,000, adding his own barb. 'I am afraid, however, that those casualties are being dwarfed by those involved in the liberation of Caen and other Normandy towns and villages.' Churchill had no answer. Nor did he complain about the failure of Charnwood.

Goodwood

Montgomery proposed another enormous aerial bombardment, to be followed by another ground advance, this one devised by Dempsey. Code-named 'Goodwood', it was an assault launched on 17 July in a blaze of publicity, to drive the Germans from the Bourguébus Ridge, south-east of Caen, but halted three days later, having suffered heavy losses. David Belchem, head of Montgomery's operations and planning staff, who later 'ghosted' his master's memoirs and published his own version of events in Normandy, claimed that Goodwood had not been a disaster, merely a holding operation while the Americans prepared their breakout.

This remarkable claim was made in 1978 of an operation that called for about 4,500 Allied aircraft, 700 artillery pieces, over 8,000 armoured vehicles and trucks and cost the British more than 5,500 casualties. Admiration of 'Monty' was furthered by Nigel Hamilton in a massive three-volume account of his whole life, in which all those who opposed his hero – not least Tedder and Coningham – were soundly trounced. Tedder was angered by Montgomery's refusal, yet again, to co-operate with Coningham, preferring the amiable Leigh-Mallory, who had taken a personal caravan to the army commander's headquarters.

Tedder thought Eisenhower could have Montgomery sacked, but Commander Harry C. Butcher (Eisenhower's naval aide and diary-keeper) disagreed. He was an experienced newspaperman in civilian life and correctly reckoned that the BBC and the British press had boosted 'Chief Big Wind' for so long that he could not be dismissed, even in the wake of a disaster. Montgomery had failed to make best use of available intelligence, 'grossly under-estimating the tenacity and resource' of his opponents. The rift between Montgomery and the American commander, General Omar N. Bradley, also impeded Allied efforts.

Brooke's Influence
Tedder asked Eisenhower on 21 July to instruct Montgomery to prepare yet another plan of attack *and submit it for approval prior to action*. Eisenhower, he thought, should take immediate personal command because since D-Day there had been 'a serious lack of fighting leadership in the higher direction' on the British side, though not on the part of the American. Edgar Williams, Montgomery's intelligence officer, and most subsequent historians agree that Tedder made valid criticisms. Brooke (head of the British Army) was largely responsible for the crisis in relations between Montgomery and his colleagues in July 1944. Instead of stroking his protégé's already massive ego, encouraging his constant sneering at Eisenhower and harping on endlessly about what he believed to be American strategic ignorance, he should have urged Montgomery to communicate openly with his essential allies.

Both Brooke and Montgomery were well aware of the fact that the British Army was desperately short of competent officers and adequate numbers of infantry, but reluctant to admit these facts either to airmen or to non-British soldiers. Since 1918, the army had been allowed to decay in every respect: doctrine; organisation; equipment; morale and recruitment and not least in realistic training for possible combat against a well-armed, highly-motivated opponent. Most British officers and men were unskilled in carrying out rapid manoeuvres calling for individual initiative. In order to hide their limitations as much as possible, and taking air superiority for granted, Montgomery's plans depended heavily on hardware – tanks, guns of all sizes and trucks – that were inferior to those available to either the Germans or the Americans.

Breakout
Then began an American offensive, under Omar Bradley, on 25 July that escalated from a breakout in the west into a triumphant sweep eastward. Hitler helped the Allies by demanding an impossible counter-offensive, mounted from Mortain, on the night of 6-7 August that led to a huge

slaughter of German troops and horses in the Argentan-Falaise area. A costly stalemate was suddenly transformed into an even more sacrificial victory. Montgomery, encouraged as ever by Brooke, the BBC and British newspapers, claimed far more than his fair share of the credit. This continual boasting placed the western alliance under severe strain for the rest of the war. In fact, Montgomery and Bradley jointly failed to close the jaws of the Falaise pocket and some 50,000 of Germany's toughest soldiers escaped to fight on another day.

A Vital Anvil

Eisenhower, backed by Tedder, insisted on activating Operation Anvil, a landing on the south coast of France. No operation anywhere from start to finish of Anglo-American efforts in the Second World War generated more animosity than Anvil, mostly because the decision to proceed made it painfully clear to the British that the Americans were now able to and willing to do as they pleased.

The disastrous Aegean adventure, followed by the horrors of Anzio, both of which were urged by Churchill, had fatally undermined his influence in important decisions. Anvil had originally been intended to begin at the same time as Overlord, but shortage of shipping ruled that out. Weeks of failure outside Caen convinced Eisenhower that it was essential, from August onwards, to supply the armies in Normandy with men and munitions by capturing the great ports of Marseille and Toulon. Churchill, however, strongly supported by Brooke, was determined to continue the Italian campaign, the 'centrepiece' of the British war effort, 'an imperial crusade holding postwar implications'. As so often, Churchill's strategic judgement was astray. He ignored the fact that the French had raised 500,000 troops in North Africa and refused to take part in any venture not on their own soil.

In Tedder's opinion, the case for Anvil was unanswerable, as Stalin told Churchill at Teheran and thoughtful historians have since agreed. How did Churchill (and his admirers) 'expect the huge armies of the Allies to be supplied without the French Mediterranean ports?' asked Gerhard Weinberg. Williamson Murray and Alan Millett agreed: 'Marseille was a logical godsend', all the more essential because Montgomery failed to clear access to Antwerp until December. The need for capacious ports, if the Allies were ever to reach the Rhine, let alone advance beyond, was becoming clearer every day. So too was the need to feed into France those French divisions being formed in Italy and North Africa: a need which should have weighed heavily with the allegedly Francophile and politically-alert PM.

Resistance forces were strong in number in the south and could more easily be armed from the Mediterranean than from Britain. German forces in that region were known to be weak and poorly trained. Not least, Roosevelt needed to ensure – in an election year – that Overlord remained at the centre of attention. Commitments elsewhere, especially those that suited only the British, must be kept to a minimum. If not, influential voices would demand greater efforts in the Pacific.

Tedder endured a six-hour lunch at Portsmouth on 5 August at which Churchill pressed Eisenhower to abort Anvil, but Admiral Ramsay was stout in his support of Eisenhower and Tedder. Churchill nevertheless summoned Eisenhower to London on the 9th, where he wept, he pleaded, he damned near died and made the absurd threat to lay down 'the mantle of his high office' unless he got his way. He even proposed a wholly pointless re-routing of the enterprise to Brittany. Gracelessly accepting the inevitable, he foolishly insisted that it be renamed 'Dragoon' because he had been dragooned into it.

Churchill then insisted on observing its launching on 15 August from the deck of a British destroyer. Commanded by an American general, Alexander M. Patch, Dragoon proved to be anything but the 'bleak and sterile... tomfoolery' Churchill had predicted. By the end of October, the southern French ports were handling nearly forty per cent of all American supplies reaching Europe and transporting them along a rail network deliberately left intact by Tedder. Without these ports and railways, the supply crisis which hit the Allies in November might well have been insurmountable. None of this impressed Churchill, who never understood the essential part played in military operations by supply and reinforcement.

Communications, Oil, Coal

Late in August 1944, Tedder learned from captured German records that the transportation plan had gravely impeded resistance to Overlord. He therefore proposed to extend the plan into western Germany, but his was a minority opinion. Most experts in economic or intelligence matters, British or American, who advised Portal in Whitehall or Harris at his headquarters advocated massive attacks on Berlin: these would shatter civilian morale and compel a surrender. Those who advised Arnold in Washington or Spaatz at his headquarters wanted to focus on oil targets. These would bring vehicles of all kinds, both in the air or on the ground, to a standstill and so compel a surrender.

Tedder's opponents gained an apparent advantage on 6 September when Eisenhower was obliged by the combined chiefs to relinquish control of the heavy bombers. The change ended Tedder's authority to require heavy bomber support either for the armies in France or for the attack on communications. From then on, he would have to ask for it. The change meant nothing because any help he got from Spaatz or Harris had always depended upon his powers of persuasion, whatever the combined chiefs decreed. Oil targets remained an American priority, just as city centre attacks were a British priority, but he persuaded both commanders to attack marshalling yards, canals and river traffic. In these ways 'a deadly coal famine' was spread from the Ruhr throughout central and southern Germany.

Tedder's opponents underestimated the difficulty of destroying oil targets, the extent of damage already done to the transport network and quite failed to grasp the overwhelming dependence of the German economy on coal: 'Six tons of coal stood behind every ton of synthetic gasoline,' Alfred Mierzejewski wrote. 'A heavy tank could rumble from the factory only after 115 tons of coal had been burned by a myriad of companies to produce it.'

Failure at Antwerp

On 4 September Montgomery called for 'one really powerful and full-blooded thrust towards Berlin' under his command. This despite the fact that he was still drawing most of his supplies from beaches north of Bayeux and there were grave dangers in a single thrust which needed to cross several rivers and left an ever-extending right flank increasingly exposed to counter-attack. Yet even if the plan had been sound militarily it was impossible politically, as Montgomery and Brooke refused to understand. Roosevelt and his people could not accept leadership by any British general in the final campaigns of the war, least of all when they had learned to regard Brooke and Montgomery as officers with a grossly inflated estimate of their own opinions and the skills of British soldiers. Moreover, by 1944 they had their own heroes in Eisenhower, Bradley and Patton.

British troops occupied the vital port of Antwerp on 3 September and found it practically undamaged, but because Antwerp lay at the head of the Scheldt estuary, many miles from the open sea, the British needed to capture both banks of the river in order to use it. Tragically for the Allied cause, Montgomery's attention was fixed on the Ruhr: its conquest was to be followed by a triumphant procession to Berlin, accompanied by adoring broadcasters and journalists. He quite overlooked the vital task of securing *access* to such an essential port. Severe Allied losses followed. As many as 80,000 German troops were allowed to escape across the estuary into Holland, where they prevented the use of Antwerp for twelve weeks. The first Allied ship did not berth there until 28 November.

Disaster at Arnhem

Against the advice of his own staff, Montgomery decided to launch a drive – Operation Market – to the Lower Rhine at Arnhem. This operation, carried out by airborne troops between 17-25 September, was intended to seize several river bridges and establish a corridor extending eighty miles into Holland. Another operation – Garden – was to advance along that corridor: a single narrow road, overlooked by enemies on either flank. Montgomery assured Frank Simpson (Director of Military Operations in the War Office) that 'we could be in Berlin in three weeks and the German war would be over'.

As numerous accounts make clear, every Allied unit involved fought hard in both operations, but they encountered experienced German commanders, with well-equipped and determined troops, who took full advantage of hasty, careless and impractical Allied planning, exacerbated by an astonishing disregard for unwelcome intelligence and inept leadership. Coningham was unable to give maximum air support because the plan forbade him to approach the landing/dropping zones while troop-carrier aircraft and gliders were about. In short, 'there is no aspect of the preparation of that tragic fiasco,' wrote Scarman to Bedell Smith in February 1945, 'that does not fill one with dismay.'

Even Montgomery admitted a mistake. 'Not only were the lives of many brave men needlessly sacrificed', wrote Hamilton, his adoring biographer, but the disaster reduced still further his influence with the Americans. Even so, Churchill had the nerve to inform Smuts that it was actually 'a decided victory', while Montgomery was soon claiming a ninety per cent success, which provoked Tedder to remark to Zuckerman: 'One jumps off a cliff with an even higher success rate, until the last few inches, but the result remains a disaster.'

Edgar Williams was appalled by 'the sheer willfulness' of Montgomery's decision to mount Arnhem before clearing the Scheldt estuary, and still more by the 'lack of grip' he showed throughout Operation Market Garden. Montgomery was guilty, wrote Ralph Bennett, 'of a strategic mistake of such magnitude that its repercussions were felt almost to the end of the war'. Harold Deutsch agreed: the two-part operation 'records persistent disregard of excellent intelligence that is probably without parallel during the Second World War or, for that matter, in the history of warfare'.

At a meeting on 5 October, Montgomery – now living in an impenetrable bubble – made 'the startling announcement,' wrote Ramsay in his diary, 'that we could take the Ruhr without Antwerp', This provoked the admiral to 'lambast' the field marshal for not having made the Scheldt estuary his highest priority. Had he done so, 100,000 German troops would have been trapped in Belgium, 'a victory greater even than Falaise', wrote Sebastian Ritchie, and Antwerp would have been opened to Allied shipping.

Luckily for the Western Allies, the army group commanded by Jacob L. Devers – supplied from southern France, thanks to Eisenhower's refusal to cancel Operation Anvil – would soon reach the Rhine. If Churchill had had his way, that valuable reinforcement and supply route would not have existed.

Overall, airborne operations in World War Two wasted resources and lives for little advantage. The Germans had success with them early in the war and Churchill therefore demanded the creation of a parachute force. He had decreed, on 22 June 1940, 'off his own bat and without any consultation with anybody about practical possibilities', recalled Slessor, that there should be a force of 5,000 parachute troops created immediately, even though the RAF had few transport aircraft, no gliders and no tugs.

The idea also appealed to some American ground commanders. But all airborne forces suffered cruelly: the Germans over Crete, Stalingrad and Tunisia; Anglo-Americans in North Africa, Sicily, Normandy and especially at Arnhem. As Slessor concluded: 'Airborne operations against an enemy unbeaten in the air are a spectacular form of mass suicide.'

21

Victory in Europe,
1944-1945

Advancing into Germany

Eisenhower told Montgomery on 13 October 1944 to cease his agitation to be appointed the single ground commander. He promised to do so on the 16th, but egged on by Brooke and others in the War Office he did not. They attempted to get rid of Tedder, backed by Churchill, who was eager to bring his favourite, Harold Alexander, home from Italy.

On 6 December Churchill urged Roosevelt to support an enquiry by the combined chiefs into the 'serious and disappointing war situation', but Roosevelt, as usual, relied on professional advice in military matters. Eisenhower and Tedder, recognising the importance of not allowing the opinions of Montgomery and his partisans to pass unchallenged into the record, arranged to meet Churchill and the British chiefs on 12 and 13 December. Brooke recommended that Montgomery's proposed thrust across the Rhine north of Düsseldorf be given maximum support, even at the expense of a standstill south of the Ardennes.

Eisenhower preferred a double advance into Germany: Montgomery's north of the Rhine and Bradley's through Frankfurt. No-one then or now can be sure that Brooke was wrong and Eisenhower right. What can be said is that Brooke and Montgomery had been seriously at fault over Antwerp and Arnhem, that Eisenhower was the agreed Supreme Commander, that his forces were now far superior in numbers and equipment, and that prominent roles for his American subordinates was politically essential as well as militarily sensible. It can also be said that both Brooke and Montgomery expressed their opinions in extravagant and offensive terms, whereas Eisenhower made his points calmly and cogently.

Brooke petulantly threatened to resign when Churchill felt obliged to back Eisenhower. Churchill shared the opinion of British generals that their strategic opinions were superior to those of Americans, but he had gradually learned, on his better days, to recognise since Casablanca in January 1943 that Britain's strength and therefore her voice were declining assets. Wiser than Brooke or Montgomery, Churchill saw that Eisenhower's famous patience was becoming exhausted and knew that he was wholeheartedly backed by Roosevelt and Marshall. No doubt he also had in mind, however unwillingly, his own part in disasters in the Aegean and at Anzio.

The Battle of the Bulge

'The enemy's situation,' announced Montgomery on 16 December, 'is such that he cannot stage major offensive operations.' Every senior commander, ground or air, British or American, agreed. They were all proved wrong that very morning when the Germans mounted a shattering attack in the Ardennes. Antwerp – at last open to receive and distribute supplies of all kinds – was their ultimate target. If it could be re-taken, there would be no Rhine crossing in the near future. With his rear relatively secure, Hitler's prospects of building and maintaining a strong defence in the east, where Russian armies had still to cross the Vistula in Poland, would improve.

Eisenhower met with Tedder and American generals at Verdun on the 19th, where he demanded only 'cheerful faces'. Their grins would have been less fixed if they had known that Albert Speer (Hitler's armaments minister) expected the German offensive to fail. 'I saw the switching yards east of the Rhine jammed with freight cars,' because 'enemy bombers had prevented the movement of supplies for the offensive.' These words would have delighted Tedder. On 23 December the skies cleared. Against forces now fully alert, enjoying total air superiority and far greater in numbers, arms and supplies, the result was certain.

Tedder in Moscow

Faced with an unexpected offensive in the west, Eisenhower had been anxious to know when the Soviet Union intended to resume its offensive in the east. He persuaded his masters in Washington and Whitehall to ask Stalin to receive Tedder and two American officers. Churchill agreed, but because Tedder was not his personal choice of envoy refused to consider the mission important. Sending Tedder, he told Colville (one of his secretaries) 'is like asking a man who has learned to ride a bicycle to paint a picture'. An amusing image, delighting the great wordsmith's uncritical admirers, but one that reveals what a very small man he had become by the last year of the war.

The journey took Tedder a fortnight, but eventually he reached Stalin's office in the early evening of 15 January 1945, where he noticed significant changes since his last visit in August 1942. Gone were the vast portraits of Marx, Engels and Lenin, replaced now by equally enormous portraits of Soviet generals. Stalin himself no longer dressed as a civilian, but was 'in full sail as a field marshal, suitably hung with red stars and similarly appropriate decorations'. Tedder offered him two cigar boxes, already opened by nervous guards. 'When do they go off?' asked Stalin. Tedder made a performance of consulting his wristwatch and replied: 'Not until after I've gone.' This little joke was well received by the Man of Steel and so all the courtiers could laugh.

Stalin spoke lucidly about current and future operations, then Tedder described the difficulty of crossing the Rhine. Engineers had assured him that the optimum period lay between mid-March and mid-April. Stalin readily agreed to keep the Germans occupied during that time. He and Tedder then had an animated discussion about the performance of various tanks and aircraft and Tedder emphasised the immense effort being made, round the clock, by strategic bombers against German targets.

Arthur Birse, the British interpreter, later commented that this interview 'stands out in my memory as one of the most satisfactory I ever attended,' and Tedder 'as the man for whom I should like to have worked more often... His manner was pleasant and at the same time businesslike.' Stalin, in fact, was pleased to welcome a *fighting* commander, rather than yet another politician. Portal sent a copy of Tedder's report to Churchill on 5 February, who chose to disregard it. However, Birse's high opinion of Tedder was widely seconded by permanent representatives of the Allies in Moscow. 'Tedder presented our plans and worries with the utmost clarity,' wrote Major-General John R. Deane, head of the US military mission, 'and made a great impression on Stalin by his blunt sincerity.'

Years later, when the western press had given up on 'our gallant ally, Uncle Joe' and realised that he was a villain in Hitler's class, Tedder was often asked about his meetings with the monster. He told McEvoy:

'I won't pretend I saw the beast within, and I won't deny the force of his personality: stronger than Winston's and stronger even than that of Smuts. He sat so still and his eyes, like a reptile's, hardly moved. What impressed me most was the silence of [General Alexei] Antonov, his chief of staff. He just sat there – I'm sure he thought he should be standing at attention – like a naughty schoolboy in the headmaster's study!'

Tedder had often observed British chiefs of staff arguing the toss with Churchill, and had had his own brisk exchanges of opinion with him. He could not believe that Stalin was advised as frankly or expertly by Antonov and his colleagues as Churchill was by Portal, Cunningham or Brooke.

Tedder was warmly welcomed in Paris by Eisenhower on 21 January because his mission had opened a direct line to Stalin. Eisenhower asked the British chiefs to arrange for details of Tedder's unique journey and amicable interview with Stalin and senior officers to be publicly revealed. Stalin had signalled Churchill on 15 January to say that 'the mutual exchange of information was sufficiently full' and that 'Marshal Tedder made a very favourable impression on me'. Nevertheless, Churchill refused to allow any publicity, making the pathetic excuse that it would 'shock the British and American public as revealing the lack of contact which existed before Tedder's visit to Moscow'.

Alexander to Replace Tedder?

On 30 December 1944 Churchill was in his sourest mood, after an ill-advised visit to Greece, where civil war was brewing between several factions, as German control weakened. Stalin chose not to back the local Communists and although Churchill's sympathies were all with an unpopular King George II, he was reluctantly obliged, in response to American, anti-Communist Greek and British Labour Party pressure, to back Archbishop Damaskinos as regent.

Churchill was far from well, keenly aware that the big decisions were no longer his to make, and anxious to assert his old authority where he could. He picked on Tedder, telling the British chiefs how much he regretted that Eisenhower, 'has not had in the last few months a deputy with some knowledge of the military art, who would have been capable of pointing out to him the faulty dispositions of the armies'.

Tedder should therefore be replaced by Alexander, a soldier whom Churchill readily supported. He spoke to Portal on 2 January 1945, suggesting that Tedder be appointed Air Member for Personnel, thus making room for his favourite. Portal replied that he supposed Churchill would discuss this proposal with Eisenhower, who would not, he thought, approve. He made it clear to Churchill that the only Air Ministry job he foresaw for Tedder was his own.

Rumours of this proposal reached Marshall in Washington. He told Eisenhower that Alexander's appointment would mean that the British had control of ground operations even though their forces were much smaller and they were suffering fewer casualties. Eisenhower found Alexander amiable, as did most men who served with him, but he preferred to keep Tedder, an officer whom he also regarded as good company. More to the point, Tedder had long been an integral part of the Allied team and was distinctly more intelligent and industrious than Alexander.

Although Brooke had, with good reason, a low opinion of Alexander's capacity for high command, he thought his further elevation 'a sound move, and one which would assist in keeping Ike on the rails in future': meaning that Alexander would do whatever Churchill, Brooke and Montgomery advised.

'The more I see of him,' wrote Brooke of Alexander on 12 January, 'the more I marvel at the smallness of the man. I do not believe he has a single idea in his head of his own!' And yet Brooke did all he could to advance this lightweight's career, and break that of a man whom he knew had made a major contribution to the impending Allied victory.

Tedder now learned that Montgomery had so offended Eisenhower during his absence in Moscow that he had been within a whisker of dismissal. He had brusquely challenged Eisenhower's judgement for the umpteenth time, bullied Bradley, shown open contempt for other American commanders and implied at a press conference on 7 January 1945 that only his exceptional leadership had saved the Allied cause in the crisis caused by the Battle of the Bulge. Even Churchill thought his words 'most unfortunate' and told the British chiefs on the 10th that his speech 'had a patronising tone and completely overlooked the fact that the United States have lost perhaps 80,000 men we but 2,000 or 3,000'. These sensible words were wasted on Brooke.

Eisenhower met with Marshall and other senior American officers at a chateau near Marseille on 28 January. Everyone knew that Churchill wanted Alexander as Eisenhower's deputy, but Marshall was sure that Tedder should not be replaced at this late hour. Eisenhower returned to Paris next day and admitted to Tedder that he had wavered, but only because Churchill insisted that he was wanted for an important post in the Air Ministry. Churchill, as ever, refused to accept any opinion other than his own. During the Yalta Conference, he secured what he took to be an agreement that Alexander should be appointed in about six weeks, when the Ardennes offensive would be 'more forgotten'. Marshall 'took a dim view' of this shabby attempt to replace an outstanding man with one who had shown only the most limited capacity for command in North Africa, Sicily and Italy; and Marshall's opinion was decisive. The days when Churchill could do as he pleased with British commanders were long gone.

On 14 February Montgomery was 'most emphatic' in resisting a change. With all his faults, Montgomery was a seasoned professional military man, well able to recognise Tedder's exceptional ability. He knew that Alexander was weak, lazy and not worth a place in the higher direction of the Allied command. Eisenhower and Tedder thereupon agreed the text of an exceptionally sharp letter to Brooke, sent on the 17th: if Tedder was dismissed, he would be replaced as air commander by Spaatz and there could be 'no question whatsoever' of finding a place for Alexander, who would have no military duties and must concern himself solely with civilian welfare and public relations.

Brooke, shocked out of his usual arrogant complacency by the tone and content of this letter, promptly passed it to Churchill, who kept on shuffling until a meeting with Eisenhower and Tedder in Reims on 5 March. After brooding for another week, Churchill sent Tedder a curt signal on the 12th: 'Eisenhower will doubtless have informed you that the change I had in mind and about which we talked will not now take place.' So failed Churchill's last attempt to sack Tedder. Just to add a final twist to this sorry saga, the cypher office contrived to omit the word 'not'!

Dresden

'The centrepiece of the war in Europe in early 1945,' wrote Biddle, 'was the Red Army's move on Berlin.' Thousands of Germans were wisely fleeing westward to escape capture by angry Russian soldiers, who had suffered so cruelly at the hands of Germans and their allies. Harris thought Chemnitz, Leipzig and Dresden were now promising targets. Churchill thought so too, on the eve of a meeting with Stalin at Yalta, and was eager to emphasise to the Soviet dictator the part played by Anglo-American forces – in the air and on the ground – in crushing the Nazi regime.

By that time, the appalling extent of the slaughter of Jews, Slavs and others was becoming more widely known, and Hitler's enemies were well aware that another vile regime was still to be overthrown in Japan. On the night of 13-14 February 1945, hundreds of British bombers in two waves struck at Dresden, swollen with refugees from battles farther east. During the next two days, American day bombers also bombed the city. In the absence of effective air and ground defences, in good weather, the raids achieved widespread destruction and generated a firestorm. At least 25,000 Germans died, perhaps many more.

British and American newspapers emphasised Dresden's importance as an industrial centre and transport hub and the help the raids gave to advancing Soviet forces. But the scale of destruction at Dresden disturbed some Britons and Americans, even at the time. About a month later, Churchill, adopting his statesman pose, issued a minute in which he declared: 'The destruction of Dresden remains a serious query against the conduct of Allied bombing.' Not surprisingly, the Air Staff and Harris were outraged at so abrupt a *volte face* by the man who up to then had been the staunchest supporter of the policy of 'area bombing'. They demanded – and received – a retraction.

The war was not yet over. The Battle of the Bulge in December 1944 and January 1945 had cost the Americans alone 135,000 casualties, and there were many more American, British and Canadian losses in 1945. Soviet forces suffered many more, so the suggestion made by some writers that the war was virtually over at the time the Dresden raids were planned and carried out is entirely mistaken. Those raids did, however, convince all but the most devout Nazis that defeat was looming. Biddle quoted a German historian, Goerz Bergander, who wrote in 1978 that after Dresden belief in the sudden appearance of a miracle war-winning weapon disappeared.

A Race to Berlin?

Churchill visited Coningham at his 'sumptuous villa' in Brussels on 2 March. There, sneered Colville, 'massed flowers, expensive furniture and rare food combine to create an effect too luxurious for the HQ of an operational commander'. Colville, an aristocrat who spent most of the war wining and dining in Churchill's wake, knew all about living comfortably even in wartime and nothing about commanding air forces. He affected to believe that there was virtue – for other people – in discomfort. Next day, Colville spent some time touring service clubs in Brussels. Never can the welfare of troops, he exclaimed, 'been so lavishly and painstakingly cared for'. These words would have pleased Coningham, who had endured years of rough living and mortal fear, finding no virtue in either.

Colville lunched with Coningham on the 4th: the latter 'let himself go about Monty who, he said, was the most egotistical man he had ever met'. He was 'indiscriminate in his ruthlessness' and demanded the 'elimination' of towns and villages in Normandy which Coningham had refused to attack. He mishandled several operations in both the Mediterranean and European campaigns, but after the war, thought Coningham, he would write a 'bombastic and highly-coloured account' of those campaigns (and did so). Colville was surprised to find that Churchill agreed: he was scathing about Monty's self-advertisement stunts and said he presumed British soldiers would soon have to be called 'Monties' instead of 'Tommies'.

Eisenhower signalled Stalin on 28 March, ruling out an Anglo-American advance on Berlin as Churchill, Brooke, Montgomery, the BBC and all British newspapers ardently desired. They did not seek the opinion of those soldiers who would be killed or injured during this advance. After the destruction of German forces in the Ruhr, Eisenhower decided that his main eastward thrust, directed by Bradley, would be in the direction of Erfurt, Leipzig and Dresden. He wanted to know Stalin's intentions in order to co-ordinate Allied action. Stalin replied on 1 April, praising Eisenhower's initiative and indicating that Berlin was now a secondary target, when in fact he was planning a massive assault to begin on the 16th.

In Eisenhower's opinion, fully supported by Tedder, the Western Allies had no compelling reason to attempt an entry into Berlin ahead of their eastern co-belligerents. Allied forces had at last crossed the Rhine (on 23-24 March) and their objectives were now to secure the independence of the Netherlands, Denmark, Norway and France, also to establish a presence in north Germany by seizing Hamburg, Bremen and Emden. Less exciting than the glorious charge to Berlin for which Churchill and his British supporters yearned, but more realistic and more likely to result in lands that would escape Soviet rule.

In short, the attempt to seize Berlin would have been a strategic as well as an operational error. Stalin's subjects, having suffered so grievously at Nazi hands, were determined to take Berlin and Eisenhower refused to risk the lives of his own men in a futile attempt to deny them the vengeance they sought: foolish as well as futile because (by agreement made at Yalta) the Western Powers were to occupy much of what was left of the German capital after the slaughter was over.

Eisenhower had assured Churchill on 7 April that it was a purely *military* decision not to advance on Berlin and that Tedder had been 'freely consulted', together with other senior British officers and they were all in agreement. Angered by yet another rebuff and perhaps overcome by drink and fatigue – as he was so often in the last year of the war – Churchill fired off to the British chiefs one of the 'worst minutes I have ever seen', roundly abusing Tedder, recorded Brooke in his diary on 12 April – and Brooke was no admirer of Tedder. Eight months later, the then ex-PM wisely ordered all copies of his minute, and the replies it provoked, to be destroyed.

On 12 April 1945, President Roosevelt died. His decisions, and those of his senior military and civilian advisers, had long mattered more than Churchill's, who most unwisely, chose not to attend the President's funeral. He paid tribute to him in the House of Commons on the 17th. Colville, a devout admirer of Churchill, thought it no more than 'adequate'. Talking to Colville in May 1948, Churchill said: 'No lover ever studied every whim of his mistress as I did those of President Roosevelt.' His ardour was not returned. Despite the photographs and public statements, their relations were always those of master and man, not of equals. Quite apart from the immense disparity in power, they were separated by Churchill's desire to recover and retain imperial power in India and the Far East, a power that Roosevelt wished to see ended. Churchill's failure to pay his last respects in person was long remembered across the Atlantic.

Surrenders in Reims and Berlin

General Alfred Jodl (representing the German army), Admiral Hans Georg von Friedeburg (navy) and General Hans-Jürgen Stumpff (air force) were sent to Reims to sign an unconditional surrender early in May 1945. By a combination of bad weather, good luck and crafty stalling, they managed to delay their arrival until the evening of the 6th, earning precious hours for countless soldiers and civilians to flee westward, away from vengeful Russians. Eisenhower and Tedder remained discreetly out of sight until the document was signed, at 2.41 am on the morning of 7 May. Only then did they emerge to face a roomful of excited journalists, cameramen and photographers in addition to numerous staff officers.

Eisenhower found a quiet moment to say that he had decided to send Tedder to Berlin next day to confirm that surrender, on behalf of the Western Allies, with the Soviet Union. No higher honour ever came his way. With two dead members of his own family in mind – his first son Dick and his first wife Rosalinde – this quietly-commanding British airman would put his name to a document formally ending years of slaughter in Europe, Africa, the Atlantic and the Mediterranean.

Four Douglas DC-3 Dakotas, with forty-two passengers aboard, took off from Reims on 8 May. They landed at Stendal, sixty miles west of Berlin, where Tedder counted 150 damaged German aircraft and noted that every hangar and airfield installation was wrecked. The German representatives

(Field Marshal Wilhelm Keitel replacing Jodl) were collected and the Dakotas, escorted by Russian fighters, flew on to Berlin's enormous airfield at Tempelhof. Tedder made a short speech (repeated in Russian) and then inspected a guard of honour: 'Having looked at them,' he recalled, 'I quite sympathised with the Germans being scared stiff.'

The Russians had taken over an army engineering school in Karlshorst, East Berlin that was surprisingly intact. It took the best part of twelve hours to get the surrender document into an agreed format and to decide who should sign it. Andrei Vyshinsky, Soviet deputy foreign minister, objected to an American (Spaatz) and a Frenchman (General Jean de Lattre de Tassigny) signing as witnesses. Tedder refused to give way and, as he later told the American historian Forrest Pogue, 'took my pipe over in a corner to sulk'. Marshal Georgi Zhukov, head of all Soviet forces in Berlin, went across to him. He did not want to be unreasonable, but argued that he represented the Soviet Union and Tedder the Western Allies: 'It isn't logical to have the other two.' Tedder replied: 'It's not a matter of logic. We have to have an American name because 140,000,000 people are involved and we have to have France because 40,000,000 are involved. We have three flags to consider, you have one.' Eventually it was agreed that the other two could sign – on a line below the two principals. The Germans were brought in to sign and bedlam followed as journalists and photographers got completely out of hand. The room was cleared for a banquet that lasted until 5.30 am.

Tedder collected his party and they were all poured into a fleet of cars for a swift tour of the ruined city en route to Tempelhof. Tedder stole a few minutes to make a sketch at the Brandenburg Gate, but it proved impossible to visit the Tilly Institute, where he had met his first wife, although he did learn that it had escaped destruction. Wandering round the rubble of what had been Hitler's chancellery, Tedder saw two or three huge swastika banners. A Russian officer pointed at one and then at Tedder, so it eventually found a place of dishonour in the Imperial War Museum, London.

Humility
On 12 June 1945, Tedder was invited to accompany Eisenhower to the Guildhall in London, where the American received the Freedom of the City. They rode in a horse-drawn open carriage, escorted by policemen on white horses. It was on this occasion that Tedder first heard, and never forgot, Eisenhower's magnificent words: 'Humility must always be the portion of any man who receives acclaim earned in blood of his followers and sacrifices of his friends.' These words are now inscribed in the Chapel of Remembrance at the Eisenhower Center in Abilene, Kansas.

Historians at Work
In May 1954 Tedder had lunch at the Athenaeum with Sir Charles Webster

and Dr Noble Frankland and approved their intention to write a comprehensive account of the strategic air offensive over Germany during the Second World War. In due course, he read their draft, which he thought 'masterly and courageous' as he told them in May 1959. 'Frankly, I had not thought that anything so near the truth would be likely to go on record.' Webster and Frankland would face persistent opposition from influential senior officers and civil servants before bringing their four magisterial volumes to the light of day in October 1961. They got no opposition from Tedder and in fact he was often praised and hardly ever criticised. He was, in fact, the one air baron Frankland found 'wholly and consistently sensible'.

Frankland found that air power had not revolutionised warfare, as some of its champions claimed. It obeyed the same principles of war that governed the conduct of land and sea power: command of the land or the sea must be won by overcoming enemy armies or fleets. The US air forces found, early in 1944, that it was necessary to destroy the enemy air force *before* bombing could have a decisive impact; and even then it required land forces capable of overcoming enemy resistance to occupy territory.

The Trenchardists, represented by Portal and Harris, had been proven wrong. 'If the war had ended in March 1944 for reasons other than a collapse of German civil morale, the Bomber Command offensive would have had to be described as almost a complete failure.' Its subsequent success did not depend upon a force hardened in battle and now better equipped, but on two extraneous factors. One, that the command be employed on a special campaign to prepare the way for the landings in Normandy and two, the American realisation that unless the Luftwaffe could be defeated, its bombing would also fail.

Both British and American bomber commanders over-estimated the effect of bombing. They under-estimated the difficulty crews would have in finding, hitting and *destroying* a target of military value. And they failed to understand the economic strength and national morale of Germany – maintained by ruthless police forces. Tedder's advocacy of using aircraft against communications of all kinds was probably more effective than bombing city centres or seeking out oil targets.

At the Bar of History

Throughout his career, Churchill was deeply concerned about how he would appear 'at the bar of history', a favourite phrase. He and his admirers would do all they could during the rest of their lives to ensure that he would shine with more than oriental splendour long after he was dead: 'His story' would indeed prevail over 'history' for many years. Richard Crossman, Oxford don and Labour politician, identified a basic weakness in the Churchill version of World War Two: 'The statesman who turns chronicler, before he retires from active politics, is always seeking to adapt the past to the convenience of the present.'

Consequently, Churchill had to show himself Stalin's staunch ally while Hitler lived and his equally stalwart opponent once Hitler was dead. He also had to assert that his Mediterranean strategy, as opposed to an invasion of France, would have ended the war much sooner, and somehow prevented Stalin occupying much of Eastern Europe. As for 'setting Europe ablaze', Churchill had an organisation created in June 1940 to promote resistance in occupied Europe. There were many heroic individuals in the Special Operations Executive (SOE) who helped to forge inspiring memories, but it never threatened German rule (except in the Balkans) and its actions provoked savage reprisals, as even Churchill realised when he was supervising the writing of 'his story' after the war and therefore it was ignored: 'a damp squib,' wrote Reynolds.

Talking to Colville in 1953, Churchill said that Eisenhower's election as President obliged him to suppress his opinion that the United States 'gave away' vast areas of Europe to please Stalin in the last stages of the war. Roosevelt was too ill to back Churchill by 1945 and died in April. His successor (Harry S. Truman) was a bewildered novice and Churchill himself lost office in July. The former Prime Minister was, however, highly skilled in the delicate art of re-writing (or simply ignoring) the past to suit whatever opinions he currently wished to be believed and many influential Britons, post-1940, admired him uncritically. Churchill kept no diary because, wrote Hastings, 'to do so would be to expose his follies and inconsistencies to posterity'. Within months of becoming PM he was already planning the account he would have written for him if the war ended in Hitler's overthrow. 'The outcome was a ruthlessly partial six-volume work which is poor history, if sometimes peerless prose.'

Churchill and his airmen would have little contact with each other after the war. When he died in January 1965 Tedder was invited to be a pallbearer at his funeral, but he was too frail to accept the honour. He dictated a tribute for *The Times*, which appeared on the 25th. 'There were times,' he said, 'when it would appear that he would almost prefer action at any cost, provided it was immediate. It was this universal urgency that often led to impatience and sometimes injustice where individuals were concerned.' His powers of inspiration and refusal to be beaten were nevertheless essential in the hardest years, 1940 to 1942; thereafter, the ever-growing strength of the Soviet Union and the United States ensured that the British people would be among the victors. Portal, not a man given to praising lightly, would describe Churchill as 'a gift from heaven'.

22

Defeat into Victory in the Far East, 1942-1946

Ignored, not Forgotten

Britain's war in the Far East, wrote Raymond Callahan, 'the war that mortally wounded the British Empire east of Suez', is completely neglected in Churchill's 'very artful memoirs': that empire about which he spoke and wrote so often and so lovingly. Only after a personal protest from Slim did he and his team of assistant writers insert a passing reference in 'his story' to the 14th Army and its re-conquest of Burma. Often referred to as the 'Forgotten Army', it was not so much forgotten in Britain as ignored, except by those who had family or friends serving there.

It was, in fact, a largely Indian and African army in which British troops were a minority. Airmen who served in the Far East could hardly be described as Churchill's. Henry Probert wrote about 'The Forgotten Air Force', but in fact it was usually ignored: more completely even than the army because it was so much smaller. Churchill's focus and that of the Air Ministry and the other armed services, was always on Germany's power in Europe, the Mediterranean, the Atlantic and the alliance with Washington.

They had good reason for this focus because Germany posed a far greater threat, the United States was an essential ally in the west and would surely overcome Japan whatever defeats were suffered initially in the Pacific, China or Burma. British-led forces must somehow manage, with American assistance, to build up enough strength to resist and then – with Chinese assistance – repel Japanese invaders. 'Unpredictable, ill-equipped, and often ill-led,' wrote Ronald Lewin, the Chinese 'nevertheless attracted during the campaign about three-quarters of the Japanese strength in Burma': a disproportion which greatly helped Britain's recovery.

Some of the RAF's finest officers (among them, Richard Peirse, Tom Williams, John Baldwin, Stanley Vincent, Guy Garrod and Keith Park) deserve great credit for the efforts they made to help Slim's army turn a complete defeat early in 1942 into an even more total victory by August 1945 in Burma, Malaya and Singapore. Unlike those air commanders who served in the war against Germany and Italy, most of those who served in the Far East rarely made headlines in the British press or on the BBC, nor did the Air Ministry compare with the War Office in ensuring that they received the decorations they deserved. Yet Tom Williams, wrote Slim, 'was an inspiring commander for his own service and an understanding and unselfish colleague to us... he was the man who laid the foundations of the air supremacy we later gained, and on which everything else was built'.

Field Marshal Viscount Slim of Yarralumla in the Capital Territory of Australia and Bishopston in the City and County of Bristol (less formally known to his men as 'Uncle Bill') was the greatest British soldier of the Second World War and commanded the greatest British-led army. That army worked closely with airmen, British and American. Superiority in the air and at sea as well as very hard fighting on the ground eventually brought about victory. As Tedder had constantly urged throughout the Mediterranean and European campaigns, only the *combined* efforts of all services would prevail either in the west or in the east against ferocious opponents.

The armed services in the Far East were always at the end of supply lines for men, material or news from home. They laboured in weather that was often vile, over vast distances, struggling to move or even communicate in dense jungle, across arid plains, through or over dangerous mountains in a land of tracks rather than roads, uncertain bridges or places of comfort and safety. Worse still, for several months in the middle of each year, a south-west monsoon would turn vast areas into swamp and quagmire. Malaria, dysentery and typhoid followed every man, diseases against which devoted but inadequately-supplied doctors and nurses had a constant struggle. Men committed to such harsh conditions hung together, as they have often done in other wars, acutely aware that otherwise they would hang separately, for they faced a merciless enemy who murdered or enslaved anyone of any age or sex whom they chose to regard as opponents.

Midway and Burma

The Far East had not been a prime concern for Churchill or for most Britons, civil or military, since long before Hitler's invasion of Poland. Brave words were often uttered about the resources and influence of a world-wide empire, but the reality in the 1930s was bleak and close to home: Germany was on the march and even with the strength that Britain mustered they could hardly resist.

Probert's 'Chain of Disaster' for Europeans, Americans and many Asians followed Japan's onslaught during and after 1941. That chain would have lengthened and strengthened had not the Japanese suffered a catastrophic defeat at sea in June 1942, a very long way from Burma. One of the war's most decisive actions was fought near a tiny atoll fortified by American forces. The atoll lay more than 1,000 miles north-west of Pearl Harbor and had been named 'Midway', reasonably enough, because it lay midway across the North Pacific between the United States and Japan.

In all, the Americans lost in the battle of Midway, one aircraft carrier, one destroyer, 150 aircraft and 307 men. But Japanese losses were far heavier: four carriers, one heavy cruiser, 253 aircraft and 3,500 men. These carriers and their experienced crews could never be replaced – unlike the American losses – and their absence would be felt, not only in the Pacific campaigns, but in the Japanese hold upon Burma, China and their threat to the Indian Ocean and India.

Before Midway, for all the miscalculations of Germany and Japan, the issue of the war still hung in the balance. Had the Americans lost this battle, the Hawaiian Islands might soon have become untenable. With his west coast exposed to Japanese attack, President Roosevelt might have been obliged to reverse his 'Germany First' to a 'Pacific First' policy, as many of his fellow-citizens demanded. This would have reduced American aid to Britain and the Soviet Union and so made it more likely that Germany would overcome them. After Midway, fortunately, Japan was obliged to pass from violent offence to tenacious defence of her so-called 'Greater East Asia Co-Prosperity Sphere'.

Burma, the largest country on the south-east Asian mainland, became a major battle ground and endured the longest campaign of the war, where British and American forces faced a resistance that would have been even more fierce had the Japanese achieved another victory at Midway. One writes 'British', but the 14th Army which Slim ultimately commanded was made up of a wide variety of peoples: Burmese, Chinese, Gurkhas, Africans and many others. Despite all hazards and the pressing needs of other theatres, Allied strength gradually increased at a greater rate than the Japanese could match. To the west of Burma lay India, to the east lay the only supply route to China, which, for the United States, was a major concern.

Ceylon Spared

In January 1942, Donald Stevenson (whom we last met in charge of Home Operations in the Air Ministry) commanded a weak air force from Rangoon, greatly aided by an American volunteer group under the command of Claire Chennault, 'Air Adviser' to China since 1937. He had skilled pilots and ground crews under his command and about 100 P-40 Tomahawk fighters, a force superior to Stevenson's, but there were few radar aids, spares or repair facilities. The Japanese – far stronger in the air as well as on the ground – took Rangoon in March 1942 and their further advance faltered only after Midway. Although they sank two British cruisers and an aircraft carrier in the Indian Ocean, they were stoutly resisted and unable to inflict a 'Pearl Harbor' on Britain's Eastern Fleet. They did not seize Ceylon (now Sri Lanka) and make it a base from which they could have intercepted Allied shipping bound for the Middle East.

Slim and Peirse

Slim had arrived in Burma in March as a corps commander and during the rest of 1942 and in 1943 headlong retreat was gradually stemmed and turned into a determined advance, on the ground and in the air. Improvisation is surely the motto for all Allied armed services in the east. An American 10th Air Force was formed under Lewis H. Brereton in India with its headquarters in New Delhi. Its chief task was support for China, certainly not for helping to restore British rule, but for many critical months the defeat of Japan was a common goal.

Richard Peirse, late of Bomber Command, had arrived in New Delhi early in March 1942 to lead the building of air forces in India and Ceylon. It was not merely a huge area for which he was responsible, but one almost devoid of the resources, except ample unskilled labour, needed for conducting military operations in the age of tanks, aeroplanes and electronic communications.

Not the least of Peirse's problems was caused by Air Ministry ignorance of the world east of Suez. In May 1942, he told officials there 'that he was trying to create an air force and a defence system in an area four-and-a-half times the size of Great Britain, and at the same time to resist an enemy who was on the doorstop'. He got nowhere until Freeman agreed that Ludlow-Hewitt (now inspector general) should visit India and see for himself. He did so and agreed that the formation of two groups (221 and 224) at Calcutta was necessary, as was the establishment of an air headquarters in Bengal. 'What India wants,' reported Ludlow-Hewitt to Portal, 'and should be allowed to have, is to be free to organise itself to meet the Japanese menace, without restrictions and interferences from Whitehall.'

There are several 'finest hours' in the RAF's history, but none outmatch the 'finest months' from 1942 onwards during which – in partnership with soldiers, seamen and American allies – a power great enough to destroy Japanese invaders in Burma was laboriously created. Churchill's influence in all this was intermittent and not always wise, as his exuberant backing for Orde Wingate reveals only too clearly.

Numerous airfields were built, air and ground crews arrived and would be given essential protection by a recently-formed RAF regiment, which prevented snipers or infiltrators from doing more than cause temporary disruption of flying or servicing work. Communications by radio, radar and watching posts were created, and arrangements made for the recovery and repair of hardware. By November 1943, there were 2,800 British aircraft in the east, as compared with about 400 in April 1942: most of them of greatly improved models. Combat types won air superiority, Japanese locations, movements and supply depots were identified from the air and, most famously, transport aircraft provided almost everything that soldiers needed. River traffic would also become an important asset. Supplies came in and casualties were taken out. The Japanese were defeated in bitterly-fought battles around Kohima and Imphal during the middle months of 1944 and then at Meiktila, a centre of communications by road and rail with supply depots and hospitals, some eighty miles south of Mandalay.

Mountbatten, Churchill, Stilwell

Lord Louis Mountbatten had been appointed head of a newly-created South East Asia Command (SEAC) in August 1943. Churchill and his British colleagues had left a conference in Washington in May of that year concerned about American intentions for the Far East. The Americans, they thought, overvalued the opening of a Burma Road and the prospects of air forces using bases in China to launch attacks upon Japan. Nevertheless, Churchill wanted to support the Americans, to keep them involved in the Far East and thereby help the British to regain their lost territories. A new allied command, quite independent of India, was needed. Its first headquarters were in New Delhi, but it would soon be moved to Kandy in Ceylon.

In June 1943, Churchill had proposed Sholto Douglas as Supreme Commander, whom Roosevelt immediately rejected because of his 'lack of experience in Allied matters and in a most difficult theatre and with certain prejudices against him, justified or not'. Portal then suggested Tedder, but Churchill, aware that Eisenhower would not agree to lose Tedder, suggested that an American soldier, General Joseph W. Stilwell, who spoke Chinese, should be assigned dual responsibility to both Chiang Kai-Shek (military leader of China) and whoever was appointed head of SEAC. As is only too well known, 'Vinegar Joe' detested the British, but he had given what was (for him) lavish praise to Slim in March 1942: 'Good old Slim. Maybe he's all right after all.'

Early in May 1944, Mountbatten was instructed by the chiefs of staff to return seventy-nine transport aircraft to the Middle East at once: this at the very height of hard fighting around Kohima and Imphal, among the bloodiest land battles of the entire war. The attention of the chiefs in London was at that time wholly given over to the imminent landings in Normandy. Mountbatten – a proud man, born to command – refused to obey and Churchill made one of his rare interventions in the Far Eastern war. 'Let nothing go from the battle [of Imphal] that you need for victory', he signalled. 'I will not accept denial of this from any quarter, and will back you to the full.'

By July 1945, the Japanese had been defeated. Hurricanes, Spitfires and American-built Vultee Vengeance dive-bombers cleared the way for DC-3 Dakotas and their cargoes. Later there would be many more American combat aircraft: P-47 Thunderbolts; P-38 Lightnings and even heavy B-24 Liberator bombers. 'Without the victory of the air forces,' wrote Slim, 'there could have been no victory for the army... the shares of the soldier and the airman were so intermingled that it was a joint victory.' A victory which extended into the Indian Ocean, as recorded by naval historians. 'The air escorts provided by the RAF commands in the theatre, from Aden and East Africa to India and Ceylon, though never large by Atlantic standards, undoubtedly contributed to the discomfiture of the U-boats and to the safe arrival of the thousands of fighting men and the vast quantities of supplies needed by the Allied land forces in India and Burma.'

Wingate

Churchill was always thrilled by war as high excitement, for he had the heart and soul of a Victorian cavalry officer. War should be, whenever possible, fun: and he eagerly encouraged those who wanted to hit and run, to 'slash and burn' the enemy, 'to set Europe ablaze', to land in Norway, to raid Dieppe, to seize the Dodecanese Islands, to regard Orde Wingate in Burma not merely as an inspiring fighting man but as 'a man of genius who might have become a man of destiny'. In his absurdly romantic way, Churchill called him the 'Clive of India' and even considered giving him command of the army there. He had made a name as a guerilla leader in Palestine and Abyssinia, but would find the Japanese far more demanding opponents.

By 1943, hard-eyed men in Britain, the United States and the Soviet Union knew that only careful planning and overwhelming force, directed at the enemy's main strength, could lead to total victory. Churchill's enthusiasm for special forces, for spectacular deeds and headlines cost many lives, none more uselessly than in Burma. 'There is no evidence,' reported John Gordon, 'to conclude that Japanese operational capabilities were terminally crippled by the very costly placing of special forces so deep in their rear.'

In June 1942, Wingate had been given a force of some 3,000 men (later known as 'Chindits') to train which he operated behind Japanese lines between February and June 1943, dependent upon air supply, but losing a third of his strength and achieving very little, except favourable publicity. During the winter of 1943-1944, he was given an even larger force, this time including American combat and transport aircraft (later known as 'Merrill's Marauders') which suffered yet more casualties. He was killed in an aircraft accident in March 1944.

Lessons, it is said, were learned about the need for constant air supply: lessons similar to those that are said to have been learned as a result of a costly shambles at Dieppe in August 1942: lessons that could surely have been learned without such heavy loss of lives. Slashing and burning excited newspaper readers and wireless listeners, but they were not the way to win 'total war', against a ruthless enemy, well armed and well trained. Only after Wingate's death did Churchill propose Mountbatten. His royal blood, inspiring personality, immense energy and low cunning made him the ideal commander of multi-national forces of all services, the more so because he had experience of combined operations and soon learned to value Bill Slim, a man who was to become one of Britain's greatest soldiers.

Park Plays the Winning Card

In September 1944, the Americans withdrew their objection to a British air commander-in-chief for SEAC and Leigh-Mallory, unwanted by senior British and American commanders in the European campaign, was appointed. He chose to leave Northolt for India in an Avro York at about 9 am on 14 November in dreadful weather with a pilot who was unfamiliar with this new machine. Shortly after midday the York crashed in mountains near Grenoble, killing everyone on board.

Who should replace him? Slessor, ardently ambitious for yet another position about which he knew nothing, was keen to go, but Portal ruled that Park had 'the better operational sense, just as Slessor has the better political and strategical sense', and at that time it was expected that the Far East war would last until at least 1946. Slessor was angered by Park's elevation and persuaded himself that he was a candidate for a chair in military history at Oxford University, even though he had never been even a student there or at any other university, and might also be found a seat in Parliament, even though he had never been a member of any party and was entirely unknown outside service circles. Common sense eventually prevailed and he returned to his spiritual home in the Air Ministry, as Air Member for Personnel. There he went far to confirm Tedder's opinion that he is 'still unstable' by proposing that Harris be appointed Governor of Bermuda. It was a gaffe that took him a long time to live down.

Guy Garrod, Peirse's deputy, had taken over when Peirse fled to England in November 1944, taking a willing Lady Auchinleck with him, and thereby bringing his RAF career to an abrupt close. As late as 26 January 1945, Park signalled Garrod to congratulate him as Peirse's successor, which had been announced in the Cairo newspapers. As ever, the Air Ministry was in a muddle: all was resolved on 27 January when Mountbatten learned that Garrod was to replace Slessor in Caserta and Park was to go to Calcutta. Neither Mountbatten nor Garrod were happy with these decisions. Park knew this and worked hard (and quickly) to win the confidence of his fellow commanders in the Far East.

He arrived on 23 February 1945, just in time to attend a conference chaired by Mountbatten. His main task would be to help the Americans to supply Slim's 14th Army – more than 300,000 men – from the air throughout its advance from northern Burma to Rangoon. If Burma had fallen, the Japanese would have been able to invade India and isolate China from Anglo-American help.

Christopher Courtney, who nearly became head of Fighter Command in 1940, but was mercifully found a far more suitable position for his abilities as Air Member for Supply and Organisation, reported to Portal in March 1945 on his recent tour of South East Asia. He doubted if the vital part being played by Allied air forces in that theatre was appreciated in Britain or in the United States. Narratives on the war in the Far East were composed by the RAF's Air Historical Branch in the late 1940s and drew attention to the daunting challenges facing American and British transport crews. An uncharted country of high mountains and dense jungle, unpredictable air currents, enemy fighters, small arms fire from the ground, primitive radio aids and long hours in the air ending with a search for tiny drop-zones.

Slim's army was almost entirely maintained by the American Combat Cargo Task Force, while Stanley Vincent's 221 Group provided most of the artillery support. Strong fighter and bomber forces, British and American, were now on hand when Park arrived and there was an effective command and control system created for all forces in India and Burma. If the Japanese could be beaten in the central Burmese plains around Mandalay by June (when the next monsoon was due), the port of Rangoon could be captured and the re-conquest of Burma would be practically complete. Properly organised air supply, recalled Bernard Fergusson (who served in Burma) 'was to prove the winning card' in that theatre.

It had begun long before Park's arrival and the Japanese never realised how vital it was. Whenever they attacked, they expected what Ronald Lewin called 'a partridge drive': a headlong retreat. Given sufficient air support, the soldiers were able to stand and fight. Everything a division would need:

'From pills to projectiles, from bully beef to boots, was laid out, packed for dropping, at the airstrips... Besides the routine requirements of war – food, ammunition, fuel, fodder for animals, water – the packing lists were flexible enough to be able to include mail, plasma, drugs, outsize boots, the *SEAC* newspaper, typewriter ribbons, socks, spectacles, razors and tooth brushes.'

Park's headquarters were in Kandy and he spoke to his new staff on 2 March. With his long experience of London, Cairo, Malta, Algiers and Cairo in mind under the command of such outstanding officers as Dowding, Tedder and Eisenhower, he appealed to everyone to have teamwork in mind: not merely at Air Headquarters, but with army, navy and American colleagues. Having delivered himself of these hard-earned opinions, he spent a week touring his enormous command with the intention of putting them into practice. He had a reputation for going to see what was actually happening in any units under his command and would fly thousands of miles during the next year from his base in Kandy, later from another base in Singapore, to Quetta in the north-west, the Cocos Islands in the south and Hong Kong in the north-east. Already by the end of March, he had travelled more than 17,000 miles in all types of aircraft, motor vehicles and watercraft. Given the primitive or isolated conditions under which most units operated, exacerbated by intolerable heat and dust alternating with rain and mud, Park's obvious concern for the living and working conditions of all ranks fitted him well for the RAF's most physically demanding command.

The occupation of Rangoon on 3 May 1945 marked the end of American commitment in Burma. 'For the RAF,' wrote Park, 'the offensive now headed down the Malay peninsula to Singapore. For the USAAF, however, the route lay across the Himalayas to China.' Park signalled George E. Stratemeyer (head of Eastern Air Command, about to 'disintegrate') on 24 May to pay tribute to the work of his command since December 1943.

He emphasised that American transport squadrons had carried the greater part of the airlift in support of British land forces in Burma. Without them, 'we could not have defeated the Japanese army so rapidly and decisively in 1945'. At that time, Park did not expect to be in Singapore before Christmas and thought Japan would not surrender before May 1946. The atomic bombs dropped on Hiroshima and Nagasaki early in August 1945, however, brought the war to an abrupt close.

'We did it Together, Old Boy'

'No army in history,' said Mountbatten in a radio broadcast after those bombs were dropped, 'has ever contemplated fighting its way through Burma from the north until now, not even in Staff College studies. The Japs came in the easy way and we pushed them out the hard way.' The Allied air forces had carried out the biggest lift of the war, 'though heaven knows most other theatres had many more transport aircraft and they didn't have the monsoon and the jungle to fight'. At a press conference on 9 August, Mountbatten praised Park, whose part in directing air forces in the final stages was proficient and enthusiastic.

But the campaign turned round the Mountbatten-Slim axis: men with little in common, save 'the power of commanding affection while communicating energy'. In December 1970, Mountbatten visited Slim, who was then near to death. 'We did it together, old boy', said Slim.

'Mountbatten,' wrote Lewin, 'could not have defeated the Japanese without Slim's military skills; during the great crises of 14th Army Slim could scarcely have survived without Mountbatten's imperious energy and intimate acquaintance with the Anglo-American corridors of power.' True enough, but the efforts of airmen in the Far East cut little ice in London. Hardly any decorations were awarded. 'Almost certainly,' wrote Henry Probert, 'the fault lay in the Air Ministry, not with Park or his predecessors, and it merely serves to reinforce the judgement that ACSEA was in too many respects "out of sight, out of mind."'

Aftermath

At the moment when Japan surrendered (midnight on 14 August), the regions for which SEAC was responsible contained well over 100,000,000 people, whose pent-up nationalist feelings were now to be released against the British, Dutch and French, who expected to revive their colonial empires. There were some 250 prison camps, containing 125,000 prisoners, civilian and military, who had suffered appalling hardship at Japanese hands. There were also 750,000 Japanese soldiers still at large, more than enough to vent their rage on anyone within range, if they so chose. Not least, many thousands of British servicemen wanted to get home immediately to escape hateful living conditions and poor food among alien people.

The arrival in South East Asia of a film, *Burma Victory*, made by the British Army Film Unit, foolishly ignored the valuable part played by airmen. Park found it particularly distressing because Slim himself had written: 'Never has an army been better, more unselfishly, or more gallantly served by an air force.' There were strikes, amounting in official eyes, to mutiny in several camps throughout the command, all of which Park handled sensibly, preventing them from getting out of control.

The fact remains, however, that during the last eight months of his service, until April 1946, he was taxed more severely and constantly than he had been in wartime with tasks for which neither he nor any other Allied commander had any experience. Neither Park nor the airmen under his command in India, South East Asia and Japan, were in any sense Churchill's. Commanders in all three services laboured long and hard to deal with the mess left everywhere that Japanese forces had ruled. One of Park's boldest decisions was to use Japanese aircraft and aircrews to supplement British resources in rescuing prisoners from remote areas of Java and Sumatra. In April 1946, not yet fifty-four, he was shattered to learn that he was to be retired. Younger men must have their chance, now that the war was over, but Park would not receive the full pension of an air chief marshal (not having held that rank for long enough), but he was to be consoled by the award of the Grand Cross of the Bath (GCB), which cost the government nothing.

23

A New World,
1945 and After

Chief Aunt Sally

Polling day for a General Election in Britain, held while war still raged in the east, was 5 July. It was the first for a decade – Hitler's onslaught prevented the one due in 1940 – so nobody under thirty had ever voted before. Results were not to be declared until the 26th in order to allow the votes of nearly 3,000,000 men and women serving in the armed forces abroad to be collected and counted. A Conservative victory, with Churchill remaining Prime Minister, was widely expected, even by members of the Labour Party. He had addressed enthusiastic crowds in many places and told Colville that he had no doubts about the result. 'I said that I would agree, if it were a presidential election.' Although Tedder was keen to succeed Portal as head of the RAF, he had good reason to believe that Churchill would insist on another officer.

During the evening of 26 July, Tedder learned, to his delighted surprise, that the people of Britain had overwhelmingly rejected the Conservative Party, though not Churchill personally. The notorious trio of Churchill's close cronies – Beaverbrook, Bracken and Cherwell – were also out of public life.

Clement Attlee, leader of the Labour Party, would become Prime Minister. Unlike Churchill, he used words sparingly, his temper was reliable, he lived a normal life, did not make unreasonable demands on others and did not regard himself either as a war lord or a master of all other skills. He was, in short, a man for Tedder, who was promoted to five-star rank as a marshal of the RAF in September. Among many congratulations was a most welcome letter from Spaatz, soon to succeed Arnold as head of the American Army Air Forces. 'I know that never will I have a post similar in happiness,' he wrote on the 18th, 'to that which I had under you and Ike in North Africa, England and Europe.' Tedder replied at once, looking ahead as always: 'Yes, it was a good team, and I hope it has done something even more permanent than winning the war.'

Tedder succeeded Portal as CAS on 1 January 1946: or 'Chief Aunt Sally', as he extended the initials in an address to the Cambridge University Air

Squadron in May 1949. One friend, Air Chief Marshal Sir Ronald Ivelaw-Chapman, wrote of him locked in the 'whirligig of Whitehall', head of the RAF in 'the House of Shame', as Air Commodore Frederick Rainsford described the Air Ministry. Tedder was also elevated to the peerage as a baron, although not as a viscount. Unlike all his successors, however, he was not appointed for a fixed term. He would remain CAS until he chose to retire.

'I am glad to see you where you are,' wrote Harris, late of Bomber Command on 2 January 1946. He was to lunch with Churchill on the 4th and intended to have 'a final row with the old boy' over the award of nothing more than the defence medal to members of Bomber Command, a scandal for which Churchill – anxious about his postwar reputation – was responsible. The ex-Prime Minister was acutely sensitive to criticism, once Hitler was safely dead, that perhaps Allied bombing had been too destructive.

In another letter to Tedder, on 6 January, Harris expressed his displeasure that Montgomery and Alexander had been made viscounts, 'and you, as their superior, a baron. Shades of Reims and the attempt to oust you.' Harris left England for Cape Town and published *Bomber Offensive* in 1947, an account that Tedder thought full of 'bitter and unbalanced comments' he told Trenchard on 20 January 1947. 'I know there is good stuff in it, and it ought to have been a great book, worthy of a great commander and a great command. Unfortunately, it is not.'

Tedder and Montgomery

From June 1946 Tedder was chairman of the chiefs of staff committee. Brooke had been anxious to retire once Hitler's Germany had been destroyed and perversely selected Alexander as his successor, an officer whom he knew to be inadequate for so demanding a role. Churchill persuaded Brooke to stay on for another year and sent Alexander to Canada as governor-general. Brooke did not support his vice-chief, Sir Archibald Nye, who 'knew how to handle the chiefs and Whitehall with a lightness of touch that Montgomery did not possess' and so cleared a path to the top for his protégé. Portal and Andrew Cunningham did not oppose Montgomery's proposed appointment, which took effect in June 1946.

From that month, Tedder took up his position and was thus brought into regular contact with the War Office and the Admiralty. Tedder, smirked Montgomery, was as bad as Eisenhower: holding conferences 'to collect ideas. I held them to give orders.' Montgomery's dictatorial approach, as even Nigel Hamilton admitted, was 'often based on inadequate advice or hasty judgement, and would be a distinct liability, casting an unfortunate shadow' over his postwar career. Harmony would not be restored until November 1948 when Attlee found Montgomery a job outside England.

There were actually many points of agreement between Montgomery and Tedder. They concurred, for example, that all modern military operations were in fact combined army/air operations. Montgomery did not claim that the army commander should direct all air forces working over land. On the contrary, he thought air power must be under centralised air control, within the framework of an agreed army/air plan. They agreed on many issues: the shortage of regular recruits for the armed forces; the lack of adequate, modern fighting equipment for them; the adverse effects of reliance on National Service men; the poor pay and living conditions of officers and men and the inept performance of A. V. Alexander as Minister of Defence.

Where Montgomery disagreed with Tedder, his case was usually strong. In February 1948, for instance, while Montgomery accepted that Britain's main weapon in a war with the Soviet Union would be air power, he argued that British troops should be sent immediately to the Continent for three practical reasons. Firstly, to hold positions on the Rhine until American support arrived. Secondly, to establish and protect air bases from which the Allies could mount counter-attacks. And thirdly, to prevent enemy forces from launching bomber or rocket attacks on British targets from bases close to the Channel coast.

Tedder believed, with Admiral John Cunningham (a cousin of the wartime Cunninghams), that British forces would be swiftly swept aside and that effective counter-attack could only come from secure bases in the Middle East. Foreign Secretary Ernest Bevin agreed with Montgomery, Prime Minister Attlee with Tedder, but even today no-one can say who was 'right'. The issues were grave and it was entirely proper that the soldier and the airman should offer their political masters stark alternatives rather than fudged compromises. Attlee and Bevin were experienced politicians, used to dealing with colleagues who detested each other.

New Alliances, Enemies, Weapons
The notorious rift between the chiefs in the period June 1946 to November 1948 had little effect on either the major policies of the British government or the wider world in which those policies were framed. Had the chiefs been blood brothers, Britain's dire financial situation throughout those years would not have improved one iota. The chiefs had no impact, for example, on the McMahon Act of August 1946 to prevent Anglo-American collaboration in atomic research or the Truman Doctrine to contain Soviet aggression or the Marshall Plan to assist west European economic recovery or worsening relations with the Soviet Union that led to the Berlin Airlift.

The arrival of Admiral Sir Bruce Fraser in September 1948 and Slim as his fellow chiefs of staff in November greatly pleased Tedder, but did nothing to hurry along the union of western powers resulting in the formation of the North Atlantic Treaty Organisation (NATO) in April 1949. The chiefs were mere observers of the Soviet Union's test of its first nuclear device in August 1949 and the proclamation of a People's Republic in China in October. Their four main concerns were the defence of Britain and Western Europe, the defence of sea links with the rest of the world, the retention of a firm hold on the Middle East, to safeguard oil supplies and provide essential bases for offensive action in the event of Soviet aggression, and to retain control of Singapore and the Malay peninsula.

Above all these concerns was the atomic bomb. A possibility of extinguishing life on earth now existed, at the moment in the hands of a friendly power, but another power, growing less so by the day, was seeking to build its own bomb, at great expense but with the help of successful espionage. Britain's safety, as well as her global influence, seemed at risk, but the American government was no longer prepared to share its knowledge or permit further joint research with British scientists, partly because of that espionage.

Tedder therefore supported Attlee's decision in January 1947 to develop nuclear weapons and planning began, under his direction, for a British jet-bomber force capable of carrying them. He thought the American stance would change as relations with the Soviet Union worsened. The thoughts of Washington and Whitehall would then turn to the restoration of long-range bomber bases in eastern England. Spaatz was thinking along the same lines, so too were his able younger colleagues, Hoyt S. Vandenberg and Lauris Norstad. A problem anticipated is one more easily solved, so the former wartime allies put their heads together during the summer of 1946.

During June and July, Tedder and Spaatz made a secret agreement of long-lasting significance. Almost from the day of their return from Moscow in May 1945, they had shared concerns about the strength of Soviet forces, Western Europe's vulnerability and the speed of demobilisation in both Britain and the United States. What was to be done?

The RAF's latest bomber, the Avro Lincoln, was an 'unenterprising' design, with an 'unremarkable' performance, utterly incapable of reaching important targets in the Soviet Union from eastern England. The superior Boeing B-29 Superfortress had the range, but could not operate from runways in that region unless they were lengthened and strengthened. Tedder began this work at Marham and Sculthorpe in Norfolk and at Lakenheath in Suffolk that would turn Britain into an unsinkable aircraft carrier for American bombers.

The first official visit, lasting a week, began on 9 June 1947 when nine B-29s arrived at Marham from Frankfurt; a total of 150 men were aboard, many of them wartime veterans, and Tedder arranged for a host of journalists and cameramen to be present. In return, he sent sixteen Lincolns of the famous 617 (Dambusters) Squadron to the United States to help celebrate the first Air Force Day, 1 August 1947.

American air commanders knew that the B-29 was nearing the end of its life as a carrier of atomic bombs and that even an improved version, the B-50, would not last long. Crew training, especially in accurate navigation at night, needed to be improved and secure, fully-equipped bases were needed in the Middle East as well as in Britain if Soviet aggression was to be deterred or answered. During 1947, Tedder learned that even Spaatz and his most senior colleagues found it extremely difficult to extract information from the Atomic Energy Commission, formed in January and holding the absurd belief that its work was 'a sacred trust', taking precedence even over the 'military requirements' of the United States.

On 17 and 18 July 1948, sixty B-29s landed at three specially-prepared airfields in East Anglia. It was the first time that the United States had stationed combat aircraft in another sovereign state in peacetime. None of them were modified to carry atomic bombs, all of which remained in the United States. Soon the B-29s were rotating through England on ninety-day tours and a major depot for repair and maintenance work was opened for these and for transport aircraft at Burtonwood, east of Liverpool.

Vandenberg, who had succeeded Spaatz in July 1948, was concerned about 'the exposed position' of his bombers and asked Tedder if American soldiers could be sent to England, with their own anti-aircraft guns, and engineers to improve the airfields. Tedder agreed wholeheartedly and began negotiations that concluded in March 1949 with the purchase of 194 B-29s to replace the Lincolns.

Friendly relations only reached so far and Britain was excluded from American thinking regarding the possible use of atomic weapons, nor was Tedder able to obtain, for the RAF, the superior B-50 or get the B-29s leased or loaned. He realised, more clearly than most other Britons in public life, that the postwar relations of the United States and Britain were those of master and man, as they had been since 1941. He supposed, however, that if war threatened between the West and the Soviet Union the best available American bombers and fighters would then be sent to England and the Middle East. Although the deal provoked adverse comment from the British aircraft industry and in the House of Commons, it went ahead. The first of eight squadrons of 'Washingtons', as the British named these B-29s, was formed in June 1950 and they survived until March 1954.

Tedder strongly influenced the conception and creation of the RAF's jet-bomber force, though why he – or anyone else in authority – supposed that Britain could afford or need three different types is impossible to say. He would be long out of office before such bombers became operational, but they supposedly gave his successors a stronger hand to play in dealing with the Americans. The Vickers Valiant appeared in May 1951, followed by the Avro Vulcan and the Handley Page Victor in August and December 1952. They only reached squadron service between 1955 and 1958: the years of maximum danger, Tedder thought, of war with the Soviet Union.

The Berlin Airlift
At the end of the European war in May 1945, the victorious allies had divided Germany into four 'Zones of Occupation', but Berlin – although

deep inside the Soviet zone – was also quartered into four 'Sectors of Occupation'. The Soviet Union insisted that American, British or French access to Berlin was a privilege, not a right; that supplies of food, fuel, medicines, clothing and manufactures for the three western sectors must all come from the western zones; and that free movement of people or goods between the western and eastern divisions of Germany or Berlin could not be permitted.

The Western Allies gradually became aware that only economic revival, in which Germany must play a leading part (despite French reluctance to help an old enemy), would permit the creation of armed forces strong enough, in Western Europe, to resist the danger of invasion by a new enemy, the Soviet Union. They therefore decided in March 1948 to link their zones into a common economic unit and introduce a new currency: clear indications that they intended to strengthen their capacity to resist the Soviet Union.

Vehement Soviet protests culminated in the closure, on 23 June, of western access to Berlin. General Lucius D. Clay, the American military governor, proposed to fight a land convoy into the city. This proposal appalled Ernest Bevin, Tedder and his fellow chiefs in Whitehall. Clay was persuaded that the British and Americans should use their unquestioned right of aerial access to fly supplies into Berlin.

No-one supposed that a city of more than 2,000,000 people could be supplied indefinitely by air: Berlin's distance from the west, too few aircraft, too few landing grounds, uncertain weather, smoke from industries and private homes were all severe handicaps. But the airlift was a triumph, under the inspired guidance of an American airman, General William H. Tunner, who created a 'steady rhythm', as he later wrote, of loading, flying and unloading, 'constant as the jungle drums'. He had a British airman, Air Vice-Marshal John Merer, as his deputy and they worked together until Stalin accepted defeat in May 1949, but flights continued for another four months to build up stocks for the coming winter.

Gail S. ('Hal') Halverson had the idea of dropping tons of 'candy' (sweets and chocolate) by miniature parachute for the children who stood all day in the rubble at the end of the runway. They deserved any candy they got. As Ann Tusa said, the food delivered was nasty: dehydrated potatoes; vegetables; dried soups, all of them barely edible. Near the end of the airlift, some Berliners 'tasted cheese for the first time since 1945', yet they accepted what they got and few responded to Soviet blandishments, nor did Stalin allow radio jamming, static balloons or aerial 'incidents' to impede the airlift. He expected 'General Winter' to wreck the airlift in spite of all that Allied courage, ingenuity and determination could do, but for once the winter of 1948-1949 was mild.

The British share of all the cargo delivered was less than one quarter, but that share included nearly half the food and most of the liquid fuel. The airlift demanded the most precise flying by thousands of American and British airmen, day and night, imposing a fearful strain on everyone involved, on the ground or in the air. Mick Ensor's experience may stand as an example. He was a New Zealander serving with the RAF who flew exactly 200 airlift missions, eighty-six of them wholly or partly in darkness, between Wunstorf and Gatow. 'In the beginning,' he later reflected, 'God created Heaven and Earth. Then he created the Berlin Airlift to cure keen pilots of their sinful desire to fly aeroplanes.'

That airlift was the 'finest hour' of Anglo-American air power in peacetime and greatly helped Tedder's constant efforts to keep alive a partnership born in wartime. The airlift's amazing success confirmed what many British and American officers had always preached: that the particular strength of air forces lay in their capacity for rapid response in maximum strength at an identified key point. By the time Stalin gave up, the United States, Canada, Britain, Iceland, Denmark, Portugal and Italy were allied; a West German republic was about to emerge and several British airfields were being actively readied for American bombers that were nuclear-capable.

Another War

On 22 May 1948, some Egyptian Spitfires attacked an airfield at Ramat David, where RAF forces were covering a British withdrawal from Haifa. Several RAF Spitfires and three DC-3s were destroyed or damaged, before the Egyptians could be shot down or driven away. The Jews were currently forming their own air force and they too attacked and destroyed RAF aircraft – perhaps in error – while defending the newly-formed state of Israel against their Arab enemies.

Tedder backed the decision of his local commanders not to escalate these tragic incidents into outright war. 'It is ironic,' wrote Bruce Williamson, 'that during the Israeli War of Independence, the RAF was attacked by both protagonists... the almost inevitable result of getting in the middle of someone else's war.'

Tedder retired on 31 December 1949 and next day began his duties as a governor of the BBC. Only ten weeks later, on 14 March 1950, he reluctantly agreed to a request from Prime Minister Attlee to accept a year's appointment as head of a joint-services mission in Washington and Britain's first representative on NATO's 'Standing Group', a newly-formed executive committee. Attlee's decision to re-activate Tedder was justified by the response of Omar Bradley, head of the US Army and chairman of the joint chiefs of staff. 'I consider Marshal Tedder one of the United Kingdom's most outstanding men', he assured Louis Johnson, Secretary of Defense, on 17 March. 'I am glad we are going to have him with us.' Lauris Norstad, head of US Air Forces in Europe, agreed. Tedder, he wrote:

'has a very strong position with Americans, both in and out of the military establishment and he has, of course, the esteem and affection of his wartime associates. The remarkable thing is that he is not considered a foreigner when in this country. We regard him as one of the family.'

Then, to everyone's surprise in Whitehall and Washington, came an outbreak of war. Not in central Europe or the Middle East, as many half-expected, but in Korea. By June 1950, a communist state existed in the north and an officially democratic republic in the south. When North Korean forces invaded South Korea on the 25th, it was widely supposed to be a Moscow-inspired attempt to draw Anglo-American forces to the Far East while the Soviet Union 'destabilised' the politically-shaky states of Western Europe: in particular, France, Italy and Greece, where there were large and well-disciplined communist parties.

Although President Truman and his advisers recognised this danger, they believed they must act in support of South Korea. Britain was anxious to help, but always had an eye on her interests in Malaya, Hong Kong and the new People's Republic of China as well as the Nationalist state in Taiwan. Tedder was immediately involved in top-level discussions and later, on Attlee's instructions, would support Truman and Bradley in opposing the attempt by a famous general, Douglas MacArthur, commanding US forces in the Far East, to escalate the conflict. Throughout the rest of his year in Washington, Tedder served as an important link between American and British services, but he was determined to escape, resisting pressure to stay on, and did so at the end of April 1951. He was then nearly sixty-one and had then worn uniform for more than thirty-five years. It was, he thought, enough.

The Global Strategy Paper

Slessor succeeded Tedder as CAS on 1 January 1950 and throughout his three years in that office was deeply concerned with the development of a British atomic bomb, long-range aircraft to deliver it at need, the development of air-to-air and ground-to-air missiles, new fighters and an improved radar reporting system. He was faced with constant pressure in Germany, the Middle East, Korea and Malaya in partnership with NATO and American forces. Churchill returned to power in October 1951 and ruled that Britain's defence policy must be revised.

He adopted the result, a 'Global Strategy Paper', largely written by Slessor. It became 'perhaps the best-known, the most often discussed, and also the most highly-regarded defence document of the post-war period'. Its basic themes were the need to win the Cold War, to complement American nuclear strength and to cut British commitments overseas. Even so, whatever Churchill or Slessor had in mind, the so-called 'special relationship' remained that of master and man, for American power was so much greater than that of Britain.

'American imperialism,' Slessor complained in September 1952, 'has become far more intolerant and selfish than British imperialism at its ripest.'

Slessor ended his career on 1 January 1953, and was not awarded a peerage, even by a Conservative government. Churchill, he wrote, 'was not the easiest of men to work under and he did not particularly care for me'. His last careful, heart-felt letter to Churchill, urging him to keep Britain strong in the air and not utterly dependent on the United States, was written on his last day in office. It was not even acknowledged, yet in his memoirs – published in May 1956 – this archest of grovellers described Churchill, in his usual extravagant language when discussing important persons, as 'by a long chalk the greatest Englishman that ever lived'.

Indecent Exposures

In 1957 Tedder referred to the fuss currently being made over the publication of an edition of Brooke's wartime diaries. Brooke was by then Lord Alanbrooke and the edition (by Arthur Bryant) was in fact inadequate as subsequent scholars have revealed. Bad as it was, the edition was vehemently criticised by civil servants and politicians who regarded as 'indecent exposure' arguments over the conduct of strategy and operations. Mistakes, it was argued, should be deeply buried, far from the prying eyes of historians and those citizens who wish to know what went on while they were enduring a global war. This secrecy would, of course, ensure that those mistakes would re-surface if or when another war loomed.

The idea of making his own 'indecent exposure' was taking shape in Tedder's mind, and correspondence with Liddell Hart encouraged him. Glowing reviews of an official British account of the Normandy campaign (by Major L. F. Ellis) 'staggered' Liddell Hart, as he told Tedder in December 1962, because it slavishly followed Montgomery's opinions and actions. Tedder was not surprised. 'I wonder if it has struck you,' he wrote to Liddell Hart in March, 'that there is a remarkable likeness between Monty and Winston in their respective attitudes towards history?' In other words, each of them determined, so far as lay within his own power, to make sure that 'his story' should record his own version of events rather than 'history'. Tedder thought the facts about Churchill's conduct would eventually become known, but Montgomery – operating at a much lower level of importance – had the record of his actions so 'skillfully adjusted at the time that I see little, if any, prospect of the truth being disentangled from the story'. Not only 'adjusted': it is now known that when Montgomery was head of the British Army he 'removed' many documents from the War Office and destroyed some.

In March 1963, Liddell Hart sent Tedder some copies of a paper he had written in 1942 entitled 'Points Supplementary to an Estimate of Winston Churchill'. In 1938, Churchill had declared that aircraft would not be a danger to 'properly-equipped modern war fleets, whether at sea or lying in harbour... This, added to the undoubted obsolescence of the submarine as a decisive war weapon, should give a feeling of confidence and security, as far as the seas and oceans are concerned, to the western democracies.' Churchill also declared in 1938: 'Those who know France well, or have long worked with French statesmen and generals, realise the immense latent strength of France'; the French army is 'the most perfectly-trained and faithful mobile force in Europe'.

As many historians have written, especially in the years since detailed information about Churchill's entire career became available, he was often carried away by his fluent pen and delight in resounding words. His strategic grasp did not extend beyond offensive action regardless of tedious concerns about supply and reinforcement. Everyone agrees, however, about his endless energy, powerful personality and exceptional capacity for leadership, especially in the blackest days of the war. Above all, Churchill saw in Hitler a man who must be destroyed, a man more deadly than any natural disaster that had hitherto struck this planet.

Tedder was helped in writing his memoirs by many former colleagues and by David Dilks, a young scholar who later became an eminent historian. Zuckerman provided detailed information, particularly on the transportation plan. On this subject, Tedder ran into trouble with 'someone in the Cabinet Office', who tried to insist – as is instinctive in British officialdom – that a bland summary of conclusions should take the place of a detailed account of who said what to whom. That was one battle won by Tedder, with the help of Dilks and the Air Historical Branch.

Tedder's book, entitled *With Prejudice*, was published by Cassell in September 1966 and widely reviewed. An anonymous reviewer in the *Economist* made the point that Tedder scorned most politicians and yet he was himself 'one of the war's must successful politicians', in that he so often survived even Churchill's wrath. Across the Atlantic, Alfred Goldberg noted that Tedder had never been dazzled by Churchill and lacked the 'intensely egocentric' focus that so grievously marred the writings of Montgomery and Brooke. Only Slim, among British commanders, had qualities comparable to Tedder's: 'He, too, was successful in leading Allied forces... and in triumphing over terribly ambiguous command arrangements.' One exceptional achievement, thought Goldberg, was to insist on the bombing of French and Belgian railway networks before D-Day against the political (not military) objections of Churchill. 'Great credit should also be granted to Roosevelt for his unflinching trust in the responsible military commanders at that critical moment.'

Epilogue

This Star of England

Britain's airmen were never, of course, 'his' in the sense that Winston Churchill personally commanded fighters or bombers, although he would dearly loved to have done so, just as it grieved him never to have taken personal command of armies or fleets. He did his best to qualify as a pilot at a time when it was a most hazardous undertaking and he was some years past his best (physically, if in no other sense) but airmen were certainly 'his' in the sense that without his support the Royal Air Force, independent from April 1918, would have been divided between the army and the navy soon after the Armistice in November 1918 that ended the Great War.

An independent British air service, with all its faults in management and equipment, proved to be of great value to all who feared rule by Germany, Italy and Japan in the critical years before and during the war that began in September 1939. Those neutral states which did not then fear that rule, or believed they could evade it, would have been taught a severe lesson had Britain fallen.

RAF officers who looked to him for help in the 1930s knew that he was merely a backbench MP, probably too old (he turned sixty-four in November 1938) and certainly too unpopular with most movers and shakers in Westminster and Whitehall to return to ruling circles. Yet his opinions, spoken or written, were widely reported both in Britain and abroad and on the outbreak of what became the Second World War he was suddenly recalled to high office, as First Lord of the Admiralty and in May 1940 became PM. By the end of 1941 he was accepted as one of 'the big three' (with Roosevelt and Stalin) in framing strategies to overcome Germany, Italy and Japan. He was easily impressed by men in all three services who were recklessly brave, reminding him of his own youth, but he never understood the importance of supply, training and reinforcement. Subordinates and allies alike found it difficult – but not impossible – to persuade him that they understood more about military realities than he did.

As a young man, Churchill had learned something, supplemented by a powerful imagination and unshakeable prejudices, about Britain's military and political history. He would have a powerful impact on British public life during more than half a century and eventually earned a world-wide reputation.

Although Churchill loved to wear uniforms, he never ceased to be a politician, writer and orator, deeply attached to a Victorian vision of the British Empire and to the course of events in France, Germany, the United States and the Soviet Union. Unlike most aristocrats of his generation, he easily assumed a common touch, especially in wartime, when showing himself to the people in military or factory service who were trying to cope with broken careers or wrecked homes.

Throughout the Second World War, his attention – and that of most Britons, even those serving in the Air Ministry – was focused upon the fight against Germany and Italy. He was shocked by the Japanese conquests in the Far East, but only rarely attended to the desperate struggle to turn the tide there. A British general, Sir William Slim, 'Uncle Bill', as he was widely known, commanded what became the most outstanding British-led army of the war. It was an army with many Asians and Africans in its ranks and depended heavily on American combat and transport air power. It triumphed with minimal resources in the harshest conditions to overcome a cruel enemy. Although it was a campaign worthy of Churchill's most fulsome praise, it largely passed him by, both at the time and later in the memoirs that he and his assistants composed. Few of the many airmen who served anywhere in the Far East had cause to think of themselves as 'his'.

Only in May 1940, thanks to Hitler, did Churchill at last become PM in default of any convincing alternative. He himself had played a leading part in the inept shambles of an Anglo-French invasion of Norway and neither the British nor the French proved able to resist a German conquest of most of Europe. A great many people will always honour him for the stand he took against Hitler in 1940, when most British politicians were ready to accept terms. Men and women far from Whitehall and Westminster in every trade or profession responded to his defiant speeches and helped to overthrow three vile regimes.

True, Britain had become since the end of 1940, as Correlli Barnett wrote, 'a warrior satellite of the United States, dependent for life itself on American subsidies'; and it is also true that the defeats of Germany and Japan were largely brought about by the forces of the United States and the Soviet Union. Even so, British-led forces were fully engaged in every theatre from the first day until the last.

After July 1945, when once again out of office, Churchill was elevated from national leader to world statesman and had little to do with Britain's airmen during the last twenty years of his life. He headed a research team during the years 1948 to 1954 that produced an officially-sponsored account of the 1930s and the war that followed. It is an extended essay in self-vindication, tempered to some extent by the arguments and objections of those who researched and wrote on his behalf. As Raymond Callahan wrote, the memoirs were 'the product of a cottage industry', as much a 'syndicate production' as the numerous volumes of the official histories that eventually appeared. Both Churchill and his aides enjoyed the advantages of hindsight and tailored what they wrote to suit current political interests. The world-wide success of the six volumes enhanced his reputation and, with the help of skilled lawyers, earned a lasting fortune for himself and his family.

The main 'cottagers' were Bill Deakin (a close friend, notable author and ultimately head of Wadham College, Oxford), Hastings Ismay (Military Secretary to the Cabinet), Henry Pownall (deputy head of the army), Gordon Allen (a naval officer), Denis Kelly (a lawyer), Frederick Lindemann (a scientific adviser) and, not least, Edward Bridges and Norman Brook, successive secretaries of the Cabinet, who ensured that no other writer had equal access to official records.

No airman was employed until late in the day and the man then chosen, Guy Garrod, was far from the top rank among those then available. No doubt the cottagers were gratified to read, as each volume appeared, reviewers enthusing over their own prose, supposing it to be the unaided work of the master.

Meanwhile, Anthony Eden – that most 'useful idiot' – toiled away as leader of the opposition and later as acting PM while the memoirs were being cobbled together. Everyone involved, including the publishers, were continually exasperated by the need to take into account Churchill's second (third and fourth) thoughts, his evasions, omissions and exaggerations. The memoirs encouraged Britons to over-rate their contribution to Allied victories and to believe that they remained a world power, a match for the United States and the Soviet Union. They were not, but their efforts and Churchill's leadership were wonderful when it mattered most, in 1940 and 1941, and he is far more deserving than King Henry V of the praise given by Shakespeare to that grim ruler: 'Small time, but in that small, most greatly lived. This Star of England.' Unlike King Henry, Churchill lived long enough to enjoy the rewards of a 'small time' of triumph against his nation's enemies.

Churchill's Airmen

Who, then, were his airmen? At least a dozen naval officers who served in the Great War would readily have described themselves as such, and so too would those in the 1930s who sent him information about the state of the service. Smuts, of course, was among the very few men close to Churchill, even though he was never himself an airman. Trenchard became an important colleague, and he too served best on the ground. During the Hitler years, Churchill worked closely with Portal and Harris. It may be, however, that he had a warmer regard for Dowding, Park, Coningham and Douglas. He never felt at ease with Tedder – one of the war's outstanding airmen – and gave no countenance to Slessor: he more than any of them pined for admittance to the Great Man's inner circle. Churchill found little time for any of the airmen who served east of Suez. No airman became a member of that inner circle and his postwar memoirs suffer from this omission.

Mercifully, for the Western Allies and their Soviet co-belligerent, they made fewer catastrophic errors in employing their land, sea and air forces than did the rulers of Germany, Italy and Japan. They generated overwhelming resources, human and hardware, and in Churchill, Roosevelt and even Stalin they found rulers who far surpassed their enemies in willingness, however reluctant, to listen to men with military, scientific, industrial or commercial expertise and be guided by them. Most of the inadequate or unlucky commanders in all services were gone by 1943, and during the last two years of the war, Churchill's influence declined. His military judgement was frequently astray or thwarted. In July 1945, the Conservative Party suffered a humiliating defeat in a General Election and Churchill ceased to be Prime Minister. No longer a 'war lord', he transformed himself – with many willing helpers on both sides of the Atlantic – into an international icon. Overall, however, it is true to say that he had less influence on Britain's airmen than he did on her soldiers or seamen.

Bibliography

All published in London, except where indicated.

Adamthwaite, Anthony P., *The Making of the Second World War* (Allen & Unwin, 1977)

Adamthwaite, Anthony P., *The Lost Peace: International Relations in Europe, 1918-1939* (Arnold, 1980)

Addison, Paul & Jeremy A. Crang (eds.) *The Burning Blue* (Pimlico, 2000)

Air Ministry, *The Battle of Britain: An Air Ministry Account of the Great Days from 8 August to 31 October 1940* (HMSO, 1941; revised ed., 1943)

Air Ministry, *The Origins & Development of Operational Research in the Royal Air Force, Air Publication 3368*

Alanbrooke, Viscount [Sir Alan Brooke], *War Diaries, 1939-1945*, ed. Alex Danchev & Daniel Todman (Weidenfeld & Nicolson, 2001)

Andrew, Christopher, *Churchill & Intelligence* in Handel, Michael (ed.) *Leaders & Intelligence* (Cass, 1988)

Andrew, Christopher, 'The Affair of the Weighted Bag that didn't Sink' in *BBC Listener*, 2 Jan. 1986

Ashley, Maurice, *Churchill as Historian* (Secker & Warburg, 1968)

Ashmore, E. B., *Air Defence* (Longmans, 1929)

Barnett, Correlli, *Engage the Enemy More Closely: The Royal Navy in the Second World War* (New York: Norton, 1991)

Barnett, Correlli, *The Collapse of British Power* (Eyre Methuen, 1972)

Barnett, Correlli, *The Desert Generals* (Pan Books, Macmillan, 2nd ed., 1983)

Baxter, Colin F., 'Winston Churchill: Military Strategist?' in *Military Affairs*, vol. 47, no. l (Feb. 1983) 7-10

Beaumont, Roger A., 'The Bomber Offensive as a Second Front' in *Journal of Contemporary History*, vol. 22, no. 1 (Jan. 1987) 3-19

Beaumont, Roger A., 'A New Lease on Empire: Air Policing', 1919-1939 in *Aerospace Historian*, vol. 26, no. 2 (Jun. 1979) 84-90

Beevor, A., *Crete* (John Murray, 1991)

Behrendt, Hans-Otto, *Rommel's Intelligence in the Desert Campaign, 1941-1943* (Kimber, 1985). Reviewed by David Hunt in *Intelligence & National Security*, vol. 2, no. 2 (Apr. 1987) 381-3

Bell, Christopher, *The Royal Navy, Seapower and Strategy* (Macmillan, 2000)

Ben-Moshe, Tuvia, 'Churchill's Strategic Conception during the First World War' in *Journal of Strategic Studies*, vol. 12, no. 1 (Mar. 1989)

Bennett, Ralph, *Ultra & Mediterranean Strategy, 1941-1945* (Hamish Hamilton, 1989)

Bennett, Ralph, *Behind the Battle: Intelligence in the War with Germany, 1939-1945* (Pimlico, 1999)

Berges, Charles, 'Dieppe' in *Quarterly Journal of Military History*, vol. 4, no. 3 (1992) 100-111

Bialer, Uri, '"Humanisation" of Air Warfare in British Foreign Policy on the Eve of the Second World War' in *Journal of Contemporary History*, vol. 13, no. 1 (Jan. 1978)

Bialer, Uri, *The Shadow of the Bomber: The Fear of Air Attack & British Politics, 1932-1939* (Royal Historical Society, 1980)

Biddle, Tami Davis, *Rhetoric & Reality in Air Warfare: The Evolution of British & American Ideas about Strategic Bombing, 1914-1945* (Princeton, NJ: Princeton University Press, 2002)

Biddle, Tami Davis, 'Winston Churchill & Sir Charles Portal: Their Wartime Relationship, 1940-1945' in Grey, Peter & Sebastian Cox (eds.), *Air Power Leadership: Theory & Practice* (HMSO, 2002)

Blake, Robert & William Roger Louis (eds.), *Churchill* (Oxford: Oxford University Press, 1994)

Bond, Brian, *Liddell Hart: A Study of His Military Thought* (Cassell, 1977)

Bond, Brian, *British Military Policy between the Two World Wars* (Oxford: Clarendon Press, 1980)

Bond, Brian & Williamson Murray, 'The British Armed Forces, 1918-1939' in Millett, Alan R. & Williamson Murray, *Military Effectiveness* (Boston: Allen & Unwin, 1988) vol. 2

Bond, Brian, 'Calm Before the Storm: Britain & the "Phoney War", 1939-1940' in *RUSI Journal*, vol. 135, no. 1 (Spring 1990) 61-67

Bonham-Carter, Lady Violet Asquith, *Winston Churchill as I Knew Him* (Eyre & Spottiswoode, 1965)

Boog, Horst (ed.) *The Conduct of the Air War in the Second World War: An International Comparison. Proceedings of a Conference in Freiburg im Breisgau, August/September 1988* (New York: Berg, 1992)

Boylan, Bernard L., 'The Search for a Long-Range Escort Plane, 1919-1945' in *Military Affairs*, vol. 30, no. 2 (Summer 1966) 57-67

Boyle, Andrew, *Trenchard: Man of Vision* (Collins, 1962)

Buckley, John (ed.) *The Normandy Campaign, 1944: Sixty Years On* (Routledge, 2006)

Bushby, J. R., *The Air Defence of Great Britain* (Allen & Unwin, 1974)

Byford, Alistair, 'Fair Stood the Wind for France? The Royal Air Force's Experience in 1940 as a Case Study of the Relationship between Policy, Strategy and Doctrine' in *Royal Air Force Air Power Review*, vol. 14, no. 3 (Autumn/Winter, 2011) 35-60

Callahan, Raymond, *Churchill: Retreat from Empire* (Tunbridge Wells: Costello, 1984)

Calvocoressi, Peter & others, *Total War: The Causes and Course of the Second World War* (Viking: revised 2nd ed., 1989)

Cannadine, David & Roland E. Quinault, *Churchill in the Twenty-first Century* (Cambridge: Cambridge University Press, 2004)

Carver, F.M. Sir Michael (ed.) *The War Lords: Military Commanders of the Twentieth Century* (Boston: Little, Brown, 1976)

Chisholm, Anne & Michael Davie, *Beaverbrook: A Life* (Hutchinson, 1992)

Churchill, Winston S., *The World Crisis, 1911-1918*, 4 vols. (Odhams, 1938)

Churchill, Winston S., *The Second World War*, 6 vols. (Cassell, 1948-54)

Churchill, Winston S., *Complete Speeches*, 8 vols, ed. Robert Rhodes James (New York: Chelsea House/Bowker, 1974)

Claasen, Adam R. A., *Hitler's Northern War: The Luftwaffe's Ill-Fated Campaign, 1940-1945* (Lawrence, Kan: University Press of Kansas, 2001)

Clark, Ronald W., *Tizard* (Methuen, 1965)

Clayton, Aileen, *The Enemy is Listening: The Story of the Y Service* (Hutchinson, 1980)

Cochran, Alexander S., 'Ultra, Fortitude & D-Day Planning: the Missing Dimension' in Wilson, Theodore A. (ed.) *D-Day, 1944* (Lawrence, Kan: University Press of Kansas, 1994)

Cole, Christopher & E. F. Cheesman, *The Air Defence of Britain, 1914-1918* (Putnam, 1984)

Collier, Basil, *Leader of the Few: The Authorised Biography of Air Chief Marshal the Lord Dowding of Bentley Priory* (Jarrolds, 1957)

Colville, John, *The Fringes of Power: Downing Street Diaries, 1939-1955* (Hodder & Stoughton, 1985)

Coningham, AM Sir, 'The Development of Tactical Air Forces' in *RUSI Journal*, vol. 91 (1946) 211-226

Cooper, Malcolm, *The Birth of Independent Air Power: British Air Policy in the First World War* (Allen & Unwin, 1986)

Cooper, Malcolm, 'The British Experience of Strategic Bombing' in *Cross & Cockade* (GB), vol. 17, no. 2 (1986) 49-61

Cooper, Malcolm, 'Blueprint for Confusion: The Administrative Background to the Formation of the Royal Air Force, 1912-1918' in *Journal of Contemporary History*, vol. 22, no. 3 (Jul. 1987) 437-53.

Cooper, Malcolm, *The German Air Force, 1933-1945: An Anatomy of Failure* (Jane's, 1981)

Cowman, Ian, 'Main Fleet to Singapore? Churchill, The Admiralty, & Force Z' in *Journal of Strategic Studies*, vol. 17, no. 2 (Jun. 1994) 79-93

Cox, Sebastian, '"The Difference between White & Black": Churchill, Imperial Politics & Intelligence before the 1941 Crusader Offensive' in *Intelligence & National Security*, vol. 9, no. 3 (Jul. 1994) 405-447

Cox, Sebastian, 'An Unwanted Child: The Struggle to Establish a British Bombing Survey' in *The Strategic Air War against Germany, 1939-1945: Report of the British Bombing Survey Unit* (Cass, 1998)

Cox, Sebastian, 'Sir Arthur Harris & the Air Ministry' in Grey, Peter W. & Sebastian Cox, eds., *Air Power Leadership: Theory & Practice* (HMSO, 2002) 210-226

Crook, Paul, 'Science & War: Radical Scientists & the Tizard-Cherwell Area Bombing Debate in Britain' in *War & Society*, vol. 12, no. 2 (Oct. 1994) 69-101

Cross, Kenneth & Vincent Orange, *Straight & Level* (Grub Street, 1993)

Danchev, Alex, 'A Special Relationship: Field Marshal Sir John Dill & General George C. Marshall' in *RUSI Journal*, vol. 130, no. 2 (Jun. 1985) 56

Danchev, Alex & D. Todman (eds.) *War Diaries, 1939-1945: Field Marshal Lord Alanbrooke* (Weidenfeld & Nicolson, 2001)

Davis, Richard G., 'Operation Thunderclap: the US Army Air Forces & the Bombing of Berlin' in *Journal of Strategic Studies*, vol. 14, no. 1 (Mar. 1991) 90-111

Dean, David, *Airpower in Small Wars: The British Air Control Experience* (Maxwell Air Force Base: Air University Press, 1985)

Dean, Maurice, *The RAF and Two World Wars* (Cassell, 1979)

Dennis, Peter & others, *The Oxford Companion to Australian Military History* (Melbourne: Oxford University Press, 1995)

Derry, T. K., *The Campaign in Norway* (HMSO, 1952)

D'Este, Carlo, *Decision in Normandy: The Unwritten Story of Montgomery and the Allied Campaign* (Collins, 1983)

D'Este, Carlo, *Fatal Decision: Anzio & the Battle for Rome* (HarperCollins, 1991)

D'Este, Carlo, *Warlord: a Life of Winston Churchill at War, 1874-1945* (New York: HarperCollins, 2008)

Deutsch, Harold C., 'Commanding Generals and the Uses of Intelligence' in *Intelligence & National Security*, vol. 3, No. 3 (1988) 194-260

Dick, Ron, 'Confronting Complacency: the RAF Girds for War, 1933-1939' in *Air Power History*, vol. 41, no. l (Spring 1974) 24

Dilks, David, 'The Twilight War & the Fall of France: Chamberlain & Churchill in 1940' in *Transactions of the Royal Historical Society*, 5th Series, vol. 28 (1978) 61-86

Dinerstein, Herbert S., 'The Impact of Air Power on the International Scene, 1933-1940' in *Military Affairs*, vol. 19, no. 2 (Summer 1955) 67

Dowding, Lord, *The Battle of Britain: Supplement to the London Gazette* (HMSO, 11 Sep. 1946)

Dudgeon, AVM Tony, *The War That Never Was* [Iraq, 1941], (Shrewsbury: Airlife, 1991)

Edgerton, David, 'The Prophet Militant & Industrial: The Peculiarities of Correlli Barnett' in *Twentieth Century British History*, vol. 2, no. 3 (1991) 360-379

English, Allan D., 'The RAF Staff College & the Evolution of British Strategic Bombing Policy, 1922-1929' in *Journal of Strategic Studies*, vol. 16, no. 3 (Sep. 1993) 408-431

Farrell, Brian & Sandy Hunter (eds.) *Sixty Years On: The Fall of Singapore Revisited* (Singapore: Eastern University Press, 2002)

Ferris, John, *The Evolution of British Strategic Policy, 1919-1926* (Macmillan, 1989)

Ferris, John, 'Ralph Bennett & the Study of Ultra' in *Intelligence & National Security*, vol. 6, no. 2 (1991) 473-486

Ferris, John, 'The Air Force Brats View of History: Recent Writings and the Royal Air Force, 1918-1960' in *International History Review*, vol. XX, no. 1 (Mar. 1998) 119-143

Ferris, John, 'Fighter Defence before Fighter Command: The Rise of Strategic Air Defence in Great Britain' in *Journal of Military History*, vol. 63, no. 4 (1999) 845-884

Frankland, Noble, 'Some Reflections on the Strategic Air Offensive, 1939-1945' in *RUSI Journal*, vol. 107, no. 626 (Feb. 1962) 94-110

Frankland, Noble, *History at War: The Campaigns of an Historian* (Giles de la Mere, 1998)

Fraser, David, *And We Shall Shock Them: The British Army in the Second World War* (Book Club Associates, 1983)

Fredette, Raymond H., *The Sky on Fire: the First Battle of Britain, 1917-1918, & the Birth of the Royal Air Force* (Washington DC: Smithsonian Institution Press, 1991)

Gilbert, Martin, *Winston S. Churchill*, 6 vols. (Heinemann, 1971-1988) & Companion Vols.: 2 part 1 to 5 part 3

Gilbert, Martin, *Churchill: A Life* (Heinemann, 1991)

Gilbert, Martin, compiler, *The Churchill War Papers*, 3 vols. (New York: Norton, 1993-2000)

Gooderson, Ian, 'Fighter-Bombers versus German Armour in North-West Europe, 1944-1945' in *Journal of Strategic Studies*, vol. 14 (Jun. 1991) 210-231

Gordon, Andrew, 'The Admiralty & Imperial Overstretch' in *Journal of Strategic Studies*, vol. 17, no. 1 (Mar. 1994) 63-85

Gordon, John, 'Operation Crusader' in *Military Review*, vol. 71 (1991) 48-61

Goulter, Christina J. M., *A Forgotten Offensive: Royal Air Force Coastal Command's Anti-Shipping Campaign, 1940-1945* (Cass, 1995)

Greenwood, Sean, '"Caligula's Horse" Revisited: Sir Thomas Inskip as Minister for the Co-ordination of Defence, 1936-1939' in *Journal of Strategic Studies*, vol. 17, no. 2 (Jun. 1994) 17-38

Greswell, Air Commodore J. H., 'Leigh Light Wellingtons of Coastal Command' in *RUSI Journal*, vol. 140, no. 3 (Jun. 1995) 55-58

Gretton, Peter, *Former Naval Person: Winston Churchill & the Royal Navy* (Cassell, 1968)

Halpern, Paul G., *A Naval History of World War I* (Annapolis, MD: Naval Institute Press, 1994)

Hamill, Ian, 'An Australian Defence Policy?: The Singapore Strategy & the Defence of Australia, 1919-1942' in *ANU Historical Journal*, 10 & 11, 10-20

Harris, MRAF Sir Arthur, *Despatch on War Operations: 23 February 1942 to 8 May 1945*, ed. Sebastian Cox. Reviewed by Brian Bond in *TLS*, 8 Mar. 1996

Hastings, Max, *Overlord: D-Day and the Battle for Normandy, 1944* (Michael Joseph, 1984)

Hastings, Max, *Finest Years: Churchill as Warlord, 1940-1945* (Harper Press, 2009)

Henderson, Nicholas, 'A Fatal Guarantee: Poland, 1939' in *History Today*, vol. 47, no. 10 (Oct. 1997) 19-25

Hezlet, Vice-Admiral Sir Arthur, *The Submarine & Sea Power* (Davies, 1967)

Higham, Robin, *Diary of a Disaster: British Aid to Greece, 1940-1941* (University Press of Kentucky, 2009)

Hinsley, F. H., with others, *British Intelligence in the Second World War*, 4 vols., (HMSO, 1979-1990; see also vol. 5, Michael Howard (HMSO, 1990)

Horne, Alistair, *To Lose a Battle: France, 1940* (Penguin, 1979)

Hough, Richard & Denis Richards, *The Battle of Britain: The Greatest Air Battle of World War II* (Hodder & Stoughton, 1989)

Howard, Michael, 'Bombing & the Bomb' in *Encounter*, vol. 18, no. 4 (Apr. 1962) 20

Hyde, H. Montgomery, *Neville Chamberlain* (Weidenfeld & Nicolson, 1976)

Hyde, H. Montgomery, *British Air Policy between the Wars, 1918-1939* (Heinemann, 1976)

Irving, David, *The Mare's Nest* (Kimber, 1964 & Panther, 1985)

Ismay, Hastings, *The Memoirs of General the Lord Ismay* (HMSO, 1960)

Jacob, W. A., 'Air Support for the British Army, 1939-1943' in *Military Affairs*, vol. 46, no. 4 (Dec. 1982) 174-182

James, Robert Rhodes, *Churchill: A Study in Failure, 1900-1939* (Weidenfeld & Nicolson, 1970)

Jones, Neville, *The Origins of Strategic Bombing: A Study of the Development of British Air Strategic Thought and Practice up to 1918* (Kimber, 1973)

Jones, R. V., *Most Secret War: British Scientific Intelligence, 1939-1945* (Hamish Hamilton, 1978)

Jones, R. V., 'The Intelligence War & the RAF' in *Royal Air Force Historical Society*, vol. 1 (Jan. 1987) 9-34

Jones, R. V., *Reflections on Intelligence* (Heinemann, 1989)

Juniper, Dean, 'Gothas over London' in *RUSI Journal*, vol. 148, no. 4 (Apr. 2003) 74-80

Kee, Robert, *The World we Left Behind: A Chronicle of the Year 1939* (Weidenfeld & Nicolson, 1984)

Kemp, Peter, *The T-Class Submarine* (Arms & Armour Press, 1990)

Kersaudy, Francois, *Norway, 1940* (Collins, 1990)

Killingray, David, 'A Swift Agent of Government: Air Power in British Colonial Africa, 1916-1939' in *Journal of African History*, vol. 25, no. 4 (1984) 429-444

Kindleberger, Charles P., criticism of Zuckerman, *Apes & Warlords in Encounter*, vol. 51, no. 5 (Nov. 1978) 39-42. Zuckerman's reply is in vol. 52, no. 6 (Jun. 1979) 86-8. Kindleberger's response, 89; supported by W. W. Rostow, 100 & Zuckerman's reply 101-2.

Kingston-McCloughry, AVM E. J., *The Direction of War: A Critique of the Political Direction & High Command in War* (Cape, 1955)

Kinvig, Clifford, *Scapegoat: General Percival of Singapore* (Brassey's, 1996)

Kirby, M. & R. Capey, 'The Air Defence of Great Britain, 1920-1940: an Operational Research Perspective' in *Journal of the Operational Research Society*, vol. 48, no. 6 (Jun. 1997) 555-568

Kuehl, Daniel T., 'Airpower vs. Electricity: Electric Power as a Target for Strategic Air Operations' in *Journal of Strategic Studies*, vol. 18, no. 1 (Mar. 1995) 237-241

Kyba, Patrick, *Covenants without the Sword: Public Opinion & British Defence Policy, 1931-1935* (Waterloo, Ont.: Wilfrid Laurier University Press, 1983)

Lambert, Max, *Day after Day: New Zealanders in Fighter Command* (Auckland: HarperCollins, 2011)

Layman, R. D., *Naval Aviation in the First World War: Its Impact & Influence* (Annapolis, MD: Naval Institute Press, 1996)

Lee, Gerald Geunwook, '"I See Dead People": Air Raid Phobia & Britain's Behaviour in the Munich Crisis' in *Security Studies*, vol. 13, no. 2 (Winter, 2003/4) 230-272

Levine, Alan J., 'Was World War II a Near-run Thing?' in *Journal of Strategic Studies*, vol. 8, no. 1 (Mar. 1985) 38-63

Levine, Alan J., *The War against Rommel's Supply Lines, 1942-1943* (Westport, Conn: Praeger, 1999)

Lewin, Ronald, *Slim: The Standardbearer* (Pan, 1978)

Lewin, Ronald, 'World War II: A Tangled Web' in *RUSI Journal*, vol. 127, no. 4 (Dec. 1982) 16-20

Loewenheim, Francis L. & others (eds.) *Roosevelt & Churchill: Their Secret Wartime Correspondence* (New York: Saturday Review Press, 1975)

MacGregor, David, 'Former Naval Cheapskate: Chancellor of the Exchequer Winston Churchill & the Royal Navy, 1924-1929' in *Armed Forces & Society*, vol. 19, no. 3 (Spring 1993) 319-333

Macintyre, Donald, *The Naval War against Hitler* (Batsford, 1971)

McIntyre, W. David, *The Rise & Fall of the Singapore Naval Base, 1919-1942* (Macmillan, 1979)

MacIsaac, David, *Strategic Bombing in World War II: The Story of the UD Strategic Bombing Survey* (New York: Garland Publishing, 1976)

Macmillan, Harold, *War Diaries: Politics & War in the Mediterranean, January 1943-May 1945* (Macmillan, 1984)

Manchester, William, *The Last Lion: Winston Spencer Churchill, 1932-1940* (Little Brown, 1988)

Marder, Arthur *Jacob, From the Dreadnought to Scapa Flow: The Royal Navy in the Fisher Era, 1904-1919, 5 vols.* (Oxford University Press, 1961-1970)

Massie, Robert K., *Castles of Steel: Britain, Germany & the Winning of the Great War at Sea* (New York: Random House, 2003)

May, Ernest R., *Strange Victory: Hitler's Conquest of France* (Tauris, 2000)

McCormack, Robert, 'Missed Opportunities: Winston Churchill, the Air Ministry & Africa, 1919-1921' in *International History Review*, vol. 11, no. 2 (May 1989) 205-228

McIntyre, W. David, *The Rise & Fall of the Singapore Naval Base, 1919-1942* (Archon, 1979)

Meilinger, Phillip, 'Trenchard and "Morale Bombing": The Evolution of RAF Doctrine Before World War II' in *Journal of Military History*, vol. 60, no. 2 (Apr. 1996) 243-270

Middlebrook, Martin & Patrick Mahoney, *Battleship: The Loss of the Prince of Wales & the Repulse* (Allen Lane, 1977)

Middlebrook, Martin & Chris Everitt, *The Bomber Command War Diaries: An Operational Reference Book, 1939-1945* (Viking, 1985)

Mierzejewski, Alfred C. 'Intelligence & the Strategic Bombing of Germany: the Combined Strategic Targets Committee' in *International Journal of Intelligence and Counter-Intelligence*, vol. 3, no. 1 (Spring, 1989) 83-8

Milner, Marc, 'The Battle of the Atlantic' in *Journal of Strategic Studies*, vol. 13, no. 1 (Mar. 1990) 46-49

Morgan, Ted, *Churchill, 1874-1915* (Cape, 1983)

Morrow, John Howard, *The Great War in the Air: Military Aviation from 1909 to 1921* (Washington DC: Smithsonian Institution Press, 1993)

Munch-Petersen, Thomas, *The Strategy of Phoney War: Britain, Sweden & the Iron Ore Question, 1939-1940* (Stockholm: Militarhistoriska Forlaget, 1981)

Murray, Williamson & A. Millett, *A War to be Won: Fighting the Second World War* (Cambridge, MA: Harvard University Press, 2000)

Nesbit, Roy Conyers, *The Strike Wings: Special Anti-Shipping Squadrons, 1942-1945* (Kimber, 1984)

Ollard, Richard, *Fisher & Cunningham: A Study in the Personalities of the Churchill Era* (Constable, 1991)

Omissi, David E., *Air Power & Colonial Control: The Royal Air Force, 1919-1939* (Manchester: University of Manchester Press, 1990)

Orange, Vincent, *Park: The Biography of Air Chief Marshal Sir Keith Park, GCB, KBE, MC, DFC, DCL* (Methuen, 1984, new ed. Grub Street, 2001)

Orange, Vincent, *Coningham: A Biography of Air Marshal Sir Arthur Coningham, KCB, KBE, DSO, DFC, AFC* (Methuen, 1990 & Washington DC: Office of Air Force History, 1992)

Orange, Vincent, *Ensor's Endeavour: A Biography of Wing Commander Mick Ensor, DSO & Bar, DFC & Bar, AFC, RNZAF & RAF* (Grub Street, 1994)

Orange, Vincent, *Tedder: Quietly in Command* (Cass, 2004)

Orange, Vincent, 'The German Air Force is Already "The Most Powerful in Europe": Two Royal Air Force Officers Report on a Visit to Germany, 6-15 October 1936' in *Journal of Military History*, vol. 70, no. 4 (Oct. 2006) 1011-1026

Orange, Vincent, *Slessor, Bomber Champion: The life of MRAF Sir John Slessor, GCB, DSO, MC* (Grub Street, 2006)

Orange, Vincent, *Dowding of Fighter Command: Victor of the Battle of Britain* (Grub Street, 2008)

Orpen, Neil, *Airlift to Warsaw: the Rising of 1944* (Norman, Okla: University of Oklahoma Press, 1984)

Overy, Richard, 'Air Power & the Origins of Deterrence Theory before 1939' in *Journal of Strategic Studies*, vol. 15, no. 1 (Mar. 1992) 73-101

Overy, Richard, 'Strategic Intelligence & the Outbreak of the Second World War' in *War in History*, vol. 5, no. 4 (Oct. 1998) 451-480

Overy, Richard, *Why the Allies Won* (Cape, 1995)

Overy, Richard & Andrew Wheatcroft, *The Road to War* (Macmillan, 1989)

Oxford Companion to World War II, ed. I. C. B. Dear & M. R. D. Foot (Oxford: Oxford University Press, 2001)

Oxford Dictionary of National Biography: From the Earliest Times to the Year 2000, 61 vols., ed. H. C. G. Matthew & Brian Harrison (Oxford: Oxford University Press, 2004)

Padfield, Peter, *War Beneath the Sea: Submarine Conflict, 1939-1945* (Murray, 1995)

Park, ACM Sir Keith, *Air Operations in South East Asia from 1 June 1944 to the Occupation of Rangoon, 2 May 1945: Supplement to the* London Gazette (HMSO, 12 Apr. 1951) & *Air Operations in South East Asia from 3 May 1945 to 12 September 1945: Supplement to the* London Gazette (HMSO, 19 Apr. 1951)

Parton, James, *'Air Force Spoken Here': General Ira Eaker & the Command of the Air* (Bethesda, MD: Adler & Adler, 1986)

Peden, G. C., 'Sir Warren Fisher & British Re-armament against Germany' in *English Historical Review*, vol. 94, no. 370 (Jan. 1979) 29-47

Penrose, Harald, *The Great War & the Armistice, 1915-1919* (HMSO, 1969)

Portal, C. F. A., 'Air Force Co-operation in Policing the Empire' in *RUSI Journal*, vol. 82, no. 526 (May 1937) 343-358

Postan, M. M. & others, *Design and Development of Weapons: Studies in Government & Industrial Organisation* (HMSO, 1964)

Powers, Barry D., *Strategy without Slide Rule: British Air Strategy, 1914-1939* (New York: Holmes & Meier, 1976)

Price, Alfred, 'Germany's Airship Spy Flights: Watching the Detectives' in *Aeroplane* (Oct. 2007) 22-26

Pritchard, John, 'Winston Churchill, the Military and Imperial Defence in East Asia' in S. Dockrill (ed.) *From Pearl Harbor to Hiroshima* (1994) 26-54

Probert, Henry, *The Forgotten Air Force: The Royal Air Force in the War against Japan, 1941-1945* (Brassey's, 1995)

Probert, Henry, *Bomber Harris: His Life & Times* (Greenhill, 2001)

Raleigh, W. A. & H. A. Jones, *The War in the Air: Being the Story of the Part Played by the Royal Air Force*, 6 vols., (Oxford: Clarendon Press, 1922-1937)

Ramsay, Admiral Bertram, *The Evacuation of the Allied Armies from Dunkirk & Neighbouring Beaches: Supplement to the* London Gazette (HMSO, 17 Jul. 1947)

Ramsden, John, *That Will Depend on Who Writes the History: Winston Churchill as his own Historian* (Queen Mary & Westfield College, University of London, 1996)

Ramsey, Winston G. (ed.), *The Battle of Britain: Then & Now* (Battle of Britain Prints International, revised ed., 1982)

Ramsey, Winston G. (ed.) *The Blitz: Then & Now*, 3 vols., (Battle of Britain Prints International, 1987-1988)

Reynolds, David, *In Command of History: Churchill Fighting and Writing the Second World War* (Allen Lane, 2004)

Richards, Denis, *Portal of Hungerford* (Heinemann, 1977)

Richards, Denis, *The Royal Air Force, 1939-1945*, 3 vols. revised ed. (HMSO, 1974-5)

Ritchie, Sebastian, *Industry & Air Power: The Expansion of British Aircraft Production, 1935-1941* (Cass, 1997)

Ritchie, Sebastian, *Arnhem, Myth & Reality: Airborne Warfare, Air Power & the Failure of Operation Market Garden* (Hale, 2011)

Ritchie, Sebastian, 'Learning the Hard Way: a Comparative Perspective on Airborne Operations in the Second World War' in *Royal Air Force Air Power Review*, vol. 14, no. 3 (Autumn/Winter, 2011) 11-33

Roskill, Stephen, *Naval Policy between the Wars*, 2 vols. (Collins, 1968-1976)

Roskill, Stephen, *Documents Relating to the Naval Air Service* (Navy Records Society, 1969) vol. 1, 1908-1918

Roskill, Stephen, *Hankey: Man of Secrets*, 3 vols. (Collins, 1970-1974)

Roskill, Stephen, *Churchill & the Admirals* (Collins, 1977)

Sadkovitch, James, 'Of Myths & Men: Rommel & the Italians in North Africa' in *International History Review*, vol. 13 (1991) 298-301

Sbrega, John J., 'Anglo-American Relations & the Selection of Mountbatten as Supreme Allied Commander, South East Asia' in *Military Affairs*, vol. 46, no. 3 (Oct. 1982) 139-145

Schmider, K., 'The Mediterranean in 1940-1941: Crossroads of Lost Opportunities?' in *War & Society*, vol. 15, no. 2 (Oct. 1997) 26-27

Serno, Erich, 'The History of the Ottoman Air Force in the Great War: The Reports of Major Erich Serno' in *Cross & Cockade*, vol. 11, no. 2 (Summer 1970) 120

Simpson, Keith, 'A Close-run Thing? D-Day, 6 June 1944: The German Perspective' in *RUSI Journal*, vol. 139, no. 3 (Jun. 1994) 60-71

Slessor, MRAF Sir John, *The Central Blue: Recollections and Reflections* (Cassell, 1956)

Smith, Colin, *Singapore Burning: Heroism & Surrender in World War II* (Viking, 2005)

Smith, Malcolm, 'The RAF & Counter-Force Strategy before World War II' in *RUSI Journal*, vol. 121, no. 2 (Jun. 1976) 68-73

Smith, Malcolm, 'The Royal Air Force, Air Power & British Foreign Policy, 1932-1937' in *Journal of Contemporary History*, vol. 12, no. 1 (Jan. 1977) 153-174

Smith, Malcolm, 'Planning & Building the British Bomber Force, 1934-1939' in *Business History Review*, vol. 54, no. 1 (Spring 1980) 40-46

Smith, Malcolm, 'A Matter of Faith: British Strategic Air Doctrine before 1939' in *Journal of Contemporary History*, vol. 15, no. 3 (Jul. 1980) 423-442

Smith, Malcolm, 'Sir Edgar Ludlow-Hewitt & the Expansion of Bomber Command, 1939-1940' in *RUSI Journal*, vol. 126, no. 1 (Mar. 1981) 52-56

Smith, Malcolm, *British Air Strategy between the Wars* (Oxford: Clarendon Press, 1984)

Smith, Malcolm, 'Harris's Offensive in Historical Perspective' in *RUSI Journal*, vol. 130, no. 2 (Jun. 1985) 62-64

Smith, Malcolm, 'The Allied Air Offensive' in *Journal of Strategic Studies*, vol. 13, no. 1 (Mar. 1990) 67-83

Steel, Nigel & Peter Hart, *Defeat at Gallipoli* (Macmillan, 1994)

Strachan, Hew, *The First World War* (Oxford: Oxford University Press, 2001)

Sweetman, John, 'Crucial Months for Survival: the Royal Air Force, 1918-1919' in *Journal of Contemporary History*, vol. 19, no. 3 (Jul. 1984) 529-547

Swinton, Lord (Philip Cunliffe-Lister), *I Remember* (Hutchinson, 1948)

Syrett, David, 'Prelude to Victory: The Battle for Convoy HX231, 4-7 April 1943' in *Institute of Historical Research*, vol. 70, no. 171 (Feb. 1997) 99-109

Taylor, A. J. P., 'Boom & Bombs' in *New Statesman*, 30 Mar. 1962

Taylor, A. J. P., *English History, 1914-1945* (Oxford: Clarendon Press, 1965)

Taylor, John W. R., 'The Crow & the Mole' in *RAF Quarterly*, vol. 20 (Jan. 1949) 6-7

Taylor, Telford, *The Breaking Wave: The German Defeat in the Summer of 1940* (Weidenfeld & Nicolson, 1967)

Tedder, MRAF Lord, *With Prejudice* (Cassell, 1966)

Terraine, John, *The Right of the Line: the Royal Air Force in the European War, 1939-1945* (Hodder & Stoughton, 1985)

Terraine, John, 'World War II: The Balance Sheet' in *Royal Air Force Historical Society*, vol. 2 (Aug. 1987) 10-40

Terraine, John, *Business in Great Waters: The U-boat Wars, 1916-1945* (Cooper, 1989)

Terraine, John, 'Lessons of Air Warfare' in *RUSI Journal*, vol. 137, no. 4 (Aug. 1992) 53-58

Terraine, John, 'Atlantic Victory: 50 Years On' in *RUSI Journal*, vol. 138, no. 5 (Oct. 1993) 53-59

Tusa, Ann & John, *The Berlin Blockade* (Hodder & Stoughton, 1988)

Villa, Brian Loring, *Unauthorised Action: Mountbatten & the Dieppe Raid* (New York: Oxford University Press, 1989)

Wark, Wesley K., 'British Intelligence on the German Air Force & Aircraft Industry, 1933-1939' in *Historical Journal*, vol. 25, no. 3 (Sep. 1982) 627-648

Wark, Wesley K., 'British Intelligence & Small Wars in the 1930s' in *Intelligence & National Security*, vol. 2, no. 4 (1987)

Webster, Sir Charles & Noble Frankland, *The Strategic Air Offensive against Germany, 1939-1945*, 4 vols., (HMSO, 1961)

Weinberg, Gerhard L., *A World at Arms: A Global History of World War II* (New York: Cambridge University Press, 1994)

Wells, Mark K., *Courage & Air Warfare: The Allied Aircrew Experience in the Second World War* (Cass, 1995)

White, C. M., *Gotha Summer: The German Daytime Raids on England, May to August, 1917* (Hale, 1986)

Wilson, Theodore A. (ed.) *D-Day, 1944* (Lawrence, Kan: University Press of Kansas, 1994)

Wilt, A., 'The Summer of 1944: A Comparison of Overlord & Anvil/Dragoon' in *Journal of Strategic Studies*, vol. 4, no. 2 (Jun. 1981) 187-195

Wood, Derek & Derek Dempster, *The Narrow Margin: The Battle of Britain & the Rise of Air Power, 1930-1940* (revised ed., Tri-Service Press, 1990)

Wynn, Humphrey & Susan Young, *Prelude to Overlord* (Airlife, Shrewsbury, 1983)

Young, Neil, 'Foundations of Victory: The Development of Britain's Air Defences, 1934-1940' in *RUSI Journal*, vol. 135, no. 3 (1990) 62-68

Ziegler, Philip, *Mountbatten* (Guild Publishing, 1985)

Zuckerman, Lord, 'Strategic Bombing & The Defeat of Germany' in *RUSI Journal*, vol. 130, no. 2 (1985) 67-70

Index